Werner Stegmaier

What is Orientation?

Werner Stegmaier

What is Orientation?

—

A Philosophical Investigation

Translated by Reinhard G. Mueller

DE GRUYTER

To Mike Hodges, for his curiosity and courage

ISBN 978-3-11-057388-6
e-ISBN (PDF) 978-3-11-057514-9
e-ISBN (EPUB) 978-3-11-057390-9

Library of Congress Control Number: 2019938704

Bibliographic information published by the Deutsche Nationalbibliothek
The Deutsche Nationalbibliothek lists this publication in the Deutsche Nationalbibliografie;
detailed bibliographic data are available on the Internet at http://dnb.dnb.de.

© 2019 Walter de Gruyter GmbH, Berlin/Boston
Cover image: Hodges Foundation for Philosophical Orientation Inc.
Typesetting: 3w+p GmbH, Rimpar
Printing and binding: CPI books GmbH, Leck

www.degruyter.com

Content

Preface

"Nothing stays for us."
Blaise Pascal

"Nothing compels us to say that there is something behind the fluid
realities of everyday life, behind the actions or operations, that is
constant and that one would have to recognize in order to comprehend."
Niklas Luhmann

Can we, with philosophy, face the rapid changes of our world that so severely confuse our orientation? Can philosophy understand how to keep up with the times? Philosophy has indeed been slowly preparing for this – but, at the same time, it has grown more confusing and uncertain than ever before. It has split into various fields: in part, philosophy now strives to establish specific standards of precision or justice; in part, it is engaged in addressing specific theoretical or practical issues; in part, it deals with its history and its specific authors or topics; on the whole, it is clustered in opposing camps that you may join alternately – beyond its name, you can hardly detect its coherence any more. Not only does our orientation about the world we live in today seem lost, but so does our orientation about philosophy, which might at least provide an initial overview and some certainty. But what is orientation? This is precisely what philosophy – as research into the fundamentals of existence, thinking, and action – should first of all be able to answer while, at the same time, drawing conclusions for how we, in everyday life as well as in the sciences and the humanities, can adequately deal with our relentlessly changing world. Such an answer has not yet been given. We will try to do so.

By now, hardly anyone, not even in philosophy, expects unshakeable and timeless orders; rather, quite to the contrary, we assume today that change in all areas of life, including its most basic conditions, will continue to accelerate, making our world ever more unsurveyable and uncertain as time goes on. But orientation is needed precisely when situations, both large and small, change to such an extent that they become confusing – when you no longer know your way around. Orientation is, in common understanding, the achievement of finding one's way in an unsurveyable and uncertain situation so that one can successfully master the situation. Orientation is not purely intellectual – animals, too, orient themselves, in some ways they even surpass human beings – but it challenges the whole person. Orientation involves finding paths both in the terrain and through all the circumstances of human life: not only our daily life but even our survival depends on the success of our orientation. We will only sur-

https://doi.org/10.1515/9783110575149-001

vive in our rapidly changing world if we succeed in reflecting on our current orientation skills and acquiring new ones.

If every orientation is the achievement of dealing with a specific situation, be it private, social, or global, then orientation as a whole is the ability to keep up with the times: the strength to make decisions in ever-new situations on how things may continue to run successfully – decisions that promise to hold for at least some time until new orientations become necessary. Orientation includes the capacity of renewing oneself. This has always been critical; but in a more stable world it was less noticed. Today, this is of crucial interest, for every individual and every society on this earth, but particularly in a country that feels responsible for the entire world.

As capacity for an achievement, each orientation is a process; over time, from the experience of countless such processes, a kind of knowledge consolidates that provides security, even if this knowledge – in changing with the times – cannot and must not ever be fully certain of itself. Structured in this temporal way, orientation can hardly be grasped with traditional terms, and it cannot be exhaustively defined in advance. For in order to give definitions, you must already be sufficiently oriented; any meaningful way of thinking, speaking, or acting must always be preceded by a variety of orientation processes, which may themselves also change. However, orientation processes may fail: from cases of momentary confusion or (to push it to the extreme) dementia, on the one hand, to those of social riots or global catastrophes, on the other, what is lost before anything else are the usual routines of orientation and the hold they provide. Orientation must constantly reckon with such disorientations.

Orientation processes always take place in individuals, even if some activities are now being performed by machines; for these machines to work purposefully, they must be controlled and employed by individuals. Individuals' orientations are bound to their standpoints, perspectives, and horizons; to the clues they hold on to and the signs that are available; to their routines, beliefs, and identities – all orientation decisions are inevitably made under these conditions. Always being singular, orientation processes may vary to a great extent. We must therefore – especially in democratic societies – proceed from individual orientations in order to understand how we generally behave and might alternatively behave in our world, or rather our worlds, which include our various social and global orientation worlds, as well as how we organize or could organize them. And only under these conditions can we clarify how individuals are able to cooperate in their orientations and thus arrive at common orientations and designs of their world (or worlds). Anything beyond individual orientations is an abstraction – springing from individual orientations.

In order to approach the question of human orientation in this way, we must re-sort and reexamine the insights that philosophy has hitherto gained and developed in collaboration with the sciences from the ground up: while philosophy has so far been oriented toward universality, timelessness, and finality, the question of human orientation instead centers on singularity, temporality, and decidability. Proceeding from the different orientations of individuals, this philosophical inquiry into orientation investigates how the structures of human orientation manifest themselves in social life, i.e. in the interactions and communications of individuals and in their functional communication systems, such as economics, media, politics, law, science, art, and religion. We will further explore where these structures gain moral and ethical significance, how they are affected by current processes of globalization and digitization, and how and why they remain disregarded by metaphysics. We do not presuppose any universals, be they alleged givens or norms; we refrain from universal reasons, justifications, or evaluations; we rely, instead, on observations. Our investigation first of all *describes* the conditions under which universalizations become possible and often necessary – for such universalizations are specific orientation strategies, too. The same applies to this book: while performing itself what it addresses, it tries to *orient* you about the conditions of human orientation. It thereby establishes the philosophical *pre*conditions for those informed orientation decisions that are required to successfully manage the accelerating changes of our world. By doing so, the philosophical investigation into the conditions of orientation itself becomes a philosophy of orientation.

Of course, no philosophy is entirely new; neither is this philosophy of orientation. Any orientation, in everyday life as well as in philosophy, is preceded by other orientations; orientations are always reorientations. This philosophy is new, however, in so far as it begins with orientation itself. Once this beginning has been made, you find many paths leading to it in the history of philosophy, starting with the very beginnings of philosophy. Particularly close to the philosophy of orientation is – besides the thinking of (the Frenchman) Blaise Pascal, who most strikingly expressed the need for orientation, and the thinking of (the German) Immanuel Kant, who situated this need in the midst of his critical philosophy of pure reason, thereby giving prominence to the philosophical term of orientation – the thinking of American pragmatism, which stands in the tradition of nominalism, empiricism, and utilitarianism. American pragmatism already proceeds in a rather sober and moderate manner. William James, who most succinctly formulated the basic attitude of pragmatism (while keeping in mind the German philosophy of his time), describes it as follows:

He [the pragmatist] turns away from abstraction and insufficiency, from verbal solutions, from bad *a priori* reasons, from fixed principles, closed systems, and pretended absolutes and origins. He turns towards concreteness and adequacy, towards facts, towards action and towards power.[1]

Theories and their respective innovations are not beyond experience but permeate and develop it further; they are never ultimate solutions adequately representing reality, but instruments for expanding human experience: "Pragmatism unstiffens all our theories, limbers them up and sets each one at work."[2] Terms, natural or artificial, are only "short-cuts";[3] they help with "linking things satisfactorily, working securely, simplifying, saving labor."[4] Pragmatism conceives of the world (and of orientation about and in it) as a network of networks that are expanded via "conductors" and limited by "non-conductors."[5] Common sense, as it develops over a long period of time, provides (in terms of the philosophy of orientation) plausibilities (*Plausibilitäten*) that are still unclarified and unorganized, but on which new knowledge must be based in order to be comprehensible. Such plausibilities, however, are in turn transformed by new knowledge; both plausibilities and knowledge have a "steering function"[6] concerning the other. Pragmatism (like the philosophy of orientation) offers "no dogmas, and no doctrines," but it allows one to explore the meanings of terms, theories, and doctrines used in one's dealings with the world.[7] In this "radical empiricism," as James later calls it, "truths" (plural) have the "function of *a leading that is worth while.*"[8] Truths are promising leads, nothing more, nothing less. As such, pragmatism also indicates "the ways in which existing realities may be *changed.*" James calls pragmatism "an attitude of orientation."[9]

Corresponding in many respects to American pragmatism, even in its later, 20th century forms, this philosophy of orientation could find particularly open ears in the English-speaking world. Nevertheless, it goes beyond American pragmatism by – following an irreconcilable dispute about the meaning of the concept of truth – no longer focusing on the problem of truth itself but instead, as mentioned above, on how individuals, with their different orientations and responsibilities, make use of the concept of truth. American pragmatism, which itself differentiated into various standpoints, influencing many areas of life, science, and the humanities, was and remains – as far as one can still conceive of it as a unity or at least as a movement based on shared conditions and goals – primarily an epistemology standing in critical relation to earlier, particularly rationalistic, epistemologies. The philosophy of orientation, on the other hand, takes seriously questions concerning the "practical cash-value" of clues, footholds, signs, terms, concepts, and truths, all of which may show up differently at different times in each orientation and may be assessed in different ways; investigating the conditions and structures of human orientation, this philosophy clarifies how individuals, despite their different orientations, are nevertheless able to find hold within their orientations, successfully communicate with each other, and, at the same time, continually renew their orientations. By emphasizing the individuality and temporality of human orientation, the philosophy of orientation deepens the basis and expands the horizons of the philosophical investigation of our thinking and acting in the world.

Nobody else characterized the force and momentum of this kind of philosophical investigation as clearly as Friedrich Nietzsche (who, for his part, hardly used the term of orientation). In the first aphorism of his most important work critiquing metaphysics, *Beyond Good and Evil*, he no longer presupposes even the "will to truth," but asks instead for its "cause" and its "value" for life. He confronts us with a question: "Granted, we will truth: *why not untruth instead? And uncertainty? Even ignorance?*" Untruth, uncertainty, and ignorance may be just as necessary for life as truth, certainty, and knowledge. If this is the case, then you are constantly forced to decide between the two, and the mere knowledge of being able to decide between them frees our orientations to new horizons of thinking, acting, and living. It may thus lead to innovations even in philosophical thinking that can help us keep up with the times. Before this, Nietzsche wrote down in a notebook: "The happiness of the great discoverers in their quest for certainty could now transform into the happiness of finding everywhere uncertainty and venture."[10]

In fact, human orientation can never be fully certain of itself, not even in cases when it is successful according to the standards of pragmatism; it always continues to be (more or less) at risk. Truth is something (Nietzsche adds later in the 5th book of his *Gay Science*, No. 355) that reassures us, calms us down; James speaks of "sublime tricks of human thought, our ways of escaping bewilderment in the midst of sensation's irremediable flow."[11] Given the alternative to truth(s) that Nietzsche establishes ("*why not untruth instead?*"), there remains a perpetual concern that dealing with truth(s) could only be a matter of tricks and that there could always be alternative (useful, if not even vital) truths or untruths, whether one likes them or not. Nietzsche especially calls upon philosophers to likewise scrutinize in the direction of untruths, uncertainties, and ignorance in order to discover what our orientations might offer us or conceal from us for the sake of current usefulness.

Here, the term of orientation gets us further than the term of truth, even in respect to Nietzsche. With the term of orientation, it also becomes clear that, despite all untruths, uncertainties, and ignorance, the widespread fear of nihilism and relativism is unjustified: human orientation does not require a final hold outside itself, which could never be verified (there is none); human orientation creates its hold(s) within itself in various ways, which we are able to investigate and clarify. These holds of orientations within themselves may fail at times because orientations are never safe from falling into disorientations. But the structure of human orientation typically allows one to gain a sufficient orientation once more. Our orientation thus creates confidence that its own hold(s) will continue to hold.

It may be an irony of history that Germany, although – or perhaps because – it failed miserably in its political orientations, has developed a particularly refined language of orientation, especially in the word field surrounding hold (*Halt*) and foothold (*Anhaltspunkt*), which provides a particularly fitting base for investigating the conditions and structures of human orientation. In Anglo-American philosophy, the philosophical term of orientation is still not common – in spite of James' reference to it. We are confident that through this book it will also find its home in Anglophone philosophies and beyond.

The *Philosophie der Orientierung* was first published – in German – in 2008. It includes many results of the investigations I have pursued ever since I discovered the topic in my inaugural address at the University of Bonn in 1990, "'What Does It Mean to Orient Oneself in Thinking?' – On the Possibility of Philosophical World Orientation according to Kant." The German original thus includes numerous excursus into the history of philosophy and contemporary sciences, which contribute to our understanding of human orientation. In the last decade, a lot of new evidence on the issue has emerged, which I have addressed in various publications. The year 2016 witnessed the publication of a volume compiling many inspiring contributions to the philosophy of orientation, to which I have tried to respond.[12]

Then, in 2017, the financial entrepreneur Mike Hodges from Nashville, Tennessee, suggested a translation of the *Philosophie der Orientierung* into English. Together, we decided not to translate the original text in its entirety, but rather an abridged version that is easily and quickly readable. Therefore, I minimized discussions on German orientation language, the history of philosophy, and the contemporary sciences (which have made considerable progress since then), and have removed most of the footnotes, where I discussed scholarly work, as well as the extended bibliography and index. The philosophy of orientation has thus attained a more essayistic form, which might be particularly appropriate for it (the scientific evidence can still be found in the original German version). To make the text particularly plausible for an English-speaking audience, I nonetheless made many textual changes and added some points on the subject matter, especially concerning identity politics and the digitization of global communication. The oftentimes challenging work of translation was accomplished by Reinhard Mueller, in close cooperation with me. Just as to Mike Hodges, for his initiative and support, I am thankful to Reinhard Mueller for his tireless efforts and patience, as well as to Sydney Sepùlveda and especially John Murray, whose thorough proofreading assisted our endeavors.

A philosophical investigation focusing on how we deal with the unsurveyabilities and uncertainties of our orientation in the current world must itself be as clear as possible in order to establish, if not certainties, then at least plausibilities. This was my task not only in this book, but also in a '25 footholds' summary that I composed as an overview for 'readers in a hurry'; our conversations with Mike Hodges (and the title of a former paper of mine) led to its title, *Fearless Findings*. For readers interested in how the philosophy of orientation was prepared for in the history of philosophy, I compiled a somewhat more detailed overview entitled *Courageous Beginnings: 25 Situations of New Orientations in the History of Philosophy*. Eventually, there will also be a very short list of *15 Conclusions from the Philosophy of Orientation for Your Everyday Life*, under the title *Successful Modes of Orientation* for those specifically asking for the 'cash value' of this philosophical approach.

The historical overview gratefully acknowledges the various philosophical inspirations I have received for this book from the 'great philosophers.' I want to highlight, besides Blaise Pascal, Immanuel Kant, and Friedrich Nietzsche, a diverse set of philosophers including, on the one hand, Ludwig Wittgenstein, Willard Van Orman Quine, Hilary Putnam, Nelson Goodman, and Donald Davidson, and, on the other, Emmanuel Levinas and Jacques Derrida, but also the sociologists Erving Goffman and Niklas Luhmann, as well as my outstanding teachers Karl Ulmer, author of a philosophy of the modern lifeworld, and Josef Simon, author of a philosophy of signs.

I am also thankful to many friends and colleagues with whom I newly discussed in detail the main features of this philosophy of orientation: besides Mike Hodges and Reinhard Mueller, these are Andrea Christian Bertino, Timon Georg Boehm, Ralf Dohrenbusch, Günter Gödde, Helmut Heit, Reinhard Malz, Melanie Riedel, Michael Wörz, and Claus Zittel. And I would like to thank Christoph Schirmer, the Senior Acquisitions Editor at De Gruyter concerning the area of philosophy, for also accepting this English version to their prestigious list of publications, Tim Vogel and Jens Lindenhain, who supervised the production of this book with exemplary care and speed.

Werner Stegmaier

Introduction

'Orientation' is today an omnipresent term in everyday, scientific, and philosophical language use. In science, and especially in philosophy, it is mostly used to define other terms while itself remaining undefined; 'orientation' is therefore a fundamental term. This is justified in two ways. On the one hand, orientation in fact precedes all definitions: one needs to already be oriented in order to define something. On the other hand, orientation is successful especially if it is not questionable, or problematic, or in need of definitions, but if it is taken for granted and as self-evident. Orientation only becomes questionable when it no longer succeeds; problematizations and definitions only arise when one is disoriented. If the very basics are secured and orientation succeeds anew, it again becomes self-evident. Philosophers take disorientations as opportunities to reflect, as in the case of this book, on orientation itself. And this is justified as well. For, if orientation precedes all conceptualizing and if the philosopher's task is to conceptualize what precedes and determines our life, then philosophically everything depends on the clarification of what orientation is.

Orientation, however, does not begin with philosophical orientation. A philosophy of orientation inevitably follows everyday orientation, which in turn does not necessarily include philosophical orientation. 'Orientation' is usually understood as an achievement in finding one's way in a new situation. One needs to orient oneself not only in every new country and in every new city, but also in every new office and in every new handbag or pocket; not only in places, but also in interactions and communications; not only in economics, politics, media, the law, science, morality, pedagogy, religion, and philosophy, but also in every conversation, in every text, on every website, and, of course, in a book like this one; and one also needs to find one's way, before everything else, with other people and – what is hardly noticed, but crucial – their faces. Orientation assures that one quickly knows with what or whom 'one is dealing with' and whether one can 'make use' of it or not; this is how it is decided whether one, at all, turns toward or away from someone or something.

In orientation, one is at first dealing with something one does not yet know about: a new situation. If addressed in research, orientation is mostly considered to already be a specific orientation that is to provide a hold or a stability in a world characterized by a loss or a lack of orientation. This kind of orientation is then supposed to be valid for everyone and for all time. But this underestimates orientation in general. It is rather easy to set standards or norms which, if followed by everyone, make their actions predictable. However, orientation must also be capable of adapting to unpredictable and surprising situations as

https://doi.org/10.1515/9783110575149-002

well, i.e. it must be able to change if the situation changes. The achievement of orienting oneself astonishes less by giving a permanent hold or stability than by keeping up with changes. For this purpose, it needs to establish flexible structures that indeed provide a hold and stability, but only for a certain time. In the words of Heraclitus, orientation needs to stay in flux, like a river that remains the same and which, at the same time, always changes; a river in which one does not step a second time without having become somebody else. Orientation is structured like a river whose banks are in flux as well, as Wittgenstein described it. While this hardly troubles our everyday orientation, it has always caused great difficulties for philosophy.

This book confronts these difficulties anew and, with regard to orientation as a whole, for the first time. It does not want to offer a specific orientation, but to clarify what orientation is as such, how it is structured and how it works. This investigation proceeds from the simple fact that one must already be oriented in everything one does, thinks, or says, in everyday life as well as in science and philosophy, and even when adopting orientations from others. To use a city map, one needs to be somewhat familiar with cities and city maps; to follow the instructions for a technical device, one needs to understand already something about technology and instruction manuals; to make good use of a piece of advice, one needs to be already well-advised about most other circumstances. Orientation always presupposes another orientation; and orientation always follows prior orientations. Thus, orientation is the beginning of everything without itself having a beginning. *As* an orientation, it is always a new orientation or a 'reorientation.' Thus, it proceeds from itself and refers, at the same time, always to something else: the new situation. We call it both 'self-referential' and 'other-referential.' As will be seen, its other-referentiality is possible only by means of its self-referentiality, and its self-referentiality is necessary only as far as it makes other-referentiality possible. For orientation is actualized only if it refers to something else, something new, something still unfamiliar.

But self-referentialities may lead thinking into paradoxes. One can truthfully say that one is lying; one can comprehend that one does not comprehend; one can eloquently remain silent; one can decide not to decide; one can, over time, distinguish an atemporal; one can predict the unpredictable; and one can, eventually, form the algebraic set of all sets which do not contain themselves; and one can prove mathematically and completely the incompleteness of all mathematical proofs. Such paradoxical self-referentialities may lead science, logic, and philosophy into crises, but they do not trouble everyday orientation, which deals with paradoxes quite naturally. Hence, while a philosophy of orientation must surely orient itself to science, it also needs to go beyond it. The term 'orientation,' which is used quite naturally in everyday life, in science, and in philosophy, may be the last and only term still taken for granted after thousands of years of philosophical and scientific critiques of everything that has been taken for granted as self-evident.

And yet orientation is also a term for something that may be lost and of which one can never be sure. What becomes 'self-evident' in orientation is no longer noticeable or specifically paid attention to. Under new circumstances it might, however, turn out that it was not as self-evident as it seemed to be. The deeper the self-evident is ingrained and the more unquestioned it has become, the more everything that was built on it may go into flux again. But if orientation is the beginning of any kind of grasping without being itself a graspable beginning, then one reaches questions so fundamental that most other fundamental philosophical questions must be raised anew and now in a new light. Perhaps this is why orientation has so far hardly been asked about.

Immanuel Kant explicitly asked about orientation in his short text from 1786, which was not meant for the 'school,' but the 'world,' *What Does It Mean to Orient Oneself in Thinking?* He wrote it in between the two editions (1781 and 1787) of his *Critique of Pure Reason* as a response to a text by Moses Mendelssohn, who had passed away in the beginning of 1786 and who had unnoticeably introduced orientation as a term in order to face serious and, for the Jewish tradition, existential challenges. For Mendelssohn, orientation must decide between 'common sense' and 'speculative reasoning' – from the specific stance of a 'point,' where this decision was to be made. In an earlier contribution *Concerning the Ultimate Ground of the Differentiation of Directions in Space* (1768), Kant started with the assumption that reason always requires a 'standpoint,' from which reason refers to what is not reason, the relentlessly changing world. To orient yourself in the world (including the reading of papers), you must be able to distinguish right and left, top and bottom, front and rear; but you can – this is the irritating point – neither define these distinctions logically without a circle nor perceive them with your senses. The standpoint, from which the distinction is made, is the 'point' of a body, to which human reason is bound and which itself belongs to the empirical world. In his later text on orientation (1786), Kant clarified this irritation by introducing the term of orientation: reason, i.e. the 'faculty of principles,' suffers a 'lack' in its relation to the world; it has 'needs' which limit its seemingly unlimited 'scope' to its 'horizon' of the sensual world, which depends on its standpoint. The orientation term became a supplement to his term of reason. Being a rather young term in the history of philosophy (only some two hundred years), it had, starting with Kant, both an inconspicuous and unstoppable career, not only in philosophical, but also in scientific and everyday language use. In this process, the orientation discourse detached itself from the discourse of reason; reason became a part and a specific faculty of orientation. In the 20th century, especially Martin Heidegger, Ludwig Wittgenstein, and Niklas Luhmann began to think of orientation as preceding reason, but they did not address orientation as a topic on its own; this was, however, endeavored by Karl Jaspers, Karl Ulmer, Ernst Wolfgang Orth, Helmut F. Spinner, and Jürgen Mittelstrass.

Chapter 1
Pre-Orientations

1.1 The Need for Orientation

At first, one does not search, but one finds. If orientation – in simple and everyday terms – is the *achievement of finding one's way,* then this finding-one's-way means to find something without having searched for anything specific. In orientation, you find or encounter something coming up to you: the actual situation you are dealing with. You perceive what it entails as you encounter it; you orient yourself when finding out where you are situated; and you find your way when appropriately ordering, organizing, and meaningfully dealing with what is found. Thus, the achievement of orientation is at first twofold: to make out the circumstances of a situation and to then order and organize them appropriately. Circumstances are initially random or 'contingent,' i.e. they lack an obvious coherence at first glance. If, in overlooking a crucial one of them, you create misleading coherences; then you are (more or less) disoriented. Thus, orientation may fail, and, in failing, it requires greater efforts. However, even then you do not search for something specific; instead, you make further efforts to establish a coherence in what you are finding: a coherence out of which you can – as the saying goes – 'make something'. For this, there is usually little time. One needs to act quickly so that, on the one hand, unfavorable circumstances do not have negative effects and, on the other hand, good opportunities are not missed. In order to act, one has to find promising opportunities for action. But even then, one does not already search for a set goal, but for opportunities for actions that offer meaningful goals. In a second step, orientation is thus to be defined as *an achievement of finding one's way in order to find promising opportunities for action,* or in everyday terms: to 'manage' or 'cope' with what arises and thus 'handle it well' and 'make headway' with it. If one cannot act with promising prospects, then one might not, as the saying goes, 'master' the situation, and will instead run the risk of being 'mastered' by it. In a third step, orientation can thus be defined as the *achievement of finding one's way in a situation to make out opportunities for actions to master the situation.*

Orientation is not only essential to human beings, but to animals and some plants as well. It is, like nutrition and breathing, a fundamental, irrefutable, and ineradicable *necessity of life.*[13] However, orientation only becomes noticeable when it no longer works. Like hunger, thirst, or dyspnea, when one lacks food, drink, or breath, it becomes noticeable as a lack of orientation. For usually one *is* sufficiently oriented and *has* an orientation; the need for orientation only

https://doi.org/10.1515/9783110575149-003

arises when orientation fails. This need first arises as an unsettling, as disorientation in a situation; this unsettling may grow into anxiety or despair when one feels 'completely lost' and knows 'no way out.' But even then, what is missing is usually not orientation as such, but only orientation in a specific area or respect. When going to a meeting and orienting oneself about who is there, one generally already knows where to go and why certain people attend the meeting; and when trying to orient oneself in a car with a GPS, one (hopefully) does not need to orient oneself about how to use a GPS. One usually tries to compensate for a lack of orientation in a situation by means of an orientation that one already has. And this can be more or less successful and more or less sufficient. If it is not successful right away, one starts looking for orientation aids: clues in the surroundings, hints and signs, or actions by others who seem to have oriented themselves successfully; if orientation problems persist, one seeks advice from trusted individuals or experts. But this still requires you to find your way with such help, since you must make use of this advice concerning your own specific circumstances, which are never the same as those of others; and this may again be more or less successful, if at all. Hence, you must ultimately orient yourself on your own. Orientation – as the achievement of finding your way in a new situation in order to find possibilities for actions through which you can master the situation – is the achievement of an *individual ability*; and with your individual ability, you may cope with one situation but not with another. Every orientation may face unforeseen and surprising circumstances, where its abilities might fail. Therefore, one can never be entirely sure of one's orientation.

Thus, a philosophical analysis of orientation needs to first assume that one is already oriented, second that one may always encounter unforeseen and surprising situations, and third that we orient ourselves individually in individual situations. However, in philosophy and science, the conditions of orienting oneself can only be investigated in general terms; and they are of general interest only as far as they are general. Being-surprised by a new situation is, in terms of a philosophy of orientation, something general too, even if the individual surprises are always different. But since orientation may altogether contain surprising structures, the leeway of its analysis should not be limited too much beforehand and one should be as cautious as possible not to make premature philosophical decisions. It is a premature decision to simply continue using common distinctions. Even – and especially – common philosophical distinctions such as cognition, action, perception, feeling, and thinking are already premature decisions about orientation in general as well as for particular orientations. One may draw these distinctions, but one does not have to. Since orientation is about dealing with what one encounters, *all distinctions are means for orientation.* They have all at some point been found in the search for orientation, and

with every new use, a decision is also made abou̲...
circumstances, however, new decisions about new...
necessary; a philosophical analysis of orientation mus̲...
sions.

And since a philosophical analysis of orientation is a *think̲...*
this is the case for the discourse about the function of thinking in o̲...
as well. In its early history, philosophy already distinguished itself fro̲...
thinking as the proper and true thinking, and it continues to deal with th̲...
ing of thinking as its own task up to the present day. In doing so, and by co̲...
ually making new decisions about its distinctions, this thinking of thinking ha̲...
changed and been expanded and retracted in manifold ways over time so that
now there is an extensive repertoire available to think thinking. And yet its definitions still seem too simplistic and too static considering the complexity of orientation and the expansion of this complexity over more than two and a half
millennia of philosophical efforts. While – or precisely because – orientation
usually occurs without any problems, it is difficult to conceive of it using our
conventional terms of thinking and cognition. Just as gravity is but one parameter with which to describe a leaf falling through the air, the flight of this leaf is
by no means fully comprehended by gravity alone: before it hits the ground, the
leaf may be floating through the air for a long time, covering quite some distance, and may even fly up into the air again. To determine where exactly this
leaf will hit the ground would be possible only under artificial conditions in a
vacuum. Just as Newtonian physics appears simplistic when compared to contemporary physics, any explanations of the complex relations of orientation
that rely on traditional terms might be quite impoverished.

Since Plato and Aristotle, thinking has been conceived in such a way as to be
universally determinative of what is – including what it itself is. But in orientation – regarded as finding-one's-way in a situation and gaining clarity about it –
nothing is initially determined and especially not universally; any kind of definition might indeed support an orientation, but it can also fix it too early and
thus impede its progress. What philosophy has called thinking, i.e. scientific
thinking in a logical discipline, is certainly indispensable for orientation. But
within orientation, thinking has much more diverse functions. When conceptualizing orientation, one needs to keep open definitions of thinking itself and develop distinctions for it that provide leeway for individual ways of thinking in individual situations.

As far as orientation is an irrefutable necessity of life, the question about it is
primarily not a theoretical but a *pragmatic* one, not a question of final definitions and propositions, but of the leeway in dealing with definitions and propositions when finding one's way in always different situations. But as far as

into an emergency, it is also an
s an integral part of orientation.
rs, then this most of all refers to
the need for orientation with a
ical orientation – here distin-
– may still be specific forms of
/day orientation. A new analysis
of the focal points of this book.

iality, and Temporality
doxes

ıd propositions, it is *primordial:*
ncipium, which philosophy has
looked for since its own origins and beginnings. But it is a principle that –
since it precedes all definitions and propositions – cannot be defined and confirmed itself. At least it cannot be conceived from something outside of itself.
Hence, everything belonging to orientation is to be conceived from orientation
itself; it is, therefore, the *inconceivable origin or beginning of all conceiving.* It
is thus an origin that not only remains questionable but also raises the question
as to whether one can still meaningfully ask for a first origin or principle. For the
question regarding a first origin of orientation is again preceded by an orientation; therefore, as one continues to ask this question, orientation is also the principle of itself: orientation is conceivable only from within itself. Thus, if it is a
principle, then it is a *self-referential principle*, and its very principle is its self-referentiality.

If every orientation is preceded by another orientation, then this also means
that orientation is *temporal in itself.* As far as orientation always deals with new
circumstances, new situations, and never-ending change, it also deals with time,
and its function is thus to find its way with time. According to Aristotle, time
raises contradictions and paradoxes; for 'now' is every time the same and different. And even the simple act of checking the time requires time; one thus always
checks a time that has already passed: if you say 'now,' now is already gone.
Thus, everything which is subject to time risks becoming contradictory or – as
far as the contradictions cannot be resolved or avoided – paradoxical. But this
obviously does not trouble our everyday orientation. For, being temporal in itself, orientation can decide to take time into account or not, i.e. to consider
things temporally or atemporally: in a self-referential way, orientation is always
an orientation *about* time *in* time or – to put it shortly – an orientation *for a time.*

If, for Aristotle, avoiding contradictions is the first principle of logic and – *as* the principle of logic – "the most certain of all principles" (Metaphysics IV 3, 1005 b 19 f.), then orientation also precedes logic and hence cannot be gathered from logic. But this does not mean that orientation is therefore illogical: it uses logic in its own – temporal and self-referential – way.

Paradoxes or antinomies, in a strict sense, arise when a binary distinction whose values negate each other is referred back to itself with its negative value, e. g. if you, as mentioned above, need time to check the time and thereby change the time you check; or if you, using the distinction of truth and lie, say it is true that you lie; or if you use the distinction of just and unjust and ask whether it could be unjust to make judgments according to just and unjust; or if (the example most debated in mathematics, logic, and philosophy) you form the algebraic set containing all sets which do not contain themselves. Then, you cannot decide between the two contradicting alternatives, though, for logical reasons, both are equally correct: if you say it is true that you lie, then it is just as true that you speak the truth as it is that you lie. Although modernity no longer dreaded self-referentialities, it nevertheless dreaded paradoxes and, up to the present day, has made every effort to resolve them. For paradoxes can make one's thinking oscillate and then block it. However, after hermeneutics discovered the productivity of 'circles,' which had previously been considered logical flaws, Niklas Luhmann regarded the oscillations and blockages of thinking caused by paradoxes as new *means for* thinking: for, if paradoxes block thinking, it cannot 'go behind' them – and this is why they can become a new beginning of thinking. Then, you may not only start with them, but they can also be productive for thinking because now you can operate with both alternatives and explore new leeways of thinking. Similarly, Aristotle had rejected infinite recourse as a sign of false conclusions. In the modern era, Newton and Leibniz used infinite recourses to develop the infinitesimal calculus, which made it possible to calculate movements.

1.3 Orientation under Uncertainty: Relying on Plausibilities

Unfamiliar circumstances in a new situation become familiar if one orients oneself about them. Then, they are known. But even when knowing them, the situation still remains uncertain. It is explored in orientation only as far as you are able to find your way and cope with it. Usually there is not enough time to gain final knowledge about all circumstances. In order to act quickly and master a situation, one needs to rely on a few clues, without being totally certain of them; the rest remains all the more uncertain. But this is usually sufficient. It is the *basic condition of all orientation to operate under uncertainty.* In orientation, one needs to rely for the most part on simple clues as footholds while always anticipating the risks of their uncertainty and remaining attentive toward them. Even when checking and reassuring these footholds, you can never be certain that you will be able to continue to hold onto them when the circumstances change. The certainties of an orientation are *its own* certainties, which were initially acquired under the condition of uncertainty; but since orientation can never be sure about all the circumstances that are relevant for its certitude, these certainties are always under the condition of uncertainty. It is the persistent risk of orientation that something new could always come up that is relevant and that was not seen before; and orientation consists of dealing with this risk.

Orientation, as a temporary orientation, copes with its risks by relying on something only for a time or only until something else comes up. Under the pressure of time, orientation needs to quickly accept many things; therefore, it keeps the option open of letting go of these things when the time is right. Orientation operates with tentative certainties. What is immediately and tentatively certain is called 'plausible.' The word 'plausible' comes from the Lat. *plaudere*, i.e. to clap and applaud with hands, feet, or anything else in order to agree right away. Something is plausible if one agrees immediately, without further questions or justifications; plausibilities are assumptions that are not in need of being justified. They are, in a word, self-evident. *Every orientation relies on what it regards as plausible or self-evident.*

Being self-evident, plausibilities are usually not articulated or made explicit, but relied on without question. If they are articulated, they become questionable. For the most part, one leaves them 'as they are.' To articulate them, specific circumstances are needed. Then you may ask for justifications with *arguments*. The word 'argument' comes from the Lat. *arguere*, i.e. to make clear or transparent. Arguments are to make something clear or explicit which was obscure or implicit. For this purpose, they have to be plausible themselves, particularly for those whom they are trying to convince. But what is plausible for one person may not be plausible for another; therefore, one argument may convince one person, but not another. If one argument does not convince somebody, then you need to use different arguments in the hopes that they will now be plausible for him or her. Or you 'maintain' an argument by 'supporting' it with further arguments, sometimes with a long line of arguments. In everyday orientation, such lines of argument must not be too long if they are to maintain their clarity and persuasiveness. For, in everyday orientation, argumentations are under the pressure of time as well: the shorter and the more easily surveyed (*übersichtlicher*), the more plausible they are; the most plausible is the one 'striking' argument that 'strikes down' all doubts at once and that needs no further arguments – i.e. it is immediately plausible. In this way, argumentations return to plausibilities as well. This is the same for scientific justifications: for pragmatic reasons, they must end somewhere as well; they also end with plausibilities. *Precisely because plausibilities do not need any further justifications, justifications can end with them and proceed from them.* In science, plausibilities are always in effect as well, when one is – or must be – satisfied with certain reasons at some point. And you could even consider plausibilities, where arguments end, as paradoxes too: as unjustified justifications.

Plausibilities hold until they are called into question. But plausibilities must not be called into question endlessly. When they are called into question, other plausibilities develop: plausibilities for questioning plausibilities, i. e. standards for what constitutes a meaningful question or what is to be dismissed as a pointless inquiry ('that's just the way it is'). We call them *plausibility standards.* Groups or societies are used to getting along with them without question; they protect their respective plausibilities in their ways of life against further questions and maintain their implicit legitimacy. Whereas implicit plausibilities allow for the self-evident orientation of individuals, implicit plausibility standards allow for the self-evident orientation to another individual orientation in a group or society, not only pragmatically but also and especially in a moral respect. But what is self-evident for one group or society might not be the same for another; the plausibility standards of one group or society might then become questionable when encountered by members of another group or society. But if different groups or societies continue to live together and deal with each other, then plausibility standards will again develop for this, etc. Eventually, it all goes back to plausibilities and plausibility standards, which are in effect for a certain time.

Just like orientation itself, the plausibilities of orientation have hardly been addressed in either philosophy or theory of science, which usually only deal with probability or evidence. But what is plausible is neither probable nor evident in the sense of being 'clear in itself.' For probability is understood as a truth which is only partially reliable and which includes doubts, while evidence excludes doubts. Plausibilities, however, may certainly be doubted; but, remaining in the background, they are not pronounced at all. As long as they are plausibilities, they go unnoticed; as soon as they are noticed, they may indeed be called into doubt. *If something is plausible, one does not ask for either probability or evidence.*

Even defined and justified terms often require support by plausibilities that can no longer be explained. Then images and metaphors are used. In the beginning of his treatise *What Does It Mean to Orient Oneself in Thinking*, Kant emphasizes that especially "pure concepts of understanding" are "suitable for *experien-*

tial use" only if they are connected with "*image* representations," which "procure sense and significance" for them. Images and metaphors are as such not defined; their meanings are not fixed and they can thus keep language in flux. They are in the literal sense – 'metaphor' comes from the Gr. *meta-phérein*, i.e. 'to move something from one place to another, to transfer, to defer' – what keeps language 'in motion' and what allows for its leeway to expand and to defer. The usage of language depends on them to meet the demands of relentlessly changing situations. Here Nietzsche took a radical approach: with him, terms can altogether be conceived as temporarily fixed metaphors that can be set back in motion in everyday as well as scientific language use. *To allow for definitions on the one hand and for the movement of definitions on the other, both everyday and scientific languages oscillate between metaphors and terms, though everyday languages do so more than scientific ones.*

Hans Blumenberg, in his *Paradigms for a Metaphorology*,[14] developed this approach with his notion of "absolute metaphors" – connecting it with the term of orientation. According to him, metaphors are an elementary part of philosophical language. They ensure plausibility in cases where terms can no longer be explained or defined. The most striking example is the term of orientation itself. It is obviously a metaphor: the metaphor of being directed toward the orient, where – Lat. *oriri* – the sun is rising; and obviously it cannot be translated into 'pure' terms. In any case, hardly any attempts have been made so far to philosophically investigate the metaphor of orientation. Instead, it has become a vivid source of ever new metaphors, which in turn have also become philosophical concepts such as 'standpoint,' 'horizon,' and 'perspective,' and it is regularly used to make other terms plausible (and this is how Blumenberg uses the metaphor or term of orientation as well – without discussing it as such). *Absolute metaphors, and especially the absolute metaphor of orientation itself, function as unquestioned plausibilities of orientation.*

1.4 The Analysis of Orientation: Connections and Methods

A philosophy of orientation does not justify or defend a specific philosophical 'position.' Philosophical 'positions,' titled with or formulated in '-isms,' are already 'standpoints' with specific views, which proceed from specific footholds of orientation. All of them may be plausible in some way. However, a philosophy of orientation, which explicitly deals with standpoints and footholds, can go beyond such positions and ask for their orientation functions and for the standards that make them plausible for such positions. The philosophy of orientation allows one to regard the variety of philosophies as expressing the variety of possibilities for assuming different standpoints in the orientation about orientation. Not only contemporary but also historical standpoints of philosophy can be considered as discovering, coining, and passing on distinctions of orientation that are influential and plausible up to the present day. In the following, the most relevant of them will continuously be integrated and implemented.

A fundamental problem of a philosophy of orientation is the paradox of making what is plausible in orientation an object of a theoretical and methodical investigation. In doing so, it detaches itself from that in which it is embedded, running the risk of destroying its self-evidence. However, the theoretical and methodical investigation of the plausible needs to stay plausible itself. Thus, some observations and discussions will appear philosophically trivial on the one hand and audacious on the other. However, this is possible precisely with the concept of orientation, which – as mentioned – has become as plausible as hardly any other concept in both everyday as well as scientific and philosophical discourse. Heidegger explicitly began *Being and Time* with the "fundamental constitution of the everydayness of factual Da-sein," in which Da-sein *"initially and for the most part"* reveals itself.[15] 'Everyday' refers to what happens not always but on a regular basis for a certain time so that it appears to be plausible for those who experience it. Heidegger also called the everyday what is "average" as far as it neglects anything special, which is noticeable *as* special only in comparison to what is plausible. Therefore, what is average or plausible (for a group or a society) can best be understood negatively as what is inconspicuous (for it). In the mode of "inconspicuousness (*Unauffälligkeit*)," "inconspicuous familiarity (*unauffällige Vertrautheit*)," or "self-evidence (*Selbstverständlichkeit*)," appears, Heidegger says, in "what is at hand nearest (*das nächst Zuhandene*);" the more inconspicuous it is, the greater are its "stubborn and primordial" effects. Heidegger defines orientation as the "circumspection of heedful association (*Umsicht des besorgenden Zugangs*)" of what is at hand.[16] A philosophy of orientation can accept this concept as well as Heidegger's suggested method of investigating the average and everyday being, i.e. his phenomenology, which he defines as "to let what shows itself be seen from itself, just as it shows itself from itself," but which still needs to be discovered and made comprehensible as to how it is self-evident or plausible.[17] *A philosophy of orientation proceeds as a phenomenology of everyday orientation in this sense.* However, it does not need to, like Heidegger, push for an *"authentic* existence (*eigentliche Existenz*)."* In orientation there is no criterion of authenticity like "being toward death (*Sein zum Tode*)," which Heidegger assumed per se. Orientations are different and more or less successful, but not authentic or inauthentic. Thus, we do not speak of their "falling (*Verfallen*)" from authenticity into inauthenticity either.

What is plausible in everyday orientation is most accessible through the language of everyday orientation. If orientation is an everyday problem, then the everyday language must have its own terms for it. These terms must have established themselves through continual usage and by proving – and continuing to prove – themselves appropriate from one situation to the next. Everyone is free to speak in some way or another, and she or he can introduce new ways of speaking; but one is always dependent on others' comprehension and response. In this process, there is always new coordination regarding language use in two ways: a continual coordination between communicating people on behalf of their behavior and, at the same time, a continual coordination on behalf of the plausibility of speaking in a certain way. Hence, our ways of speaking, which have proven to be plausible via innumerable speakers and countless communicative situations, indicate how the everyday needs of orientation are expressed in a plausible way. The phenomenology of orientation is thus complemented with a *phenomenology of the language of orientation.* Just as Wittgenstein demonstrated a return from the theoretical use of terms to the everyday use of words – "don't think, but look!" (*Philosophical Investigations*, §66) –, to a certain degree, a philosophy of orientation must likewise simply 'look' at what one 'can say' about the orientation about orientation. But the languages of orientation differ too – in such a way that is difficult to survey. It will be the task of linguists to make the differences surveyable. Here, we focus on the German language of orientation in the original version of this book and on the English language in its translation.

Chapter 2
First Clues: Occurrences of Orientation

2.1 Human Orientation

Human orientation is manifold. If speaking of orientation as such, one usually refers to the

- *geographical orientation* in the open field, in houses, in cities, on the sea, in the air, including orienteering, i.e. a group of sports that require maps and compasses, and orientation in military contexts,
- *mental orientation* that may be examined after an accident, in case of poisoning, or during delirium,
- *pragmatic orientation* when using devices or fulfilling a task,
- *communicative orientation* in conversations, in reports, in narrations, in writings, in books, in science, or on the internet. In these things, one is then 'doing well,' one 'gets by,' or one 'gets a hang of it' – or not,
- *sexual orientation* when preferring the same or a different sex in the varieties of physical love,
- *educational* and *professional orientation* when choosing one's path of education or job,
- *economic orientation* when dealing with scarce resources,
- *political orientation* when making or judging binding decisions for the whole society,
- *judicial orientation* when considering the use of judicial measures,
- *scientific orientation* when taking a 'position' in scientific discourses,
- *artistic orientation* when interested in specific means, objects, and styles of art,
- *religious orientation* when confessing a certain faith,
- *moral* and *ethical orientation* – which are sometimes separated, but sometimes not – when relying on moral principles, norms, values, and their critical reflection, and eventually
- *world orientation*, i.e. orientation in a global horizon.

What all these have in common is that they operate within 'leeways,' where alternatives are possible which must be decided on, and that all these decisions are made under uncertainty and therefore require courage. Orientations thus have common structures, though they are and must not be uniform if they are to do justice to individual situations. Even if they are fixed for a long time, they still need to be open for changing contexts that may force them to reorient

https://doi.org/10.1515/9783110575149-004

themselves, if necessary. Eventually, orientations are individual orientations of individual human beings in individual situations. In different or changing situations, they are more or less successful; they may be 'disturbed' or even 'fail' completely; and sometimes one person can 'hardly understand' why another person's orientation has such a 'hard time' with what is so 'easy' for the other. The following chapters deal with human orientation and its manifold structures. But it is not only human beings that have orientations. Human beings share ways of orientation with animals and plants; and even the orientations of inanimate particles, which make up the living bodies, influence their orientations. Orientations of animals, plants, and particles are being researched step by step; but they are so complex and in many respects so difficult to grasp that the scientific study of orientation is still in its early stages. And it cannot but proceed – self-referentially – from human orientation.

2.2 The Orientations of Animals, Plants, and Particles

For humans, the most conspicuous orientation is the autonomous orientation of living beings in space. It ranges from 'orientation movements' such as reactions to immediate stimuli all the way to periodical 'migrations' between different habitats. *Orientation movements*, which are performed by freely moving humans and animals in their immediate space, are called 'taxes' in biology; and the orientation movements of plants and sessile organisms are called 'tropisms.' Tropisms are either directed toward gravity (geotropism) or respond to specific stimuli such as light (phototropism), especially sunlight (heliotropism), but also water (hydrotropism), chemical substances (chemotropism), cold or heat (thermotropism), and touch (haptotropism). They are often able to either turn toward or away from something ('positive' or 'negative' tropism); they may collaborate and establish complex tropisms. Plants develop such tropisms through growth and 'turgor movements,' i.e. an elastic stretch by adjusting the osmotic cell pressure. Some plants move only to the right, some only to the left; their conspicuous right-left-orientation was one of the starting points for the philosophy of orientation in the 18th century.

A condition for the orientation of freely moving animals is their ability to keep their *balance*. When moving, this balance – in physical terms an 'unstable balance' – needs to be continually readjusted. Higher animals mostly remain in a 'basic' or 'normal stance': they crawl on their belly; they walk on all fours; they stand on their feet, etc. Vertebrates – from fish and amphibians to birds and humans – maintain their desired stance by means of a whole apparatus for keeping balance, which is in the inner ear and part of their sense of hearing; this does not seem to be a coincidence. For the sense of hearing is – like the sense of smell, but different from the sense of sight – not already oriented to something in particular: it responds to stimuli 'all around' in the environment but can still – like the sense of sight – determine the direction of the stimuli's origin. Balance is kept by means of the movement of fluids in the so-called bony labyrinth, where three semicircular canals, perpendicular to one another, are filled with fluids: with the help of tiny hairs as receptors, the body's movements – upwards and downwards; forwards and backwards; left and right – are registered, the receptors sending corresponding signals through neurons to the central nervous system, which in turn sends the corresponding signals needed to keep one's balance. All this happens without our conscious awareness. We become aware of this highly complex physiological art of keeping-one's-balance only in the case that it fails.

Beyond this 'apparatus' for keeping balance, no special sense or organ (like the eyes or the ears) for the direction of orientation has been found. For directing one's orientation upwards and downwards or forwards and backwards a specific organ seems in fact to be redundant: orienting oneself upwards and downwards (including standing upright), is oriented to gravity; orienting oneself forwards and backwards is already determined by the direction of sight because the eyes are only on one side of the head, called the 'front side.' These orientations hardly allow for any doubts. But difficulties may arise when distinguishing between left and right, for which the body's physique and stance have no pre-established directionality. As far as one can speak of a 'sense of orientation,' the whole body is its organ. It takes into account not only the signals for keeping balance, but also the signals of the senses of sight, hearing, smell, and – highly differentiated in itself – touch; all these are complex interconnected information systems that can, if required, increase, lower, or completely ignore incoming stimuli; they are thus able to trigger appropriate body movements that may gather more information. The decentralized organization of the bodily orientation of vertebrates has facilitated differentiated evolutions of their abilities to orient themselves. In every situation, the body had to direct itself toward what was most important for survival.

In a reduced and figurative sense, even the rotational movements of inanimate beings can be regarded as orientations. As such, physics has called the continual orientation of electric dipoles to an outer field an '*orientation polarization*.' The most conspicuous polarization, which was discovered a long time ago, is magnetism. And magnetism is not limited to the orientation of materials to certain poles: 'diamagnetic' and 'paramagnetic' substances become magnetic only within a magnetic field; and 'ferromagnetic' substances can produce a magnetic field themselves. Some animals direct their orientation to magnetism, such as migratory birds, honeybees, or bacteria; and human beings use it for magnetic compasses.

Magnetic fields are already produced when elementary particles rotate around their own axis, i.e. by their 'spin.' For every elementary particle, an 'angular momentum' is characteristic; the sum of the angular momenta of all elementary particles of an atom or molecule makes up the 'total angular momentum quantum number.' All the way down to the smallest analyzable elements of nature, there are alternative directions of movements that cause characteristic behavior. It is increasingly probable that there is in the microcosm – but not in the macrocosm – one distinctly marked direction in each instance. In the mesocosm, i.e. the realm of biological life, the proteins of living organisms are composed only of levorotatory – i.e. 'left-oriented' – (L) amino acids; and there is still no sufficient explanation for this. It seems possible that the first living organism randomly selected a few molecules with an L configuration; and the following generations then inherited L amino acids.

In mathematics, *'orientability'* was sufficiently understood only in the 20th century. It was addressed in the context of the 'analysis of place' (*analysis situs*) and included the introduction of vectors as a kind of 'oriented distance' – a higher structured topological manifold – and the use of algebraic topology. The most conspicuous starting point and foothold are the human hands, which can be distinguished as left and right, and which can be rotated to the left or to the right: they are examples of congruent surfaces, whose congruence is achieved not within the surface but only by rotating in space. This requires a rotation axis – when rotating the hand, this is the arm; when rotating the body as a whole, this is an imagined 'axis' through the head and the feet – from whose 'standpoint' orientation is achieved. The problem of orientability became severe in mathematics when August Ferdinand Möbius introduced so-called 'one-sided surfaces' in his prize essay *Memoire sur les polyedres* at the French Academy of Sciences in 1861. The simplest example is what later became known as the 'Möbius strip,' i.e. a long rectangular surface that is rotated by 180° and whose short ends are joined in such a way that one can get from one side to the other without crossing any boundaries. Since the left and right side are switched when going over the strip, this surface is 'nonorientable' – and it was used in the graphics of M. C. Eschers to irritate directional orientation.

One may argue about whether the rotational movement in mathematics, physics, chemistry, or botany is comparable with the orientation of animals or human beings. In everyday language use, the defining line is the ability to move freely in space and the necessity of this free movement for survival. Free movement allows one to go 'one's own way,' but it also forces one to then find it 'on one's own'; and this requires systems of orientation which enable one to explore the environment with regard to what it offers for one's survival and a 'better' life. The basic parameters of life, however, are not only physical forces but also, and especially, other living beings that function partly as partners, partly as food, and that, by orienting themselves and each other, drive evolution.

2.3 Orientation as Interaction of Orientation Systems

It is a characteristic feature of higher animals' orientation that several *orientation systems* interact in a decentralized and nonhierarchical organization, i.e. as a network. They can thus explore different clues or footholds of the situation, which are not available for each system in equal measure. If – at least partly – independent orientation systems cooperate with each other in this way, they increase the chances for survival by establishing a greater tolerance for disruptions and for the breakdown of single orientation systems.

The ways in which animals orient themselves have been studied intensively since the end of the 19th century. Here 'orientation' was defined in both a narrower and wider sense; in the widest sense, the term referred not only to an orientation to certain places (more or less far away), so-called 'translations,' but it also encompassed the whole behavior of animals as far as it showed control mechanisms for survival and reproduction. In this sense, it excluded only startle responses. The concrete research of orientation slowly moved away from focusing on the so-called *orienting reflex*, i.e. from 'conditioning' animals to respond to certain stimuli, as studied and canonized by Iwan Pawlow. Very often, stimulus-response reactions proved to be inconstant: the response to the stimulus may have been delayed, turned out differently, or been fully absent; and therefore, what was *between* reaction and stimulus was now called 'orientation.' But in both zoology and ethology, it remained difficult to say what exactly that was. It was provisionally called the 'specific central state,' where the 'orienting response' took place (or not); and it would only occur depending on a variety of factors, such as focused attention, further exploration, growing emotions and motives, and only when exceeding a certain threshold.

Regarding the orientation of animals, humans have been especially astonished by their superior capacities for long-distance orientation, e.g. the accuracy of the 'migrations' of birds, eels, salmon, and sea turtles – and the orientation communication of bees when performing their 'dances.' Via elaborate observational series and experiments, zoological and ethological research has long explored less spectacular but no less astonishing ways of orientation in a much greater variety of animal species. A differentiated terminology for the *functions of the orientation of animals* in general and the specific abilities of the senses in particular has developed, which provides – wherever possible – verifiable measurements. In doing so, one could not avoid using metaphorical terms derived from human orientation, such as 'track,' 'map,' 'compass,' 'landmark,' 'pattern,' 'way,' 'target,' 'time schedule,' and, most of all, 'orientation' itself. It is precisely this *use of anthropomorphic language* that makes the research on animal orientation insightful – even beyond measurable results – for the exploration of human orientation as well.

As such, the study of the *long-distance orientation of animals* distinguishes between a compass-track orientation and a target orientation (also called 'navigation' or 'piloting,' respectively). Compass orientation determines the direction – or simply the 'track' – of 'migrations'; and target orientation determines the target on this 'track.' Compass-track orientation, which humans are not (or no longer) able to perform, is supposed to have been developed through evolution already by simple organisms. It allows for a so-called vector navigation, which enables an animal to go into a certain direction and, if combined with a time schedule like those of ants, to reach a certain distance, and thus – if no disruptions occur – to reach a certain target. Relocation experiments have shown that such standardized directions are often based on a genetic program; they can even include bended tracks or bows. If disruptions occur, e.g. by obstacles on the track, or if the time schedule is disturbed by a sudden tailwind or headwind or by unusual water currents, then compensation mechanisms and thus multiple compasses are necessary. They are used sometimes simultaneously and sometimes in alternation; for long-distance and close-distance orientation, they can be the same or different ones. Even closely related animals may have quite different compasses; hence, in terms of evolution, they are highly differentiated.

The most important *biological compass* that has been discovered so far is the magnetic compass which can operate even under poor – or a complete lack of – sight, e.g. during night flights. It uses the earth's magnetic field and can be found among bacteria, snails, crabs, insects, fish, amphibians, reptiles, mammals, and especially birds; it is the (comparably) simplest of all known mechanisms for *directional orientation*. Current research on bacteria suggests that there are magnetite crystals arranged in rows inside their cells which allow them to orient themselves to the earth's magnetic field lines so that they can, in the case they get washed away, return to their original habitat in the sludge of the bottoms of rivers, lakes, or seas. Birds seem to have magnetic sensors in the shape of magnetite particles in the skin of their beaks which measure the force of the magnetic field (it decreases when coming closer to the equator, and which interact with magnetic sensors in the eyes. This complex physico chemical process allows for directional navigation during intercontinenta flights. However, the earth's magnetic field is not a stable and reliable reference point because its polarity has flipped multiple times over the course of the earth's history (and there is still no sufficient explanation for this). Thus, a further compass is used by many animal species: the *solar compass* – and human beings are to some extent capable of orienting themselves to the course of the sun as well. But on long flights from north to south or from south to north, the sun compass is only reliable if the changing position of the sun is taken into account. This happens by means of an 'inner clock' (circadian periodicity) which can be adjusted in experiments. But when birds cross the equator, the sun compass runs into problems as well; and even with carrier pigeons that usually prove to be confident in their orientation it is not very accurate and allows for a deviation of about 5° – but this still seems to be sufficient. Further compasses rarely include the moon, which is quite often a source of disturbance, but more often the sunset, given its light polarization: many birds can perceive ultraviolet light as well as the polarization plane of polarized light. In addition, many birds make use of a *star compass*, which is indicated by the fact that their ability for orientation is much worse in the case of an overcast sky. They seem to use a star pattern in the north, around which heaven's vault seemingly rotates. Obviously, the usage of the *star compass* is an acquired skill, for it fails if birds cannot observe the night sky in their youth; in terms of evolution, the star compass is thus probably a younger compass. For directional orientation, birds may also make use of other compasses, such as local winds (birds seem to expect such winds and take them into account for their orientation – how this works is still unknown), the infrasound patterns of oceans and mountains, etc., differences in air pressure, and scent fields (*olfactory, smell or scent compass*).

The latter can enable or support *target orientation*. But target orientation works in a very different way, namely by developing '*cognitive maps*': on the one hand, gradient maps support compass orientation by recording the changes of geophysical parameters (such as the magnetic field or the position of the sun) when birds move over the surface of the earth; on the other hand, topographical maps register significant reference points in traversed terrain or bodies of water. But since bodies of water offer less significant and especially less stable reference points, this orientation is primarily concerned with landmarks, characteristic terrain features (mountains and rivers), vegetation, buildings, scent fields, sound sources, and much more. This so-called *orientation to landmarks* is the closest to human orientation. Recently, it was discovered that pigeons tend to follow highways and take turns over highway intersections; and sometimes they even align with roundabouts. Patterns of landmarks seem again to be particularly important because the configuration of multiple landmarks allows individual landmarks to be neglected or new ones to be added. If, in experiments with bees, patterns of landmarks and the position of the sun are competing, then the bees prefer relying on patterns of landmarks, but not on individual landmarks. But every animal must acquire this landmark orientation on its own – we would say: through experience. Bees, at least, cannot bequeath it to their descendants.

2.4 Human Orientation with Maps and Compasses

For long-distance orientation, human beings are in general fully dependent on maps and compasses. This is precisely what the phrase 'to orient oneself' initially refers to. It comes from Lat. *oriens*, i.e. 'ascending': the 'orient' is, seen from Europe, the country in the direction of the 'rising sun' (*sol oriens*), compared to the 'occident,' i.e. the country in the west, where the sun goes down (*sol occidens*); and 'to orient oneself' originally means to 'turn to the east.' Via Italian (*orientare*) and French (*orienter*), the word was adopted by other European and many non-European languages. In French, it was used especially in the expression *orienter une carte*, i.e. 'to align a map (to the east).'

Since 1200 AD, when the magnetic compass became known in Europe, maps, however, have been turned toward the north and the North Pole. But until the early modern period, the east was nevertheless on the top of the map, where the sun rises and day and life begin. Many cultures endowed the sunrise in the east with a religious aura. The east became the country of light and life, and the west the country of darkness and death; the cardinal directions each had their own gods. In the Old Kingdom of Egypt, the dead were buried with their heads to the east so that they could look toward their own country in the west (later and in different cultures, this practice was performed in reverse: the deceased's head would be buried toward the west so that they could look toward the country of life). The main entrance of Greek temples was turned to the east so that the first rays of the rising sun would enlighten the (often golden) sculpture of the god inside. The Romans built their cities according to an east-west and north-south coordinate system, which was also the foundation of the judicial delineation of properties. In some religions, prayers are directed toward the east; for the Hebrews, this is where Paradise is. And above all, Jesus Christ went – according to the Christian doctrine – to the east, in the direction of the Mount of Olives, and up to heaven from where he was expected to return one day. And this is how Christian churches were 'oriented': the altar was in the east; the devil came from the west; the south was the symbol of the Holy Spirit; and the north was the symbol for the estrangement from God, from light, and from faith. This must have had an influence on the fact that the 'aligning' of maps is still referred to as 'orienting' them rather than 'septentrionalizing' them. Lat. *septentriones* means the constellation of the Big Dipper which points toward the North Pole. But 'septentrionalize a map' would have been too difficult to pronounce.

Today, ordinary maps are called *'orientation maps.'* They do not represent what is, but they offer perspectival projections. Maps depict the curved surface of the earth as a plane and thus as a distorted image. And all one can do is choose between different distortions. Only a geographical 'globe' can be completely free of distortion; however, it can never be overseen as a whole at once; for it always has an unobserved backside. As will be seen, this is a metaphor for orientation itself.

Maps sketch out the first *basic conditions of orientation.* They offer a so-called 'situation' in the shape of an outline drawing of a ground plan, whose areas may be filled with colors – orientation always happens within a concrete situation. And into the situation, maps fill in a 'signature,' i.e. signs which create schemata for what they denote by means of object images (e.g. of trees or houses), geometrical figures (points, lines, areas, circles, triangles, squares etc.), numbers (e.g. altitude), or names (of cities, rivers, mountains etc.). Their orientation value may be increased by form, size, or color and complemented by diagrams – orientation abbreviates the world by means of signs. But maps are useful only if you have found your own standpoint in them and thus if you connect the virtual situation with the real one. And this is the case for orientation in general.

Chapter 3
The Situation of Orientation: Time Pressure
Orientation as Finding-One's-Way

3.1 Orientation about the Situation in the Situation

We initially defined orientation as the achievement of finding one's way in a situation and making out promising opportunities for actions to master the situation; or, to avoid using the philosophically charged concept of action: as an achievement of exploring a situation with respect to what must be done in order to master it. However, it is not about just doing anything, but about doing what is 'right' in a given situation, i.e. what promises to be successful or by means of which the 'most can be made of a situation.' It constitutes a 'disorientation' if a baseball team does not play together in a way to score runs, or if a businesswoman or man is unable to find ways to make good deals under favorable conditions, or if a politician cannot take advantage of an opponent's weaknesses. As a philosophical term, '*situation*' is the correlate of 'orientation': it is what orientation deals with.

The term 'situation' comes, like 'orientation,' from geography. It goes back to Lat. *situs*, i.e. the location, e.g. of countries or body parts or points to each other. While the French *orienter* denotes the aligning of maps to the cardinal directions, *situer* refers to the ordering of map entries to each other. The word was especially used within a military context for 'bringing troops or canons into the right battlefield position.' Today, it refers to 'a set of circumstances,' a 'condition,' a 'status,' or a 'state of affairs' in general.

As correlates, the terms 'situation' and 'orientation' are – like all correlations (e.g. form and content; cause and effect; subject and object) – both mutually exclusive, as far as they are drawing a distinction, and mutually inclusive, as far as each one cannot be thought without the other. The distinction that is drawn by the correlation of situation and orientation is the most basic one: it is the distinction that evokes making further distinctions. The sheer fact that a situation is perceived as new means that something relevant has changed and that now distinctions are necessary – whatever they may be – for responding to this change. *The correlation of situation and orientation is the distinction evoking distinctions.*

This means: The first distinction an orientation draws is the distinction between itself and the situation. If an orientation is fully 'absorbed' in a situation, then there is no leeway to orient itself 'about' it; therefore, an orientation must always somehow be different from its current situation. Only within a certain dis-

https://doi.org/10.1515/9783110575149-005

tance from the situation, i.e. by being or setting itself apart from it, can orientation turn its attention to it. Thus, orientation's being or setting itself apart from its situation is its beginning as an actual or new orientation; it is precisely in this sense that the distinction of the orientation from the situation is the premise of all further distinctions. Therefore, this distinction cannot be justified with further reasons because this would again only be possible by means of further distinctions.

A situation, in which one must find one's way and get by, *is* a new situation, i.e. a changed set of relevant circumstances. In fact, *every situation is more or less new* because one cannot assume that everything will always stay the same; instead, one can expect that everything has a (more or less) limited time. But for every orientation in a situation at a certain time, different things (or their relevance) can be new. What is new for an orientation is that what makes a difference for it. That the weather has changed today may make a difference for *one* orientation in *its* situation, but not for another in its situation; for yet another one, the fact that the global climate is changing (or not) makes a difference. Different orientations are more or less alert to certain changes and more or less interested in them; and situations may thus appear to be more or less new – requiring more or less new orientations.

The situation that requires orientation is – as one calls it – that which is 'given.' Everything that is 'given' is given in a situation; the situation encompasses all that is given for an orientation. Such 'givens' or circumstances of a situation are, one says, 'found'; one 'encounters' and 'comes up against' them without having searched for them. They are just there; and now one has to deal with them. What (or who) 'gives' them remains anonymous at first: the giving, as it first appears, is a giving without a giver. In philosophical terms, what is given is 'contingent'; Lat. *contingere* just means 'to encounter something; to touch; to come up against; to find; to experience.' *As far as orientation deals with what is given in a situation it deals with contingency.*

However, as mentioned above, you are not dealing with everything given in a situation. There are always only a few things in it that you are concerned with and that are thus 'of concern' or 'relevant.' Lat. *relevare* means 'to free or relieve oneself from a displeasing or distressful situation.' In a situation, what is relevant is what may create hardship or distress, which you are (more or less) forced to deal with in order to eliminate, remedy, or prevent it. Therefore, *orientation means dealing with relevant contingencies.*

When 'encountering' and 'entering' a situation, it is initially unknown what will be of concern or of interest in it. In each situation you are in, you must 'find out' about it. But the situation is not limited – neither in space nor in time. What is relevant may be very far away or very near in space and time: a noise in your ear; voices that reach the ear; stories that are told; news distributed by the media; political decisions that are announced; scientific discoveries and calculations that are published (among which, e. g. global warming may have a strong impact on life on earth). And behind everything that you pay attention to, further – more or less – relevant issues may arise; their realm may suddenly be widened or narrowed. If, when discussing more or less trivial matters during breakfast in a hotel, you suddenly hear your name from the neighboring table, the realm of relevant matters widens; if, when expecting intrigues from a new colleague or competitor, he or she proves to be cooperative and loyal, the realm of relevant matters narrows. The relevant matters of a situation are not given in a way that would allow one to determine them once and for all. Every relevant circumstance can suddenly appear or disappear; and they can always lead to further relevant circumstances. And since in some way 'everything is connected with everything else,' it is unforeseeable what 'in the end' is relevant in a situation of orientation. Therefore, *the situation of orientation can eventually be defined only negatively as that from which nothing may be excluded as irrelevant.* It is the entirety of contingent and relevant circumstances that have not yet been conceived of or defined in terms; and it can never be fully grasped in concepts. In positive terms, it is singular and individual; and this means again that *one can conceive of it only negatively as that which escapes all conceiving.*

However, even perception cannot grasp the situation – it cannot survey all the possibly relevant matters that may arise. Perception, as a perception of something specific, already presupposes something that is demarcated, distinguished, and isolated. But for an orientation in a situation, it is still open as to what (and from what and how) something is being demarcated, distinguished, and isolated: e. g. the babble of voices in the hotel's breakfast room from the noise of construction machines on the street, or the voice of one's interlocutor from the babble of voices or the peculiar tone in his or her speech which has strangely changed since yesterday. Thus, what Kant said about the left-right distinction seems to be true for the situation as such: *it is neither 'given' for thinking nor for perception.* This very distinction is also only drawn in the situation – as far as it offers an orientation.

Despite being in principle unlimited, inconceivable, and ungraspable, situations of orientation are in fact spatially and temporally limited, conceivable, and graspable. They are limited because the relevant matters that one is dealing with always end somewhere; and the capacity to grasp them is limited in each orientation at each time. Thus, each orientation limits itself to focus on those matters that it can oversee for a certain time. Later, under new circumstances, it may extend or move or shift its focus. *An orientation limits the situation which it is to explore and widens it as needed at a time.* In other words: the current situation is always the 'here and now'; but this 'here and now' is not simply the present moment in place and time. Instead, the spatial and temporal realm of relevant matters in a situation can vary greatly: e. g. children playing in a sandbox and forgetting everything else; a rare family celebration that was therefore long-expected and that will have a lasting effect; a country making efforts for sustainable political reforms; a continent striving for economic and political unification, the entire earth with the uncertainty of future life on it; or the whole universe that is expanding and perhaps collapsing again. The situation can last a few seconds or billions of years – how far it is expanded depends on the orientation it self. But in any case, the situation includes a (more or less long) past that is relevant for the future, such as the pat given from one child to the other who took his or her toy away; political decisions made by former governments; or scientific calculations whose theoretical foundations were established centuries ago. In the situation of orientation, *the present consists of relevant matters from the past for the future*; and as far as the future is 'open,' the present is 'open' as well

Orientation about a situation however takes place *in* the situation that the orientation explores; and it changes the situation that it explores. If a situation is explored, then one 'sees clearer'; one 'knows what one is getting into'; and a situation that is made 'clear' is different from a situation which remains 'unclear.' It is the *starting paradox* of orientation that it already *changes the situation it explores*. Thus, it always renews the need for orientation and thereby continuously renews itself. By renewing itself it continuously makes recourse to its own results from orientations in former situations. This continuous recourse is called recursiveness or recursivity. As such, *to orient oneself about a situation in the situation means recursively dealing with the relevant contingencies of the situation*

Recursivity is self-referentiality combined with other-referentiality: the recursive orientation refers to itself in its former shapes up to the present moment and, at the same time, to the current situation; and in both regards (its self-referentiality and its other-referentiality), it changes more or less all the time. To summarize: orientation, which appears to be quite simple, self-referentially and other-referentially deals with relevant contingencies in its current situation limited by its own capacity to grasp the situation, it temporarily widens and reduces its focus on the situation, evokes distinctions to conceive it, and through all this, changes the situation that it explores. Traditional philosophy has hardly – if at all – addressed these differentiations.

They have been, however, addressed in military contexts where recursive orientation has become particularly relevant, as we learn from Wikipedia. John Richard Boyd (1927–1997), a highly decorated United States Air Force fighter pilot (with no combat kills), military strategist and Pentagon consultant, made the recursivity of orientation the core of a very successful military theory. Beginning in the 1940s, he developed the concept of the so-called *OODA loop*, which entails recursively **o**bserving, **o**rienting, **d**eciding, and **a**cting. From the start, he conceived of orientation as a process that can change the situation at any point. 'To orient oneself' is the second step after 'to observe': it involves, according to Boyd, genetic heritage, cultural traditions, previous experiences, new information, and their analysis and synthesis. Orienting yourself prepares your decision and your action, which both create a new situation and require new observations – the loop thus makes recourse to its beginning. But making a decision can also involve canceling an action for the time being or creating new situations that the opponent does not expect. The pilot who goes through the OODA loop in the shortest time prevails because his opponent is caught responding to situations that have already changed. Boyd applied the loop to all intelligent organisms and organizations; to him, a decentralized organization could be more successful – given a high degree of mutual trust. Though Boyd never wrote a comprehensive text about the OODA loop, his ideas have been highly influential in sports, business, and litigation. Throughout his life, Boyd also expanded the concept scientifically and philosophically; he integrated mathematical, physical, and logical theories into his concept, such as Kurt Gödel's incompleteness theorems, Werner Heisenberg's uncertainty principle, the second law of thermodynamics, cognitive science, and game theory, trying to expand his theory to a general theory of litigation strategy; in the sense of Darwin's theory of evolution, Boyd considered the orientation loop as the crucial mechanism for adapting to ever-new situations. The key to survival is therefore not perfect adaptation to given circumstances, but rather the ability to adapt to change as such, and this survival is challenged and fed by radical uncertainty.[18]

3.2 The Basic Mood of Orientation: Being Unsettled by Time Pressure

To put it simply: dealing with relevant contingencies means dealing with surprises. In each situation, orientation tries to cope with something that it does not yet know anything about; and if it knows, it is no longer the same as it was before. In short: orientation must always encounter surprises. There is no identifiable correlation of cause and effect. The correlation of cause and effect presupposes that cause and effect are distinguished as separable entities that are connected by a general law. This cannot be assumed for the correlation of situation and orientation. Instead, there are 'irritations' of orientations by situations: Lat. *irritare* means 'to stimulate, to unsettle, to excite.' An irritation is a disturbance of the established orientation whose causes are unclear. Therefore, *irritations unsettle* and prompt one to *search* for their causes – not knowing *where* one is to look for them and without ever being certain that one has found them. A strange noise that one cannot locate; a behavior that one cannot explain; a comment one does not know what to do with; a contradictory direction sign; coinciding events indicating that unusual things are going on – these are all (more or less) disorienting especially with regard to cause and effect. They spur an orientation to find out what is 'behind them'; they create orientation needs and make them noticeable.

Irritations – they may be more or less strong in more or less new situations – keep orientation in perpetual agitation. *Agitation or unsettlement is the basic mood of orientation.* It is not a kind of knowledge because nothing can be known yet; it is not a feeling either because nothing can be felt. It is a mood (*Stimmung*) that – like the tuning (*stimmen*) of a musical instrument – brings all tones to a different pitch. In different moods, situations are experienced in different ways; and thus, their orientations vary as well. Even science, which seems to be without a mood, still presupposes a certain mood: the mood of sobriety, earnestness, and asceticism – all of which must be created with substantial effort, e.g. quiet areas; bleak offices and lecture halls; chilly laboratories; a disciplined language; inconspicuous clothing, etc. Moods can quickly shift; and this already creates an unsettlement: suddenly everything may look different. If the unsettling increases, it can grow into *anxiety* or *angst*; and if the anxiety continues, it may even become *despair* (*Verzweiflung*): *doubts* (*Zweifel*) about one's own opportunities to 'get by' may grow and then paralyze all action. If the desperation persists, it may result in *depression:* i.e. the 'pressing-down' of all prospects for coping with one's life. Anxiety is the basic mood that one's orientation will not succeed in a certain situation; despair is the mood that it will not succeed in returning situations; and depression is the persistent despair that one's orientation can no longer master any relevant situation. If an orientation succeeds and if opportunities for getting by are sufficiently explored and successfully actualized, then one feels reassured, calmed down, and at ease. *Calmness through reassurance is the hallmark of a successful orientation and is already its criterion.* Every orientation that succeeds calms down; and it calms down because it succeeds. In reassurance, the need for or the necessity of orientation ceases.

In perpetually new situations, which must each be mastered anew and which are generally mastered with success, the unsettlement and reassurance (*Beunruhigung und Beruhigung*) of an orientation constantly take turns: they oscillate. However, in the *oscillation of orientation between unsettlement and reassurance,* unsettlement is not per se the negative value nor is reassurance the positive one. For unsettlement not only arises when something surprising happens that disturbs an orientation's established functioning, but also when nothing surprising happens and orientation appears not to work. Orientation is set in a way – and experiences itself in this way – that something irritating and surprising is happening continually; in a word: there is always 'something going on' that orientation is continually dealing with. Thus, it is unsettling as well, if 'nothing is going on.' Just like we are afraid of change, we also welcome change. Change is, of course, especially pleasing if a situation is somehow displeasing, troublesome, or no longer bearable; and it is pleasing too, if a pleasant situation is calm for such a long time that boredom arises. In this case, one is looking for 'entertainment'; and entertainment is first and foremost the *maintenance of the orientation process*. The pleasure of change is the pleasure of the liveliness of orientation. One is looking for this pleasure (more or less often) in 'adventures' – athletic, touristic, political, economic, scientific, artistic, or religious – which can turn out to be (more or less) productive and creative.

Thus, both calmness *and* unsettlement may cause irritations: one can be unsettled by calmness or calm in the face of persistent unsettlement. Whether something is experienced as unsettling or calming depends on where the cause of surprises is suspected. If the cause is attributed to a situation that is not yet sufficiently overseen and that is therefore unpredictable, then the surprise is considered a *danger*. If one can to some degree assess the situation and 'make something' of it, then possible surprises are perceived as *risks* that one is willing to take.[19] Because every orientation is under uncertainty, new situations always require one to take such risks; if everything were for certain, then nothing new would happen and one would not need to orient oneself.

That something new can happen presupposes *time* – time in its most unlimited sense that all things can change (including the sense of time). Precisely this is why everything is always (more or less) uncertain. In situations of orientation, time is experienced as *time shortage* and *time pressure*. Time shortage means that orientation needs time to oversee the situation and to find opportunities to deal with surprising circumstances. Time pressure refers to the fact that time 'pressures' one to do now in this situation what can be done successfully. The time pressure of orientation is so normal that its temporary lack is noticed – and the lack of time pressure is (mostly) experienced as pleasing: as leisure or 'free time' (i.e. a time free from time pressure). Science and particularly philosophy – as far as they are not expected to produce any 'cash value' but basic research – enjoy special arrangements to lower the time pressure; they are (or were) allowed to 'take time' for their research. This privilege could be one reason why philosophy has so far mainly ignored the needs of orientation.

However, new relevant occurrences in a situation do not only put one under pressure. They can also become *opportunities*. Opportunities are favorable, but temporary, occurrences to succeed in a situation; they must be recognized and made use of in the situation. For what makes up an opportunity, there is again no higher criterion: it arises now for this orientation in this situation; it is an opportunity only in this situation; a slight change of circumstances can already make a situation 'look worse' again. Despite the pressure of time, it may sometimes therefore be better to 'wait for opportunities.' They come 'over time'; one needs to grasp them 'at the right time' and then use them in the right way. As far as orientation uses opportunities, it is a matter of *kairos*, which the ancient Greeks greatly appreciated. Making good use of the favorable time when opportunities arise leads to the desired balance in each situation; continually making good use of these opportunities provides psychological assurance in the form of a long-lasting self-confidence and can ethically create a balanced character. Balanced characters stand out by staying calm even in difficult situations; they are able to curb the oscillations between unsettlement and reassurance. A person who has learned to confidently orient him or herself in his or her circumstances will become altogether calmer over time; a person who has learned to deal even with the oscillation of unsettlement and reassurance develops composure. Today, we might simply say they are 'cool.'

3.3 The Basic Attitude of Orientation: Attention and Courage

Orientation responds to an unsettlement (pleasing or displeasing) with an increase of attention. Attention is experienced as a state of tension that can increase and decrease or wear off and cease. In orientation, it never fully ceases. If it ceased completely, orientation would come to an end: death. Attention is essential for life in order to face dangers. It can be completely absorbed by something involuntary; and it can voluntarily focus on something. Since it is at first unclear where dangers may originate, attention must initially be without a particular focus; it relentlessly scans the situation for possible dangers. One's attention decreases if it is not stimulated by something relevant in the situation – it then needs to be kept up with conscious efforts. To keep up one's attention is easier in an eventful environment than in an uneventful one; but an eventful one can also distract one's attention. It may then 'jump' or be 'divided.' If it is divided, one's attention may either weaken when taken from one aspect to the other or it may increase and become tenser. However, the increase of its tension is effective only within limits. Attention has – depending on the person and the situation – a limited capacity (just like orientation as a whole) and can therefore sometimes be overwhelmed.

Whenever situations exceed the capacity of attention, one's orientation tries – seeking relief – to find regular patterns. But it focuses only for a short time – usually for a few seconds – on the same occurrences and then involuntarily digresses; thus, when an object is to be fixed, it needs to be recalled as often as needed. This is where the voluntary sustainment of attention begins. William James, who intensively dealt with the manifold research on attention in his time, described it as follows:

> What is called sustained voluntary attention is a repetition of successive efforts which bring back the topic to the mind. [This means] that it is not an identical *object* in the psychological sense, but a succession of mutually related objects forming an identical *topic* only, upon which the attention is fixed.[20]

Thus, the digression of attention that is scanning the situation for what is relevant is not its lack but its primordial mode; and the voluntary focus of attention is effective only in a limited way as well: if something is rigidly stared at, it loses its contours, and if a word is repeated several times in one sentence ('a rose is a rose is a rose is a rose...'), it loses its meaning. Hence, attention must – to be effective for orientation – keep itself within a certain leeway of increasing and decreasing as well as focusing and digressing; and thus, attention is more an attitude than an intention: *Orientation responds to the basic mood of unsettlement with the basic attitude of paying more or less attention.*

Intention is a focused and oriented attention; but this focus is only a result of orientation: it requires a prior non-directed and non-oriented attention. Like in a situation where 'something' is not just given as a distinguished or defined identity, attention in a situation is not already focused on something specific. In neurophysiology and psychology, attention and intention are distinguished as non-selective and selective; philosophical phenomenology uses the less felicitous distinction of passive and active attention. But it is less a matter of passivity and activity and more a matter of going ahead and proceeding: the non-selective attention that is open for irritations and surprises of all kinds precedes the selective one, i.e. 'intention': when orientation focuses on certain things, it monitors the situation to discover matters that prompt an orientation to focus its attention – and become an intention. While the non-selective attention (sometimes called the 'passive' attention) ranges between the extremes of lethargy and indifference on the one hand and interest, alarm, and shock on the other, the selective attention (sometimes called the 'active' attention) or the intention needs to sustain its focus despite always being in danger of digressing.

For the psychological state of the tense (and paradoxical) expectation of the unexpected that constitutes the pre-selective attention, everyday language uses the terms attentiveness or vigilance. It has become an object of brain research as well. And research results highlight that the brain is never calm, but continuously generates highly complex excitation patterns, even if external stimuli are missing.[21] Vigilance is not limited to what is called consciousness. Instead, the whole body is part of it, not only its five senses, but also all its organs and especially its skin (sometimes this holistic orientation is called the 'sixth sense').

The structuring of attention is also the structuring of orientation. It is the topic of the following investigations. As far as attention makes one's orientation aware of dangers and risks as well as of favorable opportunities in a situation, it also includes *courage:* the courage to face dangers, to take unavoidable risks, and to grasp promising opportunities – in each case without any certainty of success. Courage is the courage to act under uncertainty – and as far as orientation is always under uncertainty, it always requires courage.

Chapter 4
The Selectivity of Orientation: Views
Orientation as Overview

4.1 Viewing the Situation

One orients oneself with all one's senses. But in the everyday language of orientation, sight has priority: the alignment of attention is articulated primarily by the word field of seeing, viewing, and sighting. This seems to be due to the prehistoric living conditions of humans: when tracing what was necessary for survival and when searching for the paths that led to it, the human being had to rely mainly on the ability of sight; and walking upright allowed for a clear view. Human beings had to – and still have to – view the situation, scan it, spot anything conspicuous, and, at the same time, select what is relevant in it. When viewing or scanning or 'sifting' the situation in this manner, orientation shifts from a non-focused and non-selective mode to a focused and selective one. Something specific then moves into the center of the field of vision; everything else goes to the edge, to the periphery. When sifting the situation, orientation focuses, i. e. it 'centers,' 'concentrates' itself. This concentration (in the case of hearing it becomes a focused listening), and that means, *the distinction between center and periphery*, is a basic condition for the operation and self-structuring that orientation follows.

Even science and philosophy are kinds of viewing in this sense. 'Theory,' by which both are sometimes defined, is derived from Greek *theoreîn*, which originally means 'to come to view' something, and this viewing happened particularly in a place specifically designed for it: the theater (Gr. *théatron*). Its ascending rows and ranks allowed for an increasing overview of everything that happened on stage. By analogy, scientific and philosophical theory was assumed to have a particularly sublime position over events. But orientation in a situation is different from such a theory; the analogy between orientation and theory in the theater is misleading. It makes one believe that the circumstances of an everyday situation can be completely surveyed.

Everyday orientation rather proceeds from the – probably – primordial situation of hunting, where the hunter always puts him or herself at risk of becoming the hunted. Thus, when on the watch, one tries to avoid being seen and one therefore stands still. Moreover, when standing still, it is easier to track whatever is moving. Whatever or whoever is moving becomes conspicuous while the viewer remains inconspicuous. In the primordial situation of hunting, moving in-

https://doi.org/10.1515/9783110575149-006

creases one's visibility while resting decreases it; the perception systems of animals and humans usually respond more strongly to moving objects than to resting ones. Nevertheless, the observer always remains part of the situation and he or she can, at any time, be observed and discovered as well. But in the situation of hunting, one can quickly lose sight of what is moving. In this case, the hunter needs to start moving as well in order to pursue the hunted. It is much more complicated to observe something which is moving while oneself is on the move, and this also applies to our everyday orientation: while viewing the situation, we are 'moved' by the situation itself. The perception system of the viewer must continuously recalibrate the viewed movements in reference to its own moving view. The views multiply, and new needs for reorienting oneself arise through the multiplicity and diversity of views. Thus, there is not a sublime, stable, and protected point of view like in a theater. Orientation is not like a scientific theory: the viewers are also viewed, the observers observed, and the hunters hunted. As a result, viewing what is moving while moving oneself significantly increases the pressure of the situation and the requirements for coping with it.

4.2 The Direction of Attention while Viewing the Situation: Meaning

Your orientation does not begin with goals you want to attain; instead, it begins with the viewing of the situation in order to look for promising options and opportunities for action, which then allow goals to be envisaged. In orientation, promising options and opportunities for action must first be 'found'; you must find them among unlimited possibilities that are offered in every situation. You find them through limitation: by restricting and focusing your attention on what may be relevant for you in the situation. What is relevant for an orientation in a situation is the beginning of 'meaning' (*Sinn*): *for an orientation, meaning is that with which it can 'make something'* (*etwas anfangen können*). Meaning arises in the situation itself; it is not given and fixed in advance. Thus, like the term 'orientation,' the term 'meaning' cannot be reduced to any other term; just as understanding the meaning of 'orientation' already presupposes orientation, understanding the meaning of 'meaning' already presupposes meaning. And both terms obviously belong together: orientation is initially successful when it finds meaning; wherever and whenever meaning is found, there is orientation; the meaning of orientation is to find meaning.

But finding meaning does not coincide with finding the *'meaning of life'* (*Sinn des Lebens*) in general. Seeking and finding the meaning of life in general would go beyond what is possible and necessary for orientation, which is always an orientation in a certain situation. In order to seek and find the meaning of life as such, the orientation of human beings would need to possess an overview of life as a whole; and this would include not only the life of the individual orienting him or herself, but also the lives of all others with all the circumstances they have to deal with in some way and who might influence the individual's life. From 'life' in this sense, nothing can be excluded; it encompasses everything that might be there or that might happen; and therefore, it can never be fully available for any orientation. Nobody can have an overview of his or her entire life or even of 'life as such' so as to 'find' *one* meaning in it or 'give' one to it.

Of course, this does not preclude that you search for such an all-encompassing meaning of life and thereby give your life a direction. You will try to do so as long as you are unable to reconcile important concerns of your life (or whatever of your life you may observe): when long-cherished wishes and demands have not been fulfilled; when great and continued efforts do not lead to success; in sum, when your orientation is, in the long run, unsuccessful and when anxiety and despair arise.

However, even though anxiety and despair may urge your need for orientation, they usually do not help you in finding a good orientation; instead, they limit this even more. Decisions on new directions of your life, if made under their influence, become questionable again when the situation has calmed down. Yet, even in calmer periods, life often forces you to again change the decisions you have made and the directions you have taken on certain occasions.

The 'meaning of life' will most likely be different for a young woman asking about it when trying to make plans for her future than for this same woman in the middle of her professional career – perhaps being responsible for her own children then – and different again when she has retired and her children have grown up. Thus, the 'meaning of life' will always be a temporary one – not one for your entire life or even the lives of all human beings. In addition, every 'meaning of life' will have alternatives at any moment in time, and that means: *One does not* find *a meaning of life, but one* decides for *a certain meaning and thus* against *others; this decision or selection is made in a situation that may change and that therefore may also require changing one's decision.* Committing oneself to a certain decision made in a certain situation for the whole duration of one's life may provide a stable orientation for this life; but it also impedes orientation from 'keeping up with the times' and thus deprives orientation of its own meaning.

The question of the meaning of life, if it arises in a situation, is usually not answered positively or definitely, but rather in a way that it is simply no longer asked. It usually resolves itself as soon as new fitting options and opportunities for action emerge – as soon as you succeed in orienting yourself again in such a way that everything fits together to some degree. For this, it is not necessary that you have an overview of everything in the situation and be able to specify criteria or reasons for the fitting of its relevant circumstances. And the options and opportunities for action, which now provide sufficient meaning, need not be options and opportunities for action in all stages of your future life. Wittgenstein, a persistent searcher for meaning, wrote near the end of his *Tractatus logico-philosophicus:* "The solution of the problem of life is seen in the vanishing of the problem. (Is not this the reason why those who have found after a long period of doubt that the sense of life became clear to them have then been unable to say what constituted that sense?)." (*Tractatus Logico-Philosophicus*, 6.521; transl. by D. F. Pears and B. F. McGuiness)

4.3 Gaining an Overview: The Paradox of Seeing-Everything-and-Nothing

With a clear view, an orientation remains calm; with an unclear view, it becomes unsettled. If something is clearly in sight, one does not pay attention to one's vision, but only to what is in sight. The viewing conditions are noticed only when they are hampered, just as balance is only noticed when it is at risk of being lost; then one needs to strive for a clear view. The same accounts for 'meaning': meaning mostly occurs without further ado, 'automatically'; the search for meaning only becomes noticeable when it is troublesome. When, in a situation, meaning cannot be easily found and one runs into difficulties trying to make something of the situation, one strives to 'gain an overview' of it: at first an overview of the circumstances and of the potentially relevant matters in the situation, i.e. of what in it could provide meaning, then an overview of the possible views themselves that could make sense. The latter kind of overview is a second-degree view: a view of views, whereby each may give a direction, disclose a way, or offer an option or an opportunity for action in order to make headway. This overview is thus once again self-referential; and this self-referential view of views makes different views visible in the first place and allows for decisions between them.

The first-degree overview has a threefold meaning in and for orientation.

(1) When seeking to gain an overview of the circumstances of a situation, one tries to *overlook everything that is relevant in this situation.* In geographical orientation, this is possible through an elevated view, spatially above everything else. One 'surmounts' or 'transcends' in a literal sense the situation in order to arrive at a 'panorama,' literally an 'all-seeing' position. This is how gods were usually imagined: sitting high above, be it on Mount Olympus or in heaven at

the highest point of the heavenly vault, with a full overview of human matters; this is what theaters were built for; and this is how the ideal philosophical or scientific theory was envisioned. But in the everyday orientation of humans, there are only preliminary and intermediate stages to this: at first the range of view disclosed by upright walking or by sitting in the upper ranks of something like a theater, then the extended overview of towers and mountains. But even from there, panoramas are still limited, and towers and mountains can block each other's view. At last, beyond the highest towers and mountains, there is the 'bird's-eye view' from paragliders, balloons, helicopters, airplanes, and – with even more technical effort – spaceships. This last overview, which we would also appreciate in everyday orientation, is, however, itself moving and usually very fast. Thus, it allows the field one wants to survey to be seen for only a few short moments. But in everyday orientation we prefer an overview that is, on the one hand, effortless, and, on the other, enduring.

If in geographical orientation simply 'looking around' is not enough, you can turn to maps for help. Orienting oneself with maps is a second-degree view as well; but it affords, moreover, another kind of orientation, which we will discuss later in chapter 7: the orientation by means of characters and signs. Maps containing characters and signs can be held in one's hands in front of one's eyes and, at the same time, over the area in which one seeks to orient oneself; in doing so, one can look over both the map and the area. With a map of the area in which one wants to orient oneself, one gains an overview by oscillating between both the overview of the map and the overview of the terrain – without climbing towers or mountains or flying in balloons or aircrafts. Gaining an overview with maps is the everyday transcendence of orientation today; it is an overview that is (comparably) easy to make use of.

However, you must also orient yourself in the map itself; and it can be difficult to identify your own location on the map. For maps are not photographs and their signs only symbolize the circumstances of the area and greatly abbreviate it. This in turn requires new ways of orienting yourself (if not modern navigation systems).

(2) 'To overlook' (just as in German *übersehen*) means both 'to see everything' and 'to miss something' in this seeing. This creates an everyday paradox that is philosophically interesting: by seeing everything, one sees nothing. When trying to overlook everything, you cannot and may not focus on something specific. When focusing on *something* specific, you exclude everything else. As a result, when taking an overview of a situation, one is overlooking (i.e. missing) all of it. This is the well-known paradox of the whole and its parts or – to take another example from geographic orientation – of the forest and the trees. Certainly, the whole consists of its parts and the forest of its trees. But when seeing the

forest, one overlooks (or skips in viewing) the single trees; when seeing single trees, one overlooks (or skips in viewing) the forest. This simultaneous 'seeing everything and nothing' or 'seeing and not seeing' while viewing a situation usu-ally does not trouble our everyday orientation, even if it is paradoxical. Orienta-tion resolves the paradox by temporalizing it: once again, by oscillating – in this case between focusing and defocusing or looking at something and looking away from it. At one point, we see the forest, at another, the trees, keeping both views present almost at the same time. And this is also how we arrange the forest and, next to it, the hill and the church spire in the terrain, or the words in a sentence or the sentences in a text, etc.

(3) The third meaning of 'having an overview or a survey' is the most com-mon and the most important one for our orientation. It is the aforementioned re-sult of the oscillation. When oscillating between looking at certain circumstances of a situation and looking away from them, it becomes apparent how they fit with each other and interrelate: connections between circumstances and con-texts of meaning arise. These connections and contexts are what we need to see when orienting ourselves; and this is what Wittgenstein in his *Philosophical Investigations* (§ 122) called "a surveyable representation" (*übersichtliche Darstel-lung*). He defined it as "that kind of understanding which consists in 'seeing con-nections'" (*das Verständnis, welches eben darin besteht, dass wir die 'Zusammen-hänge sehen*; transl. by G. E. M. Anscombe, P. M. S. Hacker, and Joachim Schulte). Gaining such a "surveyable representation" or an overview, as we call it, of a situation that we have not been able to cope with so far enables us to make something of it or to start acting.

4.4 Distinguishing Views Ethically: From Aspects (*Hinsichten*) via Intentions (*Absichten*) to Confidence (*Zuversicht*)

The overview as a second-degree view, a view of views, allows one to distinguish between different views. In the German language of orientation, these are usual-ly formed with the word *Sicht*, i.e. 'view' – in English, they are sometimes, but less frequently, formed with various words belonging to the field of viewing – and some of them are ethically distinguished. At first, there are different aspects (*Hinsichten*) of a situation, i.e. views on what matters in a situation from differ-ent points of view or perspectives. Depending on these selected aspects, the cir-cumstances of a situation gain different senses or meanings. If a certain sense is followed, an intention (*Absicht*) is connected with this aspect. The intention pur-sued may again require taking further aspects into account in order to arrive at a more detailed view (*Ansicht*). If, for a certain intention, one aspect proves to be more promising than others, one can – even when disregarding them – still continue to keep them in consideration (*Rücksicht*). The other aspects become the periphery of the aspect connected with one's intention.

A complete survey of all aspects is neither possible nor necessary in an orientation. Aspects may remain limited or be increased from case to case and from time to time. When the overview is at risk of being lost, they may be disregarded again. Any overview that can be gained can also be lost; therefore, it must be secured. This happens at first through careful circumspection (*Umsicht*). While the aforementioned views belong to every human orientation, careful circumspection is a special achievement and is therefore regarded as a virtue of orientation, in which one person may be more skilled than another. It consists – after involuntarily choosing one aspect and connecting an intention with it – in 'looking around' for further aspects that might be relevant in the situation for yourself and – especially – for others; in doing so, you can keep them in mind or 'respect' them and thereby avoid troubles and conflicts. If this happens in the anticipation of matters and views that may arise in the future and if you therefore hold back in judging and acting, the circumspection becomes precaution (*Vorsicht*). If you can confidently predict promising prospects, you prove to have foresight (*Weitsicht*). Whenever you cannot expect any or sufficient circumspection, precaution, or foresight (e.g. from little children), then this requires supervision (*Aufsicht*): i.e. taking responsibility for the safe orientation of others.

The view that we consider the most secure and in which we therefore would like to trust forever is insight (*Einsicht*). But it is also most prone to unnoticed metaphysical assumptions. The word 'insight' suggests a view into an alleged 'interior' of things, against which all other aspects are believed to be just 'external' throughout different situations and different contexts. Such an insight would make all other aspects and respects superfluous; it would completely transcend them and make them appear like surfaces of a depth, in which the 'true essence of things' is supposed to be. But in our human orientation and in all the knowledge we are capable of, there are no true essences; if there were any, they would be, as Thomas Nagel once put it in his famous book,[22] beings in a 'view from nowhere.' This does not exclude – to continue the philosophical metaphor of depth – looking 'deeper' and 'deeper,' or in other words, recognizing preconditions that remain hidden for others. 'Interior' is – more than 'depth' – a metaphor that seduces one into making metaphysical assumptions. The 'interior' is visible only in thought – and the 'insight' into it sees invisible things.

When views relate respectfully to the views of others, they become ethically significant. This begins with the aforementioned ethical consideration (*Rücksicht*) of others, which urges one to continuously take into account the intentions of others. It includes the precaution (*Vorsicht*) when dealing with others: ethically, this entails constantly refraining from using them for one's own intentions. If you are being used for the intentions of others and you indulge this, we speak of leniency, forbearance, or even indulgence (*Nachsicht*). While consideration applies to the present and forbearance to the past, confidence (*Zuversicht*) relates to the future. Confidence is the expectation that good orientations will continue in an unforeseeable future.

Chapter 5
The Self-Arranging of Orientations by means of Horizons, Standpoints, and Perspectives

Orientation as Arranging Things within Leeways

The beginning of orienting oneself is finding meaning in a situation; to choose a direction in finding meaning is the beginning of ordering one's orientation. Order, in the simple sense of 'arrangement,' comes from Lat. *ordo*, i.e. the 'thread in a texture.' Orders, like seats in a row or sequences in a narrative, indicate continuing connections in what is given; they lead the observer's view to find a specific direction and succession of these connections allowing him or her to make headway: *orders simplify and accelerate an orientation* (and as far as orders are essential for life, there may be something 'imperative' about them, the quality of a command). Yet, orientations, in their basic conditions, are not arranged or ordered from the outside, but arrange themselves on their own: they are self-arranging. The first or basic order is their self-arrangement by means of horizons, standpoints, and perspectives. 'Horizon,' 'standpoint,' and 'perspective' are classic terms in the philosophical and everyday language game of orientation. They have become – just like 'orientation' itself – absolute metaphors.

5.1 The Paradoxical Limit of Sight: The Horizon

Just as orientation is a nominalized verb, 'horizon' is a nominalized participle: Gr. *horízon* means 'limiting'; and the horizon is a *horízon kyklos*, a 'limiting circle.' *Horízein* meant, in its transitive usage, 'to limit, to delimit, to define by means of borders' and in this sense 'to distinguish,' a basic word in the ancient Greek language of orientation. The Greek *kósmos* was still enclosed in *one* horizon or sheltered in it. In the modern age, horizons multiplied and the shelter inherent in any limitation was lost.

In orientation, a horizon limits an overview. To gain an overview, you can 'let your eyes wander across the horizon,' you can 'explore' it with your (sensory or mental) eyes, and you can give others an overview about a topic area by means of a *'tour d'horizon.'* Based on the model of the 'heavenly vault,' horizons are envisioned as (more or less metaphoric) spherical halves, 'before,' 'in,' or 'from' which one sees or understands something. The horizon is noticed especially at

https://doi.org/10.1515/9783110575149-007

the coast, where the land is flat and the sea is open; here, the horizon seems to become visible as a demarcation line behind which nothing can be seen. However, this horizon, at the same time, turns out to be a *paradoxical limit:* as the limit of delimiting as such. When viewing something *before* a horizon, you can see and, at the same time, not see the horizon. For, when looking *at* it, it is no longer the horizon; instead, you see what you then see *before another horizon.* This is the same for 'understanding a statement *in* or *from* a horizon:' when addressing a horizon, you already understand it in or from another horizon. *'Horizon' is the concept or the absolute metaphor for the fact that one can see or understand something only if one limits or restricts one's view, if one 'concentrates' it and if, when doing so, one does not at the same time look at the limit or the restriction, but leaves it in the margins, the periphery, the 'background.'* Thus, by being neither a visible nor an invisible limit of viewing or understanding, a horizon first of all allows one to view or understand something. The horizon is the 'excluded third' of the distinction between the visible and the invisible: it is the unity of and condition for the possibility of this distinction.

However, the horizon of seeing and understanding is not a graspable ground or reason (*Grund*), but only their background (*Hintergrund*). A ship disappears at the horizon, another one emerges from the background; one views a picture before the background of a wall; one understands an event before the background of history: the (absolute) metaphor of the background resolves the paradox of the (absolute) metaphor of the horizon or, as we now say, 'de-paradoxizes' it. The *distinction between foreground and background* in turn orients the distinction between center and periphery, which is entailed in sight as such: the background is the periphery in a certain direction. Without seeing the horizon, one can look up to the point of the horizon, which always remains far away. When advancing toward it, it draws back too; one cannot cross and transcend it, but only defer it. As such, it is a spatial boundary, but only for a certain time – it is a moving boundary. Horizon is where orientation ends; but behind every horizon, a new horizon arises. As such, horizons are *temporary limits of delimiting spaces of viewing or understanding.*

5.2 The Center of a Horizon: The Standpoint

The standpoint of an orientation is the (metaphorical) 'point' one 'stands' on in a horizon and from which one sees and understands what one can see or understand within this horizon. This could be a geographical, political, scientific, moral, religious, or any other type of standpoint; in each case, one can 'enter' it and 'leave' it, 'adopt' it or 'abandon' it. In this respect, one can 'have' multiple standpoints at once. But one always has a standpoint that one cannot 'adopt' or 'abandon': the *standpoint of one's own body in the world*. It is the reference and starting point for any kind of orientation; even all actual reasoning is bound to it. In respect to it, all kinds of orientation are – in a word – 'relative' to it; it is therefore *'the absolute' in orientation*. And with one's body, one does not only 'stand' in a situation, but one's mood, the psychophysical state of one's orientation, also depends on it. Depending on how healthy, capable, and attractive one's body is, it already presets a considerable portion of one's opportunities for action and living; and depending on its shape on a good or a bad day, one's orientation succeeds with more or less effort. One can work on and improve one's body, one's health, one's capability, and one's attractiveness – but only within limits (an unathletic person cannot become an Olympic champion). Beyond one's body, this is also true for one's living conditions in general: the talents one 'has'; the social and family setting in which one grows up; the influences one 'falls under'; and the character one develops throughout all of these. One can indeed do something about them, but what one can do or what one does is already shaped by them. To the extent that such living conditions shape a human being, they take part in making up the standpoint of one's orientation. In this sense, the standpoint where an orientation starts is *everything somebody 'brings' with him or her to his or her orientation and from which he or she can distance him or herself only within (more or less narrow) limits*. As such, in the language of orientation, the word 'standpoint' is currently used most frequently. The 'standpoint' of an orientation presets the 'points of view,' according to which this orientation explores what can be done.

The standpoint of the body, to which the current metaphor connects, only *appears* to be a point. For one cannot stand on a point; and even as a point, the body is not fixed because one can move with it and change the place where one stands. Nevertheless, it is still the absolute standpoint. For if one moves – be it when turning on one's own axis to have an overview of one's entire surroundings, or when taking a new position to get an overview from there – one always takes one's standpoint along. No matter how one changes one's standpoint, one sees what one sees (and understands what one understands) only from one's standpoint – and other people see (and understand) different things from their standpoints.

However, the metaphor seems to be misleading or it at least makes things too simple. The standpoint is only a point because it is not simply the (big or thin) body that takes this position. For one can view one's own body, without a mirror, by looking down at it; but one then still views it from a standpoint – and even when sitting or lying down (and not 'standing'), one still has a standpoint. Then, the standpoint is not the spot where one's feet stand, but it would have to be the eyes which one sees with and which one cannot (without a mirror) see themselves; in this regard, it would then again rather be the point of view from which one is (physically) viewing. As such, the standpoint would be, like the horizon, a *paradoxical starting point of viewing*, from which one can see everything, but which itself cannot be seen: the 'blind spot' of orientation that is literally localized at the blind spot of the eyes. However, nobody would consider one's standpoint to be in one's eyes; and if one were to locate it in one's eyes, the blind would be completely disoriented. Thus, the standpoint of one's orientation is neither one's body nor one's eyes. Likewise, it is not the physical center of gravity (for it would then change when sitting or lying down). It has no specific place in the body, one cannot localize it there; it seems to be an *imaginary center* in or on one's body.

However, it is still paradoxical. Like the horizon, it is unquestionably 'given' (one 'has' a standpoint) and, at the same time, not given (it is only an imaginary one); one cannot leave it (one always takes it along) and one can leave it (one can move and change it). One 'has' it without actually having anything; one 'takes' it along without actually taking anything. That means: *Each standpoint of orientation is at the same time absolute and contingent: it is, paradoxically, a contingent absolute.* The contingency of the absolute standpoint of orientation is the origin and beginning of all further contingencies.

To the extent that everything inevitably merges into one's standpoint and proceeds from it, *a pre- and extra-moral egocentrism* is inherent to it. Maurice Merleau-Ponty analyzed this egocentrism in detail in his *phenomenology of perception*. For him, the 'Ego,' which explores its world, proves to be neither unified nor fixed. For already the horizons and directions of our senses, all of which in fact refer to *one* reference point of orientation, differ significantly and thus need to be integrated in orientation. The different senses reach different distances; they have different operational capabilities and different sensibilities for risk and danger, and they are connected with different feelings of distance. With our hands and eyes we can move in various directions: we can act and react rather spontaneously and take risks; with our noses and ears, we perceive rather observantly and watch out for dangers. When in a threatening situation, one is calmer if one can still see and grasp something rather than having to rely only on smelling and listening. Hearing and sight can be enhanced with technical devices like amplifiers and spyglasses, which, however, make it more difficult to relate the senses to each other. Usually, taste, touch, and smell cannot be improved; one must rely fully on one's own sensitivity. The senses in their specific qualities work in specific ways; they converge neither in a fixed center that would precede and control them, nor do they converge in consciousness, which in fact only registers a very small amount of the work of the senses and which interferes in even fewer occasions. Rather, they interact like different orientation systems that – in part genetically programmed and in part shaped by experience – are synchronized with each other moment by moment; they complement and help each other if one of them fails; and they influence each other in manifold ways (something might be pleasing to touch, but startling in sudden light; sounds may – in everyday language terms – take the shape of colors, smells, and contours; colors may appear to be cold or warm, etc.). The different sensual orientation systems make the starting point of our orientation (the imaginary center of its standpoint and its contingent absoluteness mentioned above) impermeably complex – but this does not mean disoriented.

5.3 The View from a Standpoint: The Perspective

The field of vision between the standpoint and the horizon is the perspective. The 'perspective' term relates to sight and the direction of viewing: the 'field of vision' of a directed view is a limited sector of the circle around a standpoint, i. e. of the scope of vision (this also applies to the metaphorical standpoints – in a metaphorical sense as well). The word 'perspective' comes from Lat. *specere*, i. e. 'to view, to see'; *perspicere* means 'to look through something; to look into something; to inspect; to see through something.' Starting around 1600, one was able to see with more precision what was far away by looking through a telescope (also called a *Perspektiv* in old German language); and this telescope also made – and still makes – manifest the sectional and selective character of natural sight. Perspectivity, as far as it delimits one's view, seems to be a partial loss in orientation. But it is at the same time a gain in orientation. Perspectives that one adopts are selected aspects (*Hinsichten*) connected with intentions (*Absichten*). Since perspectives can be complemented or substituted with further or other aspects, they abbreviate sight and, at the same time, multiply it: thus, they differentiate sight. *Perspectival viewing, as we know it, always has alternatives; it is the ability to view something in various ways that exclude but also complement and enrich each other.*

At the dawn of the modern age, the art of painting drew special attention to perspectivity. Beginning at the end of the 14th century, efforts were made to represent the 'depth' of space; 'perspective' meant at first '*ars perspectiva*,' 'perspectival art,' and it retained this sense up until the end of the 18th century. This art was about representing three-dimensional objects on a two-dimensional plane – so that it appears natural to one's eye. If, for example, someone is being depicted turning sideways, stretching out one arm, his or her arms and hands must be presented as different in size if they are to appear of the same size; if you want to show the depth of a landscape, the horizontal lines must be shortened and shadowed. Things appear 'correct,' 'true', 'natural' only through perspectival foreshortening, i. e. through an artificial illusion – which, in fact, shows the 'natural' foreshortening in our everyday views of things. Thus, natural things are illusionary and illusionary things are natural; the illusion is natural, and nature is an illusion – perspectival art makes clear, by using geometrical and technical procedures for creating its illusions, that our natural sight works with foreshortening procedures as well. From the viewpoint (or 'distance point') of an observer, the 'lines of perspective' in the picture must run – for the picture to appear natural – toward a 'point of sight' or a 'vanishing point' on a 'horizon line'; and all represented objects must be shortened in proportion. How this is to be done was explained in numerous instructional guides that were increasingly refined. They showed: the eye does not *see* depth, but it only *constructs* it – also in nature. *By way of perspectival painting in the modern age, 'natural' optics became manifest as perspectival artistry.*

Already in Greek and Roman antiquity, attempts were made to represent *bodies in perspective* (the representation of figures through foreshortenings and oblique views) as well as *spaces in perspective* in prospect paintings. Perspectival art was – as with optics – part of projective geometry; based on Euclid's geometry, it was, in modernity, mathematically developed by Desargues, Pascal, and Leibniz. In the medieval ages, the 'status perspective' or 'hierarchical perspective' was prioritized over the illusory representation of God's creations: what was significant, meaningful, important (Christ, Mary, the Saints) was painted bigger than what was insignificant, less meaningful, unimportant. The breakthrough to the *central perspective* came in the early Italian Renaissance around 1420 with Filippo Brunelleschi (the master builder of the Florence Cathedral) and his circle; Masaccio (among others) was part of it, whose 'Holy Trinity' fresco in Florence's Santa Maria Novella is considered the first painting entirely designed according to the central perspective (around 1427). Soon after, Leon Battista Alberti gave the first theoretical account of the *prospettive legittima* that also introduced the point of sight (around 1435). Between 1490 and 1500, the first perspectival drafts of ideal cities were endeavored; at the same time, painters in France, in the Burgundian Netherlands, and in Venice developed the *aerial perspective:* i. e. making use of gradations of color and light for perspectival representations. By aligning what was important with the vanishing point, the former status or hierarchical perspective was enriched in a new way. Leonardo, Raphael, and Dürer all mastered this – the latter himself wrote *Four Books on Measurement* (*Underweysung der Messung*) in 1525. Leonardo, building on his own theoretical investigations, e. g. of the anatomy of the eye, further developed the *perspectiva artificialis* (which assumes a single fixed eye) via his *sfumato* to a *perspectiva naturalis,* according to which he blurred the contours of represented objects in relation to their distance from the viewer. In doing so, he was able to take the air's opacity into account. As such, *perspectival dimness (mezzo confuso)* was created: it not only allowed figures to appear more vividly, but it also gave them an 'atmosphere.' Perspectival art was also increasingly applied in architecture when designing interior spaces, halls, and ceilings. As such, it has become self-evident and normal in everyday living environments.

In philosophy, perspectival art gained a certain prominence especially by means of Johann Heinrich Lambert's *Free Perspective (Freye Perspective)* and Johann Georg Sulzer's *General Theory of Beautiful Art.* This also shifted the traditional distinction between rationality and sensibility. It showed rationality *within* sensibility, as the construction principle of the sensible – and thus rationality was no longer the 'atemporal,' 'essential,' and 'interior' in contrast to the sensible as something 'temporal,' 'contingent,' and 'exterior.' In this way, perspectival art paved the way for Kant's constructivism and made it plausible. While the perspectivist Nietzsche recommended that future philosophers learn producing perspectival art from artists (*The Gay Science,* No. 299), painters like Van Gogh and Cézanne, as well as cubism and constructivism, were already beginning to detach themselves from perspectival art – which was then conspicuous again: because it was now intentionally violated after it had become self-evident. Art drew, through creative disorientation, attention to perspectivism as a condition of orientation.

5.4 The Flexibility and Mobility of Horizons, Standpoints, and Perspectives

In everyday orientation, a multiplicity of perspectives is always at work: corporeal and intellectual perspectives that can both complement each other as well as overlap and interfere with each other. Every reorientation also changes the texture of perspectives: a reorientation is also a re-ordering of perspectives; *the movement of orientation is also a movement of its perspectives.* And as far as orientation is – and has to be – always in movement in order to keep up with the times, fixing one perspective is an exceptional case that requires special reasons.

However, horizons, standpoints, and perspectives cannot simply be changed or substituted with others; they are not objects of a transcendent subject that could decide about this change from beyond all perspectives. Every subject is itself a perspective. What we really observe is this: one perspective leads to the next; perspectives connect with each other, merge with each other, and continue each other; their movements happen as a continuous crossover; instead of a fixed superordinate control center, there is a continuous crossing over of perspectives. This can be understood within the contexts of horizon, standpoint, and perspective themselves. A perspective changes if its horizon or its standpoint or both change; and in everyday orientation, they can change, to some degree, independently from one another as well. From one's standpoint, one – 'one' itself being conceived as a part of a texture of perspectives – can envisage a narrower or a wider scope: one can 'look at' something specific to view it in a narrower horizon; and one can then 'look up' again to view it in a wider horizon. But one can also fix one's gaze on it and change one's standpoint, e.g. when going around it. Even though the horizon and the standpoint are in principle dependent on each other (the horizon changes together with the standpoint), a standpoint can still be changed *within* a horizon without *significantly* changing the horizon. Similarly, the horizon may be widened or narrowed from a standpoint fixed for some time. But if a standpoint is being changed more and more, at some point a new horizon arises, in which the standpoint is then reoriented. In everyday orientation there is, so to speak, an *elastic relationship between standpoint and horizon:* they may be pulled apart from each other or move closer together; and if their current relationship is overdone, they can suddenly jump into a new one. In this way, continuous change is possible.

The urge to change perspectives (including their standpoints and horizons) is, again, due to something new and relevant 'coming up' along the current horizon, i.e. from the periphery of the perspective. Orientation then focuses on what came up and narrows the horizon on it to take a closer look; afterward it broadens the horizon again in order to also explore the surroundings of what is new and to see what it is about. And then an orientation might also change its standpoint by approaching closer to it – thus changing the horizon as well. In this way we can understand that reorientation happens as a *continuous shift of perspectives* – the continuous shift of perspectives is orientation's mode of continuity. If in orientation everything may be subject to reorientation, then the only hold of orientation is its own continuity – which allows continual shifts and where nothing necessarily remains the same. Later (chap. 9.5), we will introduce the term 'fluctuance' for this, meaning a 'substance in flux.'

5.5 Spatializing Time and Temporalizing Space in Orientation

Every horizon of orientation is also a horizon of space and time; every perspective is also a perspective of space and time. The space of orientation is not premeasured in yards or meters, nor is its time pre-measured with a clock. These metric classifications of space and time already presuppose specific orientation worlds. *The spatial and temporal horizons of orientation are the first horizons relevant for the exploration of a situation.* But initially, there are no metrics: instead, there are more or less 'narrow' or 'broad' spatial horizons or more or less 'short-' or 'long-term' temporal horizons – always with regard to what is to be done and to the emerging opportunities and risks. Therefore, orientation times are most of all times that have an end, i.e. times under pressure: 'deadlines,' 'time limits,' 'terms'; you can 'still have' time – or simply 'run out' of it; sometimes you can try or hope for more time to be 'given.' The relevant matters of a situation themselves induce case by case a narrowing or broadening of spatial and temporal horizons. In general, this happens quickly, without notice, through routine, and likewise 'over' time, which puts orientation under pressure because everything is temporally limited, even the spatial and temporal horizons one relies on in one's intentions and plans.

As such, everyday orientation is concerned with at least three kinds of time: first, the time that every orientation is pressured by and in which all their perspectives are temporary as well; second, the limited times in a temporal horizon; and third, technically measured time or clock time, i.e. a socially institutionalized time, in which 'appointments are scheduled.' The last kind of time is – for us – the most obvious one; but it is also the 'youngest' in the development of humanity and the maturation of individuals. The first kind of time was spoken of, for example, in the Hebrew Bible in Kohelet's 'there is a time for everything' (3:1–8). The second one was substantially analyzed in Edmund Husserl's *On the Phenomenology of the Consciousness of Internal Time* (1893–1917). The third one is dealt with in physics with regard to measuring it and in sociology with regard to its social liability. In between these, further kinds of time may be added that likewise influence orientation: cultic times, which shape cultures in specific ways, whose scheduling was once the responsibility of priests, and which are explored by religious and ethnological studies; historical times, in which history is divided into periods, which are marked by developments and events, and which have become subject to reflexive theories of history; the times of biological rhythms in corporeal processes, including the times of the brain's neurophysiological rhythms: times not consciously perceivable but that can be scientifically studied; the time of the evolution of life altogether, in which all these rhythms and all these cultic, historical, and physical distinctions arise and where sciences and philosophies also try to formulate atemporal or supratemporal laws; and eventually the time of the universe, in which even the time of this evolution is limited and evolves as well.

Time is where everything, even every notion and concept of time, is temporally limited. Thus, time makes all attempts to envision, understand, and conceive time self-referential and turns them into paradoxes. As a consequence, orientation has to look for notions and concepts of time that in turn resolve these paradoxes. What all these notions and concepts have in common is that they spatialize time. The most basic notion in conceiving time is *succession*; for space it is *juxtaposition*. But the image of succession also becomes – as far as the succeeding moments are in turn imagined to be at once – ineluctably an image of juxtaposition; and since anything permanent in time is only possible as something recurring always anew, and since we track what recurs in countable units, which are again juxtaposed side by side, any image of something permanent in time is also and especially imagined as a spatial juxtaposition. As such, traditional clocks (with hands), which – up until a short time ago – have shaped the picture of time, show time as if it passes by in circles measured in hours, minutes, and seconds; and from Newton, we learned that this is the "absolute, true, and mathematical time." Since this kind or image of time was to function as a universal parameter for the physical laws of motion, Newton regarded it as running "in a uniform way (*aequabiliter*) in itself and in nature and without relation to anything exterior"; and he in turn declared all time understood in any other way to be mere "popular opinion," only a "relative" or "apparent" time.[23] But in doing so, he declared an image or a conception of time for specific purposes – in this case to formulate the universal laws of motion – to simply be the 'true time.' But in the development of modern physics, the conception of an absolute and true time was no longer tenable; it was necessary only for the physics of classical mechanics; and with relativistic physics, its time was over too. *By spatializing time orientation disregards the inconceivable time in which everything is temporally limited – including all images and concepts of time; but it does so, again, only for a limited time.*

Time, in which everything is temporally limited, cannot only be disregarded for orientation purposes; it can and must also be kept off – although, again, only for a limited time. The paradigm for this is everything living. Due to negentropic processes, animate beings are capable of building structures that resist the relentless attacks of time by relentlessly reproducing themselves (*autopoiesis*). They in turn are – or appear to be – spatial shapes that take a place in space and move autonomously in it – as spatial entities. Entities, from which time is kept off, also include long-term habitats such as nests and houses that are to be continually 'maintained,' i.e. kept with constant care in a certain shape. But these entities are also experienced through the change of perspectives – thus in orientation they are again temporalized. *In orientation, the spatializing of time is again followed by a temporalizing of space*; and as far as horizon, standpoint, and perspective are also spatial metaphors this accounts for them as well. Eventually, they too are indispensably necessary illusions of orientation: i.e. images without which we could barely orient ourselves to orientation itself in the relentless 'flux' of time; and 'flux' is also a spatial metaphor for time.

5.6 Flexible Leeways of Orientation

For movable limits, like horizons, and mobile spaces, like the perspectives of orientation, the German language of orientation offers another immediately plausible word, which is difficult to define in terms: '*Spielraum.*' *Spielraum* is referred to differently in different languages. The Latin words *campus* (open field), *spatium* (free space), *latitude* (width, e.g. of a trench) have military connotations and leave out the *Spiel* (play). The French language, however, can choose between space (*champ libre*) and play (*jeu*). In English, there are many different words: there is 'free play,' but also 'elbow-room,' 'wiggle room,' and 'room to move'; additionally, there is '(full) scope,' 'range' (of a gun, of influence, of oppositions, of temperature), 'clearance' or 'clear space,' 'leeway' (from nautical navigational language: to allow or give somebody leeway), 'allowance' (an allowance 'conceded' to someone, e.g. luggage allowance on flights or an allowance for errors).

A *Spielraum* is a space (*Raum*) in which there is play (*Spiel*), though not play in the common meaning of the term. When connecting space (*Raum*) and play (*Spiel*), the meaning of both words changes. And, as one might expect by now, the *Spielraum* metaphor likewise conceals and hides a paradox. A *Spielraum* is a 'space' that limits movement by means of regulations, a space within which a 'playful' movement is allowed that does not follow these regulations – in this sense, it is 'play' free from regulations. In short, *a Spielraum is a regulated limit of an unregulated behavior.* Of course, a game played usually follows rules. But as far as it is a game, it allows leeway or 'room for maneuver' in the handling of these rules – and this leeway is what makes the game interesting. Playing chess requires more than just mastering the rules: the rules are quite simple, but what can be done with them is very sophisticated. In games, the room for maneuver is the room allowed by the rules of the game.

Spielraum – or let us now call it 'leeway' – was (and is), in German military language, the space in a gun barrel required for the bullet to fly freely. If a shot is to hit its target, this space must be perfectly measured: the bullet can neither have too little nor too much space in the barrel. Such a leeway is also necessary for a door in its frame, for a wheel in its bearing, etc., for everything that is to move within a certain 'frame' of something. One can try one's best to pre-calculate it, but eventually, one has to try it out; this also applies, more or less, to the leeways that parents (must) give their children, employers their employees, and governments the governed. They are not fixed, either, but change over time.

As limited (or regulated) spaces for free (or unregulated) movement, perspectives of orientation are leeways of orientation. Due to the elastic relationship of their standpoints and horizons, they are furthermore leeways with movable limits; they not only allow for movement, but they also move themselves. This applies in turn to the aforementioned leeways as well: over time and after much use, gun barrels and wheel bearings 'wear out.' Children, employees, and the governed become, if given more leeways, more independent and self-responsible; they then not only wait for allowances, but they 'take' them themselves. Furthermore, leeways for actions (*Handlungsspielräume*) that open in one direction may close in another (when gaining influence in an elected office one becomes dependent on bureaucracy). And lastly, the regulated limits of leeways as such can, over time, become so loose that they eventually dissolve entirely (like 'loosely handled' regulations).

In addition to 'finding one's way' and 'gaining an overview,' the self-arrangement of an orientation within the leeways of horizons, standpoints, and perspectives is another basic feature of orientation. It specifies its kind of freedom. The freedom of orientation is limited by rules or regulations, but these rules or regulations apply only 'regularly' or 'as a rule' under certain conditions, not unconditionally. Its freedom is not and does not need to be metaphysically founded or justified. It is not atemporal nor supratemporal, but temporal; and as a temporary leeway it is necessary for an orientation to keep up with the times. *Spielraum* or leeway is – like horizon, standpoint, and perspective – an irreplaceable and thus absolute metaphor; it is the concise and succinct 'term' for the always limited and always changing freedoms we have in orientation, for the fact that we are not free in every way, but only in some ways, i. e. that we sometimes find certain opportunities to decide for certain actions – and we sometimes do not. The leeway for action that orientation allows is not a uniform one following uniform rules; rather, it is a versatile and multi-faceted leeway connected to diverse 'freedoms' that differ case by case; in each situation, they have to be found out first and used under the pressure of time. In this respect, Jean-Paul Sartre's 'condemned-to-be-free' is unrealistically exaggerated as well. In everyday orientation, one is rather condemned to play – not 'for fun,' but as seriously as a gambler who must continuously place bets under persistent uncertainty. This is then less about *freedom* of action than it is about *certainty* in action: the 'hold' in orientation.

Chapter 6
Hold in Orientation: Points of Reference, Clues, Leads, and Footholds
Orientation as Hold

To gain an overview of a situation, to find one's way in it, and to make out promising opportunities for action in it – all this is called to 'gain,' to 'find,' or to 'create' a 'hold' (*Halt*) in orientation. A 'hold' stops something from moving, from falling, from collapsing, or from decaying: *the language of hold is indicative of the enduring risk of any orientation that it might slip, fall, collapse, or decay.* Besides metaphors for sight and self-arrangement, metaphors for hold most strongly characterize the language of orientation – particularly in the German language, but in many others as well. They are used in great variety and with great frequency. In verbs alone, their meanings range from the (intransitive) 'coming-to-a-halt' and 'coming-into-being' via the (transitive) 'bringing-to-a-halt' and 'hindering-from-falling,' from (the intransitive) 'persisting' and 'resisting-deterioration' and (the reflexive) 'conducting-oneself' to (the transitive) 'setting-oneself-into-a-relationship-with' and 'holding-something-to-be-something.' In its primordiality and self-referentiality, orientation must – and is able to – attain all these varieties of hold solely on its own. If it needs something stable and lasting, e. g. permanent objects, regulated word meanings, reliable characters, or stable institutions, then it creates them, but only as far as it needs them and only for a limited time. What is lasting in orientation does not have to last *forever*: it need not be something absolutely atemporal or timeless that persists in all situations and beyond all possible situations 'in all possible worlds.' Something absolutely atemporal could exist only beyond the bounds of orientation; it would be something metaphysical – and even to such metaphysical things, orientation could only refer for a limited time. We thus need to ask how there can be, in orientation, paradoxically once again, something like a *temporary atemporality.*

6.1 The Hold of Points of Reference

Where English has multiple words (point of reference, guide, clue, lead, indicator, pointer, sign, – and foothold), the German language uses, in most cases, only one, but a very concise one: *Anhaltspunkt.* One says that orientation 'holds onto' – let us say now – 'footholds'. But the 'hold' of footholds is of a special kind. One relies on them and, at the same time, does not rely on them; one

https://doi.org/10.1515/9783110575149-008

holds onto them only for a limited time, only temporarily: for footholds that appear tenable can always turn out to be untenable. Accordingly, one calls them – in English too – points (*Punkte*): like geometrical points, they do not actually exist, but are arranged, defined or constructed by a certain orientation within a certain situation; like geometrical points, they only make sense when connected to other points. For what a new situation brings is not yet certain; it must first be made surveyable; and it is made surveyable by means of such points of reference. As constructed points, they are abstractions: specific *abbreviations* or *short-cuts* of a situation by means of a specific orientation. Given the pressure of time, under which orientations usually operate, such abbreviations are a basic need. Just as physics focuses on the gravitational points of a body where the forces of inertia virtually attack, orientation proceeds in the same way with points of reference, where the relevant matters of a situation virtually appear to converge. In this way, orientation can, for the moment, neglect other matters, just as physics neglects other circumstances when calculating force.

This kind of reduction from something 'overly complex' to something 'simple' allows for an especially rash *overview* of what is relevant in a situation for a certain orientation. Points, being indivisible, are 'surveyable' per se: they can be arranged side by side and always anew – in this way, they temporarily spatialize that which occurs in a situation. By providing an overview, these points in turn partake in the paradox of 'overlooking': they make the whole visible at the cost of individual aspects.

As a result, points also enable *networks*, topological arrangements or orders in both a geometric as well as a figurative sense. They establish a new kind of clear visibility and vividness in outlines, schemata, or pictures – indeed a reduced one, but nevertheless a transparently ordered and thus orienting vividness. The (more or less) schematic figures that develop from the interconnected points can in turn be filled out, e. g. with 'illustrations.' In this respect, they do *not* appear schematic.

But points of reference are abstractions of a special kind. They are not suitable for arrangement in logical 'term pyramids,' hierarchical relations of conceptual superordination and subordination; their only purpose is to attract the special attention of a specific orientation in its specific situation. They 'concentrate' an orientation in this sense. We can therefore call them *contractions*. Logical abstractions and orienting contractions are intertwined with each other. Abstract terms start with points of reference as well.

Orientation *encounters* points of reference. They proffer themselves, standing out from the other circumstances of the situation. Which reference points an orientation gets involved with – which it holds onto or relies on – depends on its particular needs. A hunter will not orient him or herself in the same manner as someone going for a walk: for each of them, different things are *attractive*. 'Attractive' is literally what 'draws' attention 'to itself' (from Lat. *attrahere*, 'to draw to itself, to lure') and what, if it binds the attention for a considerable time, 'fascinates' (from Lat. *fasciare*, 'to enwrap, to captivate, to enthrall'), e. g. a tower in a vast, empty landscape or the cry of a raptor. *A contraction – from which an abstraction is derived – is itself triggered by an attraction.* The degree to which points of reference are attractive manifests in the efforts required to turn away from them. They may be irresistible for some time: a beautiful picture, an interesting combination of colors, a rapid movement, an exciting melody. The attractiveness of such points of reference can be specifically increased – any kind of 'advertisement' takes advantage of this. Advertisements advertise for attention by means of particularly attractive points of reference.

6.2 The Leeway of Points of Reference, Clues, Leads, and Footholds for Knowledge

Points of reference become clues for new orientations if they point to additional points of reference. They then open up larger contexts in a situation that one has to deal with. When clues themselves become instructive to a greater degree, they in turn become leads, which are able to 'lead' one's circumspection to additional points of reference, clues, and leads. In growing contexts, where new attractive clues arise that attract the attention of an orientation, this orientation gains a stronger hold. Every point of reference, clue, and lead provides leeway for additional points of reference, clues, and leads. The elastic relationship between standpoints and horizons allows an orientation to move from one point of reference to another point of reference, from clue to clue, and from lead to lead. In this way, by means of threads or chains of threads, an orientation establishes its initial forms of continuity. These threads continuously refer to the standpoint of the given orientation, which itself may continuously change and, in doing so, create even more leeway. The points of reference, clues, and leads may be *exchanged* as well; an orientation may let go of some and take others into account – like on a boat trip when one is relying on changing navigation signs along the banks. And by experiencing how points of reference, clues, and leads change in changing situations, orientation experiences time itself: as a *continuous change of points of reference, clues, and leads in ever changing situations.*

But orientation can also return to specific leads and does so when it becomes apparent that such leads are particularly relevant. When several clues and leads point to the same thing, they *condense* into what is called a 'foothold,' which the process of gaining an overview of a situation 'pauses' in and 'sticks

with' in a way, e. g. when you perceive the sound of your name repeated in a babble of voices at the neighboring table. However, even then your orientation does
not stop paying attention to further clues and leads, which could strengthen the
foothold.

When, during the process of orientation, enough footholds come together
and sufficiently fit with each other, then that which we call *'knowledge'* arises –
knowledge that appears as knowledge of something 'given.' For when one believes that one has reached a certain knowledge one forgets the process of orientation that led to it – when 'knowing' something, one tends to believe in things
as already given per se. This seems obvious, for instance, when one perceives
clouds, thunder, and lightning: there is no doubt that a thunderstorm is coming.
However, when one perceives the friendly voice, the smile, or any other inviting
gesture of another person, then there may still be doubt: all that does not necessarily constitute flirting and certainly not love, though you may be eager to
suppose that it does. It is – to give another example – similar with evidence
of guilt, which also remains largely a matter of clues; countless stories, especially
criminal stories, give a telling account of this. Thus, orientation has to distinguish between points of reference, clues, leads, footholds, and knowledge,
and our thesis is that all knowledge eventually emerges from the evidence provided by points of reference, clues, leads, and footholds. None of these, including knowledge, is ever completely certain – all things are a matter of getting to
know them, and we always get to know them through the clues, leads, and footholds of our orientation. This may be how our orientation acquires knowledge (if
it is represented as a continuous process, one that can go on in very complex
ways, including bypaths and loops): acquiring knowledge at first means to
find some points of reference in an unsurveyable situation; then, proceeding
from these points, to look for more clues; then, among them, to discover
leads; then, to condense several leads into footholds; then to condense several
footholds into an alleged simple knowledge, which appears as 'given' from the
outset like the 'things' of which it is supposed to be a knowledge of.

However, in the long run, 'things' change and 'knowledge' changes. We experience this (more or less) all the time, and we are therefore always aware that
our orientation can rely on certain knowledge only within limits. Even if there
are heavy clouds, thunder and lightning, the thunderstorm does not have to happen; even if you believe you have perceived some clear evidence of love, you
could be mistaken; even if there is every reason to believe that the stock shares
are rising, they could still fall. The indicators of a thunderstorm, of love, or of a
market price always leave room for different continuations and interpretations.
And this is fundamentally no different for scientific observations, e. g. physical
observations of forces or astrophysical observations of black holes and gravita-

tional waves. We only ever have points of reference, clues, leads, or footholds, and can never know whether we have the right ones or enough of them. Thus, there is always concern as to whether additional footholds have not been overlooked, which could be of further and perhaps greater importance. The unsettling of orientation drives us to look beyond all the footholds that we have so far relied on for further (and perhaps redundant) footholds in order to become assured and calm whenever something important is at stake. But orientation can only rely on points of reference, clues, leads, and footholds when establishing any kind of knowledge, and it must decide between them case by case in order to ensure this knowledge.

6.3 Paradoxical Decisions between Footholds

Let us now, for the sake of abbreviation, use the term 'foothold,' which best resembles the German '*Anhaltspunkt*' as an umbrella term for all kinds of points of reference, clues, leads, footholds, and related evidence. Footholds are chosen – like the views on them – largely without an awareness of the choice being made. If the *selection* is noticed, it becomes a *decision*. It is, however, not already a decision based on clear reasons, but is instead experienced as a *coercion to decide*, a coercion that forces a decision between the initially uncertain footholds being offered in the course of orientation, which lead to alternative ways of acting. Our next thesis is: when exploring a situation, all decisions between footholds (and what belongs to them) are at first *decisions* made *under uncertainty*; they are thus made tentatively and with reservation. As far as they have led to failures, more attention is given to the decision itself, fostering a more careful circumspection when dealing with footholds. If the uncertainty itself has become conspicuous, the pressure of the situation on further decisions between footholds increases as well.

Decisions have always been described metaphorically as decisions between geographic paths (e. g. Hercules at the Crossroads). Decisions are 'difficult' if two viable paths are offered, yet you can only walk on one of them and will thereby irreversibly lose sight of the other, which seemed equally promising (for Hercules, it was either a life full of pleasure or a life filled with labor and toil, but also full of fame). If you make a decision, you decide between footholds for a way of acting that seems better to you in your situation, but of which you do not yet know whether it is better with regard to future situations. How is it that you decide then? If the different footholds seem to have equal or almost equal weight, you need an additional foothold. Thus, it is not really you who decides, but the additional foothold that does – coming into your view as an especially attractive one (for Hercules, perhaps his longing for fame). This is also true for decisions between different rules, values, norms, and principles, all of which demand that you follow them at the same time: in situations in which they conflict with each other, you eventually need further footholds, as well, be they further rules, values, etc., or other footholds in the given situation. However, if something is decided in a situation that must be dealt with under the pressure of time, it is irreversible: it can only be changed again at a later time by means of new decisions that must be made in a changed situation.

As such, decisions also lead to the establishment of a distinction between *past* and *future*. In orientation, the past is what has already been decided, while the future is what still needs to be decided. The present is part of the future as far as one still needs to make decisions in it; it is part of the past as far as one no longer decides in it. The thesis following from this is: for orientations, the past and the future are, respectively, the horizons of the decided and the decidable, while the present is the time for making decisions. Whereas decisions made under uncertainty may unsettle, the past is 'settled' and 'calm.' However, one cannot simply let it be 'at rest.' Since the future depends on the past and since the past (although not all of it) has an effect on the future, the past is at times 'unsettling' – it then needs to be 'taken up' again in order to be newly decided upon in a new context. The past is, for orientation, only past if it has no more effects on the present and if one can 'start anew' with something and 'newly decide' upon it. But new decisions – with hardly any influence from the past – are also the most uncertain and thus the most unsettling.

When making a decision under the condition of uncertainty, one 'pauses' the uncertainty and, in doing so, gains a 'hold'; one calms down. But again, only for a limited time: by making a decision in one 'point,' a new situation develops that may unsettle you once again; this oscillation between reassurance and unsettlement returns in every decision made between footholds (you decided for a path you did not yet know, and now new uncertainties arise – and not everyone is Hercules). The uncertainty of orientation is ineradicable; thus, every new decision between new footholds is likewise made under uncertainty. In addition, as Jacques Derrida highlighted, decisions made under uncertainty are paradoxical – they are *decisions about something that is in fact undecidable*. For, under uncertainty, there are no sufficient reasons to make a decision; and yet you have to decide precisely when you lack sufficient reasons to make a decision. When everything is certain and the preferences are clear (if, for Hercules, there were only the path of virtue and not the path of pleasure), there is nothing to decide. And even when one has 'good reasons' to make a decision (the so-called 'decisive reasons'), one must still be first convinced of them with arguments before one follows them (while others might decide *against* these reasons and the arguments supporting them). Since there might always be counter-arguments for any argument, all arguments are only footholds, too, between which an orientation must decide.

In uncertain decisions made in uncertain situations, the outcome remains uncertain. Therefore, it would seem only plausible to make short-term decisions and to decide anew in new circumstances with regard to new footholds. However, this would not allow for a sustainable long-term arrangement of orientation; or, psychologically speaking, it would lead to an extreme 'uncertainty orientation,' i.e. a constantly exaggerated and unbearably restless orientation. Instead, we are urged, not only by this restlessness, but also by others we are dealing with, to 'hold onto' decisions once they are made. This leads to the *'resoluteness' or 'decisiveness' of orientation*. Resoluteness or decisiveness (*Entschiedenheit*) is an attitude of no longer changing a decision (*Entscheidung*) in one 'point' and thus no longer taking further footholds into account even if the situation suggests it (you then have, one says, a 'determined opinion,' or a 'determined will'). Hence, decisiveness is a *self-referential decision about decisions*. It is a second level decision. It again provides a hold *within* an orientation.

6.4 The Affective Assessment of Footholds

Thus, the courage for an orientation under uncertainty involves the courage to decide for footholds and to be determined to hold onto them despite persistently unsettling conditions – to know you could have always decided differently, and you might have been better off that way. To reach a lasting calmness, orientation needs to find lasting relief from perpetually new decisions about perpetually new footholds. It finds relief by means of learning: by learning to distinguish between sustainable and unsustainable footholds. Orientation can be taught only in a very limited sense; it has to learn most things on its own, by acquiring a feeling for something that is sustainable and that it can hold onto for a long time. Physiologically, orientation can rely on a vast number of innate and thus evolutionarily proven *reflexes:* the healthy organism responds automatically and as quickly as possible to outer and inner impulses with reactions for preserving itself, especially if one's survival, and particularly the survival of one's genes, are at stake (involving, e.g., defense mechanisms, nutrition, and reproduction). According to Ivan Pavlov, orientation reflexes can also be purposefully conditioned and trained; they then function in a similar way to innate reflexes. However, most automatic actions are learned by means of random experiences, which prove to be either beneficial or detrimental. As a child, you might burn your hand on the stove and then keep away from it for some time; you might upset your stomach with a certain kind of food, which you will then loathe afterward; somebody might experience such devastating social disappointments that he or she becomes unable to commit to long-term relationships. On the other hand, the love one experiences might turn one into a loving and lovable person; enjoying fine delicacies might turn one into a gourmet; and the successful handling of tools might turn one into a skilled craftsman. All this is mostly not a matter of one's will or intention – the experiences themselves drive one to them over time. They incorporate themselves into the formation of an orientation at a time, and they determine the standpoint of it later on: a kind of *affective reaction* develops. Such reactions might trigger automatic behavior similar to that of reflexes; they often go hand in hand with substantial changes in pulse, blood pressure, respiration, facial expression, or gesture; for the time being, they demand one's full attention and hardly leave room for anything else. In this way, they *limit* the orientation and, in doing so, relieve it as well. An orientation that is trained in this way takes fewer footholds into account, and hence does not need to decide about them. *Reflexes and incorporated affective reactions relieve an orientation from making selections between footholds.*

Incorporated affects are more than attractive footholds: they do not leave a choice; as such, footholds that trigger such affects are *strong reference points for distinguishing between what is called in morality good and evil.* These affects express themselves in the feelings of being pulled toward or rejected from something, and they involuntarily affect moral judgments too. They are *paradoxical* as well: they strictly direct an orientation in a situation, but they leave little room for an overview of it. They bias an orientation and control its reactions in such a way that it is difficult to control them again; they are hardly noticeable, yet when one becomes aware of them, they can quickly be changed.

6.5 The Fitting of Footholds: Sustainable Schemata

Meaning or sense arises, as we have seen, by virtue of multiple limitations or selections of the occurrences in a situation:

- the limitation of focusing on footholds that are attractive and relevant for an orientation in a given situation,
- the limitation of finding and choosing footholds due to the standpoint of an orientation,
- the limitation due to the arrangement of footholds (each one arising in the context of another),

- the limitations due to the decisions between footholds, the distinction between past and future, and the resoluteness or decisiveness after a decision
  is made,
- the limitation in the choice of footholds due to orientation reflexes and affective reactions.

These limitations only sometimes occur one after the other, more often occurring
simultaneously. Limitations are the most significant way for an orientation to
gain a hold.

Beyond the basic need of finding one's way in a situation in order to find
promising opportunities for action and to gain a sufficient hold for both, these
limitations are not based on any shared principle that would give reason to expect a systematic relationship between footholds. Sustainable coherence of orientation is to arise from the mutual support of contingent footholds which are
able to change from one situation to another. *Across changing situations, orientation can gain its hold only by dealing with its situations in an economic manner,
broadly speaking: by considerately saving time and energy so that it can quickly
and easily do what needs to be done.*

The most economic and adaptive criterion for the selection of footholds with
the fewest preconditions is whether they 'fit' with each other or go well together
case by case: their *fitting*. That footholds fit with each other presumes nothing
beyond the footholds themselves and an orientation that can 'make something'
of them. Such fittings are quite variable and are able to adapt to ever-changing
situations. And they themselves are limiting too: when trying to find your way
you look around for footholds that fit with each other, and if they seem to fit,
you hold onto them and neglect the others. In doing so, you can quickly
'move on,' though you may continually look for additional clues to condense
and confirm the previous footholds. The denser the clues become and the
more footholds there are that are confirmed, the lower the risk and the greater
the readiness to act.

Such 'fittings' are more helpful for an orientation the less they depend on
each other. When asking for a street that is difficult to find in an unfamiliar
city, you would rather rely on two independent passersby than on a couple,
where one person might support the (perhaps false) information of the other.
The more independent footholds are from each other, the less probable but
the more significant their fitting is. Clues, leads, and footholds are contingent:
that they fit is in principle unlikely, but when they fit, they are more likely to
be tenable than if they are dependent on each other. Two pieces of information
that are independent from each other can certainly both be false, while two that
are dependent on each other can both be correct. But in the second case, the two

footholds are in fact reduced to one that now must be relied on alone. In the case of independent footholds, the footholds might challenge each other; then you may be warned and have to look for additional ones to support the previous ones – or to disprove them: then you would go on looking for further footholds. *Fittings of footholds are contingent, too, but they are less so than footholds by themselves.* The fact that footholds fit together is not due to any external criterion – they prove their fit only by finding other footholds that fit. As soon as they fit, the fitting becomes a criterion itself, a criterion for the selection of further footholds.

Fittings without a criterion beyond their own fitting must be, in a word, immediately plausible. They are plausible as they are in art, where works follow the criterion of fitting as well: when creating a work of art, you can start at random, but everything that follows must then fit. The more you add to it that fits and the more the artwork gains shape, the more everything unfitting is excluded and the more the developing artwork itself becomes the criterion for what is fitting or unfitting, until eventually everything fits, and you can add nothing more to it (if you understand the art). The work's fittings are always only fittings to itself and for itself. For a different work of art, something else can fit and there can be different criteria for fittings. The same accounts for orientations and their footholds. In sum: the plausibility of fittings is of an aesthetic nature in art; thus, one could also call the plausible fittings of footholds to be aesthetic in everyday orientation. But logical evidence – as the fitting of logical determinants – also has to be plausible on its own. What is logically not plausible may be analyzed in logical terms to make it, in this way, logically plausible – but such analyses must eventually be plausible as well. Logical analyses begin with and end in plausibilities as well. Therefore, fittings, having no criterion for their fitting beyond themselves, are the criterion for *any* orientation.

Fittings as such make sense. As often described, sense – as fittings of footholds – suddenly arises after you may have searched for it for a long time. It 'catches the eye' when, in a perspective, there are many clues that, at first, do not fit to each other, then an additional clue appears, – and suddenly they all fit together like pieces of a jigsaw puzzle. And then you feel delighted: finding something that fits is one of the most remarkable events of an orientation. Detective stories and films commonly profit from this: they increase the tension by providing many pointers or indicators that are obviously relevant but initially do not show any connection, and they release this tension by providing a final clue or lead through which it becomes clear how all the other points of reference or footholds fit together. In his films, Alfred Hitchcock, the 'master of suspense,' often questions again what seemed already clear, thus disturbing the fitting of footholds and raising a new one by means of new clues. In doing so, he demonstrates how every single foothold is significant for a fitting. Similarly, in everyday orientation, too, *every fitting remains in suspense:* it is the suspense regarding whether an orientation will hold when new footholds arise, which, in their context, cannot be neglected.

Fittings that establish repeatable contexts of meaning become *patterns.* Patterns are models or designs that can be transferred from one situation to the next. They are sustainable fittings allowing for the *recognition* of something that lasts. When footholds recur in similar connections, the first emerging foothold of a pattern already known is sufficient for 'automatically' predicting the other ones – this is especially obvious in recognizing faces or reading texts. Nietzsche gave a remarkably precise phenomenological description of such an orientation based on patterns:

> Just as little as today's reader takes in all the individual words (or especially syllables) on a page (he catches maybe five out of twenty words and "guesses" what these five arbitrary words might possibly mean) – just as little do we see a tree precisely and completely, with respect to leaves, branches, colors, and shape. We find it so much easier to imagine an approximate tree instead. Even in the middle of the strangest experiences we do the same thing: we invent most of the experience and can barely be made *not* to regard ourselves as the "inventor" of some process. – What all this amounts to is: [...] people are much more artistic than they think. – In the middle of a lively conversation I will often see the other person's face expressing his thoughts (or the thoughts I attribute to him) with a degree of clarity and detail that far exceeds the power of my visual ability: – such subtlety of muscle movement and ocular expression *must* have come from my own imagination. In all likelihood the person had an entirely different expression, or none at all. (*Beyond Good and Evil*, No. 192, transl. by Judith Norman)

If patterns prove successful when recognizing something in changing situations, they are 'tenable' both in the sense of 'sustainable' or 'lasting' as well as in the sense of 'credible' or 'plausible.' However, patterns are perceived to be rigid; but in orientation, they also shift over time, and change according to what is recognized, e. g. a face that ages over time. For changeable patterns, the term *schema* seems to best fit; it also suggests an outline without sensory content, but not a transferable model. In orientation, changeable schemata are tenable as well and even more tenable than rigid patterns because they can exchange footholds and thus keep up with the times. In them, the interconnectedness of the footholds remains elastic and supple; as such, since no situation fully equals another, they allow for a leeway to change footholds: they can take into account the fact that faces change, that trees grow, and that words can take on new meanings. But after a certain point of changing, even schemata that make recognition across changing situations possible become no longer recognizable themselves. Then, they are untenable and will themselves deteriorate.

6.6 The Leeways of Orientation in the Brain

Neurophysiological brain research has begun to explain the conditions for the activities of human orientation. For a philosophy of orientation, it is particularly insightful. Even though human orientation cannot simply be reduced to brain functions, it can only work within their limits and the leeways they provide. However, brain research also inevitably operates within the circle of orientation, given that researchers are also subject to the conditions of human orientation.

The current state of research – which is still in its early stages in light of the vast complexity of the brain – shows strong analogies between the analyses of the operating principles of the human brain and those of human orientation. According to Wolf Singer,

> it is best to envision the brain as a *distributively organized and highly dynamic system* that organizes itself instead of subordinating its functions to a centralist instance for assessments and decisions; as a system that accesses its coding spaces by means of the *topology of its connectivity* and in a *temporal structure of its activity patterns*; that expresses relations not only through the convergence of anatomical connections, but also through the *temporary coordination of discharge patterns*; that can represent contents not only explicitly through highly specialized neurons, but also implicitly through *dynamically associated ensembles*; and, eventually, that *relentlessly formulates hypotheses about the surrounding world based on its prior knowledge*; thus, a system that can take initiative instead of just responding to stimuli.[24]

As such, the brain is "never calm, but it continuously generates highly complex neural activity patterns even without external stimuli." These include "spatio-temporal patterns of coherence" that are physiologically composed of "fluctuations in the activity of greater cell populations." Here, the signals from the sensory organs are ordered in a meaningful way. Through "telecommunications" – electrical signal transmissions in the brain – quasi simultaneous activity patterns arise in neuron populations, which have "almost always a periodical, oscillatory structure" and which discharge synchronically.[25] This leads to the temporary "statistical bindings" by means of which the brain responds to its environment. "Very diverse operations of grouping with maximum degrees of freedom" oscillate with a frequency of 40 Hz and function as rhythmically acting "feature detectors."[26] In this way, the human brain is able to detect very different and rapidly changing footholds in its environment, of which the body is a part as well.

The way the human brain is organized is the result of evolutionary selection processes that are quite clearly comprehensible, and it operates through selection processes itself. Here the thought processes are in principle no different than the sensory processes because they too are based on the functions of the cerebral cortex, which works "always according to the same principles."[27] The "stimulus-response-behavior" that also shapes the orientation reflexes primarily takes place in the evolutionarily older regions of the brain: the cerebellum and the brain stem (drawing strict distinctions is as foreign to the brain as it is to orientation); in these regions, operations take place for the most part according to genetically programmed serial selections. However, the cerebral cortex, the youngest and by far most voluminous part of the brain, primarily makes use of parallel selections that create the leeways experienceable in human orientation. They become possible by means of a topological distribution of functions in areas that are in turn interconnected in manifold ways: thus, by means of a network. From the time when a child engages with his or her environment until about sexual maturity, these interconnections are consolidated in accordance to the frequency of their use. Here, too, selection processes take place: genetically, the brain keeps ready more options for interconnection than it generally uses. The ones permanently used are consolidated, while the ones permanently not used are erased; as such, "'trying out' [...] is the most economic – and perhaps the only viable – way."[28] The architecture of an individual brain develops based on the leeways of a genetically predetermined repertoire and according to effective use – but it is not defined by any given logic.

The "plasticity" of the "brain's architecture" thus provides the conditions for arranging the functions of orientation according to the needs of each individual's experience. The realized structures function then as "determinants of the subsequent changes":

> This means that the whole prehistory takes part in the decision about which branch will be taken at the next junction in the ontogenetic process of development. A result of this chain of conditioned probabilities is that within the myriad of possible branches the predictability of the final state is still limited, even if every single step of differentiation is certainly determined. This in turn drastically restricts the possibility of distinguishing between what is innate or acquired.[29]

Surely, the plasticity is bought at the cost of "greater vulnerability": a "deprivation of experience" leads to the standstill of development processes.[30] This holds true even for the mature brain. After sexual maturity, the plasticity indeed decreases, but it never ceases fully: in the orientation of adults, individual structures are usually stabilized, but not fixed.

Regarding the concrete processing of irritations from the environment, brain research has, so far, best explored the activity of sight as well. Research has discovered strategies of "segmentation" and "overlapping." Segmentation means: movement, color, brightness, etc., are registered by different neuronal ensembles and recombined to identify objects with respect to the needs of a situation. Overlapping means:

> At different points in time, a specific cell may become a member of different populations and therefore participate in the representation of many different features. This in turn may be used to drastically reduce the number of neurons needed for the representation of different features. Also, the representation of new features does not lead to difficulties because all it requires is changing the combination of the neurons activated in each case. Establishing new connections is not necessary; it is enough to activate new constellations of already existing, interacting neurons.[31]

The recombining of segmented and overlapping footholds and patterns develops again according to "criteria of coherence." The human brain seems to orient itself especially to the continuous movements of coherent contours. Hence, patterns of movement can be recognized particularly well:

> When an already stored pattern constellation reappears, established connections are preferably activated, and the pattern is recognized. Even if only partial aspects of the originally acquired pattern are available, the whole pattern can still be reactivated based on the already consolidated connections. This is also true if the new pattern shows only some similarities with the already stored contents. Adaptable neuronal networks thus function like an associative storage: they are capable of generalizing based on only partial aspects.[32]

From evaluated and consolidated activity patterns, further "criteria for adequacy and behavioral relevance" are derived. Therefore, one could also speak in brain-physiological terms of decisions made by the brain:

> Decisions arise in the brain as the result of self-organizing processes, where competition among different probable groupings is the driving force and where coherent system states make up the converging points for the trajectories of the decision.[33]

Decisions by the brain are thus made with respect to fittings as well. They are again selected and stabilized by means of calibrating the locally active patterns with each other through "the interaction of numerous evaluative functions that are spread out over the entire brain" – hence, again, by means of a "distributive decision-making process."[34]

Chapter 7
Signs as Footholds: Orientation as an Art of World Abbreviation
Orientation by means of Signs

Signs are footholds that are specifically made to attract attention. They might be indicators for something beyond themselves that is not conspicuous or noticeable on its own; to make something noticeable, signs themselves need to be particularly conspicuous. They might be conspicuous just by themselves (e.g. a blushing face as an indicator of shame); but they can also be made conspicuous for a specific purpose (e.g. pointing with one's outstretched arm in a certain direction or emphasizing a word). Being particularly conspicuous, signs are especially attractive for an orientation; it can easily hold onto them. But their conspicuousness and attractiveness may also be easily used to divert or deceive someone's attention, or they can be misused to lead someone in a false direction. Thus, they simplify an orientation, but they also increase its risks.

However, signs (*Zeichen*) do not have to be signs of something already given; they are not always 'indicators' (*Anzeichen*) of something that can be perceived on its own; indeed, most of them are in fact not indicators. For signs can also stand for themselves and refer to nothing else. This is true for a lot of gestures or facial expressions, but especially for a huge amount of the signs that belong to languages (e.g. the signs 'and' and 'not' or 'hello' or 'I beg' or 'I apologize'). Here, all we have are signs. Since such signs, which stand only for themselves and which have no foothold in anything else, may be even more deceptive, orientation deals with them all the more circumspectly and carefully: whoever perceives signs must again distinguish and decide which of them are, in his or her situation, relevant or irrelevant, reliable or deceptive.

As particularly noticeable footholds, signs quickly and deeply etch themselves into one's memory; they are the most important elements of the memory (or of the different memories) of our orientation. Our memory retains them throughout changing situations; in doing so, signs allow an orientation to detach them – and thereby the orientation itself – from the specific situations in which they are used. Just as footholds refer to other footholds, signs refer to signs: they build referential contexts that can – as far as they are remembered or persist in memory – be re-traced. In this way, one can capture the past by means of signs; and by means of signs, one can build entire worlds with new spatial and temporal horizons – worlds built entirely of signs.

https://doi.org/10.1515/9783110575149-009

At last, signs, too, can be abbreviated – again by means of signs (e. g. the signs of a long text into a short title). The abbreviation of signs into signs may continue almost endlessly. It permits abstractions through which an orientation gains footholds for the future – and by means of which it has a future in general. Theories and philosophies of signs have made signs conceivable in multiple approaches. A philosophy of orientation will conceive of them primarily from the need to abbreviate and, thus, to accelerate orientation.

7.1 From Footholds via Markings to Signs

In orientation, signs connect to footholds. Footholds can smoothly transition into signs. Since orientation always already operates with signs (even in these sentences), it is difficult for us to observe such transitions. All we can do is reconstruct what is semiotic in our orientation by referring to our orientation's signs themselves: the signs of our orientation are – like orientation in general – self-referential.

When the occurring footholds and patterns of footholds, which provide a first overview of the situation and which give meaning to it, become themselves too complex or too confusing due to their variety and diversity, then orientation needs to gain another overview of them. It maintains the economy of footholds by further selecting footholds and patterns and by holding onto particularly characteristic or distinctive ones that mark what is at stake. In German one says 'markante Anhaltspunkte'; let us call them 'distinctive footholds' in English. Distinctive footholds are especially conspicuous. It is not necessary – at least for the most part – that they be particularly important. But all of them are particularly useful for an orientation: e. g. a river or a mountain in a landscape, an obelisk in a square, a color spot on the wall, striking facial features, a rough or shrill voice. Such distinctive footholds are not only attractive, but also obtrusive: an orientation can hardly bypass them; rather, it automatically returns to them again and again when trying to gain an overview of a situation. In doing so, other footholds are blocked from one's attention; the distinctive footholds intensify the processes of selection between footholds.

Distinctive footholds can, to strengthen and fix them, moreover be highlighted or *marked* as signs. At first, this may happen, for instance, by tracing the contours of a figure or by putting emphasis on a word. However, one can also mark a foothold that is not already striking by itself, but that is relevant for the orientation in recurring situations, e. g. an inconspicuous entrance to an important room in an administrative building. You then mark the door by painting it with a striking color, for example. One does that on pieces of paper as well, more easily and more frequently: if possible, one marks important 'points' by means of circles, colors, highlights, and underlines – in sum: by *markings*. The most common marking is a *cross:* the X with its crossing lines marks the point that is at stake or the foothold into which an orientation abbreviates something. For example: you have to dig into the ground at this point which is marked by a cross to find something hidden – and yet, it need not be exactly this point where the spade must be set; the perimeter is just abbreviated to a point. With markings we repeat and reinforce that which we already attained with points of reference.

This also applies to more complex contexts: if a more complex context of footholds is traced, complex markings make it surveyable, e.g. a subway system. To make the context of such markings clear, it is put into a *schema*. Schemes are especially useful in recurring situations: for example, as means of facilitating orientation at major airports or on screens with a digital interface. In order to make these schemes even more understandable, one uses pictorial symbols for them: *icons* that everyone can understand immediately and independently from the language spoken. Icons that can be combined in schemes are explicit signs for orientation. Lastly, when dispensing markings of pictoriality, these markings become *codes*, like numbers or written characters. Codes are, in a way, pictures too; but it is no longer their pictorial quality that helps one orient oneself; and usually, you need not and cannot decipher or retrieve the pictures to which the codes once connected.

Surely, written characters are signs, drawn and composed of mere strokes like pictures; and in all cultures, they have developed from pictures. But as far as they no longer allow one to recognize pictures, or rather, figurative depictions of something one already knows, they become mere *signs* – in Asian pictorial scripts, the transition is still noticeable. Since mere signs do not follow clues or footholds in the immediate surroundings, they have to be specifically learned, and for this purpose, you need other people who already know them. They are introduced by society; they are social signs and serve the purpose of social understanding, i.e. orientation in society. But once you have learned them, they are easy to read and to understand, easier than most other clues and footholds. Even those who cannot understand such signs (e.g. if they belong to another language) still recognize them as signs. Since they do not occur in the natural environment, but are specifically painted, mere signs differ markedly from their surroundings (just think of the famous Hollywood sign on Mount Lee), and because they differ markedly from their surroundings, they are especially conspicuous and attractive for our orientation (of course, this also concerns in particular written signposts on roads and paths).

Once the meaning represented by the signs that were once markings has faded away, the signs themselves appear as random and *arbitrary* in relation to the signified. As shown by structuralism, their meaning, instead of being connected to and dependent on the signified, becomes clear only in contrast to other signs and, in consequence, to their place in *systems of signs*. Along with the arbitrariness of signs, systems of signs become independent and autonomous from the situations in which they are used. By means of arbitrary systems of signs, our orientation detaches itself even more from the situation and, in doing so, gains new leeways in it. As such, orientation is largely an orientation by means of signs – and more: an orientation within signs.

The arbitrariness of signs becomes manifest in the fact that the signified can always have a different signifier, and indeed, other languages mostly have different signifiers. Therefore, it seems that signs are just random and that they do not provide any hold for an orientation. This has triggered a mistrust of signs within the metaphysical tradition of Western philosophy. According to this tradition, signs are 'only' signs and must therefore stand for something that exists independent from them and that has, different from signs, a hold per se. Apparently, this can be made plausible with simple examples: a table is still a table even if we call it *Tisch*. But such apparently striking examples are not tenable. For the table can in turn be distinguished from the signs 'table' or '*Tisch*' only by means of signs: you can only speak of things or objects, in opposition to signs, by making use of signs ('thing' is a sign of an alleged thing which you cannot distinguish without using a sign like 'thing'). Instead, the hold that signs give in orientation functions – to state it once again – is a kind of social support: it is based on the fact that people use signs in similar situations in a similar way.

Nevertheless, arbitrary signs and systems of signs whose use is independent from specific situations are still in need of connecting with footholds somewhere in the experienced reality beyond the signs, be it in the current situation or in memory. At some point, signs, even the most complex mathematical signs, have to connect with an everyday orientation, at least in order to be learned. They never completely detach themselves from it, nor float in the air, nor somehow become transcendent. But they do not need to 'stand for' special clues or footholds to which one can directly point; signs are useful and understandable, even though they are not signs *for* certain things that you can point to. In orientation, one can go, just like from foothold to foothold, from sign to sign; but systems of signs need to stay connected with footholds – even if they are quite remote.

7.2 Persistent Signs – The Leeways of Changing Meanings

In signs, orientation finds something that persists even when situations change; in signs, one can capture something and return to it at any time in later situations. This is true for markers, for words in a conversation, and especially for written characters. One can take writings along and bring them up again throughout changing situations; their signs do not fade away, they visibly persist (on paper or wherever). They relieve our memory; you only need to remember where they are, and you can then check there again later. You can in fact point with your finger at them. They are organized spatially and, therefore, available simultaneously – so you can move forward and backwards between them, skip passages, or focus on more specific aspects of their meanings. As such, they already offer an overview of the meaning of their signs and thus allow for new patterns: in writings, even what is written far apart can be seen together.

If the use of signs (whether markers or oral or written signs) has been learned, they are not only, like other footholds, (mostly) understood immediately, but also used routinely. Thus, they are likewise no longer conspicuous as signs. Only if a single sign is not – or not immediately – understood (if it is surprisingly new or if a new sign is being used) does one ask about its meaning (if one does not wait for it to become clearer in what follows), and the sign is then noticed again as a sign. In this way, signs oscillate between inconspicuousness and conspicuousness, depending on how routinely they are understood. But to ask, at all, about the meaning of signs, one must have already understood that they are signs meant to convey something, and one must already be able to use other signs in order to ask this question. Thus, on this level, we are always dealing with signs, too, and with footholds or with additional signs that can clarify the meaning of the signs in question. Answers to questions about the meaning of signs are signs again – but now different signs that one hopes the other will better understand.[35]

Signs that are not immediately understood are *in need of interpretation*. The less familiar you are with the situation in which the signs are being used or with the person using these signs, the more they require interpretation. Over the time in which they themselves persist, signs are inevitably understood in always new and different ways – their meanings can change and shift, and they can even shift so far that they are no longer sufficiently understood. However, signs must be able to shift their meanings if they are to be useful in orientation. For as far as they do not come up in a situation (like simple footholds), but need to be learned, and since they can only be learned in a limited number over a limited amount of time, they can be used in innumerable situations only if their use allows for room for different meanings in different situations. Thus, their meanings can change more and more over time. However, they must not change all of a sudden; the room or leeway for changing meanings must also be limited. The signs may only change and shift their meanings to the extent that they are still understandable and plausible; if signs were being used and their meanings changed at random, then they would no longer be useful in orientation. In sum: signs do not need to have *one* meaning across all situations and for all time, but they need to be sufficiently clear and unambiguous in a certain situation – and therefore, they must be able to adapt their meanings to changing situations (within certain leeways).

Signs become clear or unambiguous in situations themselves. In Wittgenstein's famous language game of two pavers working closely with each other (*Philosophical Investigations*, § 19 f.), the simple word 'slab' is sufficient for one of them to hand a new slab to the other when he is done preparing its base. This is not ambiguous as only one kind of slab is being used. But if there were different kinds of slabs available, then further signs would have to be used ('big slab,' 'small slab'). Conversely, if signs are too ambiguous in a situation, you narrow down the leeways of their meanings by adding further suitable signs in the respective situations. If one says, 'let's meet in New York City tomorrow,' this would only be sufficient if both interlocutors meet there on a regular basis at a certain place at a certain time. However, if it is not always the same time and the same place in New York City, one would need to specify when and where, e. g. the street and the location on this street, the floor, the room, etc. But we always add only as many signs as are needed to make them sufficiently clear or unambiguous in a certain situation ('meet you tomorrow'). How wide the leeways of meaning can be depends, again, on the situation. By narrowing down the leeway of the meaning of the signs being used by adding further signs, everyday orientation needs no general definitions of signs to transcend all situations. Definitions are also nothing more than supplements of signs by means of further signs. But they include the demand that all signs being used be understood by everyone in the same way throughout all possible situations – a demand that can hardly be satisfied anywhere (with the important exception of mathematical characters that may only be used in a strictly regulated manner; therefore, they neither connect to specific situations, nor can they adapt to them; *if* they are connected to specific situations, e. g. when applied in physics or other sciences, they must again be interpreted and, in doing so, can become ambiguous as well).

The supplementing signs may be of very different kinds. When saying 'slab' the paver might also nod, and later on, this nodding might alone be a sufficient sign. In every conversation, systems of various signs come together and overlap with each other: beyond verbal and written language signs, there are vocal, mimic, and gestural signs; appearance and behavior, etc. Such systems of various, overlapping signs may amplify or question each other; but there is no overarching or superior system of signs – nor is there a need for one. Orientation can do without it.

7.3 Orientation as an Art of World Abbreviation

As a sign of approval, one can, instead of nodding, just expressly close one's eyes; as a sign of admonition, one can, instead of raising one's finger, just give an austere look; to tell someone to stop driving or walking one can, instead of using barriers, give a red-light signal. For our orientation, this means: signs can be abbreviated by means of other signs that take less time and are therefore more efficient. But, in the long run, it may be easiest, fastest, and most efficient to abbreviate many different signs with verbal and written signs. To quote Wittgenstein once more, who provides a famous example of this:

> A child has hurt himself and he cries; then adults talk to him and teach him exclamations and, later, sentences. They teach the child new pain behavior. [...] the verbal expression of pain replaces crying. (*Philosophical Investigations*, § 244)

By using words, one can usually make clear what is at stake in a faster, less ambiguous, and more sustainable way. But, what is even more important: language signs can again be abbreviated with other language signs. Where many words are needed to describe something, they can themselves be substituted with names or labels as far as they have been introduced before (e. g. one can say 'I have a migraine' instead of telling a long story about headache, nausea, vomiting, sensitivity to light, noise and odor, perceptual problems, loss of appetite, indigestion and so on). At first, we abbreviate with *names* (general and proper names) things, events, procedures, etc., which must be identified quickly by oneself or by others (and this is what children first learn when acquiring speech); and what we need to identify quickly is what we deal with all the time: human beings, ways of acting or behavior, technical devices, natural events, public places, etc. Since, for instance, the weather might strongly influence daily operations, we have started using names for high- and low-pressure areas, tempests, hurricanes, typhoons and the like. Names do not reveal what something is; they only allow for returning to the same thing or event in different situations; everything else, they leave open. As for general names, they refer to individual entities as well, whether they are meteorological high- and low-pressure areas or living creatures, or social institutions; and by using names, they can quickly be connected with other individual things ('hurricane Harvey became a low-pressure area over Tennessee and may bring heavy rain on Monday and Tuesday'). In spite of being arbitrary, names are – once introduced – sufficiently clear in their contexts. As signs, we try to keep names as short as possible: long names are, over time, abbreviated, e.g. by means of acronyms. In everyday orientation, sign use is more a matter of efficiency than definitive description.

From names onward, the *abstraction of terms* may further proceed. It abbreviates semiotic signs even more. At a later point, we will deal with the significance of abstractions for logic and the significance of logic for our orientation. For now, we focus only on the issue of effective *abbreviations* or short-cuts: in light of its ability to abbreviate what is occurring in a situation into footholds, signs, names, and terms, orientation altogether becomes an *art of world abbreviation* (*Weltabkürzungskunst*). 'World' is, in a philosophy of orientation, the term for all situations one has dealt and deals with, including the memory of what one dealt with in the past and the expectation that one will deal with always new and different situations in the future. All these situations require short-cuts to conceive of and describe them, and they will continually require new short-cuts in order to always maintain an overview. According to Kant, the need to maintain an overview in times of increasing complexity calls for a "genius." If the world knowledge that has been acquired throughout history is not to become too complex and confusing, geniuses must be able to "abbreviate" it again and again (*Logic*, Introduction, AA IX, 43f.; our transl.). According to Kant, Newton formulated, in this sense, common laws for the movements of masses on earth and in the sky and thus made the movements of masses in the whole physical universe surveyable. Nietzsche generalized this and called science, in a note, altogether an "art of schematizing and abbreviating" (Notes 1886/1887, 5[16], KSA 12.190; our transl.). In *Beyond Good and Evil*, No. 211, he wrote:

> It is up to these researchers to make everything that has happened or been valued so far look *clear, obvious, comprehensible, and manageable*, to *abbreviate* everything long, even "time" itself, and to overwhelm the entire past. This is an enormous and wonderful task, in whose service any subtle pride or tough will can certainly find satisfaction. (Transl. by Judith Norman; emphasis changed)

Chapter 8
The Self-Stabilization and Self-Differentiation of Orientation: Routines, Transposed Continuities, and Orientation Worlds
Orientation by means of Routines

8.1 The Self as the Self-Referentiality of Orientation

Until now, we have provisionally used the expression that 'an orientation' does something, e. g. it seeks, finds, sights, arranges itself, holds onto something, decides for something, and so on. When Martin Heidegger asks in *Being and Time* the "existential question about the who of Da-sein," he emphasizes the metaphysical baggage of the responses traditionally given to this question, which he now tries to critically take back. For him, this concerns the terms 'I,' 'soul,' 'consciousness,' 'person,' and 'subject': 'I,' as far as it is conceived of as a 'being' that "maintains itself as something identical in the changes of its modes of behavior and of its experiences"; 'soul,' as far as it means a "substantial soul (*Seelensubstanz*)"; 'consciousness,' as far as it assumes a "thingliness of consciousness"; 'person,' as far as an "objectivity of the person" is involved; and, as the unity and foundation of all these, "*subjectum*," as far as it is believed to be an "always already and constantly objectively present (*Vorhandenes*)," an "underlying base in an eminent sense (*in einem vorzüglichen Sinne zum Grunde liegende*)" (*Being and Time*, §25). Heidegger's criticism of such concepts concerning the 'who' of 'being (*Dasein*),' which goes back via Kant to Hume and Locke, was in fact already articulated even more pointedly by Friedrich Nietzsche. The latter simply sees 'superstition' at work, which he does not get tired of enlightening and which he also detects in the 'reason' of the former period of Enlightenment. The very question of 'who' thinks, perceives, and recognizes betrays, for Nietzsche, a "prejudice of reason" which has "our *language*" as a "constant advocate" and which "forces us to assume unity, identity, permanence, substance, cause, thingliness, being" (*Twilight of the Idols*, 'The 'Reason' in Philosophy,' No. 5). Ludwig Wittgenstein eventually suspected in this case "not facts; but, as it were, illustrated idioms"; and he delivered the warning: "The question itself includes a mistake." (*Philosophical Investigations*, § 295 and § 189) If the Indo-European languages with their propositional subject-predicate structure suggest that everything that happens, even lightning and thunder, is to be understood as a 'deed' by a 'doer' (Nietzsche, *Beyond Good and Evil*, No. 17),

https://doi.org/10.1515/9783110575149-010

then this, too, may be a way to stabilize our orientation; if European philosophy followed this way of supporting its orientation with metaphysical concepts (like 'I,' 'soul,' 'consciousness,' 'person,' and 'subject') in order to attain final foundations for it, then these must have been footholds which it needed, at least for a certain time. But since then, in the process of the self-enlightenment of philosophy, such metaphysical footholds have been questioned; and by way of their critique, orientation as such has been conceived of more and more critically. At the same time, its self-referentiality has been understood step-by-step – i.e. as a condition of its other-referentiality, which all the while makes, as we have seen, this self-referentiality necessary.

(1) The exploring of the 'who' of orientation essentially begins with Aristotle's term *soul* (*psycháe*). He conceives of the soul as a substance (*ousía*) and distinguishes it from the body, which he considers without question to be a substance as well because of its bodily distinctiveness and its independent mobility (*chorismós*). The soul, which is not given to the senses, is distinguishable only in thought; in this respect, it is, in its later term, a 'metaphysical' substance. It is, for him, the source or the principle (*archáe*) of the vitality of living bodies, manifesting itself in the fact that bodies grow and move, perceive, and have desires. However, in order to be the principle of a living body, the soul, too, must not only be independent (*choristáe*) and living, but also a substance and more (*mâllon*) than the body; it thus must be a substance of a substance, and thus a self-referential substance. The question as to whether the soul as the principle of living bodies can also live without the body and the question as to whether immortality can thus be ascribed to it remains unanswered by Aristotle (*De anima* II, 1–2). But he emphasizes that it is the soul through which everything that exists is perceived or conceived; and therefore, it is for him "somehow everything that exists" (*hae psycháe tà ónta pós esti pánta, De anima* III 1, 431 b 21).

(2) The fact that the soul is somehow everything that exists is regarded in the early modern period as *consciousness*. Consciousness is the being of self-referential knowledge; the Lat. term *conscientia* and the French and the (now obsolete) meaning of the English term *conscience*, which the German philosopher Christian Wolff (who preceded Immanuel Kant as the most important philosopher of the 18th century) translates as *Bewusstsein*, means literally 'with-knowledge' or 'joint knowledge,' or a 'knowledge of knowledge'; it is initially the term for moral 'conscience.' Descartes introduces the term as a being, which is able to question all other beings, but not its own being; it is thus to be the only certain being. Thus, the being of consciousness is to come into being through thought – and *in* thought by negating everything else. By thinking it in this way, Descartes continues to rely on the metaphysics of substances. As far as questioning or

doubting is a deed or a kind of action, he still presupposes a doer or an agent in the shape of a substance; as such, he conceives of consciousness as a substance, too, but now as a declared metaphysical substance, whose immortality one is also able to prove. Now, it is moreover a declared self-referential substance, which can be distinguished from the body precisely because of its self-referentiality. As such, it is, according to Descartes, no longer the principle of the body's liveliness; for him, it does indeed communicate with the body, but only by means of humors and glands that belong to the body, which works like a machine. But for consciousness, everything corporeal is to exist only through ideas (*ideae*), which this consciousness arranges in orders according to its own rules and which, according to Descartes, it ought to methodologically order in a way that the ideas of all things become as clear and distinct as consciousness' insight into the completely clear fact of its own being. Hence, within the self-referential substance of consciousness, the 'order of things' (*ordre des choses*), which will always remain questionable, is replaced by an 'order of reasons' (*ordre des raisons*), over which consciousness has sovereign control.

(3) Kant then critically emphasizes that the self-referentiality of consciousness must not be conceived of as a substance. Rather, 'substance' is, for him, one of the categories by means of which consciousness conceives of objects and among which it chooses. Therefore, it cannot be a category, which constitutes its own being. As such, Kant abolishes the metaphysics of consciousness. Instead, Kant – following Locke and Hume – connects the givenness of objects in consciousness with sensible and corporeal perceptions which 'affect (*affizieren*)' consciousness: i.e. they stimulate it to give them an order of thought in Descartes' sense. The self-referentiality of consciousness finds its purpose in reference to these affects, which it works out in its own way: 'autonomously.' Consciousness – which after being affected by the senses conceives of something *as* something (as a substance, among other things) – 'only' has an idea of itself; and as an idea of itself, it is '*self-consciousness*'. Self-consciousness exists, according to Kant, only as a self-referential idea; and this self-referential idea creates "the idea *I think*" (*Critique of Pure Judgement*, B 132).

(4) According to Kant, the 'I' itself is otherwise completely empty. It is at first only a pronoun, but it has a special grammatical function. In communication, it indicates who *speaks*; and it thus indicates that a consciousness speaks *to other consciousnesses* – in the terms of orientation, it refers to the standpoint of a speaker. However, Kant does not refer to such communication with the term 'I,' but rather wants to justify the objectivity of objects with it. For the pronoun 'I' is at once absolutely singular as well as absolutely general: one can only say 'I' about oneself; but everyone can say 'I,' even if one is in all other respects different from everybody else. In this way, the shift from subjectivity to objectivity is

possible. The 'I' indicates at once a singular as well as a general subjectivity; the (paradoxical) fact that the singular subject is at the same time a general subject is what enables objectivity.

(5) For this simultaneously subjective as well as objective 'I,' Kant makes use of another term from Aristotle: the *'subject' (hypokeímenon)*. A 'subject' is literally that which 'underlies' a statement: that about which something is being predicated. This term is also conceived of within the context of communication about objects. However, Kant uses the term 'subject' not only for that about which something is predicated, but also for that which predicates: i.e. the consciousness that makes statements about objects outside of itself (outside of consciousness) based on its ideas. The "empirical consciousness," which is affected by its subjective perceptions, becomes the "transcendental subject" as far as it objectifies these perceptions via "logical functions to judgments" (*logische Funktionen zu Urteilen*) or "categories," which are presupposed as general ones. The consciousness as a subject is "transcendental" regarding the fact that it literally 'transcends' its subjective "perception judgments" (*Wahrnehmungsurteile*) by transforming them into objective "experience judgments" (*Erfahrungsurteile*). This leads, according to Kant, to the "paradox" that the subject affects itself in the "inner sense" through perceptions of itself, before affecting these perceptions with its own terms again. The self-referentiality of the subject as a transcendental subject necessarily entails an other-referentiality to the subject itself as an empirical subject that is always concerned with newly surprising affections. By grasping these affections with universally valid or objective terms, the subject de-subjectifies itself.

(6) With the term *reason*, Kant attains the simultaneity of self-referentiality and other-referentiality. Since it is, according to Kant, reason that has 'needs' for orientation, it has to be reason, too, which is the 'who' of orientation. As that which presets the laws for the objectification of what is sensuously given, reason itself cannot be anything sensuously given, nor can it be, as such, an empirical reality. It constitutes itself by distinguishing itself from nature (the term for everything given to the senses); and the (self-)critique of pure reason consists in the fact that reason also always needs to, in its self-referentiality, take into account its other-referentiality to nature. The "entire philosophy of pure reason" is always concerned with the "negative use" to erect "under the name of a discipline, as it were, a system of caution and self-examination out of the nature of reason and the objects of its use," as a caution against "an entire system of delusions and deceptions" (*Critique of Pure Reason*, transl. by Paul Guyer and Allen W. Wood, p. 629, A 711/B 739). The goal of this discipline is the "*self-preservation* of reason" in its orientation (*What Does It Mean to Orient Oneself in Thinking?*, transl. by Daniel Fidel Ferrer, p. 21 [note 7]; AA VIII, 147, note).

(7) Thus, for Kant, reason is the 'who' of orientation only in accordance with nature, as distinguished from it, on the one hand, and as dependent on it, on the other. The unity of the distinction between reason and nature is, for him, the *human being*. After German idealism (Friedrich W. J. Schelling relies primarily on the distinction between reason and nature, Johann Gottlieb Fichte on the distinction between 'I' and 'Not-I', and G. W. F. Hegel, in his *Phenomenology of Mind*, on the distinction between consciousness and object [*Gegenstand*]), philosophers and scientists were determined to explore and empirically research the human being as a unity of reason and nature. Charles Darwin makes the fundamental divide between the human being and the animal obsolete as far as it is to be based on human reason. He observes continuous transitions and uncertain boundaries between the human being and (other) animals, which are also and especially evident in the orientation skills of humans and animals. Consciousness and reason, which human beings had reserved only for themselves, turn out to be not only an advantage, but also a problem for orientation. Whereas Kant writes: "In the natural predispositions of an organized being, i.e. a being arranged purposively for life, we assume as a principle that no instrument is to be encountered in it for any end except that which is the most suitable to and appropriate for it." (*Groundwork for the Metaphysics of Morals*, AA IV, 395; transl. by Allen W. Wood, pp. 10 f.), Nietzsche now says: "The temporal state of being conscious (*Bewusstheit* – not *Bewusstsein*; cf. chap. 9.3) is the last and latest development of the organic, and hence also its most unfinished and unrobust feature." It therefore gives rise to "countless mistakes," and this new "function" could be the greatest "danger to the organism" (*Gay Science*, No. 11).

(8) With Darwin and Nietzsche, the *individual being* is prioritized over the species and thus over the universal as such, which traditional philosophy has so strongly relied on. Now, it can no longer be assumed that it is generally 'the human being' that orients itself according to the species; instead it is every individual being that orients itself according to *its own* conditions. At the same time, individuals strongly orient themselves to each other; thus, general orientations develop as well, but these are general orientations that always leave room for individual differences. And, in fact, this approach does more justice to the reality of our orientation.

(9) Kierkegaard conceives of the traditional and general definitions of the human being in a new and more rigorous way from the point of view of the situational existence of individuals. He defines the 'who' of orientation (in a somewhat obscure but at the same time resolute manner) as its mere self-reference, i.e. as a mere *self*, or as the "relation which relates itself to its own self," namely as "this feature of the relationship, that the relationship relates to itself" (*The

Sickness Unto Death, transl. by Walter Lowrie, Part First, I. A., pp. 146f.). As a religious writer, he adds that this 'self' would not "constitute itself" (unlike Descartes' 'I think' or Kant's transcendental subject); rather, it is "constituted by another," which remains incomprehensible to it. Therefore, it is in constant danger of falling into "vertigo" and "despair." Nietzsche agrees: he has his Zarathustra step-by-step 'destruct' (as Heidegger calls it) the traditional terms of the 'soul,' the 'I,' and 'reason' in order to conceive of the "self" as a "big reason" of "the body"; and he considers this self attuned to "life and earth" in such a deep and unfathomable way that it remains for the "small reason" of the philosophical tradition just as inconceivable as God is for Kierkegaard's believing self (*Thus Spoke Zarahustra* I, On the Despisers of the Body). Heidegger, who begins his 'existential analysis' with the concept of *Dasein,* also adopts in his subsequent investigations the term of the self. Emmanuel Levinas and Paul Ricœur rely on the term as well: the former emphasizes (following Kierkegaard) the dependence of the self on an unfathomable Other; the latter tries to reconcile the term of the self with theorems of the self in analytic philosophy. In both their lines of arguments, the term of the 'self' also prevails over traditional terms like consciousness, subject, and reason.

The term of the self as an abbreviation of mere self-referentiality is also the answer to the question who or what orients itself in orientation. *The self of an orientation is this orientation itself.* When speaking of 'orienting-oneself,' the self as the self-referentiality of orientation is already presumed and thus no longer in need of being justified *in* orientation. A philosophy of orientation proceeds from this term of the self, and instead of searching for something 'behind' it that would exist 'as such,' this approach takes back any proffered metaphysics. However, the self of orientation always remains a self as distinguished from its situation and from other selves; the situation requires orientation, and the other orientations are part of the situation.

8.2 The Self-Stabilization of Orientation through Self-Structuring: Familiarity, Routines, Feelings, Plausibilities, and Memories

In philosophy, sociology and psychology, the term 'self' is frequently used as a noun that then gives rise to the expectation of a specific entity; but one would hardly expect this in everyday language use. The 'self' of orientation, which is spoken of in theoretical terms, does not *speak* of itself as a 'self' (nor as a 'soul,' a 'consciousness,' or a 'reason'), because an orientation does not distinguish such a self within itself. Rather, one speaks of oneself as an 'I' when speaking to others, and one speaks as 'one' or 'you' (in German '*man*') when one does (or you do) not want to stand out – and you always keep both options open. Neither does an orientation *experience* itself as a 'self' that could somehow be separated from this orientation; rather, it experiences itself as an orientation in all its orientation processes.

Instead, the self gains shape in the self-structuring of orientation; and through this self-structuring it at the same time stabilizes itself. The self attains an initial stability through the fact that the orientation processes become regular, that they gain a certain *regularity*, and that they continue to run as they have done up until now. If something runs long enough with a certain regularity, one tacitly expects that it will continue to run like this. With the experience of regularity, an orientation becomes something *familiar*; instead of unsettlement, reassuring calmness sets in. Familiarity is the tacit expectation that regularity will continue. Familiar processes then become stable footholds of an orientation: one no longer needs to decide or talk about them; as soon as they are familiar, they are only noticed if they suddenly 'stop running.' *Familiarity (Vertrautheit), which develops when everything 'runs as usual,' is the basic stability of orientation.* Orientation obtains its first kind of confidence: it gains a *routine*. The word 'routine,' too, comes from the language of ways, from the French and English 'route,' which in turn originated from the Latin '*via rupta*,' which is 'a way broken or paved through the area.' Paved ways are familiar and easy to follow – one trusts (*vertraut*) in what is familiar (*vertraut*). The 'knowledge' that allows one to easily proceed on paved ways, or – avoiding the language of ways – the 'confident mastery' of well-established orientation processes is then a 'routine,' which one 'has.' You usually have one in many things, but never in everything; one does not have something like 'routine as such,' but one only has 'routines' in this or that; and every orientation has *its own* routines.

In its routines, the structure of an orientation begins to differentiate. Everyday orientation is densely interveined by routines, and it gains its main foothold in them. This starts with bodily routines, like body movements and postures, gestures and facial expressions, all of which develop largely without control and which are characteristic to each individual. It continues with routines of actions and work as well as daily and weekly procedures, which are more directly determined by social factors. And it goes all the way to highly controlled social routines, such as pedagogical, workout, economic, bureaucratic, judicial, political, religious, artistic, and scientific routines. They can develop just like something familiar and trusted, but they often have to be acquired through effort and practice. Then, they become noticeable, especially if somebody is particularly bad or very 'skilled' at them. If routinization is successful, it is experienced with pleasure, e. g. by children who learn how to walk or speak. The pleasure of acquiring routines gives wings to your routinizations: the trust in routines once acquired encourages you to acquire more routines and trust in them (you learn how to ride a bike, how to roller skate, how to ski, and how to drive a car, etc.) – the self-stabilization and self-structuring of orientation accelerates. Since routines are not determined in any way, but develop gradually, they leave room for their further development and, thus, for the continued self-structuring and self-stabilization of one's orientation.

Routines that have once developed become – as complex as they may be and as much effort as it may have taken to acquire them – as one says, 'natural' over time. One then 'feels' with an 'instinctive certainty' what one needs to do. Such feelings – let us call them *orientation feelings* – can only partially be compared with other feelings. As with the left-right-distinction, one does not actually 'feel' anything; they do not 'feel' like feelings. This also applies to those feelings for which we do not have any simple or common names, e. g. the sense of balance (*Gleichgewichtsgefühl*), the feeling of one's body (*Leibgefühl*), the awareness of life (*Lebensgefühl*), self-assurance (*Selbstgefühl*), and the feeling of home (*Heimatgefühl*). They constantly support an orientation; like routines, one does not feel them positively, but one only becomes aware of them if they are interrupted or are absent. It is impossible to explicate or 'give reasons' for the assurance that orientation feelings give. You have to rely on them and therefore trust in them; only when trusting them are you able to successfully orient yourself with them.

Orientation feelings that spring from reliable routines are a kind of knowledge (*Wissen*), if knowledge consists of sufficiently certain knowings (*Kenntnisse*) that prove reliable throughout changing situations. *Orientation knowledge* is mostly not explicit (let alone explicitly justified) knowledge. It is an implicit or a non-propositional knowledge about how to use or deal with things (*Gebrauchs- oder Umgangswissen*), a 'knowing-how,' as one says: as easy as it is to walk, it is all the more difficult to explain to somebody in theoretical terms how exactly you need to use your legs in order to make headway quickly and still keep your balance. On the other hand, you can, after you have learned something through explicit instructions, forget this explicit knowledge again as soon as a routine develops. In familiar situations, orientation knowledge is something like a *self-forgotten* knowledge; it leaves out articulations, explications, and justifications, even if they were possible. *Plausibilities* are modes of such a self-forgotten knowledge as well, and as far as scientific orientation eventually relies on plausibilities, as mentioned before, it also includes orientation knowledge.

'Self-forgotten' (and thus paradoxical) also describes how our memory works, or rather – according to current memory research – the *memories* of orientation. As a short-term or working memory (for shorter periods) and as a long-term memory (for longer periods), memories structure our orientation in a way that it escapes our present orientation. You forget most of what you have seen, heard, and thought; but some of it remains in your memories without you noticing it; some of it reappears, if you look for it, and some of it powerfully intrudes on your consciousness on its own. You cannot freely dispose of what you remember; you only have a limited power over it; nor do you have an overview of everything that you 'have in your memory.' That means: your memories are also engaged in your current orientation without always involving your consciousness; by the very fact that they take most of what you have previously experienced away from your current attention (the capacity of which is always limited), they enable your current attention to work at all. It is, in fact, a kind of disease to remember too much of what happened in your past life. In short: memories work economically as well; they usually only retain what might afterward be relevant for one's successful orientation. Of course, this encompasses, for shorter periods, the currently relevant clues, leads, and footholds and, for longer periods, the experiences that were somehow crucial and took part in shaping our lives and orientations – we may remember them gladly or reluctantly. However, most remains forgotten: our memories discard it, screen it out; and this forgetting itself happens unnoticed – it is forgotten as well. But what comes back usually connects to present clues; it is attracted by them and forms new patterns with them. Memories also operate mainly with clues, previous and current ones; one clue leads to another, some of them appearing in the current situation, some coming back from past situations.

Thus, it is not about giving a correct rendition of things, but rather it is about fitting and adapting that which is remembered to the current orientation. What one remembers, and how one remembers it, depends on each situation. It is, at the same time, adapted to the context and the relevant matters of the respective situations. In other words: the affective assessments, which permeate that which was kept in memories, are reassessed (you remember something severe with greater ease if it no longer affects you), and the contents are selected accordingly. This leads to shifts in meaning and value as well – in the interest of the present orientation. Thus, you can only partially rely on the 'fidelity' of your memories. But you can all the more count on the fact that they, too, move with the times and support new orientations.

The short-term or working memory already takes part in how we perceive and identify something as something; because it has a rather limited capacity, it is forced to do a high degree of selection. One already identifies everything at the service of the current orientation. From what is perceived and identified only a small amount is retained for a short period; and from this small amount, that which is particularly relevant for one's orientation goes into one's long-term memory. The long-term memory probably developed as a memory for places which were relevant for the orientation of animals in their habitats; it mostly connects events with the context in which they happened (and is thus called 'episodic memory'). This, at the same time, prevents too extensive shifts of meaning. However, the 'engrams,' by means of which the long-term memory enshrines in the brain that which is to be retained, are still subject to transformational processes as well – they probably consolidate very slowly over months and years. Therefore, one can often retrieve past contexts only with great effort and intense concentration. This may create gaps, which in turn may be closed in different and mostly unnoticed ways – and if this fails, such gaps may be noticed. Only this noticeable forgetting is typically thought of when we speak of 'forgetting.'

8.3 Changing Routines, Transposed Continuities

There is a young man who every day drives home from his office, picks up a few groceries for his family on the way, and then goes for a half-hour run once he is home – everything as usual: a life oriented through routine or, as we will call it, a routined life. The young man's routines, as they have developed, form a sustainable pattern, in which he can smoothly shift from one routine to another one: he can *routinely shift routines*. One day, the young man notices a new construction site while he's on his run. He has, in fact, always been interested in engineering and in construction sites. Now, he runs by the site every day and observes the progress of the construction. One day, he stops and enters the construction site, and by chance he meets the construction developer: a businessman who is always looking for reliable managers for his extensive network of department stores. The young man agrees to take a position offered to him and quickly becomes the regional manager; he moves to another city; and now, he drives to work every day within this city, picks up a few groceries on his way home, and goes for a half-hour run each evening. Routines create leeway for something new; they allow for new orientations even when the situation does not require them or make them attractive. Not everything is made new in such reorientations: established routines are reinstated under new conditions; they are somewhat changed, but not conspicuously. Routines can continue to operate under changed conditions. But not all of them. When the young man who is now regional manager of a department store chain moves to the new city, his family does not want to come with him. He only sees them now for short times on just a few days each month. But routines that do not continue can be replaced by others – although not all of them and not all of them at once. Instead of spending time with his family, the young man now goes out more often, twice a week to karate practice, once a week to chess club; he becomes a routined karate fighter and chess player, and, over the course of this, he forgets his longing for his family. Replacing, one by one, individual routines with other ones does not altogether harm the stability of an orientation as long as a sufficient number of routines endure. The pattern as a whole has continuity; but since the individual routines in it are only partially replaced and transferred, it has a *structure of transposed continuities*. It endures because of the continuity of the individual routines which the young man has learned not only to change, but also to exchange with other routines. His new routines involve making new acquaintances; his short visits with his family become less frequent; and instead, he is now often seen with a new person on the golf course. The marriage falls into crisis and a separation ensues. On the golf course, he meets businessmen who are always looking for young, dynamic employees for their aspiring companies: people who are willing to risk established routines, their own as well as the routines of others. Now the young man, a member of the executive board of a construction company listed on an important stock exchange, is completely wrapped up in the business world – and thus he no longer has any time left to walk home, pick up groceries, run for half an hour, or go to karate practice or chess club. He has also undergone major changes in appearance and character. Over the course of exchanging his routines one by one, he has eventually become 'somebody else'; the day on which he entered the construction site, 'a new life began' for him, as he himself says. He indeed misses a few things, but altogether his self-confidence has grown considerably. By means of transposed continuities, he also acquired a *routine for replacing routines*; he now has not only orientation routines, but also *reorientation routines*. His orientation did not lose its stability; instead, it is now able to endure in the course of quicker and quicker transposed continuities of reorientation routines.

8.4 The Self-Differentiation of Orientation: Orientation Worlds

Having routines in changing and exchanging routines is possible if routines connect to each other and link with each other: for instance in family life, there are daily routines as well as routines of education, leisure, or holiday; in one's working life, there are routines about when and how to work, take a break, have meetings and discussions, and find agreements; in social life, there are routines regarding conversations, invitations, having dinner, and so on. These can each include entirely different orientation processes, which are, however, in belonging to each other, perceived as coherent orientation areas or as 'worlds of their own,' where you feel 'at home' and where you 'know your way around' and can 'move confidently.' Patterns of orientation routines connect with each other to form *orientation worlds*, which are often, like in the case of family and work life, spatially and temporarily separated from each other ('on the one hand, her world was mathematics, on the other hand, it was her garden'). Our everyday orientation differentiates into orientation worlds whose importance may differ depending on the time of day. We usually stay only in one orientation world at a time and forget our other orientation worlds during this time. This relieves our orientation altogether. In other words, while one orientation world is the center of attention, the other ones go out toward the periphery. Orientation worlds are usually separated to such an extent that if one world is noticed in the other one (e. g. your children call at the office), this is experienced as an irritation, as a pleasant or an unpleasant surprise.

An orientation's ability to stay in one of its orientation worlds is supported by attention thresholds, which imperceptibly separate the different orientation worlds from each other. While working hard at your desk in the open-plan office you do not hear the babel of voices or the ringing telephones around you (one calls this 'concentration'). And only this, in fact, allows you to complete tasks. Completing tasks requires undisturbed routines, and attention thresholds ensure your undisturbedness. They impede switching from one to another orientation world with different routines; they delay this switch by keeping your attention from being easily irritated and from turning too quickly to other stimuli or clues (we describe this; brain research has to explain it). As a result, the self-differentiation of orientation into orientation worlds functions as an additional selection of clues – it makes our orientation even more effective.

However, attention thresholds can only block out irritations to a certain extent. When working at home on the computer, the thresholds still need to allow one to hear one's baby in another room. Our orientation is organized in a way that clues – here in the form of signals – that are particularly relevant to it surmount the thresholds between orientation worlds and continue to irritate, be it by coercions (the baby cries and may need something: you need to promptly check) or by allurements (the baby is laughing, and you long to be there too). But strongly irritating signals are also only clues: you may or may not respond to their coercions or allurements. One has to decide, and it is precisely these decisions that make noticeable one's switches between different orientation worlds and the fact that there are different orientation worlds at all.

The ability to keep to a certain orientation world despite other coercions and allurements varies from person to person. It also depends on the orientation worlds themselves and the situations where they become relevant. Goethe was famous for living in multiple orientation worlds: He was a poet, a lover, a minister of state, a scientist, a painter, a landscaper, an architect, and a valued partner in conversations and correspondences (to name only his most obvious regular activities), and he managed to separate these worlds masterfully and to connect them as well if he wanted to. On the other hand, Napoleon was famous for being able to do various things at once and confidently act in multiple orientation worlds at the same time. To a lesser degree, most people can do this. For orientation worlds are, even if clearly separated from each other, often interlaced in multiple ways in an orientation; they are not always spatially and temporarily separated. With sufficient routine, you can simultaneously do several simple actions in different orientation worlds without any trouble, such as: preparing lunch while listening to the news on the radio; driving a car through heavy traffic while having a lively conversation with the passenger; entering a plane while doing business on the phone, etc.

Every orientation differentiates its orientation worlds in its own way. However, orientation worlds can still be differentiated more generally, especially in a communicative respect about who is participating in them or whom one is dealing with in an orientation world. These are:

(1) The *individual orientation world* of one's own body, one's hygiene, health, and diet; one's education at school or work, and one's economic livelihood. In modern democratic societies you in principle take care of yourself as long as you do not need the help of others. In each individual orientation world, one tries to fulfill one's own wishes, plans, and life rhythms and to make from one's life what one wants. Here, individual routines develop.

(2) The *interindividual or communal orientation world*, in which one adapts to the living conditions and needs of other people with whom one has chosen to 'share one's life': the friends you make, the family you start, the colleagues you prefer to work with, and the acquaintances you visit and that visit you and with whom you do things with. In communal orientation worlds, one is in (more or less) continual and immediate contact with others; here, inter-individual or shared routines develop through which communities stabilize and by which they can be identified.

(3) The *societal orientation world*, in which you must adapt to the living conditions and needs of other people, who you yourself have *not* chosen: classmates, military comrades, members of clubs or political parties, and – less and less surveyable and with increasing distance – the members of the whole society in which you live. You may seek to get in touch and communicate with them (or some of them), but you can also avoid it to a certain degree. In any case, you have to adopt certain common routines that developed previously: societal routines, such as politeness and conversation routines. You are raised toward respecting them; and if you do not respect them, you are penalized. In in-

creasingly complex societies, the routines that coordinate how people live together are at some point no longer sufficient: they have to be made explicit in rules and codified laws.[36]

(4) The *global orientation world*, which you share with all people on earth: people who you are for the most part not only ignorant of, but whose cultures are also unfamiliar and strange to you. It is the world of the world society, which consists of a hardly surveyable number of societies, all of which follow different routines, rules, and laws. Here, routines are noticeable especially for visiting strangers: they need to first know how to deal with these routines; they need to acquire reorientation routines.

8.5 Disorientations and the Evolution of Orientation

In the routined course of transitioning between different orientation worlds, while we forget in each world about the other ones, we do not notice and cannot locate any central instance that would select, activate, or trigger the respective orientation routines and orientation worlds. It is not necessary to assume that there is one. An orientation is usually limited to one orientation world at a time (though sometimes in multiple); if it transitions between different orientation worlds, this happens in response to strong signals. They seem to be sufficient to allow an orientation to slide back and forth. An orientation obviously does not need a governing center: it operates in a decentralized manner. Its decentralized organization does not lead to disorientation – quite the contrary: it helps to contain disorientations and to keep an orientation stable even in disorientations.

Disorientations are always possible due to a lack of footholds, misleading clues, disrupted or failing routines, untenable plausibilities, fragmentary memories, or infelicitous orientation decisions. Disorientations, too, appear under situational and individual conditions. However, they can also be differentiated into general types, namely:

(1) *Local disorientations:* These are the most common. You suddenly do not know where you are; you cannot find your way in your surroundings, or on a map. Then you look for clues that might help; you first try to make use of one, and then another, and eventually you ask another person, if someone is around.

(2) *Communicative disorientations:* If you ask others for directions, you cannot always rely on them giving you correct and helpful information. If the problems persist when communicating with others, you can try to solve them in more intensive conversations; but this can also lead to new and worse disorientations,

which cause distrust, anger, and disappointment. If relationships, friendships, work teams, or political relations enter a state of crisis, crisis talks may help – but they may also worsen the crisis.

(3) *Existential disorientations:* Crises may spread from one orientation world to another, and they may eventually threaten one's orientation as a whole; then they might make you helpless, cause anxieties, and eventually drive you into despair; you might feel completely lost. Despair is the doubt about one's own abilities for orientation and actions as such; it may trigger an 'identity crisis.' Martin Heidegger describes "*Angst*" as something that puts us in front of the "nothing (*Nichts*)," the loss of all meaning (*Being and Time*, § 40).

But our orientation does not so easily reach the 'nothing,' not even in existential disorientations. Its decentralized organization keeps the nothing away. Even in *Angst*, everyday routines still mostly remain intact: you can still walk and stand, have breakfast and ride your bike, talk and act reasonably, and you can still seek support and find help – and eventually you may recover and regain your balance. This happens when disorientations arising in *one* orientation world are balanced by means of other orientations in *other* orientation worlds that are still intact. During a serious crisis in your work life, your family life may give you renewed confidence to not only continue on your life path, but also to orient yourself in a new and more appropriate way at the workplace; during a deep crisis in your work life *and* your family life, you might still be able to rely on friends; and if even this foothold breaks away, you can still rely on your own established routines until the anxiety and despair settle down. If this is not successful either, you may run the danger of falling into persistent confusion or depression, or of splitting your personality, in which you will continue to need the help of others. However, in most cases it is successful, and it is successful because of the decentralized organization of orientation. Just like our orientation does not reach the 'being,' it also does not reach the 'nothing' – except in death.

Orientation is possible as long as it can somehow connect somewhere. It finds its stability in the transposed continuities of connected routines, which have developed over the course of changing situations. In this way, orientations evolve. The *evolution of orientation* proceeds via the succession of self-stabilization, destabilization, and re-stabilization: routines and routine patterns develop, fail, and develop in new ways. If the re-stabilization of routines or of whole orientation worlds (like politics, sports, or family) fails, they can be dismissed. Not only footholds and routines, but also orientation worlds are selected at the cost of some and the benefit of others (preferring one's family life over sports, sports over politics, or politics over one's family life). Instead of a "lack of orientation," one should, as Luhmann argues, "rather speak of a permanent need for reorientations."[37]

Chapter 9
The Self-Reflection of Orientation: Leeways of Thinking
Orientation as Fluctuance

In the tradition of Western philosophy, 'thinking' is that which distinguishes the human being. Hence it has been alluring for philosophy to also begin with thinking itself and to disregard its conditions in orientation and its functions for orientation – as such, it has been thought to be the beginning or the principle of everything else. Thinking is then conceived as something which not only thinks itself, but which also exists in its self-referentiality independent from everything else. However, from its very beginning, philosophical thinking has fallen into paradoxes, which keep disorienting it and thereby keep it moving. The paradoxes of self-referential thinking have forced it to think itself under the conditions of orientation, especially the variety of what it thinks. In this way, a phenomenology of thinking, which includes its multifarious skills in our everyday orientation, becomes both possible and necessary.

This phenomenology has to also begin with the self-referentiality of thinking. For even those conditions, in whichever way they may be thought, are *thought* conditions: they are inevitably thought of by thinking itself. The circle persists, but it does not remain empty, if the self-referentiality of thinking is conceived of as a self-referentiality mediated through an other-referentiality, referring to 'non-thinking' or 'other-than-thinking.' The achievement of thinking in orientation is based on a self-referentiality via an other-referentiality. However, the specific achievement of what we call 'thinking' is not that it can become independent from its conditions and objects. Instead, it is only its ability to distance itself from them. Through this limited distance, thinking creates a new kind of overview, which makes possible foresight, planning, and calculation. Thereby orientation again gains time. Thinking establishes this distance by drawing distinctions based on features that are held onto across changing situations, but which also – *as* distinctions – leave room for alternatives. The drawing of such distinctions goes largely unnoticed. It is noticed as 'thinking' only when assessments based on distinctions become questionable through their alternatives, i.e. when one has to 'consciously' decide on them.

However, thinking is not identical with consciousness. Consciousness is indeed self-referential too; but thinking is, on the one hand, not always conscious; and moods, feelings, and perceptions can, on the other hand, be conscious too. What thinking does is retain distinctions in terms. Terms are consolidated when

https://doi.org/10.1515/9783110575149-011

people urge each other to hold onto them, as Plato's Socrates demonstrates, and when they are interconnected via definitions – i.e. defined with other terms – and systematized into theories. Orientation gains a new kind of hold in theories, a hold no longer limited by spatial or temporal horizons. But terms and theories, too, have a limited time. They too need to stay in motion if they are not to block necessary reorientations; they also move in the form of transposed continuities: as fluctuances.

9.1 The Self-Referentiality of Thinking and Its Paradoxes

(1) The Thinking of Being – The Being of Thinking. – After 'water' and other 'materials,' European philosophy thought thinking itself as a first beginning, origin, or principle (ἀρχή). According to this approach, thinking thinks that which 'is,' namely as that which is what it is at all times, in all its aspects, and without contradictions. Hence 'being' is that which thinking thinks, and thinking is that which being thinks. This is Parmenides' conclusion: "the same is thinking and being" (fragm. 3). The sameness of thinking and being is the self-referentiality of thinking mediated through a thought kind of being. However, such a self-referentiality is paradoxical: thinking and being must be the same as far as being is that which thinking thinks; at the same time, thinking must distinguish itself from being in order to think it *as* being.

(2) The Human Thinking of God – God's Thinking of the Human. – The thinking of being has been understood as the essence of humankind: the orientation skills of humans have been supposed to find their fulfillment in it. At the same time, however, thinking has been experienced, as far as humans are able to perform it, as conditional and limited, as something that may also fail, err, tire, and pause, as something at which humans are more or less successful. This has been attributed to the fact that thinking is bound to a body which, as Plato had his Socrates expound, hampers thinking in various ways and which only completely releases it in death. Under such impediments, thinking can therefore never be fully certain about the being it thought. Only as divine thinking can it be certain of being, freed from all corporeality. Aristotle therefore makes the divine thinking of thinking (*nóaesis noáeseos*) his yardstick.

But this divine thinking was another kind of thinking thought of by humans. After increasing uncertainties occurred when thinking the divine (now the Christian God) in the Middle Ages and, in nominalism, it became possible to think that the thinking of being and the being of thinking could just be about words (*voces*) and names (*nomina*), Descartes sought, at the onset of the modern era, to secure in a new and unquestionable way the possibility of beginning with thinking – now at the cost of conceding its temporality. As far as he proceeds from the act of doubting, he no longer determined thinking in its positive reference to being, but in its ability to negate being. Doubting means to be able to think that something, of which you think that it is, *is not*; and, in this sense, you can doubt everything except for the act of thinking that doubts itself. What then remains is thinking in its *mere* self-referentiality, without an other-referentiality to a being – except for its own being.

Descartes makes *this* self-referentiality of being his criterion of being: I am as far as I cannot doubt that I doubt and, therefore, think. This is the case, according to Descartes, "as long as (*quamdiu*) I think that I am something," and the statement (*pronuntiatium*) "I am, I exist" is necessarily true only "*as often (quoties*) as it is proffered (*profertur*) or thought by me (*mente concipitur*)" (*Meditationes* II, 3). As such, thinking is a mere temporal self-performance. But Descartes draws another metaphysical conclusion: for him, the temporal performance of thinking furthermore needed an atemporal thinking substance.

However, the being of this atemporal thinking substance remained problematic. For it can only be secured via God, who had created it. But the existence of God can be questioned as well; hence, thinking must first prove it. Given the necessity of this proof, the mere self-referentiality of thinking becomes a self-referentiality mediated by God's thinking and being. But in Christian thinking, this self-referentiality becomes paradoxical again. For if the limited human thinking tries to think the unlimited thinking of God, then it thinks, according to Descartes, something which transcends it and which is thus more than it is capable of thinking. And since the Christian God is thought to be the substance that brings all other substances into being, it must have been Him, too, who brought into being the thinking substance, which I am and which in turn has to prove the being of God; and this, according to Descartes, must happen not only once as a historical event, but again and again through continual creation (*creatio continua*). As such, the thinking substance is to be thought of as being simultaneously temporary and timeless.

(3) The Thinking of the Brain (as Subject and as Object). – After dispensing with a thinking of thinking in terms of a timeless being and an infinitely thinking and creating God, the contemporary thinking of thinking finds itself (after numerous intermediate stations) referring to the brain. In light of brain research that is as prolific as plausible, it has become a largely unquestioned certainty that it is our brain that thinks (as subject) when 'we' think. But it is also certain that it is our thinking that thinks our brain (as object) and that it can think the brain only in a limited way, as far as it indeed depends on the brain when thinking. Thus, the former paradoxes reappear: on the one hand, our thinking thinks itself as a brain, and, on the other, it distinguishes itself from the brain – just like

in its ancient reference to being. And thinking newly thinks of itself as emerging from the brain as from something that always makes it possible again and again – through a continual creation just like the one of the medieval God. Thus, the thinking of thinking easily falls back into metaphysical conceptions of itself.

The metaphysicizations of the inevitably paradoxical self-referentiality that occur in the thinking of thinking spring from the isolating of thinking from orientation processes and their conditions. But just as European philosophy created forms of metaphysical conceptions, it also critically dissolved them. It thereby prepared a phenomenology of thinking that includes the skills of thinking in our everyday orientation.

9.2 Thinking as a Skill of Orientation: The Distancing from the Situation in the Situation

Descartes already addresses his new beginning in the thinking of thinking as a problem of orientation. From the hopeless situation of someone completely lost in a forest, a certain method is to lead out of it. It includes four rules. The first is to not accept anything that is not as clear and distinct as the insight of thinking into its own being; the second, to resolve unclear problems into such clear insights; the third, to bring the acquired insights into one's own order; and forth, to bring these insights together in complete lists (*dénombrements entiers*) and general overviews (*revue générales*) so that absolutely nothing is omitted (*Discours de la méthode*, chapter 2). However, Descartes has thinking itself, while on its way to securing a full overview, once again plunge into a complete loss of hold: in his *Meditationes*, he deprives thinking from the hold, too, which it had gained on the forest's firm ground, and has it "slip down into a deep vortex," in which it is "swirled around in a way" that it "can neither put a foot down" (*in imo pedem figere*), nor "swim to the surface" (*enatare ad summum*) (*Meditationes* II, 1). In doing so, he aggravates the mere local disorientation into an existential one. A thinking detaching itself from everything by casting doubt on it loses all orientation. Descartes can absorb the disorientation only by relying on traditional metaphysics: the substantiality of thinking and God being their "ground" (*fonds*). Only on this ground can thinking "found" (*bâtir*) itself because this ground alone is to fully rest in itself (*Discours de la méthode*, chapter 2).

But in this way, according to Wittgenstein, thinking can no longer be located and identified:

It is misleading [...] to talk of thinking as of a 'mental activity.' We may say that thinking is essentially the activity of operating with signs. This activity is performed by the hand, when we think by writing; by the mouth and larynx, when we think by speaking; and if we think by imagining signs or pictures, I can give you no agent that thinks. If then you say that in such cases the mind thinks, I would only draw your attention to the fact that you are using a metaphor, that here the mind is an agent in a different sense from that in which the hand can be said to be the agent in writing. – If we talk about the locality where thinking takes place we have a right to say that this locality is the paper on which we write or the mouth which speaks. And if we talk of the head or the brain as the locality of thought, this is using the expression 'locality of thinking' in a different sense.[38]

But if thinking is brought into speaking, writing, and acting, and if it is localized in this way, it then becomes unsurveyable for itself. Thinking is then no longer an absolutely self-evident means for orientation, but one skill of orientation among others – a skill that again comprises a multitude of functions.

In fact, thinking, which philosophically has long been considered a solid unity, appears highly differentiated in everyday language use. The differentiations correspond to functions of orientation. As such, you may

- 'think of something,' remain attentive to something: thinking as a temporarily fixed *attention*;
- 'think that something is like this or that,' have an opinion or a *belief*, which may prove to be false;
- 'think something,' 'think something in this or that way': thinking as *imagining*;
- 'think something up,' invent, contrive: thinking as *phantasy;*
- 'think of something when doing something,' take something into account: thinking as *consideration*;
- 'think back,' remember something: thinking as *memory*;
- 'think yourself in someone else's place,' imagine yourself in someone else's shoes: thinking as *empathizing*;
- 'think ahead,' take future situations into account: thinking as *foresight*;
- 'think about something,' bethink, reflect, ponder, contemplate: thinking as *meditation*;
- 'think something over,' think before doing: thinking as *deliberation;*
- 'think something through,' 'think something out,' scrutinize the relevant matters of something: thinking as purposefully *exploring*; this includes the methodical thinking of *science;*
- 'rethink something,' check and review something that previously appeared clear, think it over from other points of view: thinking as *testing* and *assessing*;

- 'think to do something,' have an *intention*, come to a decision to do something: thinking as *will*;
- and, eventually, you can simply 'think' in the sense of 'think in a characteristic or typical way,' e.g. think 'deeply' or 'on the surface,' 'politically' or 'nonpolitically,' 'morally' or 'immorally,' 'stereotypically' or 'differently': thinking as the *overall shape or style of the judgment* of a person, group, or society, which is in turn *morally distinguished* as 'thinking well or badly about or of something or somebody.'

'Thinking,' in everyday language use, thus comprises the entire spectrum of orientation's achievements, which traditional philosophy divided into 'thinking, feeling, and wanting'; it encompasses their affective and moral assessments as well. However, 'thinking' excludes perceiving as referring to something immediately given. All modes of thinking involve a *distancing from the given situation*. This distancing allows one to come up with alternatives to the current situation and keeping them in one's 'memory' or 'in the back of one's mind.' What is called 'thinking' allows an orientation to 'see' situations 'differently' and to thereby open up new leeways for opportunities to act in them. If there is an overarching function of thinking in orientation, then it is *to expand the horizons of action*.

For the *phenomenological* exploration of that which we call 'thinking,' speaking and writing are not the only distinct clues and signs. You also surmise thinking to be taking place when somebody pauses with a tense facial expression in the midst of routined actions, e.g. he or she hesitates in speaking or writing and adopts an inward gaze. However, thinking is neither speaking, nor writing, nor pausing during actions. It differs from speaking as far as thinking can happen silently – which gives it the appearance of *speechlessness*. It differs from writing as far as it controls writing as a 'non-natural,' a (more or less) hard-learned and conspicuous movement – which gives it the appearance of *causality*. On the other hand, pausing makes clear that nothing visible has to happen while thinking, at least no visible effects have to occur – which at the same time produces the appearance of *ineffectiveness*.

Thinking as suspension of other actions can also be observed as an action 'by other means'; for, after a certain time, it can indeed result in effects. One then considers it a *calm* or *reassuring action*; accordingly, we call on each other to 'quietly think things over'; an agitated 'thinking-things-over' would be perceived as contradictory. In orientation, calmness means a decrease of the pressure of time and the pressure to act. Decreasing the time pressure and the pressure to act, however, in turn requires 'having time': thinking and reflecting need time and, during this time, physical relaxation, be it sitting or standing still (think of Socrates, who was supposed to have sometimes stood in one place for many hours when thinking), or a calm, steady movement, such as going for a walk or a hike (think of Nietzsche, who often emphasizes how conducive walking and hiking are to thinking). In physical relaxation or routine one can also observe one's own body from a certain distance; and since your body can remain externally calm even when you think exciting things, thinking appears to be *bodiless*.

These initial phenomenological indicators together form an image of thinking as something speechless, calm, relaxed, and bodiless: an action without immediate effects, but which generates impactful effects in the long run – which is not perceived as paradoxical because time goes by in between. For thinking needs time on the one hand, while on the other it can, during this time, 'gain' even more time. This happens just by pinning down footholds, marking them with signs and thereby detaching them from the changing situations, linking them into patterns or schemata according to (more or less explicit) rules, and retaining them for future situations where they, given new connections, can quickly 'provide a new orientation.' *Thinking provides an orientation with projections of orientations, which can, in different situations, be applied in different ways.* It does not record 'what is,' but only what has the chance of abbreviating future orientations; it connects to the 'art of abbreviation' by means of footholds, markings, and signs. This suggests the appearance of its *constructivity* and *creativity*. Here, you gain time by passing time, i.e. by anticipating alternative continuations of what is given. As far as thinking seems to be 'ahead of time,' it provides the appearance of *timelessness*; as far it succeeds in maintaining projections that prove tenable in ever-new situations, that which is being thought also appears as timeless; and as far as thinking timelessly maintains timeless things, it finally appears to be *void of a standpoint*, or rather, its *standpoint* is supposed to be *theoretical*, capable of providing a timeless overview detached from every situation.

Calmness, speechlessness, (immediate) ineffectiveness, bodilessness, timelessness, and the lack of a standpoint are negative determinations; they denote ways of distancing oneself from the given situation. By contrast, causality, constructivity, and creativity are positive determinations: they indicate that thinking, too, is experienced in a positive way. Thinking is experienced as pleasing whenever it is obviously successful, and as displeasing when it fails or creates difficulties. Causing pleasure and displeasure, it appears as a self-contained and autonomous action that evades one's will in following its own fittings and rules. You can focus on 'thinking,' or not. If you focus on it, you perceive a certain force to obey its laws, wherever they may come from: this produces the *appearance of coercion*, on which logic and mathematics rely. But this too is a coercion, which you can submit to, or not. You can also let your thinking wander around and experience that, in doing so, it becomes unexpectedly creative.

The fact that thinking can fail and that it sometimes takes efforts to focus on it and to remain consistent in it means that thinking is conditional – in multifarious ways. It is not only dependent on available signs, on memories retrieving fitting signs at the right moment, on knowledge requiring consideration when making expedient plans, and on ideas which help to solve problems, but it also depends on physical, chemical, and biological processes, without whose functioning thinking cannot function, either. And these processes can in turn operate in different ways and be dependent on temporary corporeal states and momentary moods. For some, it is obviously easier, while for others, it is harder to consistently pursue thoughts and chains of thoughts in order to gain a clear overview or come up with good ideas and useful solutions; and at one moment this is more difficult than at another. Thinking can also divert itself, and, rather than clarifying anything, become entangled and confused. But only when it no longer operates in a routined way, when it is difficult and when it comes under the pressure of time and success, does it become noticeable, and it thinks of itself: it is then called conscious.

9.3 Being-Aware of Thinking as Becoming-Aware of Decisions about Distinctions

In the philosophical tradition, thinking has been associated with consciousness, and consciousness with the self. Thinking, consciousness, and the self share their self-referentiality. Not only are thinking and (*per definitionem*) the self self-referential, but so is consciousness: when you *are* conscious of something, you can *make* yourself conscious of this being-conscious. But you do not have to do so, and in most cases, you do not; consciousness can, but does not have to be a consciousness of consciousness, or rather a self-consciousness; its self-referentiality may be actualized, or not. However, consciousness can make itself into its own object (then becoming self-referential) only in its own horizon and from its own standpoint; it is only accessible in its own way; it inevitably objectifies itself subjectively. This produces the *paradox of the subjectivity of all objectivity of consciousness*. For a consciousness can only objectify itself, as well as everything else, under its own conditions of orientation; thus, it is itself always already implicated in what it becomes conscious of. The subjectivity of all objectivity was one of the most crucial insights of the philosophy of the modern era. Following this insight, it must in principle remain open as to what and how things, according to Kant, are 'in themselves' – and this includes consciousness as well.

The paradox of the subjectivity of all objectivity of consciousness can be resolved by distinguishing the self-reference of consciousness and its other-reference to objects (including consciousness itself) as *different perspectives*. Today's philosophy and science of consciousness conceptualize self-reference, in which consciousness 'experiences' itself, as the 'first-person perspective.' This perspective is accessible only to itself and closed off to other consciousnesses. Thus consciousness has been metaphorically located in an 'inside' for which other consciousnesses are 'outside.' But this spatial metaphor for something non-spatial can easily mislead us: for 'inside' is here something *un*observable (like Wittgenstein's beetle in the box: *Philosophical Investigations*, §293). The observation of consciousness 'from the outside' is located in a 'third-person perspective,' in which one is dependent on 'outside' clues and signs. Such clues and signs are primarily the behavior and the words of others, but also scientific observations following neurobiological, brain physiological, and psychological methods.

But in this distinction between perspectives the paradox continues. For the first-person- and third-person perspectives remain irreconcilable: as is known, consciousness subjectively experiences itself in a completely different way than is objectively observed. You can explore the brain functions that make your consciousness possible, but only generally and indirectly; and you cannot observe the brain functions that are at work at the very time you are exploring them. Hence, consciousness appears to itself *either* in the first-person *or* in the third-person perspective, but not in both at the same time; you can only oscillate between the two.

In everyday orientation, the paradox of the subjectivity of all objectivity of consciousness is hardly a problem. For, on the one hand, orientation is only to a small degree conscious of itself, and, on the other, it is used to oscillating between perspectives. In orientation consciousness and thinking are indeed closely connected to each other. In addition to the possible self-referentiality and immediate unobservability, consciousness shares with thinking the appearance of speechlessness, (immediate) ineffectiveness, and bodilessness. But whereas thoughts are considered communicable, as something that one can have in common with others (Lat. *communicare*), this is not the case with consciousness, from which these thoughts originate. Consciousness is indeed conscious of other consciousnesses. However, it cannot communicate with them. For every consciousness can become conscious of another consciousness only in *its own* consciousness; hence it communicates with itself when believing it communicates with others. Like thinking, it does not have an identifiable location; but as 'my' consciousness, it is connected to that simultaneously absolute and contingent standpoint from which 'my' orientation cannot detach itself, not even when thoughts are communicated with signs and other hints. In the very action of trying to communicate thoughts, you experience that others may understand what you communicate differently than how you 'mean' it. As Wittgenstein puts it (to quote him once more):

> But if someone says, "How am I to know what he means – I see only his signs?", then I say, "How is *he* to know what he means, he too has only his signs?" (*Philosophical Investigations*, §504, transl. by G.E.M. Anscombe, P.M.S. Hacker and Joachim Schulte)

The speech of *'having'* or *'conceiving of'* an idea in turn suggests that consciousness is something which *controls* its ideas, which has to have or be a 'center' from which this control is exerted, and that thinking would be this center of control. But although 'ideas' (*ideae, idées, Vorstellungen*) can become 'objects' – which thinking grasps, isolates, distinguishes, defines, and puts in order, thereby 'objectifying' them, as the philosophy of the modern era taught us – consciousness nevertheless, as we later learned, does not 'possess' or 'control' them. Even if consciousness may 'control' its ideas in thinking, they must have occurred and arisen previously – and most of them do so in an uncontrolled way. And faced with a vast number of ideas that continually arise, a consciousness must again initially *orient* itself in order to select the ideas that are fitting to hold onto, connect with others, and communicate as thoughts. Without or before such achievements of thinking that make ideas clear and distinct in order to record and communicate them (and, at the same time, shape and assess them in appropriate ways), ideas are (or are considered) vague, indeterminate, ephemeral, or, in short, vivid. In this vividness, ideas are ungraspable; they stay in consciousness for only a limited time, and then they involuntarily and imperceptibly vanish from it once more. Hence, ideas cannot be representations in the literal sense of making the 'outside' reality present again through them. Instead, in new orientations, ideas are rather adapted to new situations of orientation, and they *must* be adapted to them; otherwise they could not contribute to an orientation. In the philosophy and science of the mind this is sometimes neglected, especially when computational theories of the mind are used. However, most recent results of neuroscientific and psychological research have firmly substantiated the processes of adaptation we describe above.

A philosophy of orientation need not solve the 'riddle of consciousness'; the riddle could arise from confusion in philosophy itself, as, again, Wittgenstein particularly emphasizes. Instead of a 'conscious being' (*Bewusstsein*), which suggests a being of its own, we are better off speaking of an 'awareness' (*Bewusstheit*), as Nietzsche does following Leibniz (*Gay Science*, No. 11; cf. chap. 8.1 [7]). The ontological problem then turns into a question of attention and the awareness of attention. In our orientation, in which most things happen unnoticed, only a few things attract special attention, as we have shown; and through routinization that which was once noticed can become unnoticeable again. But if routines have not yet developed or if they are disturbed, then further attention, reflection, and *decisions* are required. Such decisions are the ones we are most likely to call 'conscious' – as long as they have not been made or been proven successful. With them, thinking sets in: where decisions are to be made one has to think about the chances and risks of possible alternatives. And this also accounts for the routines of thinking themselves: thinking itself may stand before alternative 'paths,' needing to decide between them. Thinking does not operate in a self-referential way all the time, but it becomes self-referential if this is necessary for an orientation. For precisely this 'pausing to think,' at a 'crossroads' with alternatives needing to be decided on, Mendelssohn introduced the term 'to-orient-oneself' into philosophy.

Alternatives require orientation. As such, every orientation has alternatives; otherwise it would not deserve the name. Alternatives in thinking are initially offered in the mere use of distinctions: thinking can then decide for one or the other side of a distinction, for instance, whether something is to be judged as true or false, just or unjust, beautiful or ugly. Moreover, distinctions may themselves be a matter of decision. In a certain situation it may be necessary to decide whether, in order to assess the state of affairs, one distinction or the other is more appropriate. When distinguishing distinctions and deciding between them, distinctions themselves become points of reference which thinking itself provides from memory. In this way, thinking becomes self-referential or 'reflecting' – without being more certain of its decisions. In fact, the situation of making a decision under uncertainty is a situation of irritation; and when, in situations of deciding between distinctions, thinking becomes conscious of itself, it is a self-irritation. *Conscious thinking as an achievement of our orientation would then be the achievement of self-irritation in thinking, through which our orientation can create and control alternatives between its distinctions.*

9.4 The Calming of Irritations by means of Orders: The Hold in Terms via Logical Discipline

By means of an overview, which thinking gains by distancing itself from a given situation, by means of its distinctions, which disclose alternatives, and by means of its memories, which keep alternatives available, thinking provides an orientation with a new kind of hold, a hold in what we call terms or concepts. This hold is experienced as having terms or concepts at one's disposal or command. Terms are presupposed in all kinds of planning and reckoning; they are a condition of the 'rationalization' of orientation. Questions about what terms or concepts are, how they exist, in which way they are formed, and why or to which degree they can be valid, have been a matter of concern for European philosophy from the very beginning. In orientation, terms are to be thought of via footholds, signs, and names: situations are abbreviated into clues and footholds; footholds can be marked as signs; signs can be used as names for something that often recurs in situations of orientation; and names can be defined through which they become terms.

Names, general and proper names, are signs that pin down something we deal with again and again; as such it becomes necessary that one can quickly identify it. In the distance of thinking from its given situation, names become footholds for its projections. They come into play when the footholds of a given situation suggest it; they then 'come into mind' from memory. In using them, they must fit into the context; you have to 'hit the right word' in order to do anything with it in the situation. The language of orientation speaks of 'points' that are at stake in a situation and which one can return to if needed. By referring to names as points in this way, the thinking of one person can connect to the thinking of another. Thus, our orientation not only takes a new step in gaining an overview of a situation, it also improves the possibility of connecting different orientations to each other – at the cost of reducing precisely their differences. In thinking (and speaking), individuals can pass beyond the individuality of their orientations by holding onto common signs.

However, this does not make thinking something common to or uniform for all, existing independent from individuals. Commonality among different orientations must be continually created. Based on names, this happens by means of *terms*. Terms or the concepts they express exceed names as far as they can not only be used in different situations and different orientations, thus being 'general,' but their use is also 'defined,' which literally means 'delimited.' It is a defining characteristic of terms or concepts that they are defined, or that they, if need be, can be defined. While signs can (more or less) shift their meaning in every new use, definitions help to avoid such shifts in meaning. By defining them, the meaning of signs is tied to the meaning of other signs and the meaning of concepts to the meaning of other concepts, both of which can also be defined by other signs and concepts, respectively, if needed. But at some point this must end: you have to stop the series of definitions somewhere. Here, the terms are then left as provisionally self-evident, unquestioned – or, simply, plausible.

By fixing the meaning of signs to each other through fixed connections, signs can, as terms or concepts, determine something *as* something for different orientations and for a longer time. One can further strengthen the hold of terms by defining the procedures of definition, going all the way to formulate laws of thinking in a *formal logic.* If these laws are eventually formalized with specifically introduced mathematical signs, shifts in meaning are completely prevented. Thus, among otherwise divergent orientations, more and more unambiguous general terms can be corroborated.

However, it is also possible to create various kinds of formal logic. As there are various grammatical descriptions of each language, there can be (and in fact are) various logics determining what is (allegedly) one universal thinking; just as there are no things as such, there seems to be no thinking as such. Thus, the compelling force of logical thinking cannot arise from thinking as such either. Complying with a defined or controlled use of signs instead requires discipline (e. g. in the various 'disciplines' of the sciences and humanities). Such disciplining is a social procedure. It can already be found in many fields of everyday orientation; it is the minimum required for explicitly communicating solutions to problems that must be solved together, i. e. organized co-operations. In co-operative communication, we make terms 'clear' to each other in order to get along with each other in shared projects. We expect and demand reliability from each other in action as well as in the use of terms. If someone, in a surveyable amount of time, keeps acting differently and keeps using certain terms in a way that is different than usual, we accuse him or her of discrepancies or contradictions. As a result, we may no longer want to communicate with such a person, at least in certain areas, and we stop communicating and coopering with him or her. In a group or society, cooperating people mutually discipline each other in the use of the terms necessary for their cooperation.

This usually achieves what one calls error control. For example, companies, legal systems, and sciences continue enhancing and strengthening error control – but only to such an extent that a smooth cooperation is possible. This may require rules, but not an explicit logic that systematizes error control through a coherent system of explicit terms and rules for using terms. Such a system renders controlled thinking itself methodically self-referential and autonomous. This allows one to disregard all so-called 'content' that connects terms to any specific person or situation – the logic becomes 'formal.' In formal logic, thinking is the most detached from actual situations and the needs of orientations. Logic, as 'formal,' is independent of all actual situations; as far as it is orienting one, this is only within a particular 'logical situation,' where logical relations can themselves become unsurveyable.

However, logic needs to be applied. By applying formal logic to specific contents, things which an orientation draws on with names are determined by using common properties or qualities abstracted from them. By gradually abstracting – i. e. 'pulling off' – such properties, concepts become more and more general. In this way you can hierarchically order them in superordinate and subordinate terms, creating surveyable 'pyramids' of terms, which culminate in a highest term, from where the whole order can be overseen and fully reconstructed. This has been one of the main goals of European philosophy since Plato and Aristotle. Proceeding from the self-referentiality of thinking in the modern era, the idea of the 'system' developed as a *system of terms*, in which ideally all terms that are used to gain knowledge about the world and to act in the world would be compiled and ordered, allowing for a complete overview of them. The ideal of the system is a *complete hold of orientation in terms,* compared to which any other hold in orientation would be considered as secondary.

Hegel, who methodologically organized the system as self-referentially developing out of itself (creating for it a new kind of logic, i.e. 'dialectical' logic), sought to grasp in this way the 'reasonableness of reality' (*Vernünftigkeit des Wirklichen*) as a whole, which was to allow for a secure orientation all over the world. If reality is conceived as equally transparent for everyone and everywhere, then orientation would no longer be necessary at all. In fact, according to Hegel, the need of orientation is limited to the immediate and (allegedly) non-problematic spatio-temporal situation. Although the term was already familiar in philosophy in Hegel's time, orientation played no role in his own philosophy.

However, times have changed; Hegel's system itself has lost its plausibility; and there is neither a system nor a logic left that can claim sole validity. Just as orientation allows for some leeway for signs to shift in meaning, it must likewise allow for some leeway for interpretations of defined and scientifically controlled terms when applied to situations. If someone is accused of theft based on the general definition of criminal law, individual criminal judges must decide whether and to what extent the legal terms apply to this individual case. In doing so, they must rely on clues presented by witnesses or pieces of evidence during the trial. When, in the sciences, terms like force, mass, energy, particle, or wave are used in a physically defined sense and calculated mathematically, one still needs to identify what specifically they are referring to in an experiment; and such reference points can change again, as was proven in the shift from classical mechanics to the theories of relativity and quantum physics. Logical disciplining, especially in the form of the mathematization of the natural sciences, has been one of the most successful and most sustainable means for orientation. But here, too, orientation must be able to keep the terms in movement. After Thomas S. Kuhn's discussion of 'paradigm shifts' in light of 'revolutionary' reorientations in the sciences, this has in fact become almost normal. And logics, too, have been developed further, changing their very fundamentals.

Scientific terms are usually kept 'in movement' when something new is explored: you must oscillate between orienting to the new situation and finding appropriate terms (established or new ones) for analyzing it; thus, every terminological analysis requires a preceding orientation concerning the 'conceptual situation' that can in turn be analyzed. In this sense, according to Moses Mendelssohn, terminological analysis must be continuously oriented, and orientation must be continuously corrected by terminological analysis. In other words: scientific analyses are embedded in orientations, which gain precision through scientific analyses. This does not mean that orientation and analysis always complement each other harmoniously. With new orientations, the interest in analyses or their focuses can shift, and when gaining precision, certain needs of orientation may disappear. By discovering hidden dogmas on the one hand, and opening leeways in the logical analysis of language on the other, analytic philosophy, from William Van Orman Quine to Donald Davidson and Richard Rorty, in fact explored its own preconditions in orientation.

9.5 Moving Terms: Fluctuances

Terms must not impede reorientations beyond their own time. Human orientation needs, in order to avoid short-term shifts in meaning, sufficiently sustainable terms to prevent discrepancies and contradictions in communication. However, in the long run, terms must be able to shift their meanings. This happens, as in the case of routines, by means of transposed continuities.

Aristotle connects atemporally used terms to atemporally existing *substances* (Gr. *ousíai*; Lat. *substantiae*), where thinking is to 'come,' within the relentless changing of everything, 'to a halt' (Gr. *anánkae stâenai*). In order to think the relentless changing-of-everything, he conceives of atemporally existing substances as constituting 'the underlying' (Gr. *hypokeímenon*; Lat. *substratum*) beneath the contingently changing, i.e. temporally existing, properties or 'accidents' (Gr. *symbebaekóta*; Lat. *accidentia*). Thus, Aristotle splits the changing-of-everything into atemporal and temporal beings. However, it has always been difficult, already for Aristotle, to draw a general line between this *hypokeímenon* and its *symbebaekóta*. In fact, every change can only be observed in contrast to something that persists. But what persists can always be something different: the ocean stirring up waves; the waves creating whitecaps; the whitecaps dispersing into water drops; the water drops reflecting the sunlight. To observe change, there is no need for everlasting substances; the term substance can be reduced from a metaphysical to a functional one, as Kant shows. Aristotle, instead, conceives of substances not only as persisting in contrast to their changing accidents, but also as the causes of their change. Thus, substances must exist per se. But then, the problem arises that they, especially living beings, which he primarily orients to, likewise change their forms over the course of their lives – and living beings die. This coerces Aristotle to differentiate his concept of substance: he considers it, first, as matter (*hylae*) which 'underlies' all changes, but which, changing its forms all the time, cannot be grasped by concepts; second, as an individual being composed of matter and form (*morpháe*); third, only as form (*eîdos*) that persists when individual living beings are born and die, since it is, at the same time, their goal or end (*télos*); and, finally, as divine mover, which keeps moving all beings in constant motion, but is itself unmoved. We cannot explain this in detail at this point: but as a result, Aristotle's concept of substance is, ironically, in flux itself.

What, in our current orientation, remains from Aristotle's, is that we still distinguish between the persisting and the changing features of something that is given in a situation in order to find sequences and orders of change. What persists in changing situations can in fact be essential, in contrast to changing properties (e. g. a portrait in contrast to the lighting it happens to be seen in). To distinguish between the persistent and the changing and the essential and the inessential, the Aristotelian distinction between substance and accidents is still of unabated significance; orientation cannot and does not have to do without it. However, this distinction – considered as a distinction of functional categories, not of metaphysical beings – does not necessarily presuppose something essential for all time. Rather, what is essential can change from time to time. It can not only arise and pass away, but also the criteria as to why essentials become essentials can change: the portrait may come into its own only in a specific light; it might at first only be significant because of its composition and coloring, later as a memory of the person portrayed in it; at some point, as mere wall decoration; and eventually, greatly aged and rediscovered in its artistic value, as a financial investment. The properties may change, too: the color pigments might undergo such strong changes that the mood of the portrait changes. Identities can change: a dealer's shop, e. g. an art gallery, may step by step change its employees, its location, its owner, its range of goods, its name, and its listing in the commercial register. Throughout this change in all these cases, there are still reference points, which allow one to identify them. Even when the relevant issues, properties, and identities change, there is still always something that persists – because otherwise this change could not even be recognized as a change. However, what persists need not be the same in every change – it need not be an eternal essence. The essentials of something can likewise change; and there can still persist something that allows one to identify it as the same over time. Think of animals as they grow: tadpoles becoming frogs change their shape almost completely; but they do this step by step. If something is to be identified despite its ongoing changes, not everything may change at the same time. If all its properties change at the same time, it becomes something completely different, and is no longer recognizable. As a result, the art gallery mentioned above, or whatever you like, can change through transposed continuities and become completely different over time – and yet persist to be recognizable all the time.

This is not only clear concerning evolutionary theories, from which nothing seems to be excluded, but also in everyday orientation. Everyday orientation always expects that the matters it deals with change, and *it is able* to deal with ever-changing matters. 'Substances' and 'essences,' which seem to provide a steady hold, can remain in flux as well – I have called them '*fluctuances.*' Aristotle and Kant and Hegel did not yet think of substances as fluctuances.

But Nietzsche did: he grasped the category of fluctuance with the formula "The form is fluid, the 'meaning' even more so..." (*Genealogy of Morals* II, 12). The 'logical empiricist' Otto Neurath used the image of a ship being reconstructed in all its parts on the open sea. Wittgenstein further elaborated the old Heraclitean image of a river, which always and never stays the same, into the image of a river which also changes its bed by streaming through it, thereby changing its stream as well (*On Certainty*, §§ 96 – 99). And for mathematics (just for mathematics!), he created the metaphor of spinning:

> we extend our concept of number, as in spinning a thread we twist fibre on fibre. And the strength of the thread resides not in the fact that some one fibre runs through its whole length, but in the overlapping of many fibres.

He commented on it thus:

> But if someone wanted to say, 'So there is something common to all these constructions – namely, the disjunction of all their common properties' – I'd reply: Now you are only playing with a word. One might as well say, 'There is a Something that runs through the whole thread – namely, the continuous overlapping of these fibres'. (*Philosophical Investigations* § 67, transl. by Anscombe, Hacker, and Schulte)

Chapter 10
Mutual Orientation: Interaction and Communication

Orientation under the Condition of Double Contingency

10.1 The Unsettlement and Reassuring Calmness Caused by Others' Orientations

When encountering other people, they create new situations of orientation. They may irritate you more than anything else and they orient you more than anything else; they can thus unsettle or reassure you more than anything else. When you have grown out of the trustfulness of childhood, the mere physical proximity of others' makes them unsettling, whether this is experienced as pleasant and attractive or as unpleasant and intrusive. Others unsettle one because, from their different standpoints, they inevitably orient themselves differently. Thus, they remind you of the risks of your own orientation: they constantly draw your attention to the fact that, at the same time and place, one can always also view the situation differently and that there may be more successful opportunities for action. Even when others seem to orient themselves in a similar way and thereby confirm your own orientation, you can never be certain to what extent you are assessing their orientations correctly and if you are right in being reassured by them. *Whenever you are dealing with others, you are dealing with others who are dealing (more or less) with other things in different ways.* But even when other orientations run counter to your own orientation, they may still be helpful precisely because they call attention to other opportunities for action; and what initially may have had an unsettling effect can then have a reassuring and calming one.

Orientations cannot presume anything given *a priori* in all orientations: you can never be completely sure that you have anything in common with others. Expectations of any commonalities, whether they be superficial or deep, can turn out to be premature. Of course, one can and will try 'to put oneself in the standpoint of others' and empathize with their living conditions, and one can try to understand what they are 'up to,' what they say, think, or want – but one can never be certain of any of these things. You likewise can only access other orientations from your own point of view and under your own conditions. You cannot independently compare the orientations of others with your own orientation

https://doi.org/10.1515/9783110575149-012

from a third point of view; you are continually constrained by your own standpoint. This *incomparability of orientations* is the very reason they constantly unsettle each other.

Dealing with other orientations thus creates *new orientation problems*. Here, one runs the risk of not only not finding one's way, but also of getting into unpleasant and threatening conflicts, from physical collisions on narrow paths and verbal altercations to persistent hostilities and violence. The possibilities of failing here, too, reveal the difficulties of succeeding. Since you can fail with your own orientation and get into conflicts with others, you will pay careful attention to other orientations, not only for the sake of your own security but also because they can help you overcome your own orientation problems. In this way, *new opportunities for orientations* arise as well: others become important footholds. If somebody is remarkably quick, successful, or professional in finding his or her way in new situations, then others will appreciate this, trust him or her, rely on him or her, and eventually entrust their own orientations to him or her. In modern societies, we not only rely on other people, such as parents, teachers, friends, clerics, doctors, lawyers, travel guides, etc., but also, more and more, on technologies and the experts who clearly know how to use them. By means of *taking on orientations that have proven successful*, your own orientation is abbreviated; you may omit detours and errors and succeed more easily. Since, compared to other species, human beings are dependent on other orientations for a much longer time, it is for them entirely natural from the very beginning to take on other orientations and rely on them. We rely on a vast, mostly anonymous, number of other orientations; and we hardly encounter any problems when doing so.

The *separation of orientations* begins with birth, when one is separated from the mother's body. But now you are held by others (including your mother) in their arms until you can move freely on your own; and even when grown up you can, as a sign of holding on to each other, hold hands. Holding onto each other, however it occurs, is always necessary and always possible. But when the bodily distance and the difference of standpoints increase over time, it also becomes increasingly questionable as to whether orientations that have proven successful for others will also be successful for your own orientation. Children that trust their parents and teachers start asking questions about what they have been instructed to do: within reassuring holds onto other orientations, the unsettling grows as to whether these holds will hold what they promise. You learn that the more you trust in others, the more they may disappoint you; the more you rely on others, the greater the risk they may prove unreliable. Even those who have gained a reliable orientation in dealing with other people, i.e. 'people skills,' only know those with whom they share their life through how they behave in specific situations; and they can never be sure whether those people might not act surprisingly different in a new situation, in a way that perhaps surprises themselves. *Other people are the most trustworthy and reliable foothold in orientation, but they can also become the most surprising experience.* As such, we always observe each other with respect to our *reliability*.

In moral consideration, which quickly arises in philosophy when dealing with mutual orientations, it is tempting to overlook the actual circumstances of a situation: in order to observe each other or 'keep each other in sight,' human beings at first distance themselves from each other; this may date back to our prehistoric times. We only begin to come closer to each other when we have found footholds for trusting each other – or when we run into conflict with each other. Observing other people from a secure distance, we preemptively make out clues and leads of possible collisions; we hold the distance, even when knowing the other so as to clarify the specific situation of this encounter – in a word, we mostly keep an *orientational distance*.

At the same time, we usually observe whether and how others observe us, whether they are also attentive to us. Characteristic of this ongoing *observation of others' observations* is the typical *orientational gaze* that is performed when entering an area where there are already people, such as a public square, a pub, an office, a class room, an elevator, etc.: you try to quickly 'secure' the situation by finding out what others see – without looking into their eyes. Through this kind of mutual orientation, you spontaneously decide to whom you will turn and to whom you will not, whom you want to walk closer to and whom you will stay away from, and with whom you will engage and with whom you would rather not – while those around you carefully observe all of this for themselves as well.

With your orientational gaze, you not only get an overview of the situation, but you also situate yourself in it. The gaze initiates an *interaction*. 'Interaction' is a sociological term referring to the reactions among those present in a shared space who perceive each other and who perceive *that* they perceive each other, without already having to be familiar with each other. People who are present in the same place at the same time cannot but react to each other and thus interact with each other, even when they do not engage with one another. Everyone unintentionally, immediately, and almost unnoticeably changes his or her behavior when realizing that others are present. As such, our behavior is always informed by our orientation to other orientations.

Whoever observes how others observe his or her observations will also become aware of special characteristics of his or her own observations; e. g. he or she may observe someone in an intrusive way (he looks at her, but she does not want to be observed by him) or a cursory way (she wants to be seen by him, but he does not look at her), in an expectant or a bored way, in a happy or an unhappy way, etc. Via this observation of other orientations, it is possible to observe one's own orientation – and not only possible: the reactions of others *force* you to do so. And since our social behavior involves, on the one hand, establishing contacts, and, on the other, avoiding them, mutual orientation does not persist in a somehow theoretical distance, but it creates real tensions in the situation; and these tensions can then initiate *communication*, an exchange of words, a conversation, etc.

The transitions between interaction and communication are smooth. You interact, for instance, when keeping the greatest possible distance from strangers in an elevator and moving into corners in which you would not go if you were by yourself; or when, in a busy pedestrian area, you get out of the way of others without looking directly at them. But if people come too close, then communication may become necessary: now, you can pass others only with the help of gestures and, eventually, ritualized formalities ('Please, after you!'). In the tensions of interactions, you can engage with others by means of signs and words, even when you do not want to come close to them. In the medium of language, you can create a shared community – but at first it is only the medium you share with others. Of course, an exchange of information, e.g. a conversation, already shows the openness for a shared community. But through communicating, tensions can also increase and create conflict. Communication does not per se mean – as one would like to suppose with moral intentions – reaching a consensus. Much more than simple interaction, communication allows for *cooperation* in shared projects; surely, to cooperate with others requires some consensus, but only to a certain extent; cooperation takes place even when the people involved have different ideas about it and different intentions; and it can again be peaceful or troublesome. As a result, *communicating does not already solve or end orientation problems, but it creates new orientation problems in a new and more complex way under new and more complex conditions.* Since other people are the strongest footholds for our own orientation, this all the more increases the need to attain certainty about their bearings. But in communication, this is more difficult because with signs and words you can also only *pretend* to give footholds to others – you can also deceive them with signs and words. Therefore, an orientation can further be unsettled by communication – here, it is not less, but more difficult to find reassuring calmness.

10.2 Bodily Distances, Body Signs, Exchange of Glances, Interaction Rituals: Orientation Procedures in the Presence of Others

Erving Goffman, who, while frequently using the term of orientation, has made the most interesting sociological and the most inspiring philosophical contributions to this area of research, writes in his study *Relations in Public: Microstudies of Public Order:*

> When an individual is in a public place, he is not merely moving from point to point silently and mechanically managing traffic problems; he is also involved in taking constant care to sustain a viable position relative to what has come to happen around him, and he will initiate gestural interchanges with acquainted and unacquainted others in order to establish what this position is. In a public place, the individual appears to be indifferent to the strangers in his presence; but actually he is sufficiently oriented to them [...].[39]

When simply passing each other, many things can happen. In order to avoid physical collisions and their unpleasant consequences, we keep, as described above, a 'safe distance' from each other. To sum it up in a simple phrase: in most cases, we try to *avoid trouble*. This is usually in the interest of others as well; in general, you can expect people to avoid situations where they might be troublesome to each other. However, avoiding trouble with others requires one to permanently observe others, including what and how they observe; this is a co-operative interaction based on mutual interest. Thus, as far as we deal with recurring situations of conflict, *rules* develop. Rules are *orientation instruments,* too: instruments for mutual orientation. Most of them develop by themselves; for the most part they are implicit; but they can also be explicitly formulated and justified. As with routines, we hold on to rules in order to relieve ourselves from ever-new orientation decisions regarding our common life. This is the first reason for their existence: they ease our living together.

But rules also come with a price: by generalizing different situations, i. e. by treating something unequal as equal, 'gains' are made for a better survey, but, on the other hand, there are 'losses' in circumspect dealing with concrete situations. Rules thus create pressure too. When, on the subway, a great number of passersby seek to quickly catch the next subway, you are forced to fall into line, even if you are not in a hurry or handicapped in walking. Rules, including implicit ones and those developed on occasion, tend to become *norms:* they force everyone to behave and act in the same or a similar way (conveying with words or without, 'Come on, you can't stop everybody here, keep on walking!'); by referring to them, everyone can demand the same behavior from everyone.

After colliding with someone (be it physically or in a conversation), you will most likely never forget these rules again.

Once fixed in memory, rule-governed behavior in turn gains its *routine*. Having become routine, rules can also allow for leeways for complying with them; depending on the situation, the pressure to comply with them can increase or decrease. In tense situations (the subway is already there and about to leave, you want to catch it, but suddenly somebody cuts in line in front of the doors and hinders you from entering), you will insist much more on keeping to the rules than in relaxed ones (when strolling through a shopping mall, your direction and speed of walking may vary much more; you may stop before display windows, cross others' paths, or stop somewhere in the middle of the walkway to greet acquaintances, forcing others to walk around you).

With rules, there are routines for changing routines, too: when violating one rule (in this case: blocking other's paths), there are usually enough other rules to maintain order as a whole (in this case: to persist relaxed); when you must reach someone who needs your assistance (for instance, your child slipped into a subway car leaving you outside), you will cut in line and then comply with the rules again by acting in an especially correct way, moving with extra caution, offering apologies, etc.

However, what appears to be the conscious observance of rules and norms is, for the most part, 'interaction rituals,' which are hardly noticed constraints of behavior. They begin by keeping certain bodily distances, sending out body signs, and exchanging gazes. Involuntary *orientation procedures* like these have now been well researched.

(1) Bodily Distances. – Behavioral research distinguishes between species of animals that tend to keep close contact and species that keep distances from each other and from other species; human beings are categorized as keeping distances. Among the distances, one distinguishes – in regard to animals – between a 'flight distance' or 'run boundary,' whose violation triggers an animal's escape; an 'attack boundary,' where they attack other animals coming too close; and, in between the two, a 'critical distance,' where they oscillate between assessing whether they should escape or defend themselves.

Human beings, too, at first involuntarily orient themselves to each other with their bodies. Of course, they have a much larger behavioral repertoire at their disposal so that there is less need for them to escape or attack out of reflex. However, all societies have specific rules for keeping specific bodily distances, which differ only within certain leeways; everywhere they vary depending on whether someone is dealing with strangers or acquaintances, whether they are relatives or not, whether they are of a different gender or of different generations, etc. Generally, bodily distances depend on how much space is available, how many people there are (e. g. on an escalator or on a train), how long and why they are there (you may want more room on a long train ride than on a short subway ride). It also matters how attractive a person is or whether there are stigmata, uncomfortable odors, etc.; the moods and the 'climate' among those present are important factors as well. Violating the finely graduated procedures or rules of distances (mostly) creates physical discomfort so that the people around will quickly urge the violator to comply with the implicit rules appropriate to the situation. According to these rules, reducing the distance to someone is only permitted if it is explicitly desired by him or her or if the circumstances require it. For instance, there must be good reasons for touching someone: you may firmly touch somebody to help him or her get on the bus if he or she obviously needs help; or you may fall asleep on the plane and sink to the side of your neighbor when you are tired to death; but you cannot just touch someone in any given situation.

The discomfort due to unwanted physical approaches can be verified through physiological factors (elevated pulse, sweating, and the like.) Relevant experiments have determined invisible *distance zones* around respective bodies. These zones revolve around the standpoint of the body: each body's standpoint becomes, in mutual orientations, a 'bodily territory,' which is jealously guarded and defended. The bodily territory is a hardly noticed 'reality' of the standpoint of an orientation: it has an oval shape, larger in the front than in the back; when turning one's head it also turns; but it hardly depends on one's viewing direction – among the blind there are no major differences. Called 'personal space' in psychological research, it is in fact an 'interpersonal space': it only becomes relevant in the presence of others.

Distance zones vary depending on how one interacts with others. Regarding the distance behavior of white middle-class Americans, where it was first comprehensively explored, Edward T. Hall distinguished in his "proxemics"[40] an *intimate*, a *personal*, a *social*, and a *public distance*, each with a narrower and a wider scope. These distances correspond closely to the orientation worlds we distinguished earlier (chap. 8.4) and which become the horizons of our moral behavior (chap. 14.5). In body distances, too, the senses come into play in different ways. Therefore, each distance has a different quality:

- The *intimate distance* is a zero distance. Here you open your bodily territory and allow the other to 'come near,' be it when caressing someone, or playing contact sports, or during medical examinations. In the intimate distance, the senses of touch and smell are primarily involved. But here you cannot look into the other's face and you can hardly talk to him or her; to do that, you would have to move somewhat apart from each other, being in the – still intimate – whispering distance of approx. 40 cm or 16".

- Within the *personal distance*, which is (for white middle-class Americans) at approx. 70 cm or 27 ½", you can still stay in physical contact, e.g. tapping on someone's shoulder or stroking somebody's arm. Here you can easily look into the other's face, but you do not do so for a long time without a good reason. Instead, to keep contact you alternate between looking at the upper and the lower part of the face. Only when increasing the distance in a conversation (to approx. 120 cm or 47") you perceive the other's face as a whole including his or her upper body, which you do not focus on (unless you are making a benevolent or cautionary remark about the other's outer appearance, if you are close enough to do so). You speak with a softer voice so that only your interlocutor and no one else can understand you; in doing so, you mark a common territory for this personal relationship. Typically, voice volume and the perceptions of comfortable distances vary between men and women as well as between people from the South or the North (e.g. in the USA or Europe) in various ways.
- The *social distance*, which was measured (in the USA) at approx. 160 cm or 63", is adhered to in social orientation worlds when dealing with people on an occasional basis: in stores, at work, or in casual business meetings. Here physical contact is hardly permitted; it is limited to shaking hands as a gesture of welcome or goodbye (for the latter one, you come – after a successful conversation – momentarily closer to each other). But in the social distance, you can inspect others in their full appearance. Increasing the distance even further (to approx. 3 m or 9'10"), you can start drawing comparisons, but you no longer discern the small details of the face, nor the other's smell. This is the distance for giving orders and directives. To stay in touch with someone in this distance, you have to (and can) look at him or her for a longer time and raise your voice to reach him or her. But this distance also allows you to discontinue or avoid certain contacts with others. In social orientation worlds, e.g. in families or shared living accommodations, you adhere to this distance, too, if you want your own space.
- Within the *public distance* (approx. 5 m or 16'5"), inter-individual interactions are hardly possible. You are at such a great distance from each other that you must speak with a loud voice and articulate yourself carefully so that you can still be heard and understood. Beyond an approx. 8 m or 26'3" distance, you have only a small image of others within a larger frame, and you have to speak through a microphone or make use of clearly accentuated gestures, e.g. when politicians, actors, or commanders appear before their audiences.

Individual and situational deviations from these distance procedures or rules (which vary depending on culture, milieu, gender, generation, and individual conditions) are important footholds for our orientation. We attentively and carefully register them: conspicuous deviations provide helpful footholds in our very complex inter-individual orientations. Even smaller approaches can be interpreted as 'inappropriate advances,' which you may either allow, letting the other 'come near' you, or try to rebuff, hoping to keep the other at arm's length with a look or gesture of rejection. When shifting between spheres of distance, you express your intention to reconstitute your relationship with the other. When shifting from a social to a personal distance, you may want to get to know the other better; when shifting from a personal to an intimate distance, you may want to move to a more intimate relationship. Vice versa, by simply increasing your distance of interaction, you, as it were, 'distance' yourself from that person. Experiences of decreasing or increasing your distance select and direct your subsequent interactions; they are remembered as fluctuant images of their bodies.

With the territory invisibly surrounding your body, you can *occupy territories*. You then have your own 'spot' for a certain period of time, which is maintained even when left for some time: on a bus, in a train compartment, on a park bench, in the theater, in a tavern, or at a desk in the library. Here you can (more or less) 'spread out' and 'make yourself at home.' If doubts come up as to whether that spot is taken, you can mark it by putting something down and leaving it there: a bag, a program booklet, a napkin, or a book. Such things are usually not touched by others, just like the body to which they belong.

(2) Body Signs. – When the body moves, the body's territory moves with it. This territory becomes a leeway for movement which moves itself: you constantly try to maintain your body territory when walking, thereby checking your way for obstacles – above all, other people – 'on a running basis.' Since the situation always changes when walking, the orientation skills of circumspection, foresight, consideration, and caution are particularly needed. But here, too, they quickly become routine "routing practices," as Goffman calls them.[41] How they are applied depends not only on one's culture, gender, age, etc., but also on one's physical agility, temper, and the given pressure of time. In traffic, cars and their room for maneuver are also included in bodily territories. Since vehicular collisions can cause serious damage, individual orientation skills are supported by explicit and formally sanctioned traffic rules or laws.

However, such rules and laws alone do not ensure collision-free traffic. The body signs that secure mutual orientations among pedestrians are also used for traffic on the road: especially in the form of looks or gestures of resoluteness signaling 'this is my way, please let me go forward.' As such, whole bodies (and the cars around them) become *moving leads:* they make clear how to reckon with them so that you can get out of the way – or insist on your own way. Changes of direction may require more striking signs, e. g. a significant turn of one's upper body or head or a steady gaze in a certain direction. If things get 'tight,' you can point with your hand in the direction you want to go; if things become even 'tighter,' you can exchange glances and thus make clear your intentions while perceiving the other's. All these footholds and signs would be meaningless by themselves – the exchange of glances would simply be irritating; but if they fit together and help control the traffic, they orient us without any problems.

When passing someone, you (more or less carefully) scrutinize him or her. This *scrutinizing* gauges much more than what is necessary to solve modern traffic problems; it reveals the ancient caution of always anticipating potentially harmful collisions. Your attention to others increases even more, the nearer they come and the more visible they are. The leads then multiply: not only does the direction and speed of the others' movements catch your eye (how they walk, be it fast or slow, stressed or easy-going), but also how they themselves look around (intrepid or cautious, curious or turned into themselves) as well as their physique, their clothes, and their overall 'look.' All these insinuate an *initial personal assessment* of others. If there is more time, e. g. when sitting across from someone on the bus or the train, the 'impression' solidifies through their posture, gestures, and facial expressions – you start to wonder how they fit together and form a coherent picture. This 'overall impression,' emerging in this way, immediately orientates you concerning how to deal with other people in case of contact. This orientation is especially based on affects: here, you are spontaneously directed to either interest or disinterest, to liking or disliking, or to sympathy or hostility. These affects are usually not articulated. They *must* not be articulated, as you would prematurely betray yourself by doing so. Besides, it is hard to articulate them: you remember other people much more through images than through descriptions, though the affective instrumentations of both always resonate.

It can even be risky to express interest or disinterest toward others in interactions. Signs of liking or disliking someone are subject to a vast range of interpretation. You therefore usually hold back announcing your orientation to others, particularly to strangers; you control as much as possible your own expression. But this control becomes the more difficult the more you like or dislike somebody. As such, *routines and rules for controlling one's expression* develop. Here, the most basic routine is to (more or less strictly) keep one's distance, not only physically, but also in regard to potential interactions or communications. While the control of one's expression is meant to not prematurely reveal one's own orientation to others, *uncontrolled* behavior stands out even more, and its clues are more revealing: we mutually observe each other with regard to how successful this control is. 'Telling' clues include certain facial expressions, postures, hand and leg movements, voice changes, as well as blushing, turning pale, coughing, twitching, working up a sweat, etc. These allow you to guess what others do not want to be revealed, thus undermining their control.

Body signs as such are initial clues for recognizing someone's *character*. The Greek *charaktáer* was originally a sign that was 'entrenched' or 'imprinted' on coins or properties, which allowed one to more easily identify them. What is most strongly imprinted in the memory of human beings are the idiosyncrasies of others' behavior; from these you then draw initial conclusions about their character. Someone's 'affect display,' i.e. the way he or she expresses emotions, is so deeply incorporated into their behavior that it is performed even when others cannot perceive it, e.g. your gestures when you are on the phone. *Face and voice* are the most striking and characteristic body signs. As far as we know, all cultures have developed highly differentiated skills for perceiving them, largely without any verbal terms for them. However, face and voice are never just the characteristics of an individual alone, but at the same time of his or her relations to others – hence of their respective orientations to other orientations. They indicate, even when they are controlled, how one person stands to another. Just as 'personal spaces' are also 'interpersonal spaces,' faces likewise are 'interpersonal faces,' or rather, if you like, 'interfaces.'

Here it is significant, too, what is and is not controlled. An involuntarily smile arising spontaneously 'comes across' better than a fake smile. But neither is easy to distinguish: even a spontaneous smile is usually quickly controlled in the presence of others; and a controlled smile only comes across well if it appears somewhat spontaneous. As such, body signs in interactions persist uncertain; just *one* new sign may give a new twist to the whole relationship. Therefore, they require and receive the greatest attention in mutual orientations.

(3) Exchanging Glances. – When scrutinizing random passersby on the street, or people standing next to or sitting across from you, all that is permitted is an *orienting glance*, which is sufficient to orient you concerning how you can come to terms with them, in the case that you – involuntarily or voluntarily – engage in further interactions with them. You usually avoid looking others directly in their eyes. Orienting glances are to be 'fleeting'; when running the danger of encountering the glance of others, they are literally ready to 'flee,' to quickly turn away. With a purportedly indifferent gaze you look at others as if you would not look at them; you register their presence and ignore them at the same time. Commercial power- or speed-dating on the internet successfully relies on the fact that we can assess the physical attractiveness of someone in approximately one third

of a second and make statements about them after a 30-second video which equal those made by their long-term friends.

We keep other people 'in view' until they are outside of our 'range,' or until we are outside of theirs. They are perceived just like points of reference in different views: through a *side glance* you make use of the distinction between center and periphery in your orientation; you look – in a way that is visible to others – at something else, but, at the same time, you look – in a way that is invisible to them – at them. You can also have your eyelids drop in such a way that your viewing direction is completely unobservable for others; you seem to look out from behind a scenery backdrop (in German *Kulissenblick*). Here, too, women and men follow different procedures in different leeways. Regarding nurses, who are particularly trained in looking to and away from someone, research has distinguished 23 significantly different ways in which they close their eyelids.

All this takes place in the (extended) social distance of approx. 3 m or c. 9'10". If you look directly at others, you run the risk of looking into their eyes. This is a risk because such contact, in which your heads and eyes are directly facing each other, can decide on the whole relationship that is to follow; therefore, the *face-to-face situation* requires our full attention. It unsettles us like nothing else in our everyday routines; it is the most tension-filled situation of interindividual orientations: the observation of the other's observation is now directly observed from both sides. This situation is so delicate and precarious that you can endure it for only a short time.

Deviations from the usual duration of looking-into-each-other's-eyes can in turn be significant. If the glance continues for a longer time as each looks 'deeply' into the other's eyes, it becomes a sign of an increased, friendly or unfriendly, interest, leading, as it were, to a 'deepened' contact. The other then responds with a 'questioning glance' that can either mean: 'Why do you look at me (with so much interest)?' or 'Why do you stare at me (so intrusively)?' The tension of looking-into-each-other's-eyes never completely ceases: even lovers who dare to expand that look for a longer time still have to look away again – does not even love allow for an entirely direct and open relationship?

To ease the tension, implicit routines and rules for exchanging glances have once again been developed. They are, in pleasant cases, followed with ease and even amusement; in unpleasant cases they require noticeable efforts. These routines and rules may be different in different societies, too; but no society can do without them.

In fact, we do not really see anything in the eyes of others. Their color, shape, and position may be – as part of the other's overall appearance – more or less appealing. However, beyond that they do not tell us much of anything even though we believe they do. Rather, we are again dealing with orienting clues: how someone's eyes are opened and what they look at; the position of one's head; the raising of one's eyebrows; the shape of one's mouth, etc.; the combination of all these – along with a lot of other aspects – makes up one's facial expression. Hence, the others' eyes are merely the vanishing points of their facial expression – similar to the vanishing point in the art of perspectival painting (chap. 5.3).

(4) Interaction Rituals. – Such hardly noticed 'interaction rituals,' as Goffman calls them, also determine orientations among human beings. The term 'ritual' comes from religious language. It presupposes a 'higher' order, which you submit to unconditionally. Rituals develop, change, and discontinue in the given circumstances just like routines and rules; but they differ from them in that complying to rituals is 'sanctioned,' just as in the case of sacred actions; you feel seriously disturbed if they are not obeyed. Our everyday interindividual orientations are in particular characterized by such interaction rituals, which are expected to initiate and maintain long-term interactions and in which the risk of a consequential social miscue is therefore very high. For instance, rituals of welcome and farewell belong to them. Rituals are, precisely because of their sacred nature, strong *orientation signs:* if someone willingly accepts an initiated ritual (e.g. an initial question about his or her well-being or where he or she is from or a conversation about the weather), you might expect a fruitful interaction and communication; if not, then you might consider preparing for irritations or perhaps even trouble.

10.3 Taking on Other Orientations: Imitations and Adaptations

When orienting ourselves to other people, we often imitate their actions. *Imitating* someone is an attempt to repeat his or her behavior under one's own conditions when such behavior seems likely to succeed. If the attempt proves successful, the repetition is continued and the relevant behavior becomes your own routine. However, imitation is also risky; it can always fail. You need to first see whether and to what extent the imitated behavior proves successful in your own orientation; only if successful will you decide to adopt it. Imitations do not have to be conscious either: they also include 'contagious' behaviors like yawning or smiling, moods that 'spread out' like boredom or panic, and thrilling movements such as waves of applause in sports arenas or people dancing in clubs. In some cases, you can only imitate what you understand; but in other cases, you understand something precisely because you imitate it, e.g. a gesture, a facial expression, a posture, or a technique. Infants, who are especially occupied with imitating others, learn how to speak in this way; adults learn most techniques not by explanation, but rather by simply looking at how others perform and then imitating them.

In our orientations to other orientations, the realm of imitation is enormous. Imitations make your orientation easier insofar as you do not have to make and test out for yourself how various attempts to orientate oneself might work – you do not have to invent anything new for your orientation needs. *Inventions and imitations* are, according to Gabriel de Tarde already in 1890 in his *Lois de l'imitation*, "the elementary social actions." Relieving life is – as already Aristotle noticed in his *Poetics* (chap. 4) – an elementary necessity of life; whatever promises relief is imitated and incorporated through repetition.

Relieving inventions come about, according to de Tarde, largely at random and inconspicuously, even for the 'inventor.' Most of them seem like trifles: simple procedures; hunting tricks; ways of improving one's dwelling; clothing; domestication of animals or cultivation of fields; religious rites; rules and routines of interaction; ideas for new sounds, words, or signs, etc. Such 'inventions' may support, supersede, or suppress one another. For instance, horses were most likely eaten before somebody had the idea to ride them or have them pull ploughs, chariots, or carriages; after that they were hardly bred for consumption. If inventions merge into patterns, they are imitated altogether, and their spread accelerates. If imitations last only a short time, then they are considered fashions – when they last a long time, they are appreciated as traditions; nevertheless, both are imitations.

But since all is imitated in (more or less) different situations, every imitation is in fact an *adaptation*. For that reason, there are again leeways to be exploited in inventive ways: adaptations are creations, too. As such, no imitation is identical to another; but every single imitation depends on the imitating individual. Speaking in moral terms: in spite of the apparent 'innocence' of an imitation, everyone is responsible for every single imitation and thus for the spread of each 'invention,' be it a new technique, a new word, a new opinion, a new theory, a new politics, or a new morality. For you can always choose to *not* imitate something, even though everyone else does – de Tarde then speaks of '*contre-imitation*': the leeways for adapting imitations are also leeways for (noticed or unnoticed) decisions about them.

In most cases, this is forgotten: one mostly imitates something after and because others have already imitated it; in that case, not only the invention but also the imitation has already proven successful for others. You then imitate imitations; and, as such, imitations too become *self-referential and self-dynamic*. They grow in a way that individuals experience them as overwhelming, like a fate: if an invention (e. g. writing or digital devices) has been successful in your environment, you only evade it at the cost of losing your social connections. You then risk your own orientation – and may appear peculiar or stubborn.

10.4 Speaking as a Means of Gaining and Losing Orientation; Languages as Orientation Routines

You also learn to speak by imitating and adapting. In speaking, the different *standpoints of the separate orientations* are articulated in verbal or written signs by means of personal pronouns like 'I' and 'you.' We speak in ritualized bodily distances and in face-to-face situations: as such, "speech acts," as John Langshaw Austin called them, are tense interactions. Verbal communication is *embedded in non-verbal interactions*. When speaking, your body also moves through its gestures, i.e. you often move your head and eyes, your arms, hands, fingers, legs and feet when you speak (e. g. the feet often bounce up and down). Every speaker follows, in each situation, a characteristic tempo, rhythm, and intonation of speech – or to put it shortly: a prosody. When speaking, you set a mood and give emphasis; both help attune speaker and listener, facilitate exchanges in their conversation, and make it easier for them to recognize each other.

A conversation is per se an *interaction ritual*. You expect it in certain situations: when meeting an acquaintance, you say something even if there is nothing to say, as saying nothing would lead the other to suspect hostile intentions. In situations of crisis it may be your job to comment, to console, to give advice, to have an emergency talk (e. g. if your relationship is in a crisis); you may also be asked to give a (longer or shorter) speech on official occasions. Long-term relationships usually begin with conversations. The moment you start a conversation, it requires your full engagement; you have to disregard all other actions; you violate the interaction ritual of conversation if you become engaged with something else.

Over the course of conversations, you again have to follow *communication rituals*, e. g. by introducing difficult questions and delicate topics with harmless openings, by letting others speak on a regular basis, or by concluding the conversation in an appropriate time with a suitable topic, etc. The tensions present in an initial exchange of glances continue to exist in an exchange of words. According to statistics, people who speak a lot hardly look at their interlocutor in comparison to those who listen a lot. Glances exchanged throughout a conversation allow you to continually orient yourself to whether your interlocutor wants to say something or not and whether you should or may speak longer – or not.

Ritualized exchanges of glances and ritualized exchanges of words are intertwined and regulate each other. If you deviate from these rituals, you have to make apologies, or you will be considered uneducated or troublesome.

If someone initiates in a (nonverbal) interaction a (verbal) communication (e. g. starting a conversation during an act of sex), the communication then quickly moves into the foreground and dominates the interaction. The present orientation shifts to *language signs* and their art of world abbreviation. Speaking increases the distance from expressive physical behavior and thus increases one's reservations toward others (if you are greatly suffering, you can still speak calmly about your pain, and talking about the pain of others is easier than empathizing).

By speaking, an orientation can moreover reach beyond the situation of those present and include those absent. It can thereby infinitely widen the horizon of orientation and let arise the common orientation world of a common language. However, this includes all the leeways for understanding the words of others. Hence, *situations of conversations* are also *situations of orientation:* languages on the one hand extend and simplify orientations to each other; on the other hand, they create new problems in orientation. In order to understand what others want to say, draw attention to, or intend to do, or what the whole conversation is about, what is relevant in it, or what you must consider, etc., you must orient yourself to their signs – in addition to orienting yourself to the situation in which they occur and the non-verbal signs that accompany them. Conversations, too, are (more or less) under the pressure of time; their time is likewise limited; and they create their own kind of time pressure. In a conversation, you must not let pauses grow too long without 'disrupting' it; when the other stops speaking, you have to immediately take the turn and find the appropriate response from among all those possible. A continued interaction, as a ritually regulated kind of exchange, thus imposes high requirements for the classic orientation skills of consideration, caution, circumspection, and foresight. Moreover, you have to expect a great number of irritations and surprises in conversations: it is usually easier to say something surprising than to actually do it. That is why you may also 'seek' conversations: 'interesting conversations,' to which both interlocutors 'contribute,' are conversations that bring 'something new' by surprise.

We therefore often have a *desire for conversations*. In conversations, we learn about other perspectives and intentions; we get to know other orientations without having to adopt them; in conversations we also gain a distance from imitations. In everyday orientation, we are indeed sometimes troubled by the diversity and ambiguity of signs, but we also enjoy it: most people take pleasure in speaking with others who say other things than they themselves do – in this way they expand their own repertoire of orientations; many people enjoy using metaphors, allusions, double and hidden meanings. If things eventually become serious, when all the jokes are over, we again have plenty of orientations signs at our disposal: we significantly change our facial expressions, posture, voice, and gestures.

Opinions, which others express in a serious or playful tone, are again leads for their standpoints which may differ in different contexts; thus you need to orient yourself concerning how they fit together. In doing so, you get – more or less spontaneously or by reflection – an *idea of the other's mental and intellectual orientation*. With such an idea in mind, you can engage with him or her and continually confirm or change this idea. If it fits to the other's idea of him or herself, communications will again succeed more easily.

In order to gain an idea or image of the other that also pleases him or her, you may try to 'meet' him or her 'half way,' for instance by adopting his or her words; he or she will then feel vindicated in his or her use of signs. Just like it is a sign of good understanding in physical interactions to adopt the same posture, it is a good sign in communication to use the same signs. As such, we speak to different people in (more or less) different and accommodating ways. This is also true for objections, criticism, accusations, attacks – they must be articulated in appropriate ways if they are to properly 'come across.' Information may be very similar with respect to content but very different in the way it is communicated. In orientations to other orientations, we usually make use of all possible ways of differentiating. Our *speaking-differently-to-each-person* is maintained even in apparently 'impersonal argumentations.' Arguments are supposed to convince all people the same way; in actuality, they are put forward in conversations to specific people in a specific way, not only on informal occasions or in political altercations, but also in scientific discourses. Some individuals you can better convince with this argument, others with that.

The most obvious gain of an orientation through conversations is the *'holding on to what is said.'* Even if you cannot know what others were thinking when they said something, you can still hold on to what they said, bring it up again, and confront them with it anew if they no longer remember. However, holding on to what was said also entails losses in orientation. For in speaking you transform that which you perceive simultaneously or what is intuitively imagined into something said in a discourse where words have to follow other words. While you can simultaneously pay attention to a wide range of events in non-verbal orientations, you have to reproduce them successively in speech; and the more you are pressed for time, the greater is the amount of what you have to leave out. Moreover, in conversations there can only be one person speaking at a time if people are still to understand each other; therefore, contributions to a conversation must be made one after another. As such, we often contend for who gets a chance to speak at what time. This may govern the selection of topics, lead to surprising turns in the conversation, or lead it in a very different direction. However, what we retain is usually only what was said, not the conditions in which it was said; in fact, this can quickly lead to new disputes when returning to the conversation at a later point. What was remembered of what was said in a conversation and how one holds onto it may then again differ from one orientation to the next.

However, what provides hold is not only what was said but also the *language as a whole* that someone is proficient in. Being able to speak of something with routine gives you a specific kind of confidence. A language as such orients its speakers by the repertoire of its distinctions and its set of rules for using them. Routines of speaking become routines of orientation – each with their own points of reference. Indo-European languages, for instance, require a subject before a predicate even in cases where there is none (we say, as it were, 'it lightens,' 'it thunders,' and 'it rains,' but the 'it' is no real subject doing or causing anything). A word from a word family or from a word field calls for family-like words; distinctions provide alternatives; metaphors leave traces for connecting metaphors, etc. Routines of speaking continue an orientation's art of abbreviation: they mostly allow you to understand statements even before they are finished; in this way you gain time to process them and to adapt to what follows.

Here *grammars*, as explicit sets of rules, play a rather minor role: their primary purpose is not to aid the use of one's own language, but rather to help one acquire another. Their grasp of languages is always limited, distinguishing between rules and exceptions. As such, they (more or less) limit the leeways of the actual use of language via norms. But this can happen in different ways, and explicit grammars must in turn be formulated in a language that must already and non-explicitly follow the very rules it formulates. Grammars, too, do not transcend language, but they persist self-referentially in their own horizon.

Like gains in orientation, using a language also entails *losses in orientation* because a language's repertoire of signs, distinctions, and rules of use must be limited – or else be impossible to learn. "When," according to Nietzsche, "individuals have lived together for a long time under similar conditions (of climate, soil, danger, necessities, work)," they are in need of a language that allows them "*not* to misunderstand each other when there is danger." Instead, it must help them understand each other "faster and faster" by means of a "process of abbreviation": "The greater the danger, the greater the need to agree quickly and easily about necessities." But for that, it is not enough to just use "the same words"; they also have to "use the same words for the same species of inner experiences too; ultimately, people have to have the same experience *base*." In this way, speakers of a language can "indicate similar requirements and similar experiences with similar signs" – but nothing more. Through language, speakers are programmed to articulate precisely the "experiences" that can be articulated by the signs available to them: desert tribes require a large verbal repertoire for different kinds of sand, arctic tribes for kinds of ice and snow; in wine-growing areas people develop the most refined distinctions for a wide variety of nuances in the taste of wine, etc. What is plausible there may be strange or absurd here. With its speech routines, which were born out of the specific needs for orientation and which have become plausible for the speakers, each language has inconspicuously exercised its force over us, which, according to Nietzsche, "must have been the most forceful of the forces that have controlled people so far." (*Beyond Good and Evil*, No 268, transl. by Judith Norman)

Here, Wilhelm von Humboldt spoke of the "power" (*Macht*) by means of which each language, as a "formative organ" (*bildendes Organ*), conveys a specific "worldview" (*Weltansicht*) to those who use it; but he also spoke of the "force" (*Gewalt*) through which each individual can gain "leeway" (*Spielraum*) within or against his or her language. For every language "expands," in its use, "unintentionally to all objects of the random sense perceptions and inner processes"; in doing so it can continually be adapted to new requirements and possibilities. Everyone produces the "language view" (*Sprachansicht*) that he or she has gained from his or her ways of disclosing the world; it (more or less) continues to develop in each new speech situation; and everyone needs to find a language which also fits to others, thus a language which must "necessarily belong to two." As such, languages are always "partly solid, partly fluid."[42] They too are *fluctuant*.

However, in this way the inevitable losses in orientation that language use entails can be compensated for whenever relevant. Not only can the distinctions of a language and the alternatives they offer be brought into play in new and different ways within the leeways of their use; but by being able to speak *in* a language *about* that language you can also distance yourself from its routines, be it through resignation ('I can't put this into words'), or innovation, using analogies and metaphors or inventing new words, etc. Of course, this brings up new orientation risks: you can 'just invent' something through language and thus disorient yourself and others (perhaps more through language than anything else). With orientation in language, according to Hegel, the "universal deception of itself and others" (*der allgemeine Betrug seiner selbst und der anderen*) becomes possible. Whatever is articulated in language can also be "inverted." While language brings harmony to experiences and facilitates agreement in judgments, it also exposes our orientation to the risk of "disruption" (*Zerrissenheit*).[43]

10.5 The Double Contingency of Communication: The Concern for Connecting with Others; the Diplomacy of Signs; Building Trust; Maintaining Spheres of Distance

(1) The Double Contingency of Communication. – In consideration of our inability to fully predict and control communication that can always be surprising, Talcott Parsons and Niklas Luhmann introduce the term 'double contingency'; it is the central point of their sociological theories of communication. For people orienting themselves to each other, this double contingency refers to the fact that individuals always proceed from different standpoints that are never fully transparent to one another, and both interlocutors can only rely on their interactions and communications in order to learn more about each other. Beyond that, they are 'black boxes' to each other. Their communication is 'contingent' in so far as their statements can always differ from what the other one is expecting; it is 'doubly contingent' as far as both anticipate this when speaking with each other. The statement by A is contingent on B; and B's response is then doubly contingent on A. This does not mean that communication is arbitrary. Quite the contrary: given this situation, you will try all the more to respond in such a way as to provide the other with an opportunity to respond in an expected way. If you succeed in doing so, continuity develops despite double contingency – though it is a continuity of the special kind that we have drawn attention to above (chap. 8.3): a continuity in the shape of a transposed continuity that allows leeways for alternatives which are not preemptively decidable. Structures of social order can also be established in this way – without predefined commonalities. Rather, they are social structures of a more complex kind, providing vast leeways for individuals. In fact, this is what we live in today or what we want to live in today.

Double contingency in interaction and communication is a problem that must be mastered in ever-new circumstances in ever-new ways. One may, from the very beginning, presume or demand truthfulness and a willingness for consensus (as Jürgen Habermas does). Then you adhere to the example of science, which in particular limits the double contingency in communication through logical discipline and methodical standards, and which sanctions non-compliance by excluding violators from its discourse. One may then also try to scientifically discipline everyday communications (as analytic philosophy does). But sincerity, the willingness for consensus, and scientific discipline are not simply given, and everyday communications work without presuming them. If you demand them, you have to communicate them, too; and among black boxes, you must inevitably communicate them under the conditions of double contingency. Statements, such as that everyone ought to be honest, come to an agreement, or follow the rules may all just be 'strategic' as well; they can be made with reservations and intentions that others cannot see.

Vice versa, strategic intentions are not necessarily hostile or treacherous. In fact, they are generally expected. Somebody may be sincerely preparing solutions and compromises of which he or she cannot convince others at the moment, but which are in the others' long-term interest; and yet the other is (better off) unaware of this: politicians as well as teachers and parents often have to proceed in this way. They do this for good reasons as far as their orientation proves superior to the orientation of others who they are to lead; this is not considered in science but used quite successfully in everyday communication. Even the distinctions of 'sincere' vs. 'strategic' and 'consensus' vs. 'conflict' are intended to justify 'domination-free discourse,' which does not really exist, being a 'counterfactual' normative ideal you may comply with – or not. In every case, you must first learn how and on which basis orientations in communications work – without already clouding your view, from the start, with idealistic preconceptions.

What in fact helps us master the double contingency of communication is our orientation to communication itself in its *self-referentiality* – the double contingency of communication can only be mastered through communication. When problems arise in understanding or believing the other, you usually simply continue to talk to him or her until you have sufficient clues as to what he or she means or intends. If communication does not move on – maybe because the other does not want to take too great a communication risk by making or affirming clear statements – double contingency as such becomes apparent. If people want to keep their distance in communication, then you can orient yourself just to this and look for other ways to convince them; or you can allow them their convictions and try, if desired or necessary, to communicate and cooperate with them nevertheless – in this way keeping your 'inner' distance as well as respecting the other's distance. It is then only a matter of remaining 'connectable' (*anschlussfähig*) to them.

(2) *The Concern for Connecting with Others (Sorge um Anschlussfähigkeit)*. – To communicate successfully, you must stay connectable for others. This means, you must speak in a way that others can connect with you: introducing topics which others can easily engage with; providing insights that interest, surprise, or fascinate them; making proposals they will gladly accept, etc. In doing so you must – as in a game of chess – assess the others' intentions, which they themselves might not even know yet. You slowly 'feel your way': step by step it becomes clearer whether the other also desires 'to connect' in communication by making supportive contributions – or not. If communication succeeds through

more and more unproblematic connections, you can also proceed to more difficult topics. If here too the connections prove successful, closer cooperations and long-term relationships may be 'established.' And from a certain point on you can then communicate with each other 'free of domination' and personal interest by exchanging apparently well-founded arguments. But you can never be sure of that. All orientation through communication continues to take place under uncertainty; and thus, the concern for an appropriate orientation to other orientations never sleeps. Normative ideals can conceal that. They abbreviate orientation via communication to a degree that you may no longer see how it works.

(3) The Diplomacy of Signs. – Proceeding in communication toward closer cooperation and long-term connection does not mean that you inevitably come to understand each other better and better. Others may, the more you know them, become more and more questionable through their statements and intentions. In order to bring different standpoints in mutual orientation closer to each other, we allow each other leeways for interpretation – also and especially – in communications. To connect through communication, we make use of the leeways for interpretation that signs provide; in order to stay in communication under the conditions of double contingency, we cultivate the art of using and understanding words and signs in various ways: we foster the diplomatic use of signs. Diplomacy is the art of establishing fruitful agreements among conflicting parties (or parties that run the risk of conflict) by using the leeways for interpretation. If such agreements are in writing, i.e. in signs that persist, then this entails a mutual awareness that they can be interpreted in different ways. Diplomatic efforts therefore quickly gain the reputation of being 'fork-tongued.' However, they can also avoid – or at least suspend –more violent altercations or, in the most extreme case, war; if these are already happening, diplomacy might help bring them to an end. Diplomatic relations cannot eradicate wars; they can, in fact, help secretly prepare them. But they can also suspend them and thus allow one to gain time, during which more measures can be taken to ward off conflict.

This is also true, in narrower contexts, for the 'diplomatic behavior' of everyday interindividual orientations. We continually make attempts to win over others in communication: instead of insisting on one's own meanings of terms, which others may reject, we tacitly allow for other meanings or look for other terms that are more palatable to others and which could therefore be used by both. Beyond consideration, caution, circumspection, and foresight, this also requires a high level of attention to the ways that others use their signs – i.e. active listening and holding back one's own opinions.

And yet, the diplomacy of signs does not save you from being deceived. However, it is not considered a deception as long as both parties see that both are striving for diplomacy. Diplomacy then becomes an everyday communication ritual, which connects with the ethical virtues of politeness, tact, nobility, and benignity. It may be accompanied by (more or less open) self-irony, in the Socratic sense of confessing one's own unknowingness, or humor, i.e. the obvious play with simultaneously ambiguous and telling words – and both of these may have ethically liberating effects. The diplomacy of signs, self-irony, and humor help, with respect to the condition of double contingency, to avoid premature definitions or severe confrontations; they create leeways for returning to other interpretations in the case of conflicts. As such they keep communication going and gain time for new and more promising opportunities for connecting with others.

(4) Building Trust. – Diplomacy establishes familiarity (*Vertrautheit*), but not trust (*Vertrauen*). Only trust – as Niklas Luhmann showed in a small but much-discussed and highly respected book from 1968 (English translation *Trust and Power*, 1979) – leads to a sustainable reassurance of communication under the condition of double contingency. In the uncertainty of all orientation, the building of trust is a necessity of life. Trust is the belief that one is able to rely on and thus trust in something or someone without any further footholds or reasons. Trust is risky because it may always be disappointed and therefore fail; trust can just as well be self-deceiving. But you are always forced to engage in a risky trust whenever you urgently need something or someone without having the time or opportunities to perform any further checkups regarding their reliability. In such situations, you have to rely on only a few footholds, i.e. on initial orientations. When trusting someone, you cannot, at least not always, expect that the other will also return your trust. If this trust and its accompanying self-deceptions persist one-sided, then others will have opportunities for (more or less) consequential deceptions. As such, trust initially increases the risks of doubly contingent communication.

This suggests *mistrust*, which is always a possible alternative; and in obscure situations of orientation, there are usually just as many clues for mistrust as there are for trust. Initially, persisting mistrustful involves fewer risks: you hold back. But as the sole strategy when dealing with the risks of communication, mistrust would make you unable to act; if you do not trust anyone or anything, you cannot start anything at all. Therefore, trust will get you further; but trust is only successful if you persist mistrustful as well; both are always necessary. Thus, we orient ourselves to them by oscillating between them: you dare step by step to build trust, and you secure it step by step through mistrust. If the first steps are successful, you take greater risks – while also paying attention to any and all helpful clues, footholds, signs and interaction rituals.

As far as every step makes you more confident in taking further steps, the building of trust is *self-referential:* trust becomes a *trust routine,* and established trust routines encourage you to have more trust. In trust routines, trust stabilizes itself, even if it persists one-sided; it then endures less significant disappointments. Through this self-referentiality, trust likewise builds thresholds that prevent it from too quickly turning into mistrust. In this way, it stabilizes itself – stabilizing our orientations as well to other orientations in double contingency.

You can secure your trust only paradoxically, by *putting yourself in danger:* in order to see if your trust is justified you have to put it at risk of being abused (think of Franz Kafka's parable *The Burrow*). This may be a successful strategy too. By putting one's provisional trust at risk of being abused you give others the opportunity to *not* abuse it and thus justify your trust: others may respond to your need for help and protection by in fact providing help and protection, to your levity with reliability, or to your openness with secrecy – and they may thus prove trustworthy. They then 'earn' your trust: the ethical dimension of trust is constituted by it not being abused or 'exploited.' Trust is not ethical per se, for it may always be careless as well. If you – in communicating with 'unacquainted persons' – encounter careless demonstrations of trust, you will tactfully evade them to avoid becoming bound to them.

If you respond to people 'putting themselves in danger' (which they risk by trusting you) with your own trust in them, then this creates *mutual trust*, which includes mutual moral bounds. Such "double trust" (Luhmann) is the *ideal solution for the problem of double contingency* – it eliminates it. This ideal solution is unlikely (otherwise it would not be ideal); but if it occurs, it is all the more appreciated. Double trust is more likely if both parties are, in their orientations, dependent on trusting each other. This may be the case only for a short time and with respect to specific situations, e.g. during an evasive maneuver in traffic or temporary political coalitions, but it may also last for a long time with respect to persons or institutions. Mutual trust in both friends and partners as well as in institutions especially encourages one's trust in a firm hold of one's orientation as a whole.

But that trust may of course also be betrayed. You may learn from this how to differentiate trust, i.e. to trust less in people as such, but more in their specific qualities, e.g. their readiness to help but not their secrecy; their technical skills but not their business acumen, etc. Then, trust is limited in a controlled way; it becomes, according to Luhmann, a "trust in trust"; and if it proves successful for one's own orientation, then it becomes a *trust in one's own skills in dealing with trust.* You then have learned how to distinguish whom you can trust in which respect and how you can do justice to the trust of others without becoming dependent on them in your own orientation. This limited kind of trust, as learned through your ways of dealing with trust, continues to stabilize your orientation to other orientations under the conditions of double contingency.

Chapter 11
The Stabilization and Differentiation of Mutual Orientation: Respecting Identities
Orientation via Respect

Individual orientations to other individual orientations are stabilized not only via trust (*Vertrauen*) but also via respect (*Achtung*). Like trust, respect is 'given' or 'gifted' to others, but not to everyone. It too must be 'gained' or 'earned'; like trust, it includes appreciation, but not necessarily goodwill, fondness, or love. It permits distance: you also respect opponents, adversaries, and enemies.

While trust quickly becomes routine, you remain attentive to respect. You pay perpetual attention to and observe what you respect. In German *Achtung* (respect), *Beachten* (paying attention), and *Beobachten* (observing) all belong to the same word field; it is, in the German language of orientation, as significant as the word fields of *Sichten* (viewing), *Richten* (directing), and *Halt* (hold). What is respected may remain in the periphery for a while; but it moves back ever anew into the center of attention. Respect attracts the attention of others and becomes the center of their orientations.

There are two opposites to respect, a weaker and a stronger one. The weaker one is *disrespect* or *contempt* (*Verachtung*): here, you believe that you need not pay attention to or to ignore him or her. The stronger opposite is *disdain, condemnation,* or *scorn* (*Ächtung*): here, someone is ostentatiously excluded from interaction and communication; the distance that is usually maintained in interaction and communication (see chap. 10) reaches its extreme. In the case of respect, in contrast, even concerning opponents and enemies, you stay connected to them, and you still communicate and engage with them: if you have respect for someone, you demonstrate this by orienting yourself to him or her, even from a (possibly great) distance, be it in agreement or disagreement. Being respected by you, others are steady footholds in your orientation.

11.1 Identities: Steady Footholds of Mutual Orientation

These steady footholds of our mutual orientation are first of all identities. But there are no identities per se: it is in every case someone who ascribes or attributes identities to people. We do so to fix our image of others (and of ourselves), and this helps us to orient ourselves to each other over a longer period of time –

https://doi.org/10.1515/9783110575149-013

we thus stabilize our orientations. In every orientation, we need identities; in individual and interindividual orientations, they may refer to bodies, outfits, mental or moral qualities, and the characters of individuals; in social orientations we ascribe 'typical qualities' to entire groups of individuals. 'Identity,' originally a philosophical term, has become, like 'orientation,' completely natural and seemingly self-evident; not only attributing identities to others, but also 'having' an identity (or identities) is for many the most important hold in orientation. But since we realized that any identity is ascribed by someone to certain intentions, we have grown used to speaking of 'identity politics.'

The discourse on identities has two sides: on the one hand, identities express what permanently belongs to someone or something; on the other hand, they implicitly indicate what is excluded from them. The *discourse of descriptions and ascriptions* is, at the same time, a discourse of *inclusions and exclusions*. In our everyday orientation, identities are created in very different ways, and we can deal with them in very different ways and with very different intentions. Identities and the discourses of them may be 'constructive,' but also 'destructive.'

Erving Goffman illustrates the diversity of possible ascriptions in a simple example (referring to John Langshaw Austin's theory of speech acts):

Take, for example (with apologies to Austin), an act that is tolerably clear: a man driving through a red light. What is he doing? What has he done? (1) Where he comes from they have signs, not lights. (2) The daylight was bad and he couldn't see. (3) He's lately become color blind. (4) He was late for work. (5) His wife is giving birth in the back seat and he'd like to get to a hospital. (6) The bank robber in the front seat is holding a gun on him and has told him to run the light. (7) He's always done this when no cops are around, figuring that the occasional cost can be distributed across the times when he isn't caught. (8) It's four o'clock in the morning, and no one is ever on the street at this hour, and in addition, he's taken a close look up and down the street to make sure his running the light is completely safe. (9) It's raining, and it's safer not to try to stop on the oil slick. (10) A policeman has waved him through. (11) His brakes gave way. (12) He just plain forgot to look at the light. (13) He's part of a funeral procession. (14) No one is about to challenge him; he's known too well for that. (15) He's an inspector testing the vigilance of the cops on duty. (16) He's driving (he claims) under a posthypnotic trance. (17) He wants to get in a race with the local cop. (18) The cop on the corner is his brother and he is putting him on. (19) Those are diplomatic plates he has. (20) The light was stuck on red, and he and the other motorists finally decided to go through. (21) The light was changing at the time. (22) He was drunk, high. (23) His mother has a lamentable occupation, and he has a psychiatrically certifiable compulsivity in regard to red lights. (24) There was a police ambulance immediately behind, sirening to go through, and the other lane was blocked with a line of cars.[44]

Each of these ascriptions entails a specific image of the driver; each of them may solidify as part of his identity (limited, perhaps, to a shorter period of time); each of them may bring about crucial consequences concerning his inclusion or exclusion in various respects. How relevant they each become eventually depends on the needs or interests and the situations of the persons observing him. What makes a steady foothold for one orientation may be irrelevant for another; in the view of one observer, the driver's behavior may affect his identity, in the view of another it may not. In orientations to other orientations, you have to co-ordinate different identities ascribed by different persons; this coordination can become a difficult process. Identities remain a matter of discourse.

Sometimes different people can become fully attuned to each other when attributing certain identities to certain things, as in Wittgenstein's famous example of the two pavers always using the same slabs. If different names are used for certain objects, as in Gottlob Frege's famous example of Venus, which some called the morning star and others the evening star, this is more difficult. You could then say that these three names mean something identical because they relate to the same object. But this already presupposes that there *are* identical objects for different orientations; this may seem obvious in the case of the morning star and evening star, but not in a case like the driver running the light.

Thus, we have to differentiate kinds of identities. Ascribing identities, we often postulate a *logical identity* 'behind' the *semiotic identity* and, to a large extent, the *real identity* of a real thing existing per se, 'behind' this logical identity. Science in particular could hardly work without such presuppositions. It needs them in order to formulate general laws; whoever studies a science is disciplined accordingly. However, we have learned that it is our orientation that separates and isolates something or someone from everything else it is related to or dependent on. Rather, there are – in everyday orientation as in science – inevitably different views on them and different ways of identifying them (think of the water you drink at dinner and H2O you use in chemical experiments); an alleged being per se exhibits (more or less) different identities. Everyday as well as scientific orientations abbreviate whatever they observe in their own multifarious ways, reducing it to surveyable and steady identities. But these abbreviations can change with changing situations and purposes; our everyday and scientific orientations can always, and sometimes must, make new decisions about identities. Thus, one must continue to keep one's eyes open to the leeways for deciding on them.

In our everyday orientation (and to a large extent in science as well), the objects proffering themselves as remaining identical are primarily dead objects, in a word, 'things' (Lat. *res*, German *Dinge*, *Sachen*), e. g. tables or chairs. We ascribe to them a *'real' identity*, which means in most cases a *corporeal identity*. They seem to remain identical because they (in general) always behave in the same way, without any surprises. But even tables and chairs may mean something very different for some people –, e.g. for furniture designers or dealers compared to those who simply use them on a daily basis (and furniture designers may shift between these views on a daily basis). And nowadays, it becomes more and more difficult to distinguish some (dead) robots from (living) humans.

With regard to human beings, despite their capacity to always surprise one another, there is, one might argue, a consistent *bodily identity*. We presume that bodies, including human bodies, remain the same when we walk around them and look at them from all sides. But in doing so, we also experience that we can see bodies only from one perspective, filling in the other views by making use of its images, signs, names, and concepts in our memory. Moreover, you are usually not able to just walk around human bodies and gaze at them (if they are not dead). For they will react and change in some ways; thus, they do not just remain the same. The interplay of bodily distances, body signs, glances being exchanged, and interaction rituals (as described above) takes place. As a result, the bodily identity becomes a *semiotic identity*.

Semiotic identities are more complex. They permit the exchange of bodily or, in general, corporeal identities. This includes dead objects: for instance, a scheduled train does not always have to be the same physical train; it does not always have to consist of the same locomotive and the same carriages; these may be exchanged for the sake of its semiotic identity. In addition, a scheduled train does not always have to leave on schedule; it is still 'the same train' even if it does not follow schedule. The semiotic identity of the announcement in the timetable only ensures that the passengers will be at the right terminal at the announced time, expecting the train to leave on schedule. Identity thus obviously consists of an expectation – it is not a fact but a norm. A semiotic identity functions as an explicit fixation of an implicit expectation: a train company's promise to its passengers. This explicit fixation of an implicit expectation works in a self-referential way: the parties involved rely on the fact that others rely on it as well, even though everyone knows that you cannot really rely on such an explicit fixation (in principle, this is also how money works: all trust in the trust all others put in its value). Thus, the self-referential semiotic identity itself falls apart if it is not connected to some concrete physical identities – there must be a physical train factually leaving at some point and, to some degree, on time (and you must be able to actually buy something for your money).

Identities of human beings are semiotic identities too. Human beings likewise have, initially, for others and for themselves, a corporeal identity. However, this corporeal identity continually and often conspicuously changes. And with respect to human beings, one must, to a greater degree (as mentioned above) make do with signs, body signs, characteristic behaviors, names, and diplomatic signs, which allow for a wide range of interpretations in the double contingency of interindividual communication. Human beings are obviously *fluctuant semiotic identities*. As such, ascriptions of *steady character identities* may quickly become visible as mere ascriptions by someone who is, on his or her part, interested in ascribing them. Thus, by ascribing character identities to others the character of the ascribing one reveals itself. For ascriptions of character identities remain controversial. Since one's ascriptions of identities or qualities to others can always refer back to the one ascribing them, their risks are so high that one usually makes use of them carefully and cautiously: you usually characterize a person present only when paying him or her compliments (which are only taken seriously to a limited extent) or when you are in a heated conflict with him or her (which makes others only take you seriously to a limited extent). Ascriptions of qualities and identities in face-to-face situations can hurt others so much that they may cut all ties with the ascribing one. Beyond this, direct ascriptions are reserved for people explicitly or officially entitled to them, e.g. teachers or personnel managers issuing certificates, physicians making diagnoses, psychologists writing personality reports, police officers providing certificates of good conduct, judges pronouncing and justifying sentences, etc.

Of course, there are also fundamental official specifications of identities: persons are given 'IDs' (identity documents or identity cards), which are used to identify them on specific occasions, e.g. when passing a national border, driving cars or paying taxes. You then acquire a *judicially legitimate identity*, by means of which you can make judicial commitments, and based on which you can also be prosecuted in the case of legal violations. The judicially legitimate identity, too, is a semiotic identity, limited to a small number of selected, standardized items. With your ID card you only prove that you are the one registered at the administration – it says nothing about you beyond that. Hence, you can physically elude even your judicially legitimate, semiotic identity by acquiring fake documents (a popular subject in many narratives and films).

As far as such changes of identity are judicially unwanted (sometimes e.g. when important witnesses are in danger, the law allows them), *identity procedures* must stop them. They become necessary precisely because the identity of a person is always uncertain. After formal identifications of persons had begun in the High Middle Ages, persons were identified in the early modern era via the clothes they wore all the time; afterward, they were identified based on characteristic physical features, which were sometimes specifically created, e.g. the branding of slaves. Today, identification technologies have been developed ranging from unique fingerprints and photos to digital biometric data and DNA analyses, which allow for distinguishing individuals with almost full certainty and detecting them among all registered people with the aid of computers in the shortest amount of time. This too is a semiotic identity, which is tied to a bodily, now *genetic identity*. However, outside the laboratory you cannot use this for identification.

Both the judicially legitimate identity and the genetic one are indeed part of a person's identity, but they are not what 'genuinely' constitutes that person's identity for either others or themselves. One's *personal identity*, which is relevant when dealing with others, instead feeds on one's bodily and character identity and most of all on one's autobiographic identity. An *autobiographic identity* is required in the form of CVs (*curriculum vitae*), which you have to write and update again and again. You write them for a specific purpose, mainly when applying for jobs or scholarships in order to earn a living. Therefore, it is not expected that applicants speak in an overly personal way in them, but they are asked to provide official credentials – steady footholds as well – regarding their education and career, which speak in their favor of getting the position or the scholarship. You thus update your CV to reflect your current position in your career and adjust it with regard to the position you are applying for. CVs are purposefully *designed identities*.

Such *public identities* then differ from *private identities*, which you put forth to your family and friends and which you sometimes put down in diaries or – usually in different a form – post on social media. They are (more or less) purposefully designed identities as well. Different from these is the *social identity*, discussed in sociology and psychology: the image of a person developing in society as such, which we will return to later (chap. 11.5).

Collective identities are proffered when you want to become part of a community: a family, a group of friends, a sports team, a school, college, university, or a political party, a religious community, a nation or a union of nations, or an organization. You then 'identify with them,' which means: you adopt the public image of this community for your image of yourself; you share their routines and rituals; you represent them by wearing their symbols (pieces of clothing, signs or colors, flags, fan gear, etc.); you are loyal to them by defending them against attacks from the outside. In the case of perfect loyalty you may unconditionally stand up for your community and, as a last resort, even die for it. You then conceive of yourself as from the perspective of the community; you say 'we' instead of 'I' (when a German Roman Catholic cardinal became pope, a German newspaper announced, "We are pope!"). You receive respect for being part of a community from the community itself and, as far as the community is respected from the outside, in your society at large. You can be proud of something for which you are responsible only to a limited extent. This kind of respect may provide a stable hold in your orientation; and this is why collective identities are so attractive and desirable. But with all this, you also draw (more or less) sharp boundaries against outsiders. As comforting as collective identities are for those who share them or are included in them, they are just as dangerous for those who do not share them or who are excluded from them.

Collective identities hold a group together. They are especially emphasized if this hold is at risk of falling apart (e. g. if someone wants to leave the group, or the group is attacked from the outside – the same is true for a union of states); then, one purposefully engages in identity politics. The hold of collective identities tightens even more if the group gains benefits over other groups by sticking together; if these benefits are at the cost of others, you would rather avoid having to articulate them. Collective identities may solidify to such an extent that they are accepted by both ingroup and outgroup as being fated (though they never are). Flagrant and yet real examples, over millennia, not only include slavery, but also the scorn and persecution of Jews, and the social split between nobility and 'lower classes.' As far as these contrasts diminished over time, others came to the fore, such as oppositions between wealthy and poor, men and women, 'white people' and 'people of color' (whose ancestors were not necessarily slaves), Christian and non-Christians, and 'straight' and LGBTQ+ people; all these have also been social relations of oppression, and they still affect people today. Different groups held together through their particular collective identity may also face each other on (more or less) equal footing, for instance, different religious communities (whose differences created centuries-long wars and amongst which there are still those that call for war today), nations and unions of nations on a large scale, or families, sports clubs, etc., on a small scale. Wherever collective identities develop, they tend to take hold in (more or less) belligerent hostilities; the ideologies they generate feed on these hostilities.

Here, that which we call footholds play a crucial role. Group ideologies (and there are in fact no others) are obviously based on footholds, which may be assessed in very different ways: for some they may be highly significant, for others completely irrelevant – things like someone's skin color, dialect, way of life, clothes, education, religious beliefs or rituals, or the house somebody lives in, or the car somebody drives, etc., etc. If, in a group ideology, such footholds (or, usually, a pattern of many) are considered to be crucial, they become such a vital part of the collective identity to which the whole group is committed that they become unshakeable – other orientation processes that could lead to completely different footholds are abandoned. These footholds are then not only steady but also fixed, leaving almost no leeways for shifts. They are made into persistent or essential qualities, which seem to justify feelings of natural or cultural superiority (Aristotle, who founded the philosophy of essential qualities, considered non-Greeks from Asia to be slaves by nature) and these feelings in turn seems to justify the discrimination, contempt, humiliation, condemnation, and even the killing of others. Fixed ideologies, based on religious doctrines, national identities, social classes, and (apparent) biological races, have brought about the worst horrors in human history.

Even the respective outgroups have, often for a long time, shared these beliefs in their alleged essential qualities. Through this, they have developed their own collective identities. These collective identities have likewise held them together as groups – and, at the same time, prepared them to defend themselves against their disadvantages and to dare riots, revolts, and revolutions, which were rare in ancient times, but more and more frequent and successful in the modern era. The groups so far excluded then revalue the collective identities ascribed to them – the despised now grow proud of what they have been despised for – in order to fight in the name of these identities against discrimination. Martin Luther performed such a revaluation on a grand scale for the protestants, Karl Marx for the working class, the women's movement for the 'second sex,' as Simone de Beauvoir called it, and Martin Luther King, Jr. for African-Americans; soon after, gay people began, during the Stonewall Inn riots, to resolutely resist their prosecution, encouraging a great number of subsequent liberation movements, now with an emphasis on their pride in their – individual or collective – identities. While everyone competes for appreciation and respect, often in the name of their identity, the ones gaining the greatest acknowledgement are those who are proud of and respect themselves. Vice versa, whoever desires to gain respect by disrespecting and discriminating against others loses the respect of those who are not in need of gaining respect in that way.

Even after these riots, revolts, revolutions, and revaluations, *discriminations* of those formerly excluded still continue (though are less open). Discriminations are, in the literal sense, simply 'distinctions.' We quite involuntarily distinguish what is conspicuous from the usual – this is just an orientational necessity; and, e. g., skin color, body size, hairstyle, and facial features *are* factually conspicuous in mutual orientations. Distinctions solidify by generalizing comparable cases – this, too, is necessary to abbreviate orientation processes and to make them a routine. However, such distinctions and their generalizations, not based on logic but on the needs of orientation, are in many cases automatically complemented with distinctions of good and bad – these are the simplest, quickest, and most extreme abbreviations, allowing you to react in the fastest possible way (chap. 6.4). But what is distinguished as good or bad (or superior or inferior) eventually depends on what is pleasant or unpleasant, welcome or unwelcome to someone in his or her situation, and thus on what somebody accepts and supports or affectively wards off. This not only happens when dealing with strangers, but also – only less obviously – between confidants.

Discriminations are thus something that we always deal with, whether actively or passively, in a stronger or weaker form. And not only in modern societies have we learned how to deal with them: an antidote is tactfulness, i. e. to considerately and respectfully deal with distinctions as soon as one encounters the other's irritation, disconcertment, or repulsion. But tactfulness cannot, given its silent reservation, prevent people in society, be they strangers or neighbors, from continuing to be affectively rejected and discriminated against because of their physical features, religious practices, sexual orientation, or the like. Initially harmless distinctions may then, as soon as they are connected with collective identities, become dangerous (the exact line is often difficult to draw), and may subsequently have harmful and, in many respects, depriving effects (above all in regard to one's education, one's search for a job or a place to live, or one's attempts to hold political office). They are thus (whether open or concealed) unjust and call for, in modern democratic societies, not only personal but also large-scale political countermeasures, such as affirmative action.

Today, the term *racism* is frequently raised within these contexts. In other languages like German or French, the term of race (*Rasse, race*) is – to just mention well-known things – generally useful in zoology for distinguishing subspecies in the field of animal breeding, where the English language speaks of different 'breeds.' But, just as with the English word 'race' today, so did the German word *Rasse* once refer to human beings, even during the enlightenment and even in the writings of Immanuel Kant; at the end of the 19th century, it became a central element of a widespread ideology of discrimination, especially against the Jews, and in the 20th century this racist anti-Semitism led, during the reign of the National Socialists, to the extermination of millions of Jews and other people, the most horrendous crime in the history of mankind. Now, that it is associated with Nazism, the evocation of racism has become the sharpest weapon against discriminations of all kinds, even when it does not fit. But by using the term racism, one risks, as we know, adopting what one fights against: one then fixates on discriminations, no matter what kind, just as discrimination fixates on its victims; one is then engaged in an abbreviating and derogatory anti-discrimination. Such procedures of anti-discrimination are, as often happens in our orientation and especially our mutual orientations, based on a paradox: by discriminating against discriminations, you at the same time support and fight against them. This may well, nevertheless, be effective in political altercations. But it again has paradoxical effects: if the terms of discrimination and racism are used too often and too broadly, they lose their distinctness and force.

It is very easy to discriminate as a member of one group against another group in order to strengthen the collective identity of one's own group and to thus assure oneself of one's own identity. It is already more complex to discriminate against discriminations and to thereby fight against them. Nevertheless, in those cases one holds on to the collective identities of anti-discrimination groups. But the structure of our orientation permits and invites us to refocus each of our own individual standpoints and to keep a distance from all collective identities, i.e. to pay attention to the affects and interests that play a part in all of them, and to pursue the fight against discriminations, if necessary for moral or political reasons, with circumspection, consideration, foresight, and confidence, which means in such a way as that one fixates neither on discriminations nor on the discrimination of discriminations.

In our orientation, which is and must be open to the fact that situations change and that different footholds may become relevant, the problem is the fixation as such, which is fortified by the forming of groups or collectives. One limits the possibilities of one's own orientation when clinging to fixed footholds, no matter when or where, but especially concerning other people. Identities are, as steady footholds in our mutual orientations, necessary; but one can be aware that these are just footholds – and not essential qualities that would justify any discrimination against others, let alone permanent discriminations like racism. Others' conspicuously different qualities and behaviors need not lead you to avoid contact with them, but they can instead make the contact with them more interesting – for your own orientation.

Prior generalizations, stereotypes, and collective identities mostly fall apart very quickly when individuals subsumed under them meet face-to-face; they may be steady but not strong footholds. By moving back from supposed essential qualities, which are the topoi of collective ideologies, to simple footholds in a situation, which allow for vast leeways for interpretation and thereby keep one from drawing premature conclusions, the philosophy of orientation has here particularly liberating effects. In this respect, it is not a sign of strength, but of weakness, when one clings to those collective identities of groups that lead to hostilities against other groups.

Instead, we can choose and decide between various private and collective identities that proffer themselves to us. We may satisfy our need to find an identity in a collective community only for a certain period of time. Our mutual orientations allow us to deal in multifarious ways with identities (with the exception of genetic identities) and, through dealing with them, perform an *individual identity*. Let us further explore how this works, beginning with individual and interindividual orientations.

11.2 Exploring Identities: Communicating about the Other and Oneself with Third Persons

In doubly contingent communication, it is of utmost interest for everyone to know more about both the personal identities of others as well as their image of one's own personal identity; you then would know what you can hold on to and rely on. However, we usually shy away from openly attributing them to others; the explicit naming of personal identities may – if they are unfavorable – hurt a person. Instead, by not explicitly pronouncing them, we try to keep open the leeways of our orientations to other orientations. We even avoid telling our names unless we have already established a certain familiarity or there is a conventional opportunity for this. It is even more aggressive to share one's assessment of others to their face without having a good reason or the authority to do so. Vice versa, you hardly ever ask someone directly what another person thinks of yourself; if you do so, the other person will try to give you a diplomatic response; confessions about oneself require a very specific situation. Even in very intimate relationships you usually refrain from telling each other how you think about and judge the other or yourself. This may continue for a lifetime. If you do it out of love or anger, you lack the distance necessary for a sober judgment; if you are in such distance, you avoid making personal judgment. That means: *when people deal with each other, personal identities are carefully protected and sometimes even made taboo.*

Hence, it makes sense to take a detour: to bypass the face-to-face situation by communicating about others and oneself with *third persons*. From third persons, you sometimes learn (voluntarily or involuntarily) how others think about you or someone else, often through statements about yet other third persons. If the person who is at issue is not present it is obviously much easier to talk about him or her. The communication about a third person has an additional side effect: by *how* the other speaks about third parties and characterizes and judges them, you may draw conclusions about how he or she may speak about you, if you were the third person. By communicating in an indirect and mediated way you may fathom the leeways of how someone assesses other people – which would not be possible in a direct way.

As such, we likewise proceed step by step and with care in these matters. Following established communication rituals, you first hold on to harmless issues, which everyone happens to deal with at that moment and which do not require any discretion, e. g. the train you are boarding together, the seats you have to look for, the beautiful scenery you will soon pass. As trivial as such subjects of conversation are, one can express oneself about them spontaneously or with hesitation, at length or briefly, as committed or bored etc., and thus indicate whether one is willing to continue the conversation. If the conversation then moves, e. g. to the current news, each side will express opinions that reveal information about his or her knowledge, interests, preferences, education, and political, aesthetic, and moral attitudes. And then it may also be possible to move on to sensitive exchanges about other persons known by both. It can then be 'very telling' whether the other, when the conversation is about a certain person, listens attentively or turns away, whether he or she asks questions or diverts the conversation, or whether he or she expresses him or herself straightforwardly or reservedly, carelessly or carefully, in a well-informed manner or by trafficking in rumors. If both interact and agree to a sufficient degree in such delicate communications, they establish trust in each other – at the expense of the persons they are talking about. If these third persons then hear about the conversation of the two, they may feel betrayed, especially in their intimate relationships. As Goffman puts it: "the tacit betrayal of the third person is one of the main ways in which two persons express the specialness of their own relation to each other."[45]

11.3 Sexual Orientation, Sexual Identities

Sexual needs are the most elementary besides eating, drinking, and free movement. Sexual orientation, one's own and that of others, is the most irritating and 'exciting' one; it is, at the same time, usually dealt with in a discreet way. Sexual relationships are, as has been scientifically well-documented, the most fascinating for human beings (as for animals); they sometimes force people to make significant decisions in their orientation. One's sexual orientation is, from one's youth onward, of crucial importance to the question of one's identity.

Human beings exist, like most (but not all) other animals, in a *sexual difference*; their procreation depends on it; most (but not all) people are biologically fixed on an alternative sex, male or female. Sexual characteristics are the most striking characteristics; the hormonal metabolisms and mental experiences of one's body differ significantly between the two sexes. In addition, most cultures specifically stress the sexual difference by emphasizing conspicuous footholds of alternative outfits and fixing social norms of sexual roles. Research has found anatomically significant deviations in the structure of the brains of the sexes; experiments have discovered different capabilities of their orientations in space or in language; and for women these capabilities fluctuate depending on menstruation and ovulation. Sexual difference may shape the orientations of the sexes in fundamentally different ways, without allowing the members of one sex to completely understand the orientation of the other. Sexual difference significantly shapes our orientations, which has increasingly been understood as *gender*;

the term 'gender' provides leeways for crossing the binary opposition of male and female in finding or reflecting one's personal and social identity (for instance, as a third gender).

Nevertheless, one's *sex identity* or *gender identity* is part of one's standpoint of orientation; it does not permit a superior or transcendent view that would allow one to draw independent comparisons between the genders. There cannot be any general knowledge about sexes or genders; everyone is already shaped and affected by his or her own sex or gender when talking about sexes and genders. Hence, the other sex is often regarded as notoriously 'mysterious' (famously the female sex for the male). Gender studies – which draws on Simone de Beauvoir, Jean-Paul Sartre, Michel Foucault, Emmanuel Levinas, and Jacques Derrida and was primarily initiated by Carol Gilligan, Judith Butler, Seyla Benhabib, and Luce Irigaray – has made it more and more plausible that sexual difference also permeates our moral and political orientations. The sexes may live in fundamentally different orientation worlds.

Even though one's sex identity does not have to be unambiguous, sexuality is mostly, despite the manifold leeways of gender, directed either toward the other sex or toward one's own sex, in so-called *heterosexual* or *homosexual orientation*. One speaks of sexual 'orientation' because there are different 'directions' for one's sexual desire, between which a choice seems possible: i.e. different orientations *toward* a certain sex. Since homosexual behavior is common even among animals, it is obviously neither 'unnatural' nor 'against nature.' This dissolves the myth of 'natural' norms: homosexual orientation has thus become a paradigm of enlightenment and emancipation.

But because we have yet to know what exactly is decisive in nature for someone to orient him or herself in a heterosexual or homosexual direction, the natural 'decision' seems random. Nevertheless, it is a decision that cannot be influenced (for all we know today). Here the will and its freedom are clearly limited. Sexual orientation is – beyond the leeways of gender – not chosen 'freely'; it cannot be changed by any known means. Thus, sexual orientation is a paradigm for learning to distinguish between the decidable and undecidable issues of one's life.

However, people who realize that they are homosexual must, under the given circumstances in most societies and cultures, make a big life decision: if they dare to 'come out,' they decide to a great extent their future social identity and thus their way of life as a whole. Such a decision may pose a heavy burden on them, but it may also liberate them to 'cheerfully' or 'gayly' act out their sexual orientation – and not only their own: gays and lesbians have, with their fight for sexual liberty and ingenuousness and against condemnation and prosecution, contributed substantially to expand the leeways for individuals in society as such.

But homosexual individuals may also decide to *not* come out, refusing to make public confessions about their private sphere. In doing so, they maintain the communicative spheres of distance in interindividual and social orientations, as they are common. They may then have to oscillate between different social identities – living the precarious identity of a double life. This may either separate their sexual orientation world from all others or, depending on how successful their decisions or non-decisions are, allow them to look for and find, in the spectrum of social identities, their own, individual identity. It may become convincing to themselves and others just through its cheerfulness or gaiety.

In the case of homosexuality, the sexual difference is still maintained. 'Lesbianism,' or female homosexuality, is experienced and lived in a different way than 'gay,' male homosexuality is, even if gays choose to act in a feminine way or lesbians in a masculine way. The social sanctions also differ: historically, female homosexuality was in most cultures less conspicuous and more tolerated than male homosexuality. *Transsexuality* does not override the sexual difference either but runs across it: transsexuals clearly belong to one biological sex, but they feel that they belong to the other, and they fight to be accepted through the social identity of this sex. To not live with a broken or double identity, they try to adhere to their sexual *orientation* by changing their biological *sex*, through hormonal treatment and gender reassignment surgery. On a social level, they are therefore perceived as even more irritating than homosexuals – and sometimes even more interesting as far as they further open the leeways of sexual orientation.

Intersexuals, who have biological features of both sexes, completely nullify the sexual difference. This complete suspension of the sexual difference is still disorienting for many today. Parents traumatized by the discovery of their child's intersexuality often decide – looking for unambiguous footholds – to clearly attribute, through likewise traumatizing surgeries, just one sex to the child, which can ultimately turn out to be the non-desired one. Trans- and intersexual individuals are at the greatest risk of suicide. Orientation obviously needs the reassurance that is produced by stable identities based on determined and socially acceptable differences. But if such differences are too restrictive in forcing one to live an undesired existence, then they will eventually be questioned too – with one's opportunity for liberation and emancipation on the one hand and one's risk of endangerment on the other.

Sexual orientations are paradigms for life orientations as such.

11.4 Performances of Acceptable Identities

Identities need not be articulated in terms; we more often stick to vague *images*. Given the precariousness and fragility of the doubly contingent communication between different orientations (especially in face-to-face situations), everyone is engaged with such images (including one's appearance, outfit, behavior, and statements) which one wants to bring up or maintain when dealing with others. In society, people routinely perform what is called *impression management*, some more, some less, some by emphasizing their good qualities, some by modestly holding back, some at the cost of others, some for the benefit of themselves – but all must do it, if they want to be accepted in some way in their societies. Impression management concerns "the presentation of self in everyday life" (Goffman), a self that becomes so normal that we mostly believe it to be our 'real' self. Nietzsche summed it up as follows: "We are like shop windows in which we are continually arranging, concealing or illuminating the supposed qualities others ascribe to us – in order to deceive *ourselves*." (*Daybreak*, No. 385, transl. by R. J. Hollingdale)

There is nothing wrong with this. Favorable self-presentations seem necessary for human beings to fruitfully deal with each other under the conditions of double contingency. To avoid embarrassing situations, which may be difficult to master, we are concerned – as again Erving Goffman showed – not only with our own self-presentation but also with the self-presentation of others with whom we are interacting and communicating. We always also work on their impression management; this is part of how we mutually pay attention to, observe, and respect each other. We then orient ourselves to a certain 'normal image,' which includes behaviors such as keeping one's balance (instead of losing it and falling over), securely orienting oneself in one's environment (and not wandering around searching for the path), being able to rely on one's memory (and not having to be reminded all the time), making clear decisions, controlling oneself, complying to social manners, etc. When another person fails in any of these capacities, you will spontaneously step in and help them and try to do this as tactfully as possible, preferably in a way the other person hardly notices: this is to 'save the situation,' and that means to preserve the situation of interaction and communication from further embarrassment.

In impression management, expectations likewise differ depending not only on gender, age, group, role, culture, and subculture, but also on the specific interactive situations. However, as far as self-presentation may involve multiples identities, these are to be kept coherent, at least to some degree: to make mutual orientations successful, self-presentations must still 'fit together.' In everyday orientation, especially under time pressure, you want to deal, as far as possible, with only one identity when interacting with others.

As such, doubly contingent interindividual orientation forces people into a routine-based and, for the most part, self-forgotten kind of *acting* in their self-presentations. This acting is, in most cases, hardly noticed – simply because most people willingly play along. But this does not mean that all people play the same game. This is not the issue, or at least not the main one. The issue is that we desire self-presentations to be striking, i.e. they must go beyond the minimal standards. Today, one speaks of a clearly distinguishable *profile*. It is not only professional actors or other celebrities who must exhibit a profile; in modern societies, individuals to some degree want to distinguish themselves from all others; hardly anyone wants to be the mere copy of another. In this way, qualities and characteristics considered especially attractive are accentuated and highlighted in order to make other and less attractive qualities less conspicuous. Profiles, with their striking contours, leave the rest unspecified: they thus invite others to 'complete' them on their own. In this way, profiles become especially interesting – human beings (and not only human beings) desire to be interesting for others. Profiles are stylized identities; and identities are only relevant if they attract and receive a sufficient amount of attention. Today, not only individuals, but also organizations, political parties, companies, sports clubs, museums, theaters, universities, and even administrations are in need of such profiles – in order to compete for attention.

Besides profiles, *stories*, or rather *narrative identities,* are also helpful in this pursuit. They must meet the needs of a *good* story, i.e. they must have a manageable amount of characters, a clear starting situation, turning and high points, and a consistent and exciting storyline; any element that might affect the story's clarity or suspense is to be reduced. Thus, you more and more adjust the stories of what you have experienced so that you can narrate them in an attractive way, and you more and more remember them in this way as well. As a result, you yourself become, over time, a well-told story, for others as well as for yourself.

Conspicuous narratives may eventually become literary stories or films. They are relevant for our orientations as well, especially for our orientations to other orientations: they gather a *repertoire of extraordinary courses of orientation,* which serve everyone as paradigms for how to find his or her way in extraordinary situations – and, in the long run, his or her identity.

11.5 Identification with Identifications: Identities in Dealing with Identities

If neither identities nor any essential qualities are given per se, one can let them develop and change over time on their own and commit oneself to them only when it is unavoidable. But one may accept or reject *ascriptions* of identities (within certain leeways); one can identify with them or not; this includes ascriptions by others as well as self-ascriptions or self-assessments. An identity that one 'has' is only an ascribed identity or an *identification* that one identifies with. The same is true especially for collective identities: depending on the societal leeways, one may or may not submit to a collective; and when submitting to a collective one may or may not identify with the respective collective identity. You can thus, in a word, *decide* on your identities.

In the double contingency of communication, identities are *doubly decidable:* as identifications of one's person by other persons and as one's own identifications with these identifications. As *(non-)identifications with identifications,* identities can be a matter of perpetually new decisions. In this way, they give leeways to a continuous shaping and presenting of one's own identity. It then depends on each individual orientation how much identification or identity it requires and to what extent it is able to find a balance between all its identifications or identities.

This eventually brings up the question of the possibility of an *authentic identity.* Under the conditions of one's inevitable self-presentation in society, the expectation of an authentic identity is again paradoxical. Even an authentic *self-*presentation is still a self-*presentation*; and what is called self-realization, self-actualization, or personal fulfillment cannot know the self it is to realize, actualize, or fulfill before it has actually been realized or fulfilled. The authentically realized self is the paradoxical vantage point of the desire for a permanent identity in relentlessly changing mutual orientations. You may orient your life to it just as you would an ideal. What is real in this case again is the self-referentiality, the possibility of keeping your balance within the leeways of your identifications with identifications, which will establish your own trust and that of others in a stable orientation. This means having an *identity in dealing with identities.* It comprises self-respect; and with self-respect (to repeat it), you most likely also gain the respect of others.

Chapter 12
Reckoning with Other Orientations: Economic, Mass Media, Political, and Legal Orientations
Orientation by Planning

12.1 The Needs for Survival and Co-Existence: Societal Orders and Individual Freedom

Rules and identities allow for orders that you can more firmly rely on in your orientation as you try to find your way in new situations with varying degrees of success: you can reckon with them. Through clearness and permanence, they produce a long-term hold, relieving and accelerating not only our own orientation but also (and even more) our orientations to each other. Basic survival needs, such as nutrition, reproduction, and safety, coerce us into following *common orders*, in which we depend on each other and which support, as much as possible, a smooth co-existence. The needs for survival and co-existence are managed through economics, media, politics, and the law. These orders create what we today call *society*. Societal orders strongly permeate the orientations of individuals, all the way down to how you deal with your own body and your own experiences. They usually develop as routines; but they can also be organized for specific purposes, and can then be enforced by select individuals or a few people, or they can be agreed upon through mutual consent via procedures, which are regulated as well. They are only maintained if the vast majority of people accept them. Through orders, which meet common needs, everyone grows more secure in his or her life and plans – at the price of losing leeways for action concerning his or her own needs. For that reason, they are also violated, repelled, and revolted against. Thus, societal orders themselves are more likely to survive if they provide *leeways* for different needs, interests, and individual orientations: i. e. *individual freedoms within common limits*. In this respect, they do not form a "shell as hard as steel" (*stahlhartes Gebäude*), as Max Weber argued: the limits of their leeways can shift (within limits as well), depending on how individuals make use of their freedom. The orders of human co-existence are likewise *fluctuant*.

Plans, which orders permit, are anticipated fixations of footholds, based on which you want to act. They remain tentative and provisional as far as they may always be challenged by a change of circumstances, making it necessary to change and perhaps abolish them. Thus, plans are – and must be – *fluctuant*; the more long-term and far-reaching they are, the higher the risk of having to

https://doi.org/10.1515/9783110575149-014

change or abandon them. The risk is low for both short-term plans and routine errands; it is high concerning individual life plans; and it is the highest when societal orders themselves are planned.

The societal orders of economics, media, politics, and law do not presume anything beyond the needs of orientation. They mutually make each other possible and limit one another. An economy flourishes only under favorable political and legal conditions; but politics and the law also need to prevent an economy from creating socially unbearable income gaps. Politics gains sufficient leeways for action only in favorable economic conditions and must stay within the limits of the law. The law can only be asserted through political power. To keep all three in balance, the media must continually report on them. *How* economics, media, politics, and law grow attuned to one another depends on a wide range of factors. Attempts to normatively construct them based on common moral principles indeed creates an overview, but their authors must largely disregard the actual interplay of things in their historical conditions. Niklas Luhmann's theory of social systems makes these systems comparable without any such principles, and it makes them comprehensible in their evolution. In this regard, it also offers the most instructive clues to a philosophy of orientation.

According to this theory, in Western civilization societal orders have developed, since the 18th century, into *functionally differentiated social systems of communication*. The former layered or "stratified" order of society, based on estates in which you would usually remain in the same position you were born into, shifted into "functional" orders, which were oriented to fields of specialization where everyone was able to develop his or her own individual skills. Traditions made way for functions, and the functions could be fulfilled most effectively if they were organized in autonomous "systems," which continued to differentiate independently within their own "environments." For Luhmann, the functional systems of economics, media, politics, and law, but also those of science, art, religion, and education operate based on their own distinctions or 'codes': economics operates according to the code of solvent/non-solvent, media to the code of interesting/not interesting, politics to the code of authorized/not authorized for the use of power, law to the code of just/unjust, science to the code of true/false, art to the code of fitting/not fitting, religion to the code of transcendent/immanent, and education to the code of better/worse with regard to certain societal requirements. What they have in common is only that they are separate systems of societal communication operating through different but comparable distinctions. In everything else, they are – according to systems theory – environments foreign to one another or – in terms of orientation – separate orientation worlds, which may influence each other in unforeseeable and surprising ways through their double contingency: Luhmann calls this "interpenetration."

Society's functionally differentiated systems of communication orient themselves to each other as well and, in doing so, also continually change themselves.

This is true not only for the functional systems, but also for the individuals who take up functions within them. Individuals too are, according to this conception, an 'environment' of a society's functional systems – they are physical and psychological systems, which both make use of the functional systems and are being used by them. Functional systems and individuals refer to each other in double contingency; they also provide leeways to one another.

The fact that individuals have leeways regarding to and within a society's functional systems is, in modern democratic societies, an essential aspect of their individuality. They can make their *careers* in them (or possibly against them). An individual's career is – in its positive meaning – his or her successfully oriented path through life. For this, one enters a functional system, via 'jobs,' where one fulfills functions; one can (in principle) move up the job ladder the quicker and better one fulfills one's functions. In doing so, one can also make the system more effective; a society's functional systems and individual careers can optimize each other (but may also destroy each other). Given appropriate skills, you may change the functional system and continue your career in a different one (a pastor may become a media star; a media star may become a governor). In modern societies, careers are (in principle) a matter of each individual's concern; as such, everyone is responsible for his or her own success or failure. Under the conditions of the functional differentiation of a society, freedom is both the freedom *from* the constraints of birth and *for* functions in functional systems, which you may be more or less suited for and in which you may thus more or less 'realize yourself.' You have the choice between the constraints of different functions; and within the leeways that remain, you may also, with appropriate skills, change the functional systems and then, if successful, be praised as innovative and creative.

For our everyday orientation, the functionally differentiated social systems of communication are *orientation systems.* The more familiar they become, the more comprehensive and reliable the footholds they provide; eventually they become separate orientation worlds, which you can alternately enter and abandon (chap. 8.4). As far as you are not engaged in one of them, you are usually occupied both with them and by them only from time to time and for a certain period of time. Their systematic orientations provide gains in orientation through *professionalization.* In functional systems, the functional professionalism can differentiate and increase without impediments, and this professionalism can be made use of as needed. However, orienting to a professional orientation generates its own paradoxes. The first and most common is the fact that, if you are not yourself a professional in a certain field, you will only have unprofessional clues by which to judge the professionalism of, e. g., a doctor, a lawyer, or a financial consultant, who you sometimes deal with. All you can do, again, is (as with mistrust) build trust (chap. 10.5); this trust will grow the more headway you make with a provided professional orientation.

Living in a modern society, you cannot escape some functional systems of communication – you *must* orient yourself to them: the systems of economics, politics, law, and – as far as it reports on these three (and more) – mass media. On the contrary, you can decide for or against taking part in science, art, or religion. In the case of education (which we have to leave out here), the alternative is not clear: you may remain resistant against the education that parents and schools provide, but you will then most likely be raised by 'life' itself. You thus orient yourself in different ways to the different functional systems, and they, too, orient you in different ways. Luhmann describes the functional systems regarding their self-organization and self-descriptions; this gives the (wrong) impression that they are, in their self-referentiality, isolated and entirely self-governed. However, functional systems must, in order to maintain themselves, connect with our everyday orientation and remain plausible and usable for it. They indeed unburden our everyday orientation from specific orientation achievements; they professionalize them. But functional systems have to provide these professionalized achievements in such a way that one can still orient oneself to them. This (and only this) is what the following chapter deals with: how, on the one hand, the functionally differentiated social systems, or as we call them, and the societal orientation systems orient us and how, on the other, one orients oneself to them in everyday orientation.

12.2 Economic Abbreviations: Goods, Markets, Money

Economics is, in the Greek sense of the word, the study of the rules of housekeeping and budget management. The ordering and planning of the household of a family, a business or a state deals with finding favorable opportunities for one's income as well as for the reduction of one's expenses. It brings a general feature of orientation to the fore: *the economic character of orientation.* Just as when managing a household you try to get by with scarce means while also seeking to use the available means as effectively as possible, orientation as such must, in order to make headway in a given situation, find the shortest and most convenient ways to seize the most favorable opportunities for action and to make use of the time available in a circumspect and farseeing way. Economics in this wider sense is a basic requirement of orientation: the *abbreviation of orien-*

tation of everything that is cumbersome, superfluous, and inexpedient. This is already true for how we deal with footholds and signs: here we also seek to quickly gain a quick overview of a situation based on as few footholds as possible, and with as few signs as possible, we try to make things as plausible as possible to others.

Economics in the narrow sense, the functional system of economics, operates with *specific abbreviations*. These include (a) the abbreviation of all that you need for living and must acquire from others, be they products or services, into *goods*. A good is meant to be sold to and bought by others; if something is or becomes a good, its use value turns, as we know, into an exchange value. Then the value depends on the needs of the people involved in an exchange: i.e. on how much *others* need a specific good; a good opens up an opportunity for exchange. Its value is determined by the needs of *others:* an exchange of goods comes about if one person needs something different than another person does, who in turn has that something which the other one needs. In this case, the bartered items have the same (exchange) value, yet different (use) values for each side – in this regard, the exchange of goods is based on a paradox, too. The exchange value is also negotiated in doubly contingent communications, during which you learn about how much the other needs the goods you possess. When doing so, you keep the other ignorant for as long as possible about how much you may need or want the goods they are offering. Thus, this specific economic orientation to other orientations is the observation of the needs involved. As far as you use this kind of orientation for your own benefit and to the detriment of others, you will, in a moral view, 'come off badly.' Vice versa, you can stand out morally when you forgo your own advantages. Nevertheless, the economic orientation in the exchange of goods is a basic necessity of life.

The doubly contingent communication about exchange values is (b) abbreviated into *markets*. Markets consist of exchange decisions (transactions), i.e. systems of selections related to each other. They may, but they do not have to be tied to certain places, certain times, and certain persons – vegetable markets more, capital markets less. At a commercial market, you focus only on the exchange value of the goods traded, while largely neglecting the individual circumstances of the people involved. The interindividual orientation to specific needs becomes less important: it is disregarded in the market orientation. One might regret this, but it also prevents discrimination: deals are made with (almost) everyone, and markets can be anonymous.

The market value of a good results from the anonymous comparison of the transactions that have taken place and are expected to take place; the economic orientation to other orientations is abbreviated into the observation of the selections made on the market. As such, in terms of orientation, *the 'market' is the situation of economics:* you have to orient yourself to and on the market if you want to act in an economically successful way. Concerning the market, you can only orient yourself as also part of the market; any of your actions on the market already change it (more or less). Thus, here too, an orientation's self-referentiality and temporality under the condition of uncertainty returns, entailing all the other basic conditions of orientation. A professional economic orientation requires making out, under the pressure of time, favorable opportunities for transactions on the market and having the courage to take risks. The market is surveyable only to a limited extent; in fact, precisely its limited surveyability (or transparency) permits different views of it and – relatedly – different opportunities to engage with it. A professional economic orientation expands or narrows its horizons depending on the available resources (chap. 5); in exchange decisions, it relies on the prices developing on the markets as footholds for the values of the goods, while avoiding affective assessments (chap. 6); it tries to establish its own 'brands' on the market which stabilize its business operations on a high price level (chap. 7); it operates with plausibilities, instead of on explicit reasonings and justifications, and trusts in business routines (chap. 8); it tries to make as far-sighted decisions as possible (chap. 9); it works on establishing long-term trust relations with business partners (chap. 10).

Eventually, the (c) exchange values of goods are abbreviated into prices in terms of *money:* everything else that goods and services can mean to someone or another is abbreviated into the one information of a scalable money value. Modern money has no (or hardly any) value by itself; it 'counts' only as a sign of value. As a system of explicit signs, which are defined by number values and other signs (images and written characters on coins and bills, watermarks, etc.), money belongs to orientations based on signs and the art of world abbreviation. Like every sign, money can have different meanings for different orientations; but on the market it keeps its fixed exchange value. Thus, it is a very strong foothold. It can exist not only in coins and bills, but also in transactions. As such, it detaches itself from materials and spaces. It can be stored for an indefinite time (as long as it is valid). Thus, it gives you more time to orient yourself, i.e. a delay allowing you to wait for more favorable opportunities in which to spend your money in the future. It relieves human orientation from the pressure of time; it reassures and increases our confidence in future opportunities for action; it allows us to more easily make plans. Money, Aristotle already argued, measures all things (*metreî*) and makes everything commensurable (*symmetron*), i.e. makes it equal (*isázei*, Nicomachean Ethics, V 8). Money makes the most different matters comparable and summable; you can calculate them according to their monetary value; and by decreasing or increasing prices, you can easily meet the other half way.

The money value of a good on the market dispenses with cumbersome communications about its different values for the interacting parties: it creates a common fixpoint for their mutual orientation. Usually (though not always), you can rely on the fact that gains in money are welcome – the more, the better. Even if money is morally disreputable when it is acquired for its own sake, it still creates the freedom to spend it on what you want – as long as basic needs are taken care of. Thus, regarded soberly, the abbreviation of goods into money entails gains in orientation, too: gains in time, trust, certainty, and freedom. Hardly anyone wants to do without this today.

However, given that the value of money is also traded on currency markets, it is not fixed, either. It, too, involves an oscillation and a balance between stability and instability. Trust in a currency may fall and be fully lost in the case of devaluations and inflations. The strongest foothold of the economic orientation may then again turn out to be the riskiest one.

12.3 Orientation in the Public: Overviews Produced by Mass Media

(1) Establishing an Anonymous Public Sphere via Mass Media. – Markets require information relevant to an anonymous public. Beyond the market economies, a public sphere is necessary for societies in which not everyone knows everyone else on a personal level anymore, but where everyone may influence the relevant matters of everyone else. What is public is what is known to (more or less) everyone; what is publicly known is the (largely) anonymous knowledge of a (largely) anonymous society. Public knowledge is part of an individual orientation's knowledge, but it involves *knowing that other anonymous people possess the same knowledge.* In its self-referentiality, it becomes independent of individual orientations: it still exists, even if this or that person does not share it. This creates a *new need for orientation:* you must continually keep track of public knowledge; and whoever is better informed may stand out. Most people can hardly influence public knowledge, but only take note of it, continue communicating it, and comment on it. They use it in a way to connect with others in communication ('Did you read that...').

Establishing a public sphere via media or mass media is a specific achievement of orientation. Mass media *professionalize communication*; this professionalization strikingly highlights another basic characteristic of mutual orientation. In modern democratic societies, mass media are also subject to *market condi-*

tions; the state's influence on the media is limited to regulating the market conditions, within the scope of which they are free; the state (above all the government) also exposes itself to the criticism of free media. Free media provide information to an anonymous market where they compete with each other, each trying to gain as many interested consumers as possible. On information markets, information also becomes a monetary good. Economic and mass media abbreviations or short-cuts thus overlap. This limits one's confidence in them. But they can also compete for truthfulness.

Mass media's development is based on new technologies, *specific distribution technologies:* book printing, broadcasting, television, electronic media. Before book printing was invented (which, along with other factors, initiated the early modern era), access to information of general relevance was controlled by the writing rooms of royal courts, monasteries, and cities. Information became public when it was, through book printing, made accessible to everyone on the markets mentioned above, which meant that it was anonymously accessible. From this public sphere, privacy then had to differentiate itself: since the uprising of mass media, our everyday orientation has had to distinguish between the public and the private. What is private is the information which you keep to yourself or which you reserve for your friends and acquaintances and which you can (more or less) control. You may on your part publicize your private information and, by doing so, re-draw the boundary. But the boundary can also be shifted by others, and your private information may be made public against your will; and what was once private and made public cannot become private again. Media establish a new mode of orientation, the mode of *irrevocable public awareness in a (largely) anonymous society*; electronic storage media increase this power even more. Contrary to interindividual orientation, it is nearly impossible to control shared knowledge in the societal orientation world. Here, anonymous others may always distribute their knowledge about you to other anonymous others wherever there is interest for it.

(2) Anonymous Orientation. – The anonymous public of mass media in turn provides the individual orientation with a new mode of anonymous orientation. With the help of mass media, you can observe anonymously; primarily via screens, you can look at others and watch them in a way that is hardly possible when interacting with them – here this would be frowned upon like peeking through a keyhole. You can shamelessly observe without yourself being observed in the act of observation. Mass media guarantee a legitimate distance when observing; they warrant a *distanced situation of orientation* in both the societal and global orientation worlds. This provides you with a standpoint where you can freely contemplate and reflect, i.e. with a special kind of freedom: you can form opinions about everything you are informed about through the media,

opinions without consequences, and you can do this as often and as long as you want, without having to do anything yourself; it is like being in a sports stadium where you can make loud suggestions to the players that they cannot hear. It is also a double distance, first to the events which the media report on, second to the media themselves: newspapers and magazines, radio and TVs as well as screens of all kinds mediate like geographical maps between the occurrences and those who orient themselves to them. We observe the media, not the reported events.

But media orientation, too, is characterized by irritations through surprises; the market conditions enforce this. Media have to periodically offer surprising irritations and thus purposefully look for them; even where information is not surprising (e. g. if the sales of a company remain unchanged, or if a celebrity marries once more), it still needs to be presented in a (more or less) surprising way. *Media render surprises an everyday routine.* To the recipients, they are usually not immediately threatening; but if you are concerned, they may have an alarming effect on you. You therefore always remain attentive to them. The routine of being regularly informed about surprises dampens the oscillation between unsettlement and reassuring calmness. It is easier to disregard media orientation than economic orientation; you cannot just put away the economy like a newspaper or turn it off like a screen; you mostly deal with mass media in relaxed situations when you are less pressed for time; in the distanced orientation to media, it is your choice as to whether you only want to acknowledge certain occurrences, or allow them to come closer to you, or if you actually want to engage them yourself: media guarantee their consumers the freedom to make use of them in whichever way they want. Just as with maps, it is 'in your hand' to take a look at newspapers and magazines or not, to turn receivers and screens on or off; and you are at liberty to switch between all of them. They are used as footholds, too, which you remain distanced from and which you rely on only with reservations.

Such *gains in freedom* regarding the anonymous orientation to mass media are routinely made use of and appreciated accordingly. However, there are also *losses in freedom.* When trying to orient ourselves in the societal and global orientation worlds we are almost entirely dependent on mass media, from community publications to global news stations, and the ways by which they select and prepare information: "Whatever we know about our society, or indeed about the world in which we live, we know through the mass media," Luhmann argues in his small, but crucial book *The Reality of the Mass Media.*[46] Since media themselves read, listen to, and watch each other, while (more or less) adopting, in the process of preparing their content, topics and tendencies from each other, they are perceived as a system ('the media'), which we are subject to or at whose mercy we are. As a system, media can be controlled in a publicly effective way only by other media. You thus feel 'manipulated' by 'the media' as a whole; you have no sufficient grasp of how much you can trust them or not.

(3) World Abbreviation by Mass Media. – By appearing or broadcasting periodically, mass media keep awake the expectation that surprises will come on a regular basis. By doing so, they put themselves under pressure, the pressure of *current actuality*. Mass media can be fast because they do not have to respond to their readers or listeners, nor do they have to wait for their responses. But as far as they operate on markets, they likewise *must* be fast, and faster than their competitors; they are the fastest and the most current if they report on current events as they happen, i. e. 'live.' However, the more current they are, the faster the newness of their information expires. Every new cycle of information makes the previous one 'look old.' The functional system of mass media is perpetually outdated and must renew itself all the time – just like orientation in general. By always keeping awake the expectation of something new, mass media continually unsettle themselves; they are thus also ready to continually transform their organizations, all the way to establishing new information channels, especially on the Internet, which are no longer controlled and operated by publishers or editors. Mass media that stick to fixed schedules of publication or broadcastings demonstrate the temporality of orientation, while simultaneously *giving a rhythm to orientation* and keeping the interims free so that you can do other things (e. g. a newspaper being distributed and read in the morning): they create temporal routines. The longer the topics persist and the less surprising they are, the more they are entrusted to books; and the more they need explanations and justifications, the more science takes charge of them. Scientific journals, too, appear in a certain rhythm, be it every week, every month, or in quarter-, half-, or full-year cycles; books are usually published according to the schedules of book fairs. As far as they bring something to light that proves to be of great interest, they may also appear on the current news.

Information media orient their consumers by selecting and preparing topics as *news*. In this way, they structure the events of the day (or the week, month, year...). News agencies and editors continually sift the current local, regional, national, or global situations with regard to occurrences of special interest, and they direct the public's attention to them. Thus, they *orient* you on a large scale without requiring any special effort from you. As comprehensive as their reports may be, they are still extremely *selective* in which events they cover; they always only report on a tiny fraction of what on a single day may be relevant in the world. At the same time, they exaggerate the relevance of what they are reporting on. Thus, the results of a local baseball game may seem to be more important than a famine on another continent. What is newsworthy is that which offers sufficiently salient, consequential, and, ideally, affectively attractive foot-holds. Such footholds are especially expected, on the one hand, from so-called 'very important persons' (VIPs), and from conflicts and catastrophes, on the other. As such, media tend toward elitism and negativism. Enhancing something from 'harmlessly new' to 'sensationally new' may be advantageous on the mass media market.

Mass media not only take up those conspicuous topics that proffer them-selves, but they are also able to *make* something into a topic; and, of course, they can also awaken the interest for new matters of relevance hitherto neglect-ed. As a result, as far as the reality that we are continually re-introduced to is a reality produced by mass media, our reality depends (at least partially) on mass media's orientational strategies. And as far as mass media make selective deci-sions, which we can discern to a limited extent but hardly control, they inevitably exert power on our orientation. As they are always ready to quickly reorient themselves in light of new footholds, they are major models of forgetfulness. As true as they may be, they do not create certainty about reality, but provide their own reality, to which we get more and more accustomed – until we believe it is the true reality. Thus, we have to trust and distrust them, as we are fed with certainty and uncertainty at the same time.

In such an anonymous, distanced, and rhythmic way, news media offer ex-emplary *overviews* – the aforementioned paradox of all overviews returns under new conditions. Traditional print media provide an overview by arranging arti-cles in a two-dimensional space, thus offering simultaneous opportunities for making selections: you have to 'skim' everything in order to find out what you want to read in detail. When you focus on some articles, the professional prep-aration of news systematically furthers the *art of world abbreviation*. News arti-cles are ordered according to relevance: the most important (or what is consid-ered thus) is on top of the front page; within articles, there is at first the current relevance highlighted by the 'headline' or 'catch line,' which is intended to at-tract attention; then there is the thematic designation, i.e. the categorizing sub-line, then the kernel of the message, the 'lead,' and eventually the compre-hensive account of the background details. The orientational distinction between center and periphery has thus already been established for the reader. You can stop reading at any moment; you can yourself decide on the selection, sequence, depth, and speed of your current orientation. However, electronic information media (radio and TV) do not offer the leeway of abbreviating by 'skimming' or 'skipping.' Rather, they preset temporal sequences, thereby demonstrating how they assess the relevance of the news. But broadcasts do permit you to separate your attention (you do not have to watch; you can also engage with something else at the same time). Television can also show events themselves in smaller clips – but of course only if the events were already expected or if people happened to be present with cameras or smartphones. In this way, you may see an authentic 'candid shot' – but of course only to the extent that pictures have been chosen in a way you cannot check yourself. The 'new' media that are working with screens and in part with short films in turn permit you to skim and skip again; but they produce so many and manifold overviews that your general overview of them may quickly be lost.

Overviews of orientation via information media are distinguished not only according to their depth (from short news items all the way to comprehensive reports and background reports, interviews with participants, commentaries, etc.) but also according to their topics: the news is classified by *sections*. Sections preset certain *orientation worlds*, such as politics, economics, culture, media, sports, technology, science, career, family, fashion, health, entertainment, travel, etc. With the help of mass media, you can flip the pages between them or change the channel. As short-lived as news items are, the sections nevertheless live on: they consolidate (or suggest) certain plausibilities (you have to keep up with fashion; you have to stay healthy in this or that respect; exercising keeps you young; everyone has hobbies; during your vacation you ought to travel); thus they shape our everyday orientation and structure our collective memories. Numerous formats entertain us with dramatic happenings providing us with *paradigmatic orientation processes* and *identification models*.

The transition to *entertainment* is fluid; 'reality shows' offer information *as* entertainment (staged with much suspense). The new social media have largely opted for mutual entertainment. Media entertainment, too, must offer, in some form, something new, be it new persons in the same course of events, be it new stories in the same formats, be it new formats for the same needs of entertainment. The most attractive entertainment media have been and largely still are professionally created *films*, which show attractive stories in attractive pictures. Films, where the viewers are sitting in the dark, may show things usually veiled by the spheres of distance in everyday routines: faces, naked bodies, sexual acts, intimate conversations, private moments of all kinds. They provide leeways by which to cast off the constraints of daily life without the danger of sanctions; they offer opportunities to reflect on one's own routines of orientation from a distance. Films may also (and simultaneously) play through moral conflicts in unusual circumstances (so-called 'fates' of characters) and test out the leeways for transgressing norms. They entertain our orientation in a double sense: they keep us from getting bored and feed us with opportunities for action and life plans, with which we may identify for a certain time (you may observe this when, after watching an impressive western, you walk around for some time with the swagger of a cowboy). With the *fluid boundary between information and entertainment*, i.e. 'infotainment' and (regarding politics) 'politainment,' the boundary between reality and fiction becomes fluid too.

12.4 Political Circumspection and Foresight: Decisions for a Society

(1) The Orientation of and through the Political System. – The political system, too, needs orientation. Politics involves making binding decisions for a society; in modern democratic societies, this must happen in agreement with the respective society; as such, politics must be simultaneously oriented for and to this. Its decisions are to ensure a society's life chances and opportunities for action in the near and distant future; and in such decisions, divergent interests and conflicts are likely to occur. Politics therefore not only requires a survey, but also a high degree of foresight in order to set goals and make use of given opportunities for action in order to achieve these goals. Whenever this is not possible in a direct way, politicians need precaution and consideration in order to bypass or overcome obstacles via short-term 'tactics' and long-term 'strategies' as well as circumspection in order to use opposing interests for their own benefit or to attain trade-offs and compromises wherever interests can be asserted only in cooperation. In short, politics involves dealing with the whole range of orientation virtues.

The further a political orientation extends into the future, the more serious risks that arise and the more its uncertainties increase. Politics faces *uncertainty* as such; it is the *planned handling of uncertain possibilities of action in a society.* The first chancellor of the German Empire, Otto von Bismarck, who has been considered one of the most gifted and cleverest politicians in history, is supposed to have described politics as the "art of the possible." There is a kind of planned handling of uncertain possibilities of action already with regard to our individual and interindividual orientation worlds as far as we are concerned with the advancement of ourselves as well as of those whom we care for; economic and media orientations cannot do without it either. However, with regard to the needs of a society as a whole, it is in turn professionalized in a specific way. Its basic requirement is the general capability of adapting to rapidly changing situations and of frequently making quick decisions under an oftentimes extreme pressure of time. That such decisions are, in the light of global interdependencies, in times of crisis, and particularly under the threats of terror and war, largely decisions made under the condition of uncertainty makes politics an extremely demanding orientation practice.

As with economics, politics too concerns the entire orientation of a society. The political system differentiates in its own way into specific domains, such as foreign policy, national defense, domestic policy, homeland security, fiscal policy, the legal system, economics, healthcare, education, etc. Depending on the current needs of a society, the domains can be augmented or reduced, the responsibilities can be specialized or generalized, and the departments can work more or less autonomously. By organizing the management of the relevant interests of a society, the government also orients the society to these interests – of course in the government's view, which is again a politically motivated one. In doing so, politicians have to decide what is relevant for the future of the society as such. They, too, decide self-referentially: they check, in each decision they make, to what extent they can expand their own influence. Thereby they must, on the one hand, demonstrate resoluteness (i.e. they must decide not to make different decisions over and over again; see chap. 6.3); on the other hand, they are particularly subject to the double contingency of communication as they are bound to always deal with other more or less combative political parties. If they do not want to permanently jeopardize the peace of a society, they must make sure that their political opponents are also able to communicate and connect with the public as far as they advocate for matters that are plausible and widespread in that society. The recursivity of orientation, too, is particularly obvious in politics: politics already changes the situation of a society by simply taking up and addressing certain matters, especially, but not only in election campaigns; it marks, identifies, and prioritizes them over other competing matters. But politicians can also to some degree evade the persistent pressure to act – by acting only 'symbolically,' i.e. by merely marking a situation that requires political action using attractive signs but without actually acting upon it. Obviously, hardly any other area of orientation makes use of the conditions of orientation as resolutely as political orientation; but it does so with specific limitations, too, at least in the case of modern democratic societies, which we will focus on.

(2) Political Representatives. – If you make a decision for yourself, you have to bear the consequences; if you decide for others, they have to bear what follows. This is the case in the interindividual orientation world in which you have taken on orientation tasks for other individuals, e.g. as a parent, teacher, advisor, doctor, psychotherapist, pastoral counselor, etc. This is even more true, although less obvious, in the societal orientation world where politicians take on responsibilities for an anonymous public, which nevertheless consists of individuals who are quite capable of deciding for themselves and who are therefore, in modern democratic societies, supposed to autonomously decide on their own matters. While informal attunements are usually sufficient for per-

sonal relations within surveyable groups (when decisions of concern to everyone must be made, the involved persons may slowly, without time pressure, come to an agreement), unsurveyable large societies require formal votes. In fact, in direct democracies, which are rare today, citizens of age are allowed to vote on factual issues, whereas in indirect or representative democracies they vote only on the representatives in parliaments, who must then decide on both factual and additional personnel matters. Even if the people are the sovereign who independently decide on their own matters, they can only do this with great organizational effort – their decisions must be organized by institutions within the political system itself. Thus, the sovereign's (i.e. the people's) possibilities of deciding about their matters are fundamentally limited: being confined to the periodic election of persons who in advance commit to specific political orientations, but who, in what follows, inevitably follow their own orientations. In addition, the candidates are usually selected by political parties, which themselves belong to the political system; but parties are organized to manage conflicts with other parties – *within* the political system again. As a result, representatives of the people are, at the same time, representatives of their parties, and usually they are more oriented toward their parties than toward the people.

(3) Political Elections. – Elections thus largely shift the leeways of the sovereign's political decisions into the political system itself and leave them only a literal marking (the check on the voting ballot) at periodic intervals. Just as the system of mass media structures, in a factual and temporal way, the orientation needs of individuals regarding societal matters, the political system does so regarding the possibilities of making decisions about them. It shapes the leeways of the sovereign's decisions – this is the paradox of the bound sovereign. This may be upsetting and frustrating. But elections also keep – provided their outcomes are not manipulated – the political system open to irritations: in modern democratic societies, the system is organized in a way that it must periodically expect surprises from voters. Even if the sovereign's participation in their political orientation may eventually only be marginal, they can nevertheless periodically bring about drastic political reorientations. As a last possibility, individuals in democracies have the liberty to engage themselves in politics (beyond simply making a mark on the voting ballot), thereby gaining leeways for deciding *within* the political system.

(4) Majority Decisions. – Through elections, divergent political orientations in a society are merged to a common orientation regarding common decisions that are to be made and then executed. Elections of parliaments are conducted as majority decisions; and in parliaments or governments, decisions are largely – formally or informally – made by majorities, too. Majority decisions bring about further crucial abbreviations of the political orientation. In the immediate or di-

rect democracy of Athens, decisions on common matters were made via – and this was an innovation – contests of speeches (*lógoi*). Thus, everyone (every Athenian male citizen of age) was able to immediately contribute to every political decision. But he then also had to carry the immediate consequences. This could entail (not uncommon) decisions on war or peace, and these could mean, in the case of a victory – one that had to be fought for by these men themselves – greater power and wealth for the city (*pólis*), and in the case of a defeat the loss of each person's family and property, enslavement, or violent death. As far as persons were running for election – and this is true for democratic elections up to the present day – they were permitted to make full use of the diplomacy of signs (chap. 10.5) and the ascription of identities and qualities (chap. 11.1) without reservations in order to gain the approval of the voters. As far as factual decisions were (and still are) campaigned for with arguments, such arguments primarily had to (and still must) be effective, whether they be true or not. Plato attacked this by distinguishing between 'sophists,' as those committed only to effects, and 'philosophers,' as those committed to the truth, or, in short, as those striving for either power or reason. That everyone agrees with each other in reason if everything reasonable concerning a decision is sufficiently made clear – this was obviously just an assumption of his. As his own dialogues, which mostly end in aporia, demonstrate, he did not in fact expect anything like this; up to the present day, we do not really expect this in political decisions either. For if that were the case, after all arguments were articulated and deliberated majority decisions would be superfluous. Politics does not operate like science. If politicians call upon science, they usually do this with political intentions that both diverge from each other and create divergent results.

Majority decisions involve processes of significant reorientations. They presuppose that the authorized decision-makers initially orient themselves from their own standpoints, form their own opinions, commit to them after debating them with others, and eventually identify with them. However, these opinions are precisely what is disregarded when a vote is taken; majority decisions are outstanding *abbreviations:* what is up for a majority decision must be abbreviated to a simple Yes/No alternative, even in the case of problems of high complexity and with greatest diversity of footholds. For only in this way can votes be added up to make a majority. After determining the *majority* of votes, the *minority* of votes can be disregarded – abbreviated, too. Those who voted against the majority now have to give up their own opposing standpoint – counter to their own understanding – for the sake of the society's common capacity for action; the minority not only have to act according to the majority, but also – as is particularly obvious in the case of ancient Greece – accept and bear the consequences, which at times include death. Thus, majority decisions entail a paradox according to which you are asked about your opinion under the condition that you are willing to disregard this opinion and follow the opposing one. They demand skilled and routined reorientations over the course of the decisions being made: from your – perhaps circumspect and farsighted – view of the common political matters to a view based on a Yes/No abbreviation, which was decided for by a majority and which you have to – for just this reason – support with loyalty. Loyalty is a commitment to a person or, in this case, a collective identity, which supersedes the desire to dissent. Through reorientations in the course of majority decisions, citizens and their political representatives learn to be considerate of other standpoints and to develop a flexible political orientation, both of which are necessary when living together with other people in cities and states. In order to achieve compromises, cooperations, and coalitions, they both must be able to resolve conflicts of different political orientations not only against others, but also within their own orientations.

(5) Gains and Losses in Orientation through Majority Decisions. – The abbreviation of complex situations of decision into mere Yes/No alternatives in majority decisions entails obvious losses in orientation. However, it also brings about significant gains in orientation. First, there are gains in time: by voting, disputes and argumentations can be broken off – decisions can be accelerated. If decisions are made faster, more can be decided on in less time, and the political realm can expand more and more. We can observe this in the modern democracies of the United States and Europe since the end of the 18th century: beyond the traditional concerns of politics, i.e. security both without (wars) and within (the administration, the police, the legal system), the levying and collection of charges and taxes, the management of immigration and the increase of economic activities (both as resources for taxes), 19th and 20th century politics also added public education, social security, the health of citizens, natural resources and energy, the preservation and increase of the labor force, and eventually, in the second half of the 20th century, increasingly equal career opportunities, the non-discrimination of disadvantaged population groups, the promotion of culture, the protection of nature, the maintenance of the equilibrium of global ecology, and the guarantee of humane living conditions for even future generations. All these require more and more decisions, which risk being no longer sufficiently surveyed and understood and which therefore no longer find everyone's support to engage in compromise and loyalty. If this support faces too high of demands, then majority decisions, which are now mostly made by representatives, jeopardize democratic processes and institutions as such. The society may then split; new parties on the fringes of the political spectrum may emerge; protests and mass movements may be organized; new kinds of revolutions may be unleashed. Yet, if, despite all these challenges, the political system still maintains its dem-

ocratic form, then these changes may trigger new evolutions that enable the political orientation to keep up with the times.

(6) The Stabilization of the Political System and the Differentiation of the Political Orientation. – However, the more the political system is subject to time, the more it must provide the means by which to maintain its stability. As a self-referential system, it likewise stabilizes itself by virtue of its own differentiations. This began with the fact that, some hundred years ago, it constituted itself in European countries as a 'state.' 'State,' from Lat. *'status'*, means, on the one hand, a current 'state' that may rapidly change and, on the other hand, a 'permanent existence.' A political state must be both: an enduring state of order that allows for more or less rapidly changing states. A political society constituted as a political state needs stability in order to be flexible: internal stability for coping with changing external situations, and external stability permitting internal change in an orderly manner. Internal stability primarily entails the containment and prevention of physically life-threatening violence (Lat. *violentia*), which is in turn only possible – again, paradoxically – by means of physical violence. According to Thomas Hobbes' epochal insight, the political state constitutes itself by monopolizing violence; but, as a violence legitimated by law, it becomes a non-violent 'power' (Lat. *'potestas,'* German *'Staatsgewalt'*) that garantuees peace, security, and order in a society. In modern democracies, this power is differentiated into the three branches of government, executive, legislative, and judicial, all of which are decision-making powers: the executive decides on political measures within the system of existing laws, the legislative on the laws themselves, and the judicial on the interpretation of these laws. Thus, they depend on and control one another. Their checks and balances create a self-sustaining network of powers, which has become the classic model for stabilization through differentiation as such.

The separation of powers also brought the *left-right-distinction* into political orientation – when, during the French Revolution, the establishing parties were distinguished as sitting either to the right or the left of the chairperson in the legislative assembly. This spatial orientation has no bearing on the goals of each party; right could have been left and left also right. The left-right distinction only symbolizes the political opposition which still persists (as in the British House of Commons) in the *distinction between government and the opposition*, which likewise is not to imply a factual or moral priority. In a democracy, the present government is not 'more right' than the opposition, nor does it have a higher moral value; instead, it is only legitimated to exert power for a certain period of time. However, to escape criticism, the government presents, as far as possible, its exercise of power as one without alternative, whereas the opposition will do everything to portray the government's actions *as* decisions, to which it can offer better alternatives. In political orientation, democracies thus visibly highlight the significance of decisions, which are crucial in any orientation. By the – at times spectacular – exchange of persons in official 'positions,' which have been established in cabinets, ministries, and the subordinate administrations to make and carry out political decisions, the political system demonstrates fluctuance as well: here, persons can not only change these positions, but persons can also create new positions and thus keep the entire political system and the political orientation in ongoing flux.

(7) The Origin of Power in Orientation Responsibilities. – Both the political orientation and the preparation of political decisions are responsibilities of the political system as a whole, which includes the opposition, various lobbies, and the media, as far as they provide political information or agitate in political ways. Making decisions, exercising them, and, if necessary, enforcing them against resistance is the responsibility of the present government, which is authorized to exercise power. But, by means of clever contributions, even the opposition can exert public pressure and, by doing so, power, too. In democracies, power arises from taking on tasks of orientation, decision, and regulation for the society; and in this sense, power is – despite the negative moral reputation it has for many – welcome in most cases. For power guarantees orders for living together, such as orders in traffic, schools, and businesses, etc.; and most people need such power-guaranteed orders; they rely in their individual orientations on them; regarding political orders, even dictatorships are preferred to anarchy. The power of a superior orientation is a positive manifestation of power and, simultaneously, the crucial foothold for political orientations. Some can indeed attain power through corruption, force, and sheer violence, and they may continue to stay in power. But such measures are less necessary the more the exercise of power is oriented to the good of the ruled. Power, too, brings about its paradoxes, as again Niklas Luhmann shows: it is stable precisely when one does not need to make manifest use of it; this is why rulers generally try to avoid making manifest use of power – for power must always reckon with countervailing power. Thus, power is primarily in effect as a "threatening power" ("*Drohmacht,*" as Luhmann calls it), i. e. a power one only threatens to exercise as long as order and peace prevail and in order to make them prevail.

(8) Assigning Political Responsibility. – Power (or those who exert it), as the crucial foothold of political orientation, is also the first address to which responsibility is assigned for everything that is perceived as unsatisfying in a society. The attribution of responsibility is often focused on the political system as a whole, but in the end it falls upon individual persons (chap. 14.4); mass media tend to amplify this focus. Assigning political responsibility to 'those in power' or to the 'rulers' is part of the usual abbreviations in political orientation.

The authorized persons have to take on the 'political responsibility' for every-thing that happens within their area of responsibility, even if mistakes were made by a subordinate employee and those in power did not personally know anything about them. This again creates a self-referentiality, a responsibility (e.g. of a minister) for others responsibilities (of his employees), and this self-ref-erential responsibility creates again a paradox: for a responsibility for other re-sponsibilities is, on the one hand, factually not in one's own power, and yet it is, on the other, an enhanced responsibility. But in truth, in modern political sys-tems the responsibility for political decisions and their implementations can be attributed to specific persons only to a limited degree. In the current exercise of political power and responsibility, not only are entire administrations in-volved, but also one's own political party or parliamentary group, possibly a gov-erning coalition and the governing cabinet, and, in addition, the electorate, the other functional systems of the society, stakeholders and interest groups, as well as the media; political decisions may furthermore include, in times of growing globalization, confederations of states (such as Mercosur or the EU), internation-al organizations (like WTO, IMF, or UN), world-wide government organizations (such as G8 or G20), etc., and eventually the morally highly-motivated non-gov-ernment organizations (NGOs). At times, NGOs offer concrete help in the case of an emergency, when governments cannot or do not want to help. But they also take on observation and orientation tasks – with the overt intent to call on others to take political responsibility without themselves taking on this responsibility and without them having the authority to do so.

As such, political responsibility becomes itself unsurveyable and confusing – it requires an orientation regarding itself. Politicians orient themselves – also with respect to future elections – increasingly to the degree of the popularity of their decisions. They now move to preemptively test crucial political projects with regard to the voters' opinions using mass media and public opinion polls. In this way, they detach themselves from ideologies and the programs of political parties, and as such, politics becomes more flexible. This may be regarded as in-creasing democratization, and it may prevent protests. However, it may at the same time feed the impression of a growing disorientation among those in power. Thus, the attribution of political responsibility is abbreviated (or simpli-fied) even more: focusing on the politicians as persons, especially the leading politicians, ends with the result that their persons, decisions, and actions are simply judged as good or evil, a judgment everyone feels entitled to make no matter how deep his or her factual insight goes. The more difficult it is to under-stand and to bring into order the factual political contexts, the more people ori-ent themselves to persons; the more difficult it is to assess the skills and achieve-ments of persons, the more people adhere to judging them in moral terms.

This too must be taken into account by leading politicians. Today, leading politicians are challenged by the extraordinary ethical demand of taking on an (in principle) unlimited responsibility for all matters of their societies as well as of the world society. Besides the aforementioned virtues of orientation, they are expected to be generally open-minded to all needs of their and the world's society and to be unprejudiced toward nearly all orientations – but, at the same time, they are to make and execute decisions according to their own standards and visions. As a result, a realistic assessment of democratic politicians and their skills and options becomes increasingly difficult – and this may have the effect that more and more autocratic politicians are – through another kind of abbreviation – idealized and elected into highest offices. One then believes in 'strong' persons with superhuman orientation skills who may provide immediate solutions for hitherto unsurveyable problems.

This in turn forces politicians to perform more striking self-displays, which at the same time are intended to meet the demands of mass media. In a personalized and moralized media landscape, politicians must stand for political goals and actions that are as simple and easy to understand as possible; by doing so in the public, they must disregard the complex contexts surrounding their decisions. Their self-display thus becomes paradoxical as well: they must, in order to appear trustworthy, portray themselves as 'authentic'; but in front of the camera they can do so only by making full use of the diplomacy of signs. Everyone knows this – or could know it. But this only further increases the politicians' responsibilities, which now include the responsibility of providing a clear orientation to the governed in contexts that are factually difficult to survey.

12.5 Securing Intentions by Law: Guaranteed Coercions for Guaranteed Leeways

(1) *The Orientation of and through the Legal System.* – The law protects (legal) intentions by using force: force against others with the help of third persons authorized by the state to apply judicial norms in order to support one's intentions and, as far as the norms' applications prove justified, to have them enforced with coercive means by the state. This guarantees some security for one's orientation. Wherever law is in effect, it prevents assaults against body, life, and property; it wards off dangers by virtue of codified commandments and prohibitions reinforced with prescribed sanctions. Through explicit rules for future actions, the law creates the most stable societal order and thus the strongest hold of orientation in the societal horizon.

The concept of the law is also controversial, but debates on legal theory and legal philosophy do not affect its operability or our orientation to it. In a modern legal order, laws are explicitly codified with defined terms for (usually) an unlimited time. Laws are *norms*, from which you can deviate or which you may violate. The concept of 'norm' comes from Lat. *'norma,'* which originally means, like Lat. *regula* and German *Regel*, an 'angle measure,' a 'yardstick,' or a 'ruler': thus, a norm is a means of orientation that directs it through previously defined points of reference. Up until the end of the 18th century, this original meaning of the term was commonly known to most people, including Kant. From the 19th century on, a sense of obligation came to the fore in the concept of norms; thus laws were understood as 'legal norms.' At the end of the 19th century, moral philosophers also adopted the term 'norm' in this sense; the sense of it as a means of orientation receded. But it was not entirely lost.

This is why the law is not an end in itself, either. Laws are needed to prevent conflicts as long as such conflicts push a society again and again into hardship; if total prevention is not possible, laws are to at least limit conflicts. In short: laws are set when hardships get out of hand. Laws, for instance, to keep the air or the water clean were passed only when the air or the water was polluted to an unbearable degree: legal norms often connect to routines and the so-called customary law, i.e. to that which usually happens anyways, but where the deviations or violations have been too frequent or too severe to be tolerated any longer. Thus, legal norms regulate how people live together in a society only in specific respects. They are therefore initially contingent, i.e. they are neither based on metaphysics, nor justified by principles, nor organized in systems.

However, as far as hardships can be controlled through legislation, guaranteed leeways of action are created for the future. The law thus brings about gains in time as well. But this is true again only for a certain time: if the occasions which brought forward new legislations disappear, then such laws become obsolete and may be changed, repealed, or abolished. As such, laws have a limited time, too. But they nevertheless provide more stability than mere routines do – with the effect that laws may remain long after the occasions that caused them have disappeared. They may have become plausible in such a way that no one afterward asks about their original meaning (this is particularly true for many administrative rules). Then, laws have attained, *as* laws, unquestioned trust; and this kind of trust is the strongest hold of a legal order.

(2) The Authority of the Law. – As long as the law is trusted, the governmental means of power used to enforce it can stay in the background – just as the governmental power itself can remain as a 'threatening power.' The certainty that it *can* be enforced if necessary is mostly sufficient for the law to be respected. It thus only needs to be claimed in critical cases. It then is claimed as *the* law,

as a collective singular, even if it is far from being a systematic unity. As *the* law, it is considered to have a position beyond humanity, originally a divine or god-like position; ancient cultures often assumed a god as the first creator of the law. In this way, the law was to be withdrawn from the ever-changing influences of human beings: it was assumed that in the long run only a god could order the notoriously litigious relations of human beings. The law was to stand as a third party above the contentious human beings, representing its own superior or supreme power, before which everyone was to be equal. The law, appearing as a kind of mystical unity, was to receive unquestioned authority. Michel de Montaigne and Blaise Pascal thus spoke of a "mystical foundation of the authority" of the law and recommended the matter be let to rest. Jacques Derrida made this mystical foundation, as a "legitimate fiction," debatable again.

(3) The Differentiation of the Judicial Orientation. – The divine foundation of the law and its mystical unity was, at some point in the process of the differentiation of the law, no longer plausible. Overly detailed legal regulations subject to constant amendment were too much to ask for from the gods. But even after the strict separation of law and religion in Western modernity, human beings could not do without a third party limiting, through its authority, their collective propensity for violence. The role of this third party was now taken up by the law itself, based on the authority it had so far acquired. The divinity was substituted by an abstract entity (often allegorized, in a nostalgic manner, as a personal entity; we are all familiar with the statues of justice in front of courthouses). In truth, the authority of the law materialized in diverse administrative bodies of justice, none of which was all-powerful, but each of which was powerful enough to guarantee permanent solutions by threatening to deploy the coercive measures of the state. In this way, the law's authority did not fade. On the contrary, it has grown even more through the separation of law and state in modern constitutional states, which base the state's power on the law and thus limit, by law, the coercive measures of the state with regard to individuals. Securing fundamental rights as fundamental freedoms likewise guarantees individuals their leeways of orientation against the very state which establishes this guarantee. According to Ernst-Wolfgang Böckenförde, a German scholar of constitutional law and at one point a member of the German Supreme Court (*Bundesverfassungsgericht*), individuals are, in a constitutional state, "put into freedom to search for their own orientation – it is this freedom which is protected and which individuals experience as a fundamental right." This freedom is no longer understood "as a metaphysical freedom, nor as a transcendental or objective freedom, but as a subjective freedom of the individuals in the sense of freedom of choice and self-determination."[47]

In a constitutional state (which in fact operates as such), everyone can expect (with more or less concern) that – besides the effective protection against private violence and the guarantee of his or her acquired rights, ensured by coercive measures of the state – his or her civil liberties, especially the rights of free movement and free speech, the right of physical integrity, property rights, the rights to personal identity and to freedom of personal development, are secured; that furthermore, everyone is treated equally without regard to the person; that anyone can bring disputes to independent and unbiased civil courts to make decisions on them; and that everyone can expect the courts to check administrative decisions if there are (or seem to be) obvious faults in them. The establishment of supreme courts in turn ensures that only the law itself can make decisions about the law – i. e. that the law can organize itself as an autonomous or self-referential system. Since the institution of the constitutional state was attained through many hard fights over the centuries, the *expectation of guaranteed coercions for guaranteed leeways* in the everyday orientation of citizens (in modern and functioning democracies) has become self-evident.

(4) Transformation and Failure of the Law; Legal Culture. – Due to its self-referentiality, the law (or the legal system via the political system) can change itself, even though it is meant to pin down permanent norms. And there is constant pressure to change laws: not only from people who are discontent with a certain legal status, but also from politicians who want to distinguish themselves by making adjustments to the law. In gaining authority, the law also increases the expectations people have for it. This leads to an expanding juridification of the living conditions of a society, which may not only set the whole legal system in flux, but which may also make it itself highly unsurveyable. As such, the law falls into a paradox, too: the more comprehensive, unsurveyable, and fluid the law becomes, the more difficult it is to enforce; and the more limited its force and effects are, the more its own authority is undermined. This may bring about a so-called 'legal failure.' Such a failure may take various forms: necessary political compromises may obscure the legislation's goals; illegalities may be tolerated by the law (e. g. abortions, in countries where they are forbidden); the number of unrecorded cases may outnumber the cases complying with the law or those prosecuted by the law. In the case of economically or politically powerful legal entities or persons, who would otherwise be difficult to persuade to comply with the law, one moves, for the sake of a cooperative state, from sovereign decrees to the negotiation of laws, in the interest of making legislative deals. The law is then no longer only the leeway *within* which but also the leeway *which* one negotiates.

Reasons for legal failure can also include, in the case of unclear laws, error-prone implementations of these laws, as well as institutions competing for their application, or inner developments within an administration, etc. In addition, there are obvious difficulties in asserting the law within a global horizon regarding the protection of human rights, the observance of the law of war, compliance with international agreements (e. g. regarding the proliferation of nuclear weapons), the condemnation of terrorists, environmental regulations, the relocation of prohibited activities to where they are not (yet) prohibited, etc. Establishing and maintaining authority in the respective fields of law therefore requires a 'legal culture,' which the law cannot ensure on its own. *Culture* is that which has become plausible for people that have lived together in certain ways; it can lend the law its own, inconspicuous authority.

(5) Orientation to the Law and to Its Decisions. – The law, the strongest foothold of orientation in the societal horizon, thus also increasingly appears contingent. The law inescapably determines the life of every individual, from birth to death (you may emigrate from one legal system, but only by entering another), and it simultaneously remains, regarding its own unsurveyability and questionable effectiveness, to some degree incalculable. Its thus has both calming and unsettling effects.

In court, litigations between individuals (natural or legal persons) are decided on by (the aforementioned) noninvolved and independent third persons, i. e. judges, and that means: individual persons again. In the framework of general laws, individuals are *authorized* to make definite decisions about other individuals. At the same time, judges are *forced* to do so. You can rely on the fact that courts *must* decide on the legal disputes that are brought to them (with possible exceptions again being regulated by the law). The courts' *compulsion* to decide most strikingly marks the need for decision in orientation as such, and, here, decisions are most clearly assigned to responsible persons. Court decisions are justified based on legal norms; if the justifications of a court seem inadequate, they can be appealed and reviewed; after passing the relevant legal instances, they are *final*. It is only in the legal system, due to its hierarchical structure, that such final decisions can be obtained. However, the law also most sharply highlights the paradox of deciding: that in the end it is something undecidable that must be decided – this means: in most cases, alternative decisions are possible, and often how the law is applied remains controversial.

For the law is just precisely when general laws, which are to be equally valid for everyone and for every case, do justice to each individual case. But there are only individual, and no equal, cases; it is only the application of laws that makes cases equal – which unjustly abbreviates their individuality. To be just, general laws must therefore, according to Jacques Derrida in his book *Deconstruction and the Possibility of Justice*, be deconstructed, i. e. questioned regarding their justice in each individual case; only a deconstruction of the general law with regard to the individual cases may create justice. Judges always decide in the leeway of this deconstruction; in doing so, they demonstrate the leeway of decision-making by subsuming individual cases under general norms.

Since ancient time, court decisions have been difficult to predict; most people are therefore cautious about appealing to the courts to claim the legal guarantee of their intentions. Legal proceedings are only instituted when a (private) plaintiff or a (public) prosecutor perceives sufficient evidence (i. e. footholds) for the success of the (private) lawsuit or (public) charge. The litigation then proceeds as an orientation process: judges can base their decision – since they are not allowed to have participated in the incriminating actions – only on the evidence of footholds like testimonies, documents, visual inspections, expert reports, indications, etc. If it is not clear under which law(s) a certain case must be subsumed, prosecutors and judges have to find out and determine which are appropriate; in this respect, laws are also only footholds for them. Finally, there is not per se a 'given' or absolutely right solution for a case; rather, the perfect judgment is the vantage point of the orientation process that a judge aims for. But in legal proceedings, the ascertainment of facts, the weighing of indicators and testimonies, the final subsumption of the case under appropriate laws, the assessment of the legal culpability in criminal proceedings, and, eventually, the sentencing are usually carried out with exemplary care, with a professional restraint from both emotions and moral convictions in the arguments and the ascription of responsibility (the presumption of innocence). Nevertheless, the judge's decision can turn out, *as* a decision, in this or that way; and this litigation risk severely limits – in civil proceedings – the ability of the law to settle conflicts. Additionally, there are (most likely) high legal costs and, in any case, great losses of time. And even if the conflict is decided in favor of the one seeking justice, this does not mean that the conflict is eliminated by the judgment; rather, the judgement may fuel the conflict even more – on the side of the adversarial party. All this again questions the promise that our orientation can find a stable foothold in the law.

Instead, in our everyday orientation, we keep open leeways regarding laws, prescriptions, and regulations. For the most part, we do not simply follow general rules and norms, but we usually assess how serious they are to be taken in each case: e. g. traffic rules when you are in the middle of nowhere; a bathing ban when a cold lake lures you in hot weather; import regulations when you return from your vacation; employment regulations when you need technical help in your private home, etc., to name a few small matters. Of course, there are smaller leeways with regard to crimes like theft, fraud, or murder; but they exist here too. In everyday life, we often 'interpret' laws and other rules, or we 'creatively' bypass them. But the laws nevertheless stay in effect, and we also wish that they do (and especially that others follow them). This is possible precisely because of norms. When you are under great pressure to act, you may be compelled to not take them as strictly; emergency situations may make their purpose entirely questionable; the desire for adventures may lead you to completely 'flout' them (here, young people are given greater leeways). In investigations of organized crime or in difficult intelligence operations, administrations may even tolerate crimes on their part. Someone who always insists on an absolute and strict observation of rules then becomes a horrifying monster, just like someone who disobeys them all the time. For whether, when, and how legal norms (besides other rules) are claimed is again a question of manifold leeways. Deviations from the law may not even be noticed; if they are noticed, they may perhaps not even be prosecuted; and if they are prosecuted, they may still be judged differently. Different kinds of leeways regarding the compliance of rules and legal norms are conditions of their functioning; what is crucial is thus to orient oneself to them, instead of strictly following them. And they pose greater challenges: orienting yourself to laws, i.e. assessing in every situation which laws are to be followed and to what degree, is a much more complex achievement than observing them without reflection. A considerate or reflective observance or compliance, however, is especially necessary when, e.g., in cases of political upheavals, the legitimacy of the standing laws is at stake. You then have to fully rely on your own orientation once more and recognize your own responsibility. Both are trained through science, art, and religion.

Chapter 13
The Critical Disciplining of Orientation, Its Creative Disorientation, and the Hold on the Eternally Ungraspable: Science, Art, and Religion
Orientation at a Critical Distance

Science (in which we also include, as in the German *Wissenschaft*, the humanities), art, and religion are also modes of the aforementioned art of world abbreviation. They profit – compared to economics, mass media, politics, and the law – much more from leeways in the use of signs and language and therefore have, or rather, create much larger leeways in the engagement with their objects. We cannot escape engagements with economics, mass media, politics, or law, but we attain a *critical distance* to them through science, art, and religion. It is at our liberty to turn to (or away from) science, art, and religion, but all three – and especially religion – can have strong and lasting impacts on our orientation. Science, art, and religion may spread all over the world (more or less) unrestrained from economic and political conditions, but they nevertheless require protection by the law, support from appropriate media, and technologies of distribution. Thus, they are, at the same time, independent from and dependent on these social systems. They have the potential for *universality*.

'Universal' literally means 'directed or oriented toward a point,' 'being turned into one,' 'being turned toward something common.' (More or less) detached from economic and political interests and from systems of law, science, art, and religion can turn people living in different societies toward something that is of their common interest; this is likewise not something which already exists, but something which results just from this shared 'turning-toward' something common. In short: what is universal is that which can be universalized; but what is being universalized depends on orientational needs and decisions. *How* science, art, and religion universalize something is also a matter of decisions. In science, you can turn toward or against certain fields and issues of research and toward or against certain scientific methods; in art, toward or against specific artistic styles; and in religion, you may also choose between a variety of practices, doctrines, or faiths.

Science allows for a critical distance from the needs of survival and coexistence by, on the one hand, taking a 'theoretical point of view,' i.e. a standpoint of observation that itself appears to be no part of the observed world, and by, on the other hand, designing theories, i.e. by purposefully restraining the leeways

https://doi.org/10.1515/9783110575149-015

of the use of signs through definitions and rules. Definitions and rules enable time-resistant, controlled, and gradually distinguished abstractions with corresponding scopes of overviews, and then, through them, controlled observations of natural processes, i. e. experiments, and, eventually, techniques for increasing the efficiency by which we cope with our world. In contrast to science, *art* expands the use of signs in a way that makes it fluid; bringing about creative disorientation, it enriches human orientation through fictional orientation worlds. *Religion* allows for the greatest critical distance from everyday orientation. It creates a leeway that transcends all other leeways of orientation, including those of science and art; in doing so, it shows them their limits. Religion provides an orientation with the strongest possible hold – or a final hold for the paradoxes of our orientation: in monotheisms, God is an unconditional hold, for which, however, there is no unconditional foothold in our orientation; God is a hold from which everything is to be comprehended, but which itself remains incomprehensible.

13.1 Scientific Orientation: Critical Disciplining of Orientation

(1) The Transparency of Scientific Orientation. – Science requires a logically disciplined use of signs. Logical discipline makes, through an explicit and controlled introduction of signs, the usage of signs transparent and thus (in principle) traceable for anyone. It excludes (as far as possible) leeways and shifts in meaning, which are necessary in everyday sign usage; wherever these restraints are successful, an orientation is particularly reliable. In light of its transparency, traceability, and reliability, scientific orientation creates a special kind of self-referential knowledge, i. e. not only a knowledge which is accessible to everyone (as in the case of mass media), but also a knowledge that can be controlled by everyone. As such, scientific orientation has become, in the Western philosophical tradition, an outstanding model and a dominant yardstick for orientation in general.

However, the (ideally complete) transparency of science (in regard to both its knowledge and the institutions responsible for providing it) is also the criterion by which it *selects its objects of study.* Something can become an object of science only to the degree to which it can be made transparent; by contrast, everyday orientation, which perpetually faces situations that remain largely unsurveyable and continuously change, is not limited by this restriction; thus, the methods of science (the various methods of various sciences) preselect the objects of science – and thus restrain the respective orientation(s). Therefore, the sciences cannot replace our everyday orientation; instead, they depend on it and are made plausible by it; this is true not only for non-scientists and students of science, but also at times for scientists themselves when they introduce new theories to each other.

Mathematics performs the utmost disciplined and reliable use of signs; it is (or is supposed to be) perfectly transparent. This is possible because mathematical signs are artificial signs, i.e. introduced, defined, and used according to predefined rules. Thus, their use does not depend on given situations of orientation, and they do not refer to anything else besides mathematical signs. As a result, their meanings cannot shift in changing situations (an A is always an A, a 4 is always a 4); they are therefore unambiguous and create certainties that are entirely time-resistant. However, to provide an orientation, mathematical signs must refer to something besides themselves, as in the natural sciences e.g. to spaces and times, bodies, particles, forces, waves, currents, vibrations, forms of energy, rays, strings, black holes, etc. And there are again, as is often seen, leeways for interpreting what exactly they refer to (e.g. to waves or particles) – or, in the language of orientation, which footholds they connect to in nature, as it is not (yet) entirely surveyable. Here, the leeways of decision-making return.

(2) The Fact-Orientation in Science. – The problem concerning the reference of signs, which was already addressed in the times of Immanuel Kant and, as a crucial issue in the theory of science, in the 20th century, persists because the 'objects,' 'things,' or 'facts' of science are neither given by themselves nor universal per se. As the history of science to date shows, 'objects,' 'things,' and 'facts' must at first be established, constituted, or constructed *as* 'objects,' 'things,' or 'facts' by specifically adjusting and directing one's orientation to them via certain methods. The terms' etymological origin indicates this: Lat. '*obiectum*' literally means 'confronted, juxtaposed, exposed, in front of someone, presented to someone' (Kant, in a related sense, used the terms 'object' and 'objective' as 'something presented to a subject' that has to discipline itself through 'logical forms of reason' in order to conceive that which it perceives in an 'objective' way); Lat. '*res*' literally refers to the object of a legal litigation, i.e. to something that is controversial and that must at first be decided on; and the original meaning of Lat. '*factum*' is simply, as a verb, 'made' or 'happened,' as a noun, an 'accomplished action, work, or event.' During the 19th century, that which proved neither different for different standpoints nor controversial became something 'objective,' 'real,' or 'factual' – proved and guaranteed by the overwhelming success of both natural and historical sciences.

The more the sciences succeeded, the more any possible alternatives disappeared; the decidability of all that one could orient oneself to receded; it became inconspicuous; *standpoint-neutrality,* as we call it, seemed itself to be a simple fact. However, an orientation must at first attain or create such a standpoint-neutrality; for this, it must detach itself from its everyday relations to standpoints and needs. Uncontroversial, standpoint-neutral 'objects,' 'things,' 'facts,' or 'realities' only come about when individuals disregard their given individual standpoints, needs, and relevancies; and this is afforded only when new needs arise for commonly referring to something as undoubtedly identical – as in the natural sciences, technical developments, or industrial productions. Which identities are being assigned to this 'something' depends on the shared needs, approaches, or methods. The needs concerning the scientific and technical innovations, as well as the historical research of the 19th century, were obvious: to obtain clear, unambiguous, common knowledge that was acquired through increasingly proven methods and which promised ongoing progress. Science, too, is not inherently true as such, but appears to be more and more true the further it progresses.

In science, as in everyday orientation, something can, over time, become self-evident, objective, factual, or real to such a degree that questions about it appear absurd ('Before we sit down at the table, how do you understand 'table'?'). But whatever *has* become indisputable *may* become controversial again ('You call this a table? I'm not going to sit there!'). Something similar happened with terms such as space, time, atom, energy, etc., which, in the 19th century, seemed completely unambiguous – until that century ended. In philosophy, it was above all Friedrich Nietzsche (in his *Gay Science*, No. 373) who warned the natural sciences against disrobing reality of its "ambiguous character" and of accepting only one "world interpretation," namely the mechanistic one: What would remain of music, for example, if one made for its yardstick "how much can be counted, calculated, brought into formulas"? Soon after, the mechanistic worldview became controversial, and the world regained its ambiguous character in mathematical physics.

Nevertheless, the more plausible it seems in everyday orientation that different orientations deal with common 'objects,' 'things,' 'facts,' or 'realities,' the more people expect from each other a reliance on 'objectivity,' 'factuality,' 'realism,' or a 'sense of reality.' In philosophy, the term objectivity is associated with Immanuel Kant's opposition between subject and object within his 'transcendental philosophy.' While Kant thinks of objectivity in such a way that the subject must de-subjectify itself in order to become objective and be able and justified to speak *a priori* in the name of reason itself, a philosophy of orientation does not assume the latter. We therefore speak of *fact-orientation (Sachlichkeit)* instead of objectivity. The ability of individual orientations to hold back their individuality only concerns their need for easier (doubly contingent) communication; the more seriously a fact-orientation restricts someone's own intentions and interests, the more it is ethically honored as being *impartial*. Once impartiality has been established as a benchmark, someone's own biases, needs, and matters of relevance, which one is inevitably urged to by one's situation, are then considered 'subjective' or 'improper.'

Being able to disregard one's own needs and interests for the sake of facts requires *self-discipline*. Nietzsche called it, in his *Genealogy of Morals*, 'asceticism,' which is oriented toward an 'ascetic ideal.' He expected it most of all from scientists and scholars: they have learned, without the pressure of sanctions, to respect facts and laws from which the scholars themselves neither benefit nor suffer. The scientist's or scholar's orientation to facts has also become a model for our everyday orientation. If constant caution regarding one's own interests and prejudices and the circumspect consideration of other standpoints (inside or outside of science) bring about an impartial self-assessment, it reduces the double contingency of communication for others; (in a respectable number of cases) it makes people reliable and thus supports interindividual trust. The self-discipline of scientists and scholars in turn bolsters the *trust* in science and scholarship itself. Trust in science and scholarship is, inside and outside of science and scholarship, always also a trust in the persons who present and represent these fields.

This appears justified, too: just as controlled traceability, based on the disciplined use of signs, is the criterion for selecting objects of science, the virtue of a disciplined orientation to facts is the first criterion for the professional selection of scientists and scholars. Starting your career as a scientist or scholar, you repeatedly have to prove via examinations and evaluations your ability to comply with standards of fact-orientation; if you are successful, you attain degrees, which in turn are to prove your expertise. But the more complex and unsurveyable science and its academic disciplines become, the more you must orient yourself (again inside and outside of science) to *authorities*, i.e. experts who have gained a distinguished reputation. You are a personal authority if you, when asked about particularly difficult problems, can propose solutions that are accepted, and if you thereby set plausibility standards. Scientific authorities are then entrusted with reviews and evaluations, with the publication of scientific journals, with the management of scientific institutions and organizations, etc. Thus, as persons, authorities represent the specific fact-orientation or scientificity of their discipline or field of research. Nevertheless, even authorities need not agree on scientific questions and may have different scientific orientations or positions. As a result, scientific fact-orientation also finds its hold in personalities who may each be distinguished by having strong scientific discipline and high self-discipline, but who are still committed to their particular orientations.

Eventually the disciplines – if we understand the word's double sense – differ. The more science differentiated over time, the more different disciplines developed – disciplines as fields of research and as ways of doing science within these fields. Every field of research needs and has its own way of practicing science. Most scientists and scholars master only one discipline (in both senses); only singular and particularly outstanding persons pursued and surveyed science in all its breadth and depth, people like Aristotle or Gottfried Wilhelm Leibniz. For this reason, among others, the different academic disciplines are united at universities – with regard to questions going beyond the limits of the different areas and disciplines. To cross the borders between them, when needed, scientists and scholars have to rely on exchanges with other experts in other areas – and again deal with the double contingency of communication which likewise arises in such exchanges.

(3) *The Theoreticity of Scientific Orientation.* – The transparency and fact-orientation of science are not only a matter of the use of signs, but also of the point of view. Fact-orientation, understood as the ability to restrain one's individual needs, views, and intentions, does not mean the complete absence of any standpoint. Scientists also take a standpoint – a standpoint *as* scientists. The specifically scientific point of view is the *theoretical point of view.* It is likewise possible only in a special situation, which must first be established with great efforts. Here, a look at the original meaning of the terms is once again useful. 'Theory' (to continue the conversation from chap. 4.1) comes from the Greek verb *theoreîn,* i.e. 'to view special things or events in an intense way'; the Greek noun *theoría* was originally a sacred delegation that traveled in order to view a sacred ceremony. Thus, *theoreîn* meant to be somewhere for the sole purpose of viewing, particularly at a place established only for that: a *théatron,* a 'theater.' In ancient Greek cities, it was carved as a semicircle into exposed slopes, often with a wide view toward the sea, and magnificently equipped; it held celebrations dedicated to gods (in Athens, to Dionysus) and was intended to provide a space for all citizens. The *theatáes,* i.e. the 'spectator,' sat there on an elevated seat (mostly flat rocks), surveying the events presented in the orchestra (originally a circular dance floor) and on the stage. He or she (the back rows were reserved for women) looked at the events from a spatial and a mental distance. Their horizon was expanded, and they could see more than the actors themselves; as far as new adaptations of old myths were concerned, they would usually know the general course of the events as well as the ending of the upsetting plot, and thus they could pay even more attention to the author's deviations or innovations. The spectator remained simultaneously calm (in his or her seat) and not calm. He or she viewed the performing actors on stage and the choir, who would comment with pleasure or concern, from the orchestra, on what the actors did or did not do, sometimes also intervening in the events. Thus, the choir represented the spectators, and neither the choir nor the spectators were *mere* spectators. They 'went along' with what was happening on stage and grew worried by it, even

if they were not unsettled in the same way or to the same extent as they would be by their everyday worries. In the ancient Greek theater, the spectator in his or her 'theoretical seat' could remain calm on the outside while watching the choir's growing unsettlement, which sprang from the performed events that reached the spectator, as well, but only at his or her distance, which dampened the unsettlement. People came to the theater in order to expose themselves to this dampened agitation, and they experienced the events with engagement but without the pressure of time or of having to act and without risking anything themselves: one was able to experience orientation without the needs of orientation in a 'theoretical view.'

Greek philosophy, from which science emerged over the course of centuries and millennia, was formed during the heyday of Greek theater, which reached its most formative shape in the time of the Athenian democracy. By virtue of the theater, 'theory' or the 'theoretical' view, i.e. the godlike overview of the most significant events in a human life, was established as a routine, no longer requiring specific justifications. Socrates – who coined, according to Nietzsche, "the type of a form of existence unknown before him, the type of *theoretical man*" (*The Birth of Tragedy*, No. 15) – went to the theater, became a subject of the theater, and committed himself, wherever possible, to theory. Living in emphasized distance from his everyday worries, he was, according to the reports, concerned for the life of others, but unconcerned about his own; always unsettled, but without ever losing his calmness; open to the beauty and prudence of the young men he encountered, but without shame for his own ugliness; all the time seeking new knowledge, but without himself claiming real knowledge – thus free for judgments concerning the matters of human life in general, based only on his 'theory,' to which he himself gave authority. Socrates as the 'type of theoretical man' – to abbreviate it to the extreme, following Nietzsche – has shaped Western culture to a crucial extent.

Since then, philosophers, scholars, and scientists have adopted – within changing contexts – the theoretical standpoint as if it were entirely self-evident, out of an 'interest in the sheer facts.' But it is, *as* an interest, still a personal standpoint that you may or may not adopt. Philosophers, scholars, and scientists, too, take the theoretical standpoint only for a certain time, just like you go to the theater only for some time. In addition, to adopt the theoretical standpoint they must create a special situation. Today, science is carried out under conditions that require great effort to establish, highly sensitive to any kind of disruption. It requires separate facilities and spaces: in ancient Greece, after Socrates engaged his interlocutors in the public, be it a public square, a *gymnásion*, or a convivial private house, special estates like Plato's Academy or Aristotle's Lyceum became the preferred spaces for science; in Hellenistic times it was groves, halls, and gardens (only in special cases, as with the Cynics, markets); in the Middle Ages, there were monasteries with their cells and halls for copying and (sometimes) debating writings or for giving lectures; then, in the modern era, universities and laboratories and increasingly growing research institutions and organizations – all of them distinctly sealed off from their surroundings. To enable discipline in science, distractions must be kept away. Its environment is thus equipped only with what is factually necessary: all kinds of aesthetic attractions and vivid moods are avoided; you dress discreetly; in addition, economic interests and political influences are to be excluded. Measures like these allow for the *leeway for conducting science;* it is not without any mood, but it is defined by the specific *mood of a calm theoretical overview and insight,* which is specifically arranged; science lives in it – and feeds from it. While it appears to look from above the world, it in fact lives in the world.

The situational conditions of science are more difficult to establish in the humanities, which deal precisely with the individual and with historical conditions, forms, and outcomes of human life, such as language, literature, social behavior, pedagogy, politics, morality, religion, and art; here theory and its standpoints are obviously more defined and somewhat less 'theoretical.' More 'theory,' more abstraction from situational conditions seems possible regarding economic research, especially if it involves mathematics. If concrete situations, needs and hardships of human life and coexistence are entirely disregarded, i.e. if the view is limited to the – comparably less complex – 'dead' nature, experiments can be conducted under 'laboratory conditions' in order to extract universal uniformities from ever-changing orientational contexts, formulate general rules and laws, and make reliable forecasts. To put it as a rule: the transparency, accuracy, and reliability of orientation grows with the degree of abbreviation, or, as William James explicitly calls it in regard to science (*Pragmatism,* Lecture V), the "artificial short-cut" involved in the reduction (or the loss) of situational complexity. Based on mathematics, the natural sciences enable us to very accurately launch a space probe into the orbit around a neighboring planet; but the best mathematics cannot guarantee the financial success of a company nor calculate the risks it poses for either society or the environment. Thus, science demonstrates, in an exemplary way, a kind of *uncertainty principle in orientation,* as quantum theory formulates it: the more precise a measurement is in one instance, the less accurate it is in other respective instances. The 'situativity' of orientation cannot be completely excluded from orientation.

When the results of science are integrated into our everyday orientation, they again become plausible in their own way: highly abstract theories in mathematics and the natural sciences are particularly convincing if one can apply them in experiments and make technical use of them, or in short: if they obviously work under concrete and practical conditions. If a certain technology, as produced by a certain science, makes our daily life easier and more secure, then this science, together with the technology, will soon be accepted as true, even if most people can neither understand nor control it. The fact that something works is usually enough to accept it in everyday orientation, where we often have no time for further questions. Scientific theories grow credible, the more they help make something work or work better; this is true not only regarding technologies, but also and above all in medicine (with all its own technologies).

But, especially in medicine, you find countless undesirable side effects of therapies or treatments that are based on scientific theories; and it may again surprise you when something that works great as a technology, e. g. an automobile running on diesel fuel, harms the environment, which you want to preserve as well. Furthermore, technologies that demonstrate that scientific theories work have often not been deduced from these theories (like the diesel engine); instead, they have been created on a different, 'new' path, e. g. by 'inventors' who had (and still have) exceptional ideas. Vice versa, the mere functioning of a technology does not yet affirm the truth of the scientific knowledge used for this technology, as we want to believe. The actual reasons for this functioning may still be different, as again medicine shows, which deals with the most complex physical and mental system that we know of, the human being. But this is also true for physics: large parts of engineering as we know it today are still based on the laws of Newton's mechanics, which were, for centuries, believed to be the laws of nature per se; instead they are, as we learned in the 20th century, laws only under limited conditions – conditions that disregard relativity and quantum theory. Under these limited conditions, you can still work with them. But that does not mean that Newton's laws are true for nature as such. And the same also applies to both the theory of relativity and quantum theory, as far as their compatibility still poses riddles, the solutions to which could once again crucially change our understanding of nature.

(4) The Evolution of Scientific Orientation. – In general, transparency, fact-orientation, theoreticity, universality, and functionality – the conditions for a particularly successful abbreviation of orientation – do not yet guarantee the *truth* of scientific theories, if truth is understood as something existing outside of any orientation with which it is supposed to correspond. Even in its scientific shape, orientation cannot transcend itself in order to attain a truth that exists outside of itself and with which it could compare itself. Truth is merely the *specific vantage point of scientific orientation,* a point which science orients itself to without being able to prove that it can ever attain it, nor that it could even clearly specify what it is by its own means, be it positively or negatively. In scientific

as well as everyday orientation, something *is supposed to be true – as long as nobody contradicts it*. Then, it is self-evidently true, 'without question.' However, at any moment someone may contradict it, or new evidence may arise. In that case, arguments must be found, considered, and weighed, and they must eventually be decided on with regard to how much they may support a supposed truth. But to question a truth that has, so far, been self-evident, there must be evidence or a foothold strong enough in given situations to be convincing. Science highlights this, too, in an exemplary way: rather than offering true knowledge it operates as *research*. It also proceeds from assumptions that are considered self-evidently true, be they pre-scientific or scientific, and it submits them – if certain observations or arguments are no longer reconcilable with them – to *examination*. Thus, science is conducted as a *critique* – as a critical distancing from assumptions so far considered true. Researchers hope to find truths, but in fact they supersede truths. *Scientific truth is then the current state of research (self-evident at a time) which is addressed only in order to be superseded.*

Karl Popper, in his theory of science, therefore described science as a process of methodic falsifications. But he still regarded science to be on the way to truth – despite knowing that all we have for a criterion is the provisional proofs of hypotheses. That scientific research does not have a graspable goal to which it 'progresses,' but merely supersedes assumptions that are at some point no longer tenable, means that it also (in principle) proceeds as an evolution that is (ultimately) based on contingency, rather than necessity. However, scientific evolution can itself also create necessities under contingent conditions.

This is where Thomas S. Kuhn's distinction between 'normal' and 'revolutionary' science comes in: once a science is 'normalized,' i.e. when certain factual and methodic assumptions are accepted as reasons for explanations, and once these assumptions are proven consistent, coherent, and logically consequential, they are indeed truths – within this frame. A normalized science removes the element of surprise from what was still surprising; in this way, it promises and achieves a *reassured orientation without surprises*. This is highly attractive for orientation as such. However, new, surprising evidence that cannot be explained with the accepted assumptions may bring about their 'revolution,' i.e. a *surprising reorientation also with regard to the criteria for giving explanations and assuring oneself of truths* – a 'paradigm shift.' From the view of the old paradigm, this shift appears as a contingent evolution; but from the view of the new paradigm, once it has become 'normal,' the surprising shift may be reconceived of as necessary progress. As such, the scientists involved may interpret the paradigm shift as both a contingent and surprising reorientation as well as one that was necessary and expected. These scientists then orient themselves and make decisions, in their scientific work, according to their individual research interests and the corresponding paradigms.

Since truth is merely the vantage point of scientific orientation, which itself can be determined neither definitely nor with ultimate certainty, *competition* among researchers remains open. In their respective areas of research, they publish their contributions, and other researchers working in the same field examine these results based on their own expertise. This is, truly (i.e. true within the frame of the philosophy of orientation), an *ideal model for orientations orienting themselves to other orientations: the ideal according to which all people involved continually and deliberately consider and engage with all factual contributions, produced with great discipline, in order to arrive at a common orientation.* For this, science is provided with the best conditions: no time pressure and no coercions to make decisions (in contrast to judges, scientists may leave questions open).

However, in the everyday operations of scientists, the usual conditions of orientation return once again. The struggle for reputation, above all the attribution of scientific discoveries and innovations to certain authors competing with each other, likewise creates time pressure and coerces rapid decisions: to be the first, you must finish research in a timely manner, publish quickly, and therefore be the first to settle a given dispute. Attaining an overview of a science's current state, even in narrowly defined research areas, is again cumbersome and time-consuming and, considering the vast number of contributions, sometimes impossible. Therefore, scientists usually proceed selectively regarding research results – often by taking 'positions' characterized by '-isms,' which pre-select the relevant evidence and arguments to be accepted or rejected. Scientists (including scholars of the humanities), who promise great certainty, inevitably orient themselves under the condition of uncertainty, too.

13.2 Artistic Orientation: Creative Disorientation

(1) The Attractiveness of Artistic Orientation. – Whereas science, with its theoretical point of view, first became self-evident through the Greek theater, only to later unfold rather inconspicuously while still operating in special situations, art generally draws attention to special or exceptional situations, making them conspicuous. It presents them under specific signs, e.g. at attractive places to exhibit fine art, in theaters, or in dance or music halls; artists (or their agents) send out attractive invitations for people to gather at these places at a certain time. To be able to concentrate on the reading of literature, you likewise seclude yourself, if possible, to special places at certain times. Artistic orientation is connected

with freedom, leisure, and pleasure. What art offers are *orientation worlds of special attractiveness:* so long as it was committed to (re)present the sacred, the well-shaped, and the mighty, artists showed them in the name of beauty; after, in Romanticism, art attained its autonomy and became ostentatiously self-referential, it was more and more the means and potentials of art itself that gained interest. The shift from representing or presenting subjects that were given (or believed to be given) to presenting art itself led to 'art for art's sake' (*l'art pour l'art*).

But besides that, an attractive art for 'entertainment' has remained and flourished. It is put into practice at many events at many locations, but it has also been taken over by a large entertainment industry, in which book publishers, the film industry, television production companies, and now also many social media participate, operating more or less under economic conditions. All of them are oriented toward surprises. But, while science seeks to resolve surprises by explaining them, art – both the so-called serious and the entertaining kind – performs them in an attractive manner. The criteria of attractivity can and must change because even the most beautiful and most interesting piece of art loses attractiveness over time (attractiveness dies from repetitive performances). Thus, just as science is driven by paradigm shifts, art needs a continual change of styles and forms, i.e. ongoing reorientations, which can and must be attractively performed. In this way, art demonstrates that both orientations and reorientations must be attractive if someone is to be interested in and follow them.

(2) Artistic Orientation as Invention. – Artistic orientation 'invents.' By means of its liberty to invent, or rather, its license to create fictions, art stands out from everyday orientation. In contrast to science, which disciplines the use of signs, art overrides all kinds of disciplines and limits, making the everyday use of signs fluid. The new and conspicuous orientation worlds that it creates out of everyday orientations are prolific in introducing attractive topics: literature, dramas, and films present either particularly stimulating or repellent, lucky or unfortunate experiences or fates; fine art, performing art, and music present particularly interesting views, movements, and sounds. All of them may use surprising materials and compose them in surprising ways: *art composes surprising orientation worlds.*

To connect to our everyday orientation, artists (more or less) likewise take up, in one way or another, what is given in it. But presenting their work in specific environments like theaters, cinemas, concert halls, museums, or on screens, they announce that they are suspending our everyday routines for a certain time, and, by doing so, they promise surprises. However, artists clearly limit their surprises in space and time: they give art performances at certain places during a certain period of time; for only in clearly limited spaces and times can attractive events be clearly performed, perceived, and conceived of *as* such events; only in art do events have clear beginnings and ends. To make them perfectly surveyable, artists abridge everything that does not support the attractiveness of their narrative, dramatic, filmic, choreographic, musical, or pictorial presentations; in this way the artistic event also shows a clear course, something that is usually not the case in everyday life. As such, art too is an *abbreviation* of orientation – now by marking and contouring with conspicuous and attractive signs both the presented topics and the means of their presentation.

Art, too, requires *discipline* in using signs. But this discipline is only to a limited extent the product of rules regarding 'technical skills.' As an artist, you need techniques and rules; but it is not techniques and rules that distinguish art as art; you cannot generalize in rules the art of surprising with new subjects, materials, styles, forms of composition, etc. As such, the discipline of artistic abbreviations is, unlike in science, not attributed to a 'community' but to *individual artists* (or indefinable 'geniuses'). They too compete, though not for the most convincing contribution to an orientation that is (in principle) equally comprehensible for everyone, but rather for individual and informal approvals of freely created orientation worlds, which some will like and others will not. The discipline of artists is their personal style, and the more one's style differs from all others, the more one is considered to be a true artist: he or she creates his or her own rules. Vice versa, the audience of art does not need general criteria for what they are interested or take pleasure in: everyone can follow their own explicit and implicit criteria. They may leave unanswered *why* a piece of art pleases them or not: art is – or is not – attractive without reasons; art is attractive through its sheer attractiveness. In this way, art also draws attention to a basic feature of orientation as such: to the fact that our orientation tends to connect to especially attractive footholds – before we even know, according to general criteria, what these footholds amount to – or, in a word, that attractiveness is one of our orientation's main criteria.

(3) Artistic Orientation as Playfulness and Seriousness. – Compositions, i.e. artistic fittings of attractive footholds, appear playful. To test the orientational potential of our perceptions, actions, and interpretations, art has special *leeways* (*Spielräume*) – (more or less) completely free rein. When entering its special orientation worlds, you leave behind your own hardships and needs, and you open up to other concerns, now for a limited time and without any pressure to make decisions; here you also distance yourself from your situation and can reflect on it. In the, artificially created, situations of art, your orientation is, for once, not serious – if 'serious' means that you have to act on your part. Nevertheless, things can be serious *within* the play, and this playful seriousness (or serious playfulness) may still pierce through to one's own orientations and change

them. If art generates awareness of the general needs of a society and gives an impetus or an inspiration to resolve them, it may become a "moral institution" (Friedrich von Schiller). Often very successfully, artists dedicate their free play to the service of moral seriousness.

The freedom of artistic orientation permits much less institutionalization than economic, media, political, legal, pedagogical, scientific, and religious orientations do. Usually there are hardly clear careers or securities for life-long income (beyond very few positions in academies, theaters, operas, museums, publishing houses, newspapers, etc.). Artists compete, exposed to many risks, with their individual skills, styles, and personalities before a picky and choosy audience and even more selective professional critics – they compete in a contest not for positions, but for reputation. With their skills, styles, and personalities, they are identified and, as it were, 'traded' on a market – something like a *personality and identity market*. Since art is eventually about pleasure and displeasure, the chances of succeeding on this market are especially uncertain. The freer an orientation, the more uncertain it is. Artists then have the choice – as far as they do not seek and find positions at institutions – of either orienting themselves to what the audience (from which they draw their living) likes, thereby abandoning surprises that are too strong, or deliberately risking them – or, with an awareness of art's autonomy, of doing both at the same time: by surprisingly dissatisfying the expectations of expected surprises. Indeed, all alternatives come with high risks on the market. If they are successful, the artists may become, in the first case, market leaders, in the second case, authorities of their art, or, in particularly fortunate circumstances, they may become both: they may then set artistic standards with almost unlimited leeways while also dominating the market, just as, for instance, Titian or Pablo Picasso did in their time in the field of fine art. These, and similar cases, fulfill the *ideal of an individual freedom to shape your professional orientation world in your own way*.

Even single artworks may provoke crucial artistic reorientations, setting standards for future creations. If they succeed in that, artworks are considered 'classic,' i.e. attractive and plausible to an extent that their field can no longer be imagined without them, e.g. in the case of 'serious' music, some pieces created by – for instance – Johann Sebastian Bach, Wolfgang Amadeus Mozart, Ludwig van Beethoven or in the case of pop music, certain songs – for instance – by Elvis Presley, the Beatles, the Rolling Stones, Bob Dylan, Aretha Franklin. Thus, like nothing else, *art emphasizes the weight of the individual over the general in our orientation*.

(4) Artistic Orientation as Irritation. – In contrast to the other functionally differentiated social systems of communication, art comes on stage, whenever it takes its autonomy seriously, as *creative disorientation*. After detaching itself

from all outside obligations, art places its inventiveness increasingly at the service of irritation: it effectively draws attention to the contingency of developed orientations in everyday life and in other functional systems. Going beyond the usual functional contexts, it (to a lesser or greater extent) disregards functionality as such – imagine, for instance, Christo and Jeanne-Claude's wrapping art or Richard Serra's conspicuous but non-functional large steel sculptures in the middle of streets and public squares. Art then attracts people precisely by having no normal function or meaning in a normal functional or meaningful context, i.e. by *being conspicuously without sense*. At first you cannot make anything of it, you cannot attribute any function or meaning to it: thus, a piece of art irritates your everyday orientation and – because (nearly) all orientations continually look for functions and meanings – will challenge your orientation to attribute a function or meaning to it as well. Whenever orientation becomes aware of a lack of function or meaning, it seeks to ensure appropriate footholds in order to put them into contexts of sense. Through its attractiveness, art invites you to do so; through its lack of a normal function or meaning, it at the same time frustrates your attempts. As a result, *through its irritations art removes an orientation from its routines of perception, behavior, action, and interpretation and thereby stimulates it to correct or reorient these routines.*

But once routines are reoriented, the irritation fades; new routines develop. This is also true for the irritating art itself: over time, you get used to its creative disorientation; your engagement with the art becomes routine. In this way, art again attains a function, and it becomes, in this respect, *inconspicuously full of sense*. It returns to a normal orientation.

(5) Artistic Orientation as Culture. – By inconspicuously attaining routine functions and meanings, art turns into culture. The word 'culture' stems from Lat. '*colere*,' i.e. 'cultivating the land, growing plants, educating human beings.' Culture requires 'care'; over the course of the long time needed for this care, this culture becomes self-evident, and vice versa: what, after a long period of attentive care, has become self-evident *is* culture. This is true not just for art, but already for everyday practical activities ('food culture,' 'conversation culture') as well as for the law, common knowledge, and all the other functional systems of societal communication. After something has attained cultural self-evidence – be it a certain custom, expectation, line of argument or reasoning, etc., in short: any context of communication – it is, inside its respective culture, noticed only if somebody disturbs, violates, or breaks the rules of this context.

Therefore, *inside* of one culture, *other* cultures that follow different rules are all the more conspicuous; they are noticed in part as pleasant, in part as unpleasant. Like art, other cultures initially appear as functionless and meaningless. If they are noticed with pleasure, they may be perceived as art, and, perceived as art, cultures may express changing 'styles' as well. If a culture reflects how it is perceived from the 'outside' by other cultures and if it performs for them through specific styles, it turns into a kind of folklore. When cultural studies deal with cultures, they usually attribute explicit contexts of function and meaning to them, thus making them comparable with and plausible for other cultures, and especially for their own: other cultures that seem to be conspicuously meaningless become (like works of art) meaningful again; when you move to a foreign country, you experience this every day. Step by step, you reorient yourself about the other culture – and thus also about your own culture. But even then (as with any perception of other perspectives in one's own perspective; chap. 5) your own culture remains the inconspicuously self-evident background of this reorientation – unless, on your part, you are ready to let a foreign culture irritate and correct your own plausibility standards. (Some) cultural scientists are working on this – to creatively disorient their own culture.

13.3 Religious Orientation: Holding on the Eternally Ungraspable

(1) Religion as Orientation. – Scientific orientation critically distances itself, with great seriousness, from everyday orientation by abstracting from the individual standpoint and adopting a theoretical one; from this theoretical standpoint, science analyzes, based on a specifically disciplined use of signs, factual givens as conditions and elements of all orientation worlds with regard to their potential laws – which, nevertheless, always remain problematic. Artistic orientation creates in a playful way – by expanding the limits of the common use of signs in individual ways – attractive and irritating contingent orientation worlds; it distances you from both the everyday and scientific orientation worlds and makes them, if not more beautiful or ideal, also problematic. *Religion* also orients people, with great seriousness, toward a world transcending the limited and temporary horizons of the everyday, scientific, and artistic orientation worlds; it provides a hold onto an eternal being that is present everywhere and all the time. While in scientific orientation fact-orientation prevails, and while artistic orientation is governed by attractiveness, religious orientation is based on an *unconditional trust in all situations, for all time.* The Abrahamic monotheisms (to which we will limit ourselves in the following) rely on an almighty, all-knowing, and all-bountiful eternal God, who has, as an infinitely skilled artist, created the world; who guides, as an omniscient sage, the destinies of the world from beyond all standpoints, where every standpoint is perfectly transpar-

ent; and who forever acts, through his infinite, but nontransparent benignity, in the interest of the human beings living in His world.

(2) Religious Paradoxes. – The Abrahamic religions start from a clearly-signified and all-governing paradox: that everything is to be grasped via God, but He Himself is ungraspable. According to the Hebrew Bible, His response to the question of His name and His essence is and is not an answer at the same time: "I am who I am" (Ex. 3:14). As the creator of heaven and earth, He raises further paradoxes, such as: what was before the beginning, before creation? Did time begin with it? Was there another time before that time? Did God create the world out of nothing? Did He then also create Himself? Or can one, beyond time, prove by pure reason that He exists and must have always existed? But would pure reason itself then have to be divine? How can God make Himself understood to human beings; how can they, as human beings, understand Him? How can He be both just and merciful, etc.? Philosophy, theology, and the criticism of religion have academically discussed these and other paradoxes. Religion itself may leave the paradoxes as God's mysteries; they have again and again inspired religious people to deal with them in a non-paradoxical way, i. e. by finding new expressions and new institutions for their religious needs. Thus, the paradoxes keep awake a vivid focus on religion itself. *Religion unsettles science, but – if nevertheless followed – reassures the everyday orientation.*

(3) Religious Conviction. – Religion does not need clear footholds – it pushes the leeways of footholds to the extreme. For everyday, scientific, economic, political, legal, and mass media orientations, something is ungraspable and therefore incomprehensible if it does not offer any observable clues, signs, or footholds. Religious orientation keeps alive what is ungraspable and incomprehensible, while insisting it may still be highly meaningful and pertain to both life as a whole and, eventually, eternal life. To resolve the paradox of grasping the ungraspable and comprehending the incomprehensible, *signs* proffer themselves: in signs, something ungraspable may show itself without being already comprehended. In the Hebrew Bible, God reveals Himself through signs, of which you can neither know with certainty what they mean, nor whether they are, in fact, *His* signs. Therefore, their religious interpretations can always be questioned, if not fully rejected. The Hebrew Bible itself continually evinces how difficult it is to ensure that certain signs are His signs and that the prophets are His prophets, called by Him to proclaim His word. This is also true for common people: somebody who wants to orient others in a religious way cannot rely on generally provable footholds either. You can only, as a person, testify to your interpretation of them; you must give proof of it as a *witness*.

This again points out another basic characteristic of our orientation to other orientations: personal witnesses are always necessary when facts and their circumstances cannot be immediately observed. In court, witnesses report on events which are not (or no longer) accessible to the court – they must prove, with their word, the existence of certain facts and their circumstances. Here, however, the authority responsible for the truth of testimonies is the court itself: it must, on its part, decide on the truth without being able to know the truth (judges, as mentioned earlier, must not have been present at the events they judge). For a (monotheistic) religious orientation, God is the authority responsible for the truth of all events and all given testimonies. But, contrary to the law, in religion it is, as Søren Kierkegaard made clear, the witness who testifies to the instance of truth: the believer testifies to God as an instance precisely by giving testimony before Him as the highest court. For this, he or she must already be *convinced* of God's existence. Whoever convinces others of something brings them to the decision of holding something to be true or untrue, with regard to something to which they do not have access without him or her. But you can also convince yourself of something by deciding for specific interpretations of specific signs; and you can convince yourself in a religious way by deciding to consider these signs as coming from God.

If you convince yourself that something is true of which you cannot know anything, then you *believe*. Here, too, religious orientation adopts a basic characteristic of everyday orientation and points to its most extreme form: as far as you cannot fully survey a situation in which you have to act under the pressure of time, your actions are always based on belief. Immanuel Kant already explained this in his *Critique of Pure Reason:* he called it a "pragmatic belief," distinguishing it from a "doctrinal belief" (*Critique of Pure Reason*, A 824 f./B 852 f.). A religious conviction or faith is a pragmatic belief that is explicitly emphasized. It can, on its part, be supported by and fixed to specific doctrines.

(4) Religious Confession. – Religious faith must – *being* religious – testify to itself, and this happens again through signs, be it someone witnessing ceremonies of religious communities, be it he or she identifying him or herself using conventional signs, or be it he or she confessing his or her faith in words. A religious confession is a *decision revealed to others about a certain religious orientation.* If understood as a binding obligation for one's entire life, it is the most far-reaching and, as far as it is publicly testified, the most conspicuous identification. It is supposed to indicate a 'reversal' of orientation, the turning away *from* an 'orientation to the world' and the turning *toward* an 'orientation to God'; it may be preceded – if initiated by others – by a 'conversion.' It is – in contrast to one's sexual orientation, which also greatly determines the course of one's life, but which is predetermined by physical features or desires – *an exemplary orientation decision.* In modern democratic societies, you are allowed to make a free decision on it.

In accounts of the Abrahamic religions, Abraham, or, as it were, Ibrahim, was repeatedly forced to make decisions concerning his faith. These included his decisions to emigrate to Canaan (Gen. 12), on the covenant with God (Gen. 15), on circumcision as a sign of the covenant (Gen. 17), and his decision to sacrifice his late-born son Isaac (which was eventually stopped by God). While Jews, springing (as they testify) from his lineage, were already born as Jews, those desiring to become Christians or Muslims had to first make a decision on their faith. Religious schisms required new, oftentimes life-threatening decisions. They were, and still are, perceived as decisions that are owed to the God one believes in, His will, and His mercy. As such, these decisions have also already been decided by God; they are thus – again, but now in a different way – paradoxical decisions regarding something undecidable. However, here too the paradox is resolved through resoluteness or decisiveness: the attitude of holding on to one's decisions without considering new decisions on them (chap. 6.3). As far as a religious decision is attributed to God Himself, a resolutely religious orientation can leave behind all uncertainties – and be calm and reassured in its faith. One then does not need to demand the same decision from others; one may let other faiths exist besides one's own; a religious orientation will seek the approval of others only so long as it is still uncertain. A religious hold, the hold of the decision to hold on to the ungraspable and incomprehensible, is based on a resoluteness that is no longer questioned or irritated by new footholds, arguments, or evidence. If irritations of faith still occur, one can understand them – in the horizon of one's faith – as signs from God meant to test one's faith (Job). In this way, one's religious faith can find an unconditional support; the religious orientation provides an *unconditional, absolute hold*. It is, if it proceeds as such, immune against existential disorientations.

(5) Religious Shelter. – As far as religious orientation goes beyond other orientation worlds, it takes away the pressing significance of immediate hardships (as difficult as they may be) and the needs that emerge from them (as urgent as they may be). It gives an orientation the *greatest possible confidence*. This was perhaps never put as concisely as it was by the German theologian and resistance fighter Dietrich Bonhoeffer, who, penned in expectation of his execution in a Gestapo basement, wrote to his mother and to his bride in a few simple lines that "By loving forces wonderfully sheltered, / we are awaiting fearlessly what comes." ("Von guten Mächten wunderbar geborgen / erwarten wir getrost was kommen mag.") Shelter is an enhanced security or safety: the confidence that one will find help in all dangers – or simply endure the dangers – and thus be safe. It is the safety offered by the certainty of faith: the certainty that even the greatest uncertainties and the gravest dangers will still have a positive outcome, a happy ending, granted by God – a certainty that no reason can ex-

plain or justify and that hardly any disappointments can shatter. It thus allows one to face much greater uncertainties in life. Religious orientation may give one the utmost courage to act, all the way up to sacrificing one's own life for others – and to maintain one's faith. Religious trust may also help one – in one's orientation to other orientations – to bear the most severe breaches of trust. "To love the human being *for the sake of God* – that has been," wrote Nietzsche, certainly the least suspicious witness of religious matters, "the noblest and most remote feeling people have attained so far." (*Beyond Good and Evil*, No. 60; our translation). Religion involves a reorientation of an entire orientation to confidence.

(6) Religious Leeways of Interpretation. – However, with the absolute hold of a religious conviction, an orientation also runs an extreme risk: the risk of holding on to something holdless. The confidence of the religious orientation is based solely on its unconditional faith in itself, which opens up extreme leeways of interpretation. But it also raises extreme difficulties of faith: if God created and rules the world as it is, why does anything exist that He, in His supposed benignity, may not want: misfortune, misery, suffering, pain of every kind and crimes including even genocide and terrorism. Attempts of so-called theodicy, God's justification for the evils in his world, have always remained questionable, if only because they were human attempts. Not only uncertain situations, but also extreme leeways of interpretation are hard to bear. In the religious orientation, too, one therefore looks for a graspable orientation – and finds it in a religious *community* that commits itself to *binding doctrines of faith*. In religious communities, confessions to God are also the members' confessions before each other; the members of a religious community oversee each other with regard to how serious and how consistent they are in keeping to their faith. This requires definitions of rules, ceremonies, and doctrines; by all of them, the delimited religious orientation is again limited and thus attains graspable holds, in addition to the ungraspable one.

For their doctrines, the text-based religions find their footholds in Holy Scriptures. But these Holy Scriptures leave open leeways for interpretation, too. Therefore, systematic dogmatics and/or selected interpreters are required to restrict the leeways for interpretation; in addition, the significance of the Holy Scriptures and the doctrines derived from them must be made clear for concrete situations. As a result, text-based religions have most strongly served to advance the art of interpretation as well as its academic discipline, i.e. hermeneutics. As far as theologies are established, any explicit formulation of doctrines puts them again to the test of arguments, criticism, and disputes. The more religions insist on firm doctrines (Christianity and Islam more so than Judaism), the greater the risk of heresy, which must then be fought against. The unconditional and steadfast decisiveness of the faith of a religious community may thus lead to religious wars – and it has done so again and again. Up to the present day, wars justified by religions remain the fiercest.

(7) Religious Tolerance. – The severe calamities that religious wars bring to humanity may eventually enforce, as was the case in Europe's modern era, religious tolerance. Religious tolerance is the strength of letting others, against one's own conviction, have other religious convictions. In this way, it renders religious convictions paradoxical, too – in some regard like majority decisions (chap. 12.4 [4]). Indeed, the need for religious tolerance has given rise to the conviction of a constitutional state that allows for the peaceful coexistence of religions and denominations, as has been exemplary in the United States. Religious peace demands not only tolerance, but also the attentive mutual consideration of religious convictions. In this way, tolerance has also become a vantage point of ethical orientation (we will come back to this). The hold of a religious conviction solely to itself may, on the one hand, produce a stiff self-righteousness and, on the other, initiate self-limitations. It can then let go of controversial doctrines, which one may insist on or abstain from; this in turn depends on the relevant religious traditions. Friedrich Schleiermacher, who dared a great reorientation in Protestant theology (and at the same time in philosophy), claimed in his *On Religion: Speeches to its Cultured Despisers* (1799) that even a person who does not believe in a Holy Scripture may be religious without any doctrines at all and that a religion may even do without God. He later defined the "feeling" that one ultimately cannot grasp or comprehend one's life situation (in all its uncertainty) as the "feeling of absolute dependence." He thus had religion emerge out of the fundamental problems of orientation.

Friedrich Nietzsche, who in many respects can be considered an heir of Schleiermacher, pushed this de-dogmatization of Christianity even further, returning to the "evangelical practice" of the "type Jesus," a practice oriented toward the God of love as Jesus understood it: this practice permitted him to keep a distance from all norms and dogmas. In the midst of his anti-Christian polemics, Nietzsche, on his part, understood Jesus as a "great symbolist," who "resisted every kind of word, formula, law, faith, dogma" and dissolved all "reality" into "parables" and "signs," into "a being floating entirely in symbols and incomprehensibilities" (*The Anti-Christ*, nos. 31–34). In doing so, Nietzsche depicted religion as emerging entirely from signs. By orienting oneself to them, a "great tolerance, that is, magnanimous self-constraint" (*The Anti-Christ*, No. 38) is still to be attained, also and especially in matters of faith. Nietzsche himself does not seem to have come to terms with Christianity in this way, least of all in the very book where he expresses these claims. But he added: "the true, the original Christianity will always be possible..." (*The Anti-Christ*, No. 39). For him, Christianity was an evangelical practice oriented solely to signs.

(8) A Culture of Gratitude. – With a critical distance from convictions and doctrines, religion transforms into a culture of gratitude. With the faith that even the decision to have faith in God is owed to God, religious orientation is eventually an attestation of gratitude. Gratitude to God excludes any retaliation, recompensation, or gifts in return for what He has given. Gratitude arises when an orientation is unexpectedly successful, when you escape a great danger, when the major risks you were anticipating are ultimately avoided, when you have 'great fortune,' but also when everything is, for once, simply calm and good. For this you want to be grateful in view of the uncertainty of all orientation. The desire to give thanks likewise, and perhaps above all, creates a need for religion. Nietzsche wrote, again in *The Anti-Christ:* religion is "a form of gratitude. One is grateful for oneself: for this one needs a god" (*The Anti-Christ*, No. 16).

Chapter 14
The Self-Binding of Orientation: Moral Orientation

Orientation through
Self-Binding

What we call moral, morals, or morality is – despite its deep impact on our orientation – difficult to grasp in terms or concepts. In the history of Western ethics, it appears in the form of *commandments* that come from the Abrahamic God (e. g. do not kill, do not lie, do not commit adultery), as the self-directed *striving* of human beings –, e. g. for justice (Plato), for happiness and reputation (Aristotle), for inner peace (Stoicism, Epicureanism), for peace with God (Augustine of Hippo), for an improvement of the general living conditions (Francis Bacon), or for the greatest happiness of the greatest number (Jeremy Bentham) –, as *pleasure* concerning the benevolence of human beings toward each other (David Hume), as an *inner coercion* to defy one's own inclinations (Immanuel Kant), as the *unlimited responsibility* of each individual for everyone else (Fyodor Dostoevsky), as the human *will to continual self-overcoming* (Friedrich Nietzsche), as the *attainment of justified consent* concerning norms to be followed by everyone (Jürgen Habermas), as a responsible response to the *call of the Other's suffering* (Emmanuel Levinas), and eventually as the *disregard of reciprocity* (Jacques Derrida) – all these are just principles that Western thought has brought forth, and that continue to have effects on its orientation. All of them are respectable, but they are hardly compatible with one other; none of them has eventually been able to prevail over the others; none of them has become the basis on which to justify all the others. Justifications of moral principles are themselves bound by these and biased by them; reasons for other morals appear just as strange as those morals themselves; reasons for certain morals are always, in moral terms, self-justifications of these morals. A lived morality, however, does not need any reasons; reasons can always be disputed, and they may thus, on the contrary, irritate one's moral routines. As such, morals seem to be part of orientation itself, something so self-evident and binding that you do not want to question it, nor are you able to do so. The fact that other morals are the strangest part of other orientations indicates how deeply embedded our own morals are in our orientation. But today we encounter other morals (like other religions) not only in foreign cultures but also in our own living en-

https://doi.org/10.1515/9783110575149-016

vironments; and we must find a way to deal with them. As part of orientation, morality is thus also a problem of orientation.

Prior to all justifications or normative demands, a philosophy of orientation starts with an *observation of moral orientation*. This is provided less by philosophical ethics, but rather ethnology, sociology, sociobiology, and psychology – as far as they are not themselves bound by a specific philosophical morality. One of the pioneers in this field was, again, Erving Goffman. By now, scientists have pursued large-scale empirical research agendas in order to observe how morals emerge and establish themselves. Already Nietzsche proposed an empirical "science of morals," tasked with "collecting the materials" and "formulating concepts and putting into order a tremendous realm of tender value feelings and value distinctions that live, grow, procreate, and perish" (*Beyond Good and Evil*, No. 186). He invited philologists, historians, etymologists as well as physiologists, physicians, psychologists, and ethnologists to involve themselves in this task (*On the Genealogy of Morals* I, No. 17, note). Michel Foucault, in particular, then adopted this research agenda.

With Nietzsche, a philosophy of orientation can assume that, on the one hand, morals limit the leeways of orientation, binding not only one's actions but also one's thinking. On the other hand, modern democratic societies allow for a pluralism of morals. Until today, we have not only morally accepted this pluralism; most of us appreciate it. Thus, in matters of morals, too, we have moved to a second-order observation, i. e. a moral observation of moral observations: we regard as morally relevant not only that people comply with certain morals, but also that they respect other morals. Therefore, what is at stake is less the universalization of a specific morality (in which case you would consider only your own), but rather how to deal with other morals, i. e. a *morality for dealing with different morals*. As such, morality not only refers to inhibition and restriction, but also to liberation and distinction. In order to terminologically separate the two, we will speak of 'ethical orientation' when addressing a morality in dealing with different moral orientations, be it your own or another.

When observing how morality contributes to human orientation, we must look for its clues or footholds in our orientation. With Nietzsche, one can assume that one's morality permeates one's entire behavior and the totality of one's orientation. If this is true, you can hardly distinguish the moral (or thoroughly moralized) orientation from the rest of orientation – but this is hardly plausible. Instead, we assume that morality manifests itself in specific situations and actions in specific ways. Here, the most striking and strongest foothold of morality seems to be the *inner coercion* to help others who are, in immediate proximity, faced with an emergency situation they cannot master themselves: the situativity of orientation – others' emergencies – immediately enforces its moral relevance.

A confused old lady goes astray, a close friend of yours can suddenly no longer take care of his family, or a child falls into a freezing cold river – being the only one present, you are the only one who can help. You will then feel compelled to disregard (and more so: to forget) all of your our own interests, even if this will bring about serious inconveniences or hardships for yourself (you may miss important appointments when taking the old lady a long way to her home; you may lose a lot of money when helping your friend; you may risk your own life when jumping into the ice-cold water to save the drowning child, and your own children may just as well lose their mom or dad). This inner coercion is something people experience again and again. It is highly respected: you find it in the Bible as well as in everyday life; it has sustained religious, societal, and philosophical transformations.

We omit any hypotheses regarding the – as it appears – overall internalization of this moral coercion; we take it for granted as an observable fact (as Kant did with the 'voice of reason' – but is there a reason speaking to you?). It is not a question of altruism or egoism: between these two, you can decide; however, in emergency situations like the ones described you do not initially decide; you immediately feel urged to help – if you are the closest to the others' emergency. But this fact is unlikely and surprising as far as orientation is primarily about pragmatically finding one's way and constantly attending to matters as to whether and how one may benefit from them. Both, the usual needs of our orientation (to look for our own advantages) and the moral coercion (to dispense with these advantages in particular situations), can only be reconciled with each other if the moral coercion, too, comes from a need of orientation. If this is the case, morality would not only be a virtue, but also a necessity – a necessity that was moralized, that was made into a virtue. Morality would then also find its measure in the needs, necessities, or emergencies of orientation. Out of respect for morality, moral philosophers usually presume that one should *always* think and act morally and can never think and act morally enough. But everyday orientation has to take into account its other options too; after suspending them in a given moral situation, it must be able to return to them. Inner moral coercion arises in specific situations of our orientation, but it also dissolves again. This has so far hardly been addressed in either moral philosophy or moral science. With regard to human orientation as a whole, we will pose and answer this question.

14.1 Closing the Leeways of Orientation: Moral Coercion

It is not in every situation that orientation is noticeably under the pressure of moral coercion. Moral coercion occurs from time to time, and it goes away as well. It may strongly coerce you in a specific situation; but the situation can change again. Under the pressure of moral coercion, you could therefore simply wait and see; such hesitation would be justified to the extent that moral actions may entail severe sacrifices. But moral coercion requires you to neglect all your own advantages and disadvantages – *it shuts down the leeways of your orientation, without reservation.* You experience that you *must* do what is morally demanded from you; just looking for a way out creates a guilty conscience. Moral coercion suspends all orientations but the moral one; it requires your full commitment.

In terms of orientation, you then adopt a moral standpoint and assess the situation only from this standpoint. Orientation is being moralized as a whole; the moral standpoint is totalized; precisely this *totalizing of the moral standpoint* is what the coercion consists of. You now distinguish everything as to whether it fits to or contradicts the moral direction of your orientation; you spontaneously assess all matters as good or evil, moral or immoral. Acting morally means acting decisively without any leeways for deciding; you exclude what does not support your moral action as immoral. Moral coercion is, in this sense, unconditional. As far as one can find no other reasons for this moral coercion, one ascribes it to free will – the freedom to act morally.

Since the moral intention suspends all other options for acting, it poses a high risk for an orientation. It can therefore only be a last resort, an emergency measure. What is the emergency or necessity it responds to? The most plausible answer would be, again, the *needs of double contingency.* More than anything else, moral action shuts down double contingency: its unconditionality means, for others, unconditional reliability. To rely on someone means to trust in him or her without reservation. The need for morality then means the *need to trust in the reliability of others* – in emergency situations, where you are totally dependent on others. Since you cannot enforce reliability (also and especially in these situations) 'from outside,' via third persons, moral coercion must come from 'inside'; its binding must be a self-binding. Bindings in orientation may develop through experiences you have with others, through education and authorities, or through contracts and laws. They then remain dependent on the people involved; such bindings are contingent. The moral self-binding, too, may mostly come from bindings to others, primarily through one's education; but once established, it makes educational measures unnecessary, and it remains in effect as unconditional – you can then instantaneously and permanently rely on it.

Self-bindings may also be of a non-moral kind; habits or routines are also permanent self-bindings that exclude other options. But we can continually shift among routines; they are themselves alternative options; and you can abolish them, if necessary, without any moral scruples. By contrast, the inner coercion of the moral self-binding excludes even this possibility of shifting, of alternating, or of abolishing your routines. Moral coercion most strongly abbreviates and restricts our orientation to other orientations. It is an unconditionally reliable hold – also and especially for others. This is why we try to raise children to this inner coercion of moral self-binding.

However, just as trust permits the betrayal of trust, morality permits the faking of morality, i. e. hypocrisy. Therefore, morality is risky, too. The moral self-binding is, for others, not a fact, but a *promise*, a commitment to future reliability. If such a promise is based on one's own conviction, it not only binds one's actions, but also one's thinking – then, hypocrisy can be ruled out, and one can expect the promise to hold true. In those emergency situations which others (close to you) find themselves in, you feel morally coerced to keep this promise; you would already be breaking your promise if you think about possibly (under certain circumstances) not keeping it; the mere thought of breaking a promise breaks the moral self-binding you committed to. Based on your own convictions, your (unspoken) moral promise of remaining reliable comes close to a religious commitment. If you are committed to something morally or religiously, you cannot even think differently: different thoughts would not even occur to you, and if others bring them up or impose them upon you, you reject them as unthinkable (e. g. 'Could I make money from the hardship my friend and his family are in?'). As a result, the inner coercion of a moral self-binding shows up not just in what you *ought* to do, but also in the fact that you are *unable* to think or act differently. It is in this way that morality, as we have conceived it here, permeates our entire orientation and can consequently govern our orientation as a whole.

14.2 Footholds for and Clues and Signs in Morally Relevant Situations

If the moral coercion in orientation occurs only from time to time, then it must be triggered by morally relevant footholds in a given situation (1). From a moral standpoint, the meaning of all footholds changes (2).

(1) Footholds for Morally Relevant Situations. – The strongest footholds for morally relevant situations are again emergencies, here the *emergencies of others*. A situation is most obviously morally relevant if somebody is in an emergency situation calling for the protection or help of others. What is morally coercing

is the emergency itself, in which someone is unable to find his or her way without the protection or the help of others, thus making him or her dependent on others; this precedes any articulated appeals or demands as well as any legal claims or moral norms. It also precedes compassion and altruism. In compassion or pity, you may still remain distanced and inactive. Pity may well play a part in acting morally. But if you are morally coerced, you immediately jump in and assist others in their emergencies, you instantaneously do something that relieves their needs, and, if the situation requires it, you risk your life in the process without considering your own benefits or the potential costs.

This is true for altruism as well: as morally pleasant as it may be, especially if it has become a permanent attitude, altruism still allows you to turn *on your own* to other people's needs (or not), thus reserving for yourself the right to decide to whom, and under which conditions, you want to turn to others' needs or stay away from them. The Other's emergency, as Emmanuel Levinas emphasized (writing 'Other' with a capital letter), allows for neither the freedom to make such a decision nor the time to assess moral reasons.

Furthermore, the inner coercion to immediately jump to the aid of others in need does not entail the expectation of *reciprocity*, either. The young woman who may miss an important exam or have to leave her children alone in order to take the old lost lady to her home would still reject any thought of a favor in return. It is thus not the expectation of rewards, but the other's concrete emergency situation itself that morally coerces us. This coercion can hardly be explained by the laws of nature as a physical, biological, sociobiological, or psychological mechanism. You experience the other's emergency as an irrefutable incitement to immediately and entirely reverse your own orientation, i.e. as the *turning point of a temporary reorientation*. Your orientation then becomes a *moral orientation*.

The needs of others, first and foremost any lack of what is most essential for life (food, clothes, housing, warmth), then physical and mental injuries, life-threatening dangers, domination, suppression, and exploitation by powerful people can morally unsettle you to such a degree that you cannot disregard them. In archaic living conditions, this was quite obvious. In the Hebrew Bible, just as in the Homeric epics, it is primarily destitute and unprotected orphans, widows, and foreigners whose needs are morally challenging; these needs involve elementary goods such as survival, physical integrity, peace, and – primarily to prevent domination, suppression, and exploitation – justice. The modern constitutional state and social securities, which have increasingly been implemented since the 19th century, have simultaneously increased the distance to these emergencies and the needs of others. Now, to a large extent, special institutions take care of them. But here, too, our sense of justice is aroused especially if individuals are not, or are not sufficiently, being assisted in their need by these institutions. However, the strongest moral outrage erupts when others' misery is exploited by third parties to their advantage, thereby aggravating this misery; the deliberate aggravation of others' misery 'cries' for justice, in both archaic and current times.

The circumstances of failing to provide help for someone in need is likewise addressed in the story of the good Samaritan in the New Testament (Lk. 10:36). By addressing the 'neighbor,' the story emphasizes *the characteristic spatiality and temporality of our moral orientation.* The 'neighbor' in the story is not one who lives in the neighborhood, but the one who is the nearest or closest to somebody's emergency; this means: the neighbor is the 'next available' who can help – in the biblical story, this means helping the man who has been beaten half to death by muggers and left to lie in his own blood. The neighbor is the Samaritan, who helps without reservation, after the priest and the Levite are prevented from helping by their religious laws, which forbid them from touching blood. The one who is temporally and spatially nearest to the suffering of another is the one who can no longer escape the coercion to offer immediate help by passing on his or her responsibility to others, but who must act him or herself. In the biblical, metaphorical sense, you are the 'neighbor' if nobody else, and above all no professional, is there to help, e. g. a doctor in the case of an accident, or a relative of the lost old lady who could come with a car to take her home. The further away one is from another's need among those who can help, the lower the moral coercion to jump to his or her aid. Thus, it is the proximity itself that morally coerces us.

However, the Christian Gospel speaks of the 'neighbor' or the 'nearest' in different ways. According to Mk. 12:31 as well as already in the Hebrew Bible (Lev. 19:17), the neighbor is also the one who is helped and who is to be loved, in the sense of the Christian commandment of 'love thy neighbor.' This sense continues to prevail. The love of neighbor, who needs help, may also get you into a situation of need, namely if the neighbor is in an emergency that also endangers the helper. As such, in the Hebrew Bible, Lot, who is himself a foreigner in Sodom, tries to divert the Sodomites from their viscous attacks on the foreigners who came to his house as guests by offering his daughters to the attackers instead (Gen. 19); his guests' emergency becomes his own emergency. The Christian Gospel inflates the 'love of neighbor' to such a degree that the neighbors or the nearest may even be enemies (Mt. 5:44), enemies like the furious Sodomites. However, this is not an inner coercion, but a commandment: if the need, which calls for help, were not to bring the helper him or herself into a situation of emergency, then the 'love of neighbor' would be easy and would not have to be commanded.

As the Samaritan story also shows, a chance meeting is enough to create the coercion to help; the Samaritan who happens to pass by does not share anything with the injured person; on the contrary, these two are even separated by belonging to different religions, which gives them more leeways of action compared to the priest and the Levite.

If it is plausible to consider the immediate encounter with the other's suffering – the proximity of the face-to-face – as the source of moral orientation, then it is quite surprising that philosophical ethics did not speak of this source before Emmanuel Levinas, a Jewish thinker who made Jewish thinking fruitful for what he called 'Greek thinking.' Christian ethics detached the moral coercion of 'love your neighbor' from the concrete needs of concrete others in concrete emergency situations, generalizing it, in the 'Greek' way, into a universal commandment. Thus, in Christianity, the supposed source of morality in our orientation is no longer clearly discernible. But the parable of the Samaritan points to it.

(2) Clues and Signs in Morally Relevant Situations. – Once a situation is observed as morally relevant, everything in it may gain moral significance. The fright caused by the sight of another's suffering becomes moral concern; the impulse to immediately do something becomes moral coercion; the torment of seeing the other's emergency becomes compassion; the rage of being powerless against it becomes moral outrage; the feeling of failure becomes shame and remorse; the satisfaction of a successful effort becomes pride. You experience all these impulses (more or less) physically, and you also observe them in others: as getting pale in fright; as a tension in the impulse to do something; as an expression of pain in compassion; as a threatening gesture in outrage; as blushing in shame; as an embarrassed turning-away in remorse; and as a beaming with pride. Given the importance of moral situations, human beings have developed the finest sensors: a barely perceptible raising of eyebrows becomes a sign of moral irritation; a brief stiffening of the gaze, the sign of moral fright; a slight hesitation or a change in the tone of voice, the signs of moral disapproval, etc.; these correspond to likewise refined signs of moral respect, appreciation, and admiration. The mood that arises together with the coercion and the decision to act morally is seriousness; it expresses itself in resoluteness.

But you can also just fake all these signs, including, and even more so, the language signs used for them: calls for help, complaints, requests, pleas, demands, claims, etc. Therefore, the morally coerced person also, and especially, needs to be vigilant for all clues, footholds, and signs in the moral situation and observe how they fit together.

14.3 The Self-Stabilization of Moral Orientation: Moral Routines, Moral Identities, Dominant Moralities, and Markets of Moralities

In specific situations, moral coercions impose extraordinary demands on an orientation. But over time, our moral orientation also becomes a habit and stabilizes itself. Since its self-binding is self-referential, it too shapes itself autonomously. It is able to immunize and taboo itself, but also to radically criticize itself. For its stabilization, it takes on the structures of orientation explored above: moral orientation develops routines (1), shapes identities (2), and adopts prevailing or 'dominant' moralities (3). In these processes, the meaning of morality changes significantly. Its footholds are subject to fluctuations on markets of moralities (4).

(1) Moral Routines. – The more you experience the reliability of persons acting morally, the more you trust in moral commitments. As such, routines – now moral routines – develop in coming to someone's aid. This obviously happens in families, among friends and neighbors, in communities, in professional and sports teams, in military units, etc., and even in global state-organized or nongovernmental disaster relief. For most emergency services beyond interindividual orientation worlds, where everyone can quickly become the next responsible person, professional institutions such as the fire department, ambulance service, hospitals, foster care, retirement centers, and nursing homes, etc., have been established along with various support groups and charitable organizations. They take on the responsibility of helping others in existential need and relieving individuals. In most cases, you can simply call emergency services in order to ensure professional care. Someone's selfless, 'self-sacrificial' succoring, e.g. in cases of addiction support or home nursing, is no longer the rule, but becomes an exceptional and distinguishing quality. But whenever moral routines develop, they create the expectation that they will continue to be fulfilled on a regular basis – and thus also the *expectation of reciprocity*. This is formulated in the Golden Rule: do to others what you would want them to do to you, or rather, do not perform any actions toward others that you would not be willing to accept from them in turn. This *limits* moral coercion: you then do not have to do anything beyond what you would expect others to do.

(2) Moral Identities. – Moral orientation based on reciprocity looks for identities as the steady footholds of mutual orientation; identifications entail, to a great extent, moral identifications: respect, on the one hand, disrespect, contempt, disdain, condemnation or scorn on the other (chap. 11, introduction). The basic moral distinction is *good or evil*. Put shortly, 'evil' is that which in-

creases needs, 'good' that which relieves or prevents them; what is good is welcome, and what is evil is warded off; both must, for purposes of orientation, be distinguished as quickly and sustainably as possible. If people have proven unreliable or even obstructive in cases when you have completely depended on them, you try to no longer involve them in anything at all. Moral identifications select a *person as a whole* ('she is ok'); they are the strongest kind of abbreviation. Based on just a few experiences with someone ('she will help me because she already helped me the other day'), one infers their *moral character*; information from third persons or mere rumors in turn influence one's own experience ('when he was with his first wife, didn't he also...').

As a next step, one quickly draws conclusions from individuals to entire groups – to societies, classes, peoples, ethnic groups, or even 'races' (chap. 11.1). Quick, and thus often premature and improper, moral generalizations help an orientation to avoid repeating 'bad experiences' with 'certain people.' What is even more dangerous is that, in doing so, one rather tends toward negative rather than positive moral identifications; in everyday orientation, morality therefore often carries a negative image. As such, explicit moral identifications of persons or groups create a specific *moral pressure:* in the negative case, the addressed persons or groups will try to defend themselves; in the positive case, they must satisfy the expectations connected with these identifications (the latter is often deliberately and explicitly intended in education).

Moral communication is therefore particularly precarious; it increases a situation's tension. If we observe each other in tense situations with regard to future reliability ('now that I am in such a bad place, will I get along with him?'), a few body signs and glances can already be crucial factors: a gesture or a look (does he look 'calmly into my eyes' or does he 'turn away with embarrassment'?) may decide whether you will continue to cooperate or not. As always, when having made the decision, the footholds in favor of it are amplified, while those that were against it are attenuated; moral communication exacerbates distortions of information after decisions are made. The enhanced moral footholds can, if positive, create moral authorities, or, if negative, defamations. Positive *moral interaction rituals* decrease risk:, e.g. a warm welcome, a handshake or a hug signalizing peacefulness, an apology or a request for forgiveness when disturbances seem to threaten an existing trust. Negative interaction rituals increase risk: ignoring or skipping over someone, provocatively looking straight into someone's eyes, etc. To gain and maintain mutual moral respect, we make use of the diplomacy of signs with special circumspection and caution. The particular tension of moral communication especially encourages engaging in indirect communication, i.e. communicating about third persons who are absent. In doing so, you can, given the explosive nature of moral judgments, learn, without any binding commitment, about the *moral standards* of others and explore the leeways of where you do not run the risk of making moral judgments that may offend someone ('you should not say something like that').

If you want to *morally identify yourself with others*, it can be enough to join *a* group on certain occasions. Alarming events that quickly spread through the media – a terrorist attack, a murderous rampage in a school, or, on the other hand, major events such as an electoral victory promising that many things will get better, the victory of your national team at a world cup, the establishment of peace after a devastating war, or the fall of a wall that long divided a nation – all these may bring people together out on the streets or in places where they will then stand together for many hours, hugging each other to express their suffering or joy. Today, you share messages on social media. You show your moral solidarity with each other, here too without being forced to morally act. During elections or ceremonial meetings, speakers publicly emphasize common moral standards. At protests for a shared concern, the participants render their own physical presence a sign for this concern; every additional person amplifies the moral weight. The public demonstration of common goals may become a moral movement, which in turn may trigger riots, uprisings, revolts, and revolutions, which may then overrun well-established political orders. In this way, a collective moral identification may develop into a dominant power.

(3) Dominant Morals. – The ensemble of the moral standards of a group or society constitutes their morals. There is no need to explicitly formulate and even less to justify or systematically work through such morals; they are in effect as self-evident, and if they come up for discussion they are presumed *as* self-evident. Children are, likewise self-evidently, raised to follow them. People become attentive to the morals of their group or society through 'scandals.' Gr. *skándalon* means 'offense' or 'trouble'; the very fact that a violation of certain morals causes 'trouble' (in the private realm) or a 'scandal' (in the public) shows that they are in effect. In their self-evidence, morals *select* people as well: if you violate their routines, rules, or standards, or if you publicly object to them, you run the risk of being excluded as 'immoral' from the group where they are in effect. In this way, morals immunize themselves against deviations and objections. They thus become 'dominant' morals within groups or societies. As dominantly accepted in a group or society, what is called *'moral' is that which would relieve their needs.*

(Most) people adopt (most of) the moral routines, rules, or standards of the morals that dominate their group or society as their own convictions. These adopted routines, rules, or standards determine what, in a given situation, coerces one to act morally. This can then not only be the 'nearest' person whom you must succor in his or her need, but also your homeland when it is involved in a war, or a religion that calls for a fight against non-believers. Dominant morals stabilize orientations as strongly as religions; therefore, it is often difficult to distinguish the two. However, morals exert greater pressure: today, it is usually easier to leave a religious community than a society – if you stay in a society, you have to obey its moral standards.

Dominant moral standards have effects similar to plausibility standards; they render questions and inquiries not only unnecessary but also inappropriate or absurd. Here, too, there is a difference between center and periphery. The periphery includes standards that still tolerate deviations and objections; the center comprises moral taboos that, as ethnological research has shown, are familiar to all societies (even if they differ among them) and where violations create moral outrage (such as, in Sophocles' *King Oedipus*, patricide and incest). You may not even articulate them: if they are articulated, the taboo is broken. Acting against taboos is 'unthinkable'; taboos prevent certain actions by means of prohibiting even the thought of them; this is how they are in effect, and they therefore constitute the core of morals.

(4) Markets of Moralities. – To become a dominant morality, a morality must be communicated. The communication of respect and disrespect in moral judgments is doubly contingent as well; before moral judgments become dominant standards, it depends – just as in the case of language standards – on each individual to accept or reject them. With dominant morals, this still applies to their periphery. Here, you can risk new moral assessments, and you will then see to what extent they permeate into the center and may 'breach the dam.' This takes time, time to test out the moral innovations and to get used to them, which may be pleasant for some and painful for others (e. g. women adopting traditionally all-male professions; homosexuals getting married; hierarchies being leveled; the moral pressure on businesses increasing; environmental concerns gaining political priority). Moral innovations must, according to Luhmann, assert themselves, as it were, on markets, small and big markets of respect or disrespect (if not contempt or scorn); innovations are demanded and offered whenever the dominant moral standards themselves cause dissatisfactions, grievances, or hardships. Markets of moralities let us also understand how individuals gain moral authority: by means of a kind of 'capitalization' of respect. If someone has earned respect from some people, he or she will more easily win it from others. Here, too, one quickly takes on orientations from others; the trust of others encourages one's own trust. Whoever enjoys the trust of many people has moral authority; whoever has moral authority receives in advance a greater 'credit' of trust, a kind of 'moral credit'; if you have moral credit, people are more likely to morally accept from you what they would not so easily accept from others: praise and blame, advice, admonitions – but also moral innovations.

Authorities represent, if sticking to the language of the markets, something like moral brands that are (more or less) independent of the fluctuations in a given market of moralities. By earning respect from others, your self-respect grows as well and increases your independence from the respect of others; this independence from the respect of others is (to repeat) highly respected, especially by those who lack it. In this way, moral authorities stabilize a market of moralities. But they do not shut the market down. Just as markets of moralities allow you to capitalize on respect for moral authority, they also make it possible for you to 'go bankrupt': moral authorities are themselves required to adhere to the high moral standards they vouch for; thus, an obvious moral misconduct can, with a single stroke, bargain away their entire moral authority, in interindividual as well as societal orientation worlds.

14.4 Moral Coercions for Submitting to Societal Rules and for Acting Responsibly

Despite its self-stabilization, the morality of a group or society can always be shaken or changed by individuals. Even if moral routines invite you to follow them and even if dominant morals force you to submit to them, thus relieving you from your individual moral coercions, neither free you from your own coercions. In others' emergency situations, individuals may still feel morally coerced to take responsibility on their own. In doing so, they may possibly break with moral routines and dominant morals, and they can thereby gain moral respect, too. Likewise, on markets of moralities, moral actions are only considered as authentic if one acts on one's own responsibility. Responsibility can be (1) 'attributed,' 'assigned,' or 'ascribed'; but one can also (2) 'take it on' oneself; it can (3) 'fall' to someone, and it finally (4) may be 'delegated.' In each case, the moral coercion and morality as such attain different meanings.

(1) Attributing Responsibility. – Attributing responsibility according to dominant standards means morally coercing others. This typically starts with the calamity caused by a damage that has occurred: one looks for a person responsible to whom the damage can be attributed. In principle, you could endlessly retrace the chain of potential causes; a car driver who causes an accident may have done this under various influences that are equally or more 'responsible' for the accident, e. g. other drivers who forced him to evade them, a preceding violent marital dispute or a certain medication that had an unfavorable effect on his driving ability. With further investigations, the orientation to the possible causes becomes ever more complex and the attribution of responsibility ever more difficult. Therefore, at some point one must stop retracing causes; one thus focuses

(in our example) on the car driver by blaming him so that he has to pay for the damage. The driver is then the 'nearest' one (as discussed before) – but in an inverted sense: as the most plausible foothold to which you may abbreviate your own orientation. The person blamed can of course refuse to take responsibility for the damage. Then, one can either look for someone else to blame (e. g. the driver who forced him to get out of the way) or one can, in less relevant cases, let the matter rest.

This mode of cutting short the search for possible causes continues in court: a judge who attributes responsibility must find plausible and legal footholds that are as close as possible to the incident that happened (chap. 12.5). In politics, responsibility is very quickly attributed to certain persons because this offers the chance of attracting public attention, and if the people involved are prominent enough, the media will gladly pick this up. Responsibility can thus be attributed for very different reasons and in very different ways – depending on the circumstances.

(2) Taking on Responsibility. – If others attribute the responsibility for some damage (be it material or mental) to you, you can also accept the attribution, identify with it, and thus 'take on' the responsibility. You then not only have to be willing to 'face the music' for what you (may) have done and thus accept the losses in assets or respect or both, but you must also assume the moral guilt. In addition, you must be prepared to bear the possibility that those who have suffered the damage or have been mentally hurt, will repeatedly blame you, make new demands based on your acceptance of guilt, and stigmatize you ('you were the one who back then...'). Therefore, the purpose of asking for forgiveness (German: *Entschuldigung*, i. e. 'de-accusation') is so that the other will no longer return to the accusation or the blame, but instead forgive or forget the guilt. Asking for forgiveness is asking for liberation from the moral pressure that has arisen from the attribution and assumption of responsibility. It includes your confession of guilt and thus provides moral satisfaction to the one who has suffered the damage or pain. In this way, the guilt is settled (at least in the eyes of third persons), and the wronged party is in turn morally coerced to accept the apology. What seems to be at stake in all this is first and foremost the settlement of moral conflicts.

In legal terms, taking on responsibility means to assume the obligation of one's liability or to accept a punishment. The responsibility or guilt is dismissed with the sentence and its execution. As such, accepting the legal responsibility for the damage (if the damage is not permanent), frees you from the moral pressure that it created. The liberation from moral pressure caused by an attribution and assumption of responsibility is increasingly desired in politics, too, and here particularly in cases of the most serious crimes against humanity. Leading representatives of states or institutions, including the Popes of the Roman Catholic Church, have publicly apologized for past wrongdoings on behalf of their states or institutions even if they themselves did not partake in the crimes – hoping that, by doing so, they will open up new political leeways for their states or institutions. One of the most famous political examples of asking for forgiveness was when the former German Chancellor, Willy Brandt, kneeled down in the Warsaw Ghetto – without speaking. His silent kneeling at the Monument to the Ghetto Heroes of Warsaw ("*Warschauer Kniefall*") paved the way for Germany's new *Ostpolitik*, a policy toward the East, and eventually for its reunification and the end of the Cold War.

(3) Responsibility that Falls to You. – You can not only assume responsibility by identifying with an attribution of it, but also anticipate the attribution by accusing yourself. You may do this out of personal or political calculation as far as you can, in this way, free yourself from the moral coercion of others. But you may also take on responsibility due to your own moral coercion, namely when responsibility 'falls' to you because you are the 'next responsible person,' if nobody else is available to whom it could be attributed. Then, this is primarily not a question of guilt: if responsibility 'falls' to you, it may (as in the Samaritan's parable), but it does not have to be, someone's fault or responsibility.

The responsibility that falls to you does not refer to anything from the past, but to the immediate present and the imminent future. Whoever happens to have the best orientation skills in a group of hikers who have gone astray in the mountains is the person whom the responsibility of leading the group falls to. If someone in great despair asks you for advice, and you *give* some advice, the responsibility falls to you for all that follows from your advice – as long as the desperate person is him or herself unable to survey the consequences. The responsibility then consists in preventing as much as possible the other from incurring any additional emergencies – whatever happens next. When others are in an emergency, he or she to whom responsibility falls must stand up for their orientations for the duration of this emergency; he or she feels morally coerced to take on orientation tasks for them as far as they are unable to orient themselves on their own.

Judicially, the person to whom such responsibility coincidentally 'falls' can be sued for 'failing to rescue' someone else only in cases where manifest damage to life and limb has occurred. In everyday life, the law is thus not sufficient; therefore, societies are, with regard to randomly arising responsibilities, dependent on a *responsibility culture*. Such a responsibility culture is again expected particularly from politicians. That politicians are the first addressees of societal dissatisfactions is based on their obligation to avert any dangers from society, no matter what happens; this is what governing politicians took their oath for. All responsibility falls to them for anything that is experienced as a common need of a society: their power – in a good and welcome sense – arises from this (chap. 12.4 [6]).

(4) Delegating Responsibility. – Those who have the authority to exercise power in a certain field of competence can delegate their responsibility to others according to certain rules. Their responsibility then becomes *leadership responsibility.* Whoever carries such an authority or responsibility – not only politicians but also, for instance, parents, business managers, or heads of institutions – is then responsible for everything that happens in his or her field of responsibility, which may include the actions of his or her employees (chap. 12.4 [8]): that means, from a moral point of view, he or she is then always the next responsible person.

If the leadership responsibility is shared, i. e. if groups or committees are making decisions, then the individuals involved are again relieved from their moral responsibility: parents, for instance, share the responsibility for their children; or the members of an executive board and, if applicable, of a supervisory board share the responsibility for their company. But such shared responsibility may also jeopardize the moral coercion to take on responsibility, as Nietzsche notes: "Guideline: only individuals feel *responsible*. Pluralities were invented in order to do things which individuals do not have the courage to do." (Notes 1888, 14[196]; our translation) But similar to the standards of a dominant morality, the member of a group or committee may also feel morally coerced to take a stance against the decisions of the group or committee. This will in most cases happen if the matters which the group or the committee is responsible for seem seriously threatened to this individual. He or she may then, as part of the group or the committee, even become a protagonist fighting for the moral renewal of the group or, if they are politicians, of the society they represent.

14.5 The Self-Differentiation of Moral Orientation: Moral Characters, Norms, Values, Orientation Worlds, and Their Leeways

Moral orientation, too, differentiates and thereby stabilizes itself. What is paramount here are the moral characters and the moral norms and values. They in turn permit for leeways of various kinds: not only the leeways of the footholds and signs in morally relevant situations (mentioned above), but also the leeways of moral characters (1), the leeways for complying with and asserting moral norms (2), and the leeways for selecting among values. In different orientation worlds, different norms and values may be in effect (4).

Moral orientation is not simply about moral characters, norms, and values, but, as Aristotle likewise emphasized, also the leeways of where they are in effect. His ethics, which has remained plausible up to the present day even if the societal circumstances have radically changed, can also be grasped through the terms of the philosophy of orientation. Aristotle already provided a *conception of ethics based on leeways of action*, of course without the conception of orientation, but also without the concept of moral coercion, which was introduced only by Christianity, especially by modern Protestantism, and, in all its strictness and with all its consequences, by Immanuel Kant. In his *Nicomachean Ethics*, Aristotle aimed less for a setting or an assertion of norms; he did not abstract from individuals' habits, but he began by addressing acquired attitudes, which come forth in action itself and which then earn respect or disrespect. He outlined typical situations of action that are of moral relevance. To capture such typical situations, he marked fields of action relevant to the citizens of a Greek polis (e. g. fighting in war; how to deal with pleasures; how to spend one's own wealth for private or public benefits; how to present one's own dignity or rank; how to appropriately deal and talk with others), and he conceived such fields of action as leeways between two extreme attitudes, both of which were considered bad (such as foolhardiness and cowardice in the case of fighting in war, or wastefulness and stinginess in the case of spending wealth).

Between the two extremes, everyone has to find what is most appropriate in each situation, or what Aristotle calls 'the middle' (*mesótaes*): thus, the two extremes are footholds for finding out the right behavior. The 'middle' does not – this is the crucial point of the whole conception – have to be in equal distance to the two extremes; in extreme situations, one of the two extremes may likewise even be the right attitude. Therefore, since all situations are different, the 'middle' cannot be defined in general terms. According to Aristotle, it distinguishes the 'prudent' man (Aristotle wrote his books on ethics only for men), who is able to *decide* in each situation how to act right, or rather, in a reputable way. What morally (or using Aristotle's term: ethically) distinguishes a Greek man is his ability to effortlessly *make decisions* on how to demonstrate good behavior in each situation. In this very ability he finds a stable moral orientation precisely because it enables him to *adjust his actions to the specifics* of each situation.

(1) The Leeways of Moral Characters. – The leeways of the footholds and signs of morally relevant situations may differ for each person. It depends on each individual which needs of others morally coerce him or her; it defines his or her moral character when, how quickly, how often, and with how much seriousness he or she adopts a moral standpoint. Moral characters, too, may

range between extremes: cynicism and moral indifference, on the one hand, moral fervor, 'harping on the principles,' and fanaticism, on the other. Here, in everyday orientation, you also need to find the proper middle – not only in building your character but also in every new moral situation. Facing the moral fervor of others may require you to adopt an attitude of reserve (or sometimes a humorous one); when encountering moral indifference all around you, it may be necessary to insist on moral principles.

(2) The Leeways of Complying with and of Asserting Moral Norms. – Factually, moral coercion varies depending on the fields of action and, in these fields of action, depending on moral norms. In contrast to routines, norms explicitly state what ought to be done in typical situations. They are intended to regulate people's moral behavior; but, like legal norms, they are, for one's behavior, only some footholds among many others. With them, too, orientation is needed in regard to how serious one must take them from case to case – which entails the risk of not being taken seriously oneself (you appear pedantic or foolish if you try to perfectly comply with every single rule, norm, or law). Their justifications and the necessity of their justification are controversial as well. But it is uncontroversial that a group or society cannot do without any moral norms. Whenever they are to be followed strictly, without leeways (e. g. in the case of murder or physical harm), they are indeed, wherever possible, formulated as legal norms and thus maintained with force.

However, the limit of the law is reached when one is required to follow the norms based on one's own convictions (e. g. to not lie or humiliate someone); here, *moral* norms are necessary. The conviction that guides one's actions is neither observable from the outside, nor is it possible to enforce it; according to Kant, we can, on the one hand, act 'out of duty,' i.e. for duty's sake, or, on the other, merely 'in accordance with duty,' i.e. only conforming to it to satisfy the outer appearance of it; and one can also just fake convictions. Thus, precisely when moral norms come into play, you can never be sure, neither regarding yourself nor others, that they are being followed out of conviction. One may indeed insist that people follow them, i.e. by morally coercing them, through emphasis, to respect the norms. But this only increases the pressure to conform to them. It thus becomes itself a moral question as to whether one ought to explicitly bring moral norms into play. If you explicitly assert them to others, you exert a morally questionable amount of moral pressure on them; if you assert them in justifications of your own behavior, you risk the suspicion of self-righteousness and self-deception. And since normative expectations can always be disappointed – they often are not complied with and even less so by everyone – you may, the more you build on them, be all the more morally dissatisfied and embittered.

(3) The Leeways for Choosing among Values. – Moral norms are on their part oriented to moral values (e. g. the prohibition to not lie to the value of truthfulness, the prohibition to not humiliate to the value of respect for everyone). Values are the vantage points of moral orientation. The term 'value' initially came up in the ethical discourse of the 19th century. Today, 'values' and 'orientation' are closely linked in our everyday language use: while we 'ought to follow the norms,' we 'orient ourselves' to values – we have leeways with regard to values as such; we can 'choose' among them. This is due to the economical origin of the term. Kant still conceived of it in economic terms – and he then turned it into a paradox, with moral intentions. In a famous phrase, he conceived of the "dignity" of the human being as a "value without price." Human dignity is a value; but morally, the economic sense of 'value' is disregarded in it and in all moral values.

Nevertheless, they are not absolute values; as far as we can choose among moral values, we compare and weigh them against each other. What is a 'higher' value for one person may be a 'lower' value for another; values allow for individual 'preferences.' Among them, 'fundamental values' or 'highest values' can be distinguished; but their number and order are undetermined, and for individuals, and for different individuals, they may have varying degrees of relevance. Moral values can be explicitly articulated, or they can be in effect as self-evident. They only need to fit together; otherwise they would be morally disorienting. *How* they fit together in an individual, a group, or a society then defines the characteristic pattern of each their moral orientations.

Such patterns of values can in turn be compared with one another. By comparing them, you can reflect on your own moral orientation and, if necessary, correct it, without being morally coerced to do so. Different than deviating from norms, deviating from values does not inspire a guilty conscience. You can of course fight for your values, just like you can for your political and religious convictions. However, values still invite coexistence rather than confrontation. They also allow for the transformation or change of values, as empirical sociology has stated ever since it came into existence. One may condemn a change of values as a 'decline in values,' but only if you expect 'eternal values'; on the other hand, you can appreciate it as a relentless moral reorientation. *The morally conceded freedom to choose among values relieves the pressure that moral orientations exert upon each other; the semantics of values creates new and wider leeways for our moral orientation.*

(4) Moral Orientation Worlds. – In different orientation worlds, different norms and values may be asserted. A female politician who is married to the CEO of an oil company and whose children are actively engaged in international environment organizations faces very different moral demands lest she continu-

ally runs into conflicts. She distinguishes between moral orientation worlds, and she switches between them according to different situations. They are *moral* orientation worlds as far as they make you see things in a morally different light in each of their horizons; this means that the different moral standards need not be consistent with each other. The mentioned politician morally succors her husband, as a wife, and her children, as a mom, without having to adopt their politics; politically, she can also act against them. Orientation worlds, which orientation generally differentiates into, have their own moral values, norms, and sanctions, too.

(1.) In *individual orientation worlds*, where everyone takes care of him or herself, norms develop for each individual to the extent that maintaining one's life rhythms, goals, and plans require efforts and discipline; not adhering to them may then produce frustrations and moral sanctions (pangs of conscience, shame, remorse). In caring for oneself, one has moral responsibility for oneself as far as everyone who is able to take care of him or herself does not depend on the help of others or does not morally coerce others to succor him or her.

(2.) In *interindividual or communal orientation worlds*, where you have to care for or provide for others on a regular basis, you are also the 'nearest,' the 'neighbor,' or the next responsible person on a regular basis. Here, 'good' is then that which attends to the needs of others, not your own; you then may – but do not have to – expect reciprocity. But since, in interindividual or communal orientation worlds, multiple people may at once place their demands on you, forcing you, at least for a certain time, to prioritize, i.e. choose one person over the other, you will have to establish implicit or explicit rules that have effects like moral norms and behavioral expectations. In this case, careless deviations will create disappointments, and deliberate violations will bring about specific moral sanctions (such as moral outrage, allegations, and perhaps withdrawals of love). What is good then becomes something good based on rules – 'good' is then considered 'just.'

(3.) In the *societal orientation world*, where you must attune to the life circumstances and life needs of those you did not choose to live with, general moral norms that are independent from interindividual bindings and that are then, more and more, explicitly formulated and legally codified become necessary. With their corresponding legal regulations, fiduciary duties are ensured by the force of the law. But they remain embedded in a culture that is self-evident for a given society.

(4.) In the *global orientation world* of the world society, the moral claims of assistance in urgent emergencies increasingly expand, in the course of globalization, beyond state borders and cultural horizons, ranging from the global assertion of universal human rights to the overcoming of morally unbearable differences in the living standards of the economically privileged societies or social classes, on the one hand, and the underprivileged, on the other. Here, what is good becomes that which is just according to universal moral rules.

Philosophies of ethics in the early modern era have primarily focused on so-called universal principles of human coexistence, at first only within the European horizon (later, much later, the horizons expanded, and the principles were no longer considered to be universal). If moral principles are supposed to be universal, i.e. 'turned to something shared by all and thus valid for all and everything in the same way,' they cannot take into account specific circumstances. They are indifferent toward any specifics. By contrast, 'global' means 'comprising the whole globe of our planet.' On the surface of the globe, all beings are turned toward each other – having various views and interests. Living on a globe suggests less the existence of higher principles but rather that one initially considers how orientations orient themselves to each other, including their specific moralities. Whereas current European philosophies of ethics strongly adhere to the idea of strict universality, the so-called communitarianism in the United States has been more accommodating to specific moralities in specific orientation worlds. Common life needs are then not the last but the first moral priority. In fact, in our everyday orientation, we initially, and as long as possible, adhere to the individual and interindividual horizons of our own or common life needs; we try to live according to our own routines, and we take it completely for granted that others (individuals as well as communities) do so too. Additional moral horizons come into play only if specific moral footholds or coercions require this.

Here, too, attention thresholds are in effect. They morally consist of the demands imposed by concrete life needs, initially in individual horizons, then in interindividual, and eventually in societal ones. Because they, too, are articulated morally, we do not let go of them up so easily. Just as your own body remains the absolute starting point of both your geographical and theoretical orientations, your own life needs are the absolute starting point of your moral orientation. You may feel morally coerced to question your life needs, but you do not do so without a good reason; in fact, it is a coercion precisely if you do not automatically follow it.

The moral standards of caring-for-oneself are surely not the highest and final ones, but based on them, you decide as to whether other moral standards come into play at all. If human beings are suppressed and suffer in another country, and vast numbers of people eventually leave this country in order to find refuge in another, the citizens of that other country may feel morally coerced to receive them. But they may hesitate wondering about the long-term effects that vast numbers of refugees entering their country will have on their own living conditions; they will hesitate even more if they are forced to not only pay for the foreigners with tax money but to also accommodate them in their own rooms in their own houses. They will then weigh the needs of the foreigners against the needs of their own community, and they will eventually decide depending on which party they feel most responsible for. They may feel more responsible for their own family members than for foreigners – but this is not necessary. When confronted with the emergency of foreign children whom no one helps, you may also feel morally coerced to put aside the interests of your own children, at least for a certain time, and you may experience great moral approval for this. But in principle, you will not put universal matters before your own or those of the people close to you.

14.6 Perspectivizing Moral Coercions

If moral orientation differentiates into different orientation worlds, it must also include an orientation about these orientation worlds. This orientation, too, is mostly carried out in a routined and inconspicuous way, with the exception of highly conflicted cases. We likewise switch back and forth, on a daily basis and usually without problems, between various engagements we are involved in, such as our family, professional, political, religious, artistic, athletic, and scientific commitments. This switch is easier if we separate our engagements into different time slots (for instance, professional ones during the week, family activities on the weekend, political and religious ones in the evening, and scientific ones on Sundays...).

By switching your moral orientation worlds, you can also change your moral standpoint. This shifting creates the *leeway that you can, at all, abandon moral standpoints again.* You will hardly announce this explicitly ('Now others should jump in as I am going to focus on my own interests again'); it mostly happens inconspicuously: through a *perspectivizing of the moral coercion.* If an emergency requires legal or political measures beyond moral engagements, the moral coercion inevitably becomes subject to other perspectives ('shouldn't it be lawyers or politicians dealing with this issue?'). And when switching between orientation worlds in this way, their different moral standards are mutually perspectivized and thus questioned. Thus, an orientation can again detach itself from its moral coercion and open up to other orientations, especially economic and political ones previously excluded from it.

In our everyday orientation, there is a vast spectrum for perspectivizing moral standpoints. It ranges from the temporal and the argumentative to the humorous perspective.

(1) Temporal Perspectivizing. – Simply repeating a moral action decreases the attention and the respect it receives. Permanently adopting a moral orientation is, over time, perceived as a routine that is then hardly considered a moral merit, either by those performing, or those observing it. People who continue to act morally for a long time must face the reality that moral attention and respect have, speaking in economic terms, a marginal utility, i.e. their appreciation decreases the more, the longer and the easier they are available.

This is true of, even more than moral actions, their communication. Whoever continually proclaims moral coercions, repeating again and again that 'I *must* do this now, I *cannot* do otherwise,' raises suspicions, and eventually risks exposing him or herself to ridicule. Strong moral statements are respected and tolerated only if they are made in a limited number and for a limited time. This frequently causes people who are morally engaged in the public to again and again let go of their involvements – it creates something like 'economic cycles' of moral activism.[47]

(2) Argumentative Perspectivizing. – The coercion to act morally, which we succumb to without a more specific justification ('I simply have to do this'), is also put into a different perspective if reasons must be subsequently given. This is especially the case if one's moral actions have led to unpleasant consequences ('now that I know what came out of it, I of course see things differently'). This retrospective moral justification is a different situation than the one in which the action was performed, and it thus follows different moral plausibilities.

Kant, who, in his moral philosophy, proceeds from the 'good will,' trying to grasp the phenomenon of moral coercion with it, already assumes the perspective of retrospective justification. We speak of a good will in cases when someone had good intentions but his or her actions led to unfortunate consequences. If an action is successful, leading to welcome consequences for those involved, there is no reason to speak of a good will; no one who is successful would emphasize that he or she acted out of 'good will.' Speaking of good intentions or of a 'good will' is already a retrospective argument apologizing for an unsuccessful action brought about by moral coercions. And, vice versa, if you claim that you acted out of good will you can make your successful actions appear even more praiseworthy (see below).

(3) Interindividual Perspectivizing. – Since moral coercions shut down other leeways of orientation, they also bring about high risks of failure. They therefore quickly encounter the skepticism of others; retrospective justifications, in the case of significant damage, often face objections ('you should have thought about this earlier'). In such an instance, both your moral coercions and your justifications are being unsettled; you observe both with more skepticism than be-

fore. Since it is always individuals who are morally coerced, and since one person may be indifferent while another feels morally coerced, interindividual relations can also have perspectivizing effects; since moralities not only bind but also separate individuals, the moralities of others may perspectivize one's own morality.

(4) Economic Perspectivizing. – The temporal, argumentative, and interindividual ways of perspectivizing moral coercion all keep awake a basic skepticism toward any moral action that is based 'purely' on moral motives or that is communicated as such – not only the actions of others, but also one's own if one is sufficiently self-critical. If someone stubbornly claims that he or she acts solely upon moral coercions, he or she seems blind to his or her own (perhaps multiple) motivations – if not morally overeager or even hypocritical. In regard to the economic risks that resolute moral actions entail, economic (in the widest sense) or "means-ends" justifications (in Max Weber's sense) are initially more plausible. As such, for the sake of your own credibility, you will claim economic rather than moral motives and downplay any moral coercions.

On the other hand, it is morally difficult to accept 'purely' economic justifications. In our everyday communication of morality, we therefore commonly oscillate between economic and moral justification. As such, they are not treated as perspectives that would exclude each other, but rather as complementing each other or as going hand in hand ('it's great that you'll stop smoking for me, and you'll also save a lot of money'). This is true not just for retrospective justifications, but also for motivating one's actions. In everyday orientation, we usually look for multiple (or multi-) motivations, which are then also more tenable in situations of justification. If an action is unsuccessful or fails in *one* perspective, then *another* perspective may help alleviate it ('my commitment to mediate in your marital dispute utterly failed, but I have learned a lot during the process' – 'Building those apartments was bad business, but at least I saved a few people from homelessness'). The economic risk of a moral standpoint is lowered by means of keeping available an economic perspective on one's actions, which may help to compensate for one's failing, if appropriate: if an action is economically unsuccessful, it may be successful in a moral perspective; if it is morally unsuccessful, it may be successful in an economic perspective.

The moral-economic double motivation is also present in the functional system of economics to the extent that business people are oftentimes engaged in moral issues. For instance, you might not only speak of generating profits but also of creating new jobs – even if these new jobs may, from an economic view, only be created if they generate profits. However, someone can also generate profits, at least in part, with the aim of being charitable to society. This can go hand in hand with the moral convictions of those economically responsible and create, over time, a kind of 'moral economics.'

(5) Political Perspectivizing. – Political perspectivizing is closely related to economic perspectivizing. As far as power grows whenever someone takes responsibility for others (chap. 12.4 [6]), power may also fall to those morally engaged, even if they do not aspire it. It can then be used for political reasons – you may join a political party or found a non-governmental organization (NGO). If by doing politics with morality, you begin to like power – despite all your moral reservations against it – your morality may eventually take a back seat.

As with economics, morality can also blend with politics. You may use morality to improve your political image, and you can even do business with morality. This does not necessarily pervert your moral motives or engagements; in this case it is just very difficult to distinguish between morality and economic or political interests. As such, moral involvements are perspectivized from a political point of view, too. Then, you can prove your truthfulness by openly admitting to your economic and political interests.

(6) Judicial Perspectivizing. – Moral engagements can, as far as existing laws permit, be asserted through legal action, or, where this is impossible, they may be successful through acts of legislation (and thus via parliaments and political parties). They then conflict with other interests, which may be articulated in a moral way as well, and may have to be reinforced with justifications of 'legal force.' This may create a morally dubious narrowing and hardening of moral convictions to the point that 'purely' judicial or 'purely' political views come to dominate the dispute. As a result, moral standpoints are, in the public, perspectivized as biased standpoints.

(7) Perspectivizing through Media. – Whoever is morally engaged in regional, national, or global organizations needs the media in order to attain as much attention and approval as possible and to urge governments to take drastic measures and pass new laws. To gain the media's interest for their goals, these organizations must stage their activities in a 'media-appropriate,' i.e. conspicuous, way. Here, moral and media interests go hand in hand: activists organize spectacular events, and the media draw attention to them and to themselves: the spectacular is of great interest to the media, who are in need of attention in order to survive; moral interests must submit to media interests. At the same time, moral organizations will, for the sake of their good cause, try to publicly present themselves in the best light possible. However, the deliberate use of the media for a good cause makes an age-old moral dilemma spectacularly obvious: that you ought not to speak or boast about the good you do. If you do, the favorable self-display will raise questions concerning your moral selflessness.

The moral coercion thus appears in a perspective that may render it morally untrustworthy.

(8) Scientific Perspectivizing. – Scientific perspectivizing is closely related to argumentative perspectivizing. However, with its theoretical standpoint, detached from the immediate necessities of life, it also goes beyond it. Science and law are both strongly committed in a moral sense to serve only the truth or only justice, respectively, and in doing so they each have to neglect all side interests in economics, politics, and the media. At the same time, they both must disregard the moral coercions of individuals: the law does so by focusing only on observable actions, leaving unobservable motives unconsidered (except for hate crime or murder), while science does so by adopting its theoretical standpoint. From here, science can, as moral science (including sociobiology, ethnology, moral sociology, and moral psychology) and from a certain distance, scrutinize morality with regard to natural and cultural rules, ontogenetic and phylogenetic evolutions, statistical probabilities, moral sensitivity, moral motivation, moral development, moral judgment, moral reasoning, etc.; or it can, as moral philosophy, submit diverse moralities to (more or less) universal principles. Therefore, examples, such as the famous one of Sophie, who is forced by a commander of a Nazi extermination camp to make a decision on whether one or both of her children are to be killed, may be debated with complete calmness according to all the rules of the art of argumentation and with regard to the most appropriate rational(!) decision-making criterion. The moral emergency fades into the background; the principles remain controversial; moral coercion becomes a question of successful rational argumentation that leaves, as it is, much room for maneuver. The sciences can indeed help to describe, as we are also attempting to do, the multifarious conditions and views of moral action. In doing so, they all perspectivize it by showing alternatives to the moral coercion.

(9) Aesthetic Perspectivizing. – In everyday orientation, we initially do not perceive moral action as an outcome of any principle, but rather, in the case of moral coercions, as an event. If such an event is striking enough, in either a good or bad way, we (privately) speak about and (publicly) report on it in a (more or less) detailed manner. It is communicated in the form of stories and thus subjugated to the orders of narration. Moral stories, too, must be told in a compelling manner in order to have any effect; they must be aesthetically convincing. They need beginnings, protagonists, and, most of all, conclusions, ideally in the shape of a (more or less explicit) 'moral of the story.' For this purpose, they must be dramatized and, at the same time, abbreviated so that they can be told in a limited amount of time. Shaped in this way, they are spread by different media: plays, novels, and films are, besides our own orientation experiences, the

primary sources of our moral orientation. In fact, the moral events in our own everyday environments hardly follow an aesthetic dramaturgy. If we are self-critical enough, we can observe ourselves perspectivizing our own moral experiences – if we communicate them – through the art of storytelling and eventually by remembering them in this narrative shape. As a result, we believe in our own stories – or, if sufficiently self-critical, we mistrust our recollection of the moral coercion we may or may not have experienced back then...

(10) Humorous Perspectivizing. – If humor is the wisdom of being able to detach oneself from everything one tends to hold onto too strongly, of not becoming too set on one thing, and of putting everything that too eagerly wants to foreground itself within the vast contexts of life back into these contexts, then humor is the wisdom of perspectivizing per se. Humor perspectivizes the seriousness of moral coercion in such a way as that one can let go of it again. Humor, too, has many nuances that create manifold moral and extra-moral effects, from cynicism, the mockery of all morality, through irony, which may keep open leeways for understanding moralities, to a relieving smile and a relaxed laughter that can immediately dissolve moral rigidity and bitter disputes – by simply letting them be.

14.7 Moral Paradoxes: Irritations for the Evolution of Moral Orientation

Both the self-differentiation and self-perspectivizing of our moral orientation encounter its self-referentiality; this leads, as shown above, to paradoxes, to the self-paradoxing that irritates morality as such:

(1) The Paradox of Unconditional Moral Consideration of Others at the Cost of Unconditional Moral Inconsideration of Third Persons. – Moral coercion appears, from the very beginning, as a paradox. To act unconditionally in moral terms not only means that you act without consideration for your own well-being, but also without considering those who depend on your well-being. A young dad who risks his own life when trying to save someone else's child from drowning risks his own children becoming orphans. Whoever helps people with great moral engagement must leave others in need: a family that, adopting orphans, makes great sacrifices must leave countless orphans in hunger and misery, who need their help just as well.

(2) The Paradox of Freedom as the Condition of Moral Coercion. – The moral coercion to unconditionally dispense with any economic or political interests must, according to Kant, assume the freedom of will. It is thought to be a freedom to do good, but it can then also be a freedom to do evil. Without a principle

of freedom, based on which you decide on the right action on your own responsibility, moral action is, as Aristotle already argues, inconceivable. Because the freedom of choice opens up the alternative of acting immorally, Nietzsche tries to conceive of the freedom of will in an extra-moral perspective – as an ascription by those who want to morally coerce *others* to do something for the benefit of themselves: by ascribing to others the capacity to decide on their actions, you yourself gain the capacity to influence their decisions.

(3) The Paradox of the Observable Unobservability of Morality. – In morality, freedom is in turn something one must take for granted, not because it is a fact, but because you observe it as unobservable: in actions themselves, you cannot observe either morality or the freedom to act morally. All you can do is draw conclusions based on the footholds of actions. But, as discussed above, these footholds give leeways for various interpretations; thus, they can also be deceptive. You must therefore, again, morally trust them and your own interpretations of them.

(4) The Paradox of Immoral Utilizations of Morality. – A morality that combats advantages or power can itself be used, as mentioned above, for your own advantage or for your own gains in power: for example, by doing business morally, by morally coercing others for your own advantage ('morally pressuring' someone), via moral humiliations (morally 'wrecking' someone), or via moral discriminations (making someone 'look bad' morally). Paradoxically, greater morality enables greater immorality. Kant condemned such utilizations as "political moralism." Nietzsche discovered in them the paradox of morality as such: morality as the power of the powerless.

(5) The Paradox of the Polemogenity of Morality. – Luhmann points out that morality, which is intended to *counter* conflicts or violence, may in fact *create* conflicts or violence if it is asserted against someone who does not share it. He calls morality 'polemogenous,' which means 'creating conflicts' – from Greek *pólemos*, 'fight,' 'war.' As it is, the stronger one's moral convictions are, the more they can 'harden' and the more they can lead to altercations or war. Its most extreme form is moral fanaticism.

All this – the moral inconsideration of third persons when acting on unconditional moral coercions, the use of a morally conceived freedom to do evil, the mere pretense of the observably unobservable morality, the utilization of morality for one's own advantage or power, as well as the polemogenous character of morality – may in turn inspire moral outrage. But it can also create moral self-critique. Moral self-critique breaks with the self-tabooing and self-righteousness of morality. If sufficiently self-critical, you see yourself as morally coerced to concede different moral convictions to different individuals. As becomes evident through its paradoxes, the self-referentiality of morality gains liberating effects –

liberating you from your own hardened morality while opening you to other moralities. This provokes an evolution of moral orientation as such, an evolution toward an ethical orientation.

Chapter 15
The Self-Reflection of Moral Orientation: Ethical Orientation

Orientation through the Reflection of Self-Bindings

15.1 The Moral Coercion to a Morality for Dealing with Different Morals: Forgoing Reciprocity

In established moralities, one expects reciprocity. Reciprocity has developed as a moral routine; this routine is often articulated as the moral norm of the 'Golden Rule' (chap. 14.3 [1]); it was called 'Golden' because you also find it in the Gospels (Mt. 7:12; Lk. 6:31). However, appealing to this rule, you can, as mentioned above, limit your moral coercion as well (you do not have to do anything for others beyond what you expect others to do for you); on the other hand, you can morally coerce others to do what you have done for them or will do – so that they forgo their interests for the sake of your interests. Both of these conclusions drawn from the Golden Rule are morally questionable. If someone exerts a great amount of moral pressure on someone else, then you may, if the latter resists, jump in to help him or her and highlight his or her own moral responsibility (the responsibility of an adult). What Kierkegaard says about religious faith is also true for morality: that the individual is in his or her responsibility "higher than the universal" (*Fear and Trembling*). For morality always arises in individual situations in which individuals act individually; therefore, it is eventually individuals who are responsible for a certain morality in a certain situation. Based on their own insights, individuals may submit to the standards of a societal or universal morality; but they may also turn *against* these standards by relying on their own moral responsibility (chap. 14.4). Your own moral responsibility and societal or universal moral standards mostly go hand in hand in the moral self-binding of your orientation. But if they oppose each other or are questioned for other reasons, a *new moral coercion* is created: to reconsider your moral self-binding. Our moral orientations – prepared by the experiences of their own leeways, of the multiple ways of perspectivizing their moral coercions, and of irritating moral self-paradoxes – then take a distanced view of themselves. You begin to ask yourself whether and to what extent the standards giving you a hold in your moral orientation are themselves tenable – now from others'

https://doi.org/10.1515/9783110575149-017

points of view. You consider *other* moral standpoints and *other* moral orientations.

What morally coerces one person in his or her moral orientation does not necessarily do the same for the moral orientations of other persons. However, others' moral orientations, from their points of view, unsettle our moral orientations more than non-moral orientations from non-moral points of view: could I have, or should I have made a different moral decision in this situation? Could I have, or should I have acted in a different moral way? But it is difficult to detach oneself from moral bindings, which often have the purpose or the effect of rejecting other moral orientations. From a theoretical point of view, this moral self-distancing may seem simple. But in our everyday orientation, a moral self-reflection and self-critique is less triggered by theoretical considerations than by concrete experiences, e.g. one's own moral coercions and moral actions may have been based on good intentions but led to dire consequences for others. You offered someone a piece of advice, and this advice brought him or her into even greater calamities; parents have strictly raised their children to be honest and disciplined, but the adolescents escape into secret drug abuse; governments have, over a long period of time, provided financial aid to developing countries, but this aid destroyed the respective domestic economic structures. Such experiences immediately coerce you to widen the – inevitably 'self-righteous' – horizons of your own moral orientation and to do justice to the moral standards of others. The moral self-binding opens up to a *morality for dealing with different morals*. This forgoes reciprocity; it *one-sidedly* dispenses with reciprocity. You morally do what you can without expecting or demanding from others that they do the same; you do not expect a favor in return, not even gratitude.

Not only among foreigners, but also (and oftentimes especially) in the most familiar relations, do you face different moralities, thus coercing you to a morality for dealing with them. Having the strength to adopt it is greatly appreciated; finding this strength invites respect, especially from those who can hardly act without the expectation of reciprocity. Forgoing reciprocity reveals an outstanding moral standard, not in the shape of a norm – one's one-sided dispensation with reciprocity cannot be turned into a norm demanding reciprocity – but in the shape of a foothold or a sign: it morally *distinguishes* you. In terms of moral philosophy, forgoing reciprocity is classified as 'supererogatory,' i.e. as something that 'goes beyond what is demanded': one may indeed morally recommend it, but one cannot demand it. As such, it is primarily exemplified by individuals such as Albert Schweitzer, Mahatma Gandhi, or Mother Theresa; and it is manifested in virtues such as beneficence, charity, favorableness, complaisance, forbearance, forgiveness, mercy, and eventually heroism and saintliness, in all of which you find a higher degree of moral sensibility, responsibility, and compulsion – beyond the 'normal level.' But 'supererogatory' actions may just as likely happen in everyday life; they are not only Mother Theresa's.

According to the Hebrew Bible, there was no equality between the moral judgments of God and the people, let alone reciprocity. After the narration of the Fall of Man (Gen. 3), God warned the human beings against desiring the ability to distinguish between good and evil, as the serpent, the 'most cunning' animal, offered it to them ('and you will be like God and you will know what good and evil is'). Based on this, human beings are incapable of distinguishing between good and evil – to even *want* this is the original sin. When, later, the incomprehensible God demanded from Abraham that he, whom God had promised a populous people, sacrifice, as burnt offering, the very son from whom this people was to spring (Gen. 22), this request must have appeared to Abraham as the utmost evil. When he nevertheless obeyed and was about to sacrifice his son, God's interruption prevented him from doing so; this moment was, according to the Hebrew Bible, the beginning of the history of Israel: God gave to the Hebrew people, through Moses, the Torah, which is an orientation – 'Torah' literally means 'orientation' – for life as such; for the Torah, according to the Jewish tradition, nothing can be given in return to God except for obedience. *The biblical history of ethics begins with the incapability of humans to distinguish between good and evil and a gift that can never be reciprocated.*

The salient commandment from the Christian gospel, *maè antistâenai tô ponerô*, 'do not resist evil' (Mt. 5:38 f.), is difficult to understand; it seems morally contradictory – for we *ought to* resist evil. It appears, in Christ's Sermon on the Mount, after the Old Testament's limiting of retaliation ('an eye for an eye, a tooth for a tooth' – this means: not more than an eye, not more than a tooth) and before the commandments to love thy neighbor and thy enemy. 'Do not resist evil' makes much more sense if it is understood as a commandment to reflect and critique one's own morality: the evil that you are not to resist is then a good for a different morality, which appears evil to your own morality (and vice versa). If, according to the examples in the Gospels, you experience something as an ignominious insult ('if anyone slaps you on the right cheek...'), as an unjustified threat with legal means ('if anyone would sue you and take your tunic...'), or encounter someone forcing you (think of a Roman soldier) to show him the way ('if anyone forces you to go one mile with him...'), then this is, from the viewpoint of the other who acts in this way, not necessarily an evil even if it appears to you as such. Jesus seems to command that you limit your moral demands (no more than ...), see the limits of your morality, and, at the same time, respect different moralities. This is hard, especially when the different moralities cause you hardship. But Jesus adds: "If you love those who love you, what reward do you have? Do not even the tax collectors do the same? And if you greet only your brothers, what more are you doing than others? Do not even the Gentiles do the same?" (Mt. 5:46 f.) People, we would say, respect the Golden Rule (according to the Gospels, where Jesus also cites it; Mt. 7:12, Lk. 6:31) within their own moral limits; but the Golden Rule fails when they deal with foreigners. Then they have to respect others' good and evil too, instead of judging them (Mt. 7:1). *To view even enemies and persecutors as human beings that have different moral convictions instead of opposing them with hostility may be the only moral path toward overcoming enmities based on different moralities.*

In philosophical ethics, too, the one-sided forgoing of reciprocity has a long tradition. According to Aristotle, although most people prefer what is profitable for themselves, it distinguishes someone if, among noble men, an 'ethical friendship' develops that lasts for a long time and if one acts in a good way without expecting a favor in return (*Nicomachean Ethics* VIII, 15). Kant, in a footnote in his *Groundwork of the Metaphysic of Morals* (second section), explicitly protests against understanding the categorical imperative in the sense of the Golden Rule of reciprocity. In fact, the categorical imperative demands that you examine *your own* moral maxims as to whether they can also be expected from everyone else. If you find that this is not the case, then you must not act according to them. However, this does not mean that *others* ought to comply to them as well: for these are still your own maxims, and you have (and Kant gives you) no right to prescribe them to others; others must test their own maxims with their own reason. The categorical imperative thus commands you to limit your own morality considering other moralities – without expecting the same from others who use their own reason in their own ways. Among philosophers, Nietzsche, in the most unequivocal way, called for a one-sided forgoing of reciprocity. In his *Genealogy of Morals*, he called the "will to reciprocity" polemically a will to "form a herd" (*Genealogy of Morals* III, 18). Levinas, eventually, proceeded in his ethics, from the very beginning, from a one-sided forgoing of reciprocity.

15.2 Ethical Orientation: Reflecting One's Own Morality via Other Moralities

In ethics, the terms *'moral'* and *'ethical'* are sometimes treated as interchangeable, sometimes as complementary ('moral-ethical,' 'ethical-moral'), and sometimes they are used as a distinction and thus with different meanings. 'Ethical' and 'ethics' stand in the tradition of the Gr. *éthos*, i.e. 'habit, custom, practice, convention,' or rather *âethos*, i.e. a 'usual behavior in a familiar environment'; the Lat. *mos*, or in plural *mores* carries the same meanings, but now with stronger associations of 'duty.' Today, in English, French, and German, 'moral' is used, on the one hand, for an inner coercion and, on the other hand, for a social coercion to act according to the norms. While in the 19th century, 'moral' and 'morals' increasingly acquired the connotation of the 'dominant morality of a society,' 'ethical,' on the contrary, remained free from this. In public debates, 'ethical' is instead currently connected with a 'good' action that is based on one's own decision and responsibility, which, in modern democratic societies, receives greater respect than if it were coerced by a dominant morality. Jürgen Habermas once more classifies the 'ethical' as the Aristotelian 'good' in the sense of an individual 'good life' and the 'moral' as 'the just' in the sense of a good that is defined in universal norms, which he found partly in Kant, partly in Hegel. Habermas does not address how morality itself comes into play. This is particularly an issue for Niklas Luhmann. He conceives of "ethics as a reflexive theory of morals" that cannot presuppose a common reason.

The ethical reflection of morals, however, not only happens in scientific theories, but also in our everyday orientation: precisely as what we call an *'ethical orientation,' which, as a one-sided forgoing of reciprocity, takes seriously the standards of other moral orientations.* It is lived on a daily basis: as open-mindedness and unbiasedness; benevolence and friendliness; tact, cautiousness or gentleness, and politeness; nobility and goodness; striving for tolerance, dignity, peace, and justice among people who follow different moral standards; and, eventually, as ethical sovereignty. As lived in everyday orientation, ethical orientation need not require any philosophical efforts – although they may help to clarify it, and provide a hold in this way. The transition from an ethical orientation self-evident in everyday life to a philosophically reflected one (and vice versa) is fluid. And this is good: for philosophy, especially as ethics, can only be plausible in connection with everyday life ethics.

As an *orientation*, ethical orientation in principle begins from the standpoint-related nature and perspectivity of all orientations. As an *ethical* orientation it in principle considers other possible moral orientations: here, you remain attentive to the fact that, even if you feel morally immediately and unconditionally coerced in a morally relevant situation, different people may find in the same situation different aspects morally relevant. In unfamiliar environments, this *ethical attentiveness* always remains awake; in familiar ones, you need to purposefully keep it awake.

For this, Nietzsche, Levinas, and Derrida created instructive terms: 'pathos of distance,' 'non-indifference,' and 'deconstruction.' They all deal with the possibility of ethics under the condition of double contingency in the communication between two separate orientations; they all forgo reciprocity:

In Nietzsche's term of *pathos of distance*, 'distance' stands in opposition to 'difference,' i. e. contrary to a terminological distinction that identifies others and pins them down. The distance is experienced as mere 'pathos,' whose meaning ranges from 'feeling' through 'suffering' and 'passion' to 'grave seriousness.' The term pathos of distance expresses that the seriousness of ethics does not reside in one's duty to follow some highest universal, but rather in the fact that others may be entirely different from what one is capable of imagining and that one must do justice to this in one's thinking, speaking, and acting.

Levinas' term of *non-indifference* contains a double negation, but it does not simply cancel itself out in a logical way and turn into an affirmation. Indifference is, as a simple logical negation, a non-distinction and, in an ethical sense, disinterest or one's actual indifference to others. Since terminological distinctions are equally valid (*gleich gültig*) for everyone and everything that they refer to, they make everyone and everything ethically indifferent (*gleichgültig*). The second negation 'non-indifference,' however, cancels this ethical indifference – again in an ethical sense: terms are used non-indifferently in an ethical orientation – especially in a face-to-face situation with another, if they are used with careful consideration of how the *O/other* may understand them in his or her situation. Your attention to your own terms – which you may use when speaking with or, perhaps, about others and based on whose meaning you then act – is the very place of your ethical responsibility for others.

Derrida's term of *deconstruction* combines, in a related sense, 'construction' and 'destruction': construction happens by means of terminological differences; destruction, at the same time, questions these differences as *mere constructions*. Identifying terms, without which communication in society would not work, are simultaneously questioned in our ethical orientation, where they are used regarding others in a carefully considerate way. Here, Levinas contrasts every act of speaking (*dire*) with a negation of this act, i. e. he proposes to detach or renounce the act of speaking (*dédire*). The identifying mode of speaking self-referentially revokes itself.

15.3 The Virtues of Ethical Orientation

As we have seen, human orientation has its own specific virtues. We call them *'orientation virtues.'*

(A) They comprise, concerning *orientation as such*, the virtues of *overview, circumspection, foresight, insight, precaution, consideration, forbearance*, and *confidence* (chap. 4.4). They are intertwined on multiple levels and support each other. Today, we call the complex of them simply *'reasonableness,'* without assuming a common reason equally shared by everyone ('in this situation, it is reasonable for him or her to act in this or that way'). At the same time, these orientation virtues require the *courage* to opt, under the condition of uncertainty, for one path of action that appears promising.

When drawing on them with courage, they help one

- to reorient oneself, whenever a new situation requires it (chap. 5 – 6),
- to use a situation's uncertainties and decidabilities, as well as the leeways provided by the clues, footholds, and signs, which arise in the situation, to creatively master this situation – thereby either restricting the meanings of signs (the extreme being the unambiguousness of mathematical signs) or expanding them (the extreme being universal philosophical signs) (chap. 7),
- to stabilize routines and differentiate worlds of orientation and to switch between them if necessary (chap. 8),
- to detach from given situations by means of thinking and reasoning (chap. 9),
- to consider other orientations in one's own, thus widening one's horizons and perspectives (chap. 10),
- to considerately deal with ascriptions of identities, i.e. to keep open leeways for identifying with them or not (chap. 11), and
- to make deliberate use of the professional orientations of the functionally differentiated social systems of communication for one's individual orientation (chap. 12 – 13).

(B) Regarding *interactions and communications with others*, human orientation mainly requires

- *trust,* i.e. the strength to rely on the uncertain footholds of others' behavior and their signs, which can always be interpreted in various ways; one therefore maintains a reasonable degree of mistrust concerning the fact that their signs may be deceptive; this ultimately creates security in dealing with both trust and mistrust and in oscillating between them (chap. 10.5);
- *reliability,* i.e. the capacity to be, given the doubly contingent orientation to other orientations, a steady and secure foothold *for others* (chap. 9.4, 10.4, 14.1);
- *resoluteness,* i.e. the power to stick to one's decisions – as long as new situations do not require new decisions, which one could then justify to others affected;
- *adherence to principles,* i.e. the resoluteness to commit to common norms and values, or to create one's own principles and ideals; since such commitments greatly abbreviate the concrete orientational processes, thus not tak-

ing into account surprising situations, this adherence also entails not blindly following norms, values, principles, or ideals, but considering what consequences they may have in concrete situations (chaps. 6.3, 12.1, 14.5);

- the ability to recognize and acknowledge superior and inferior orientation skills, i.e. a *sense for rank*; since superior orientation skills qualify for leadership in a certain field of action or in multiple fields (but usually not in all fields), and since leadership grants someone power, the sense for rank involves the ability to assess where and when the exercise of power is justified by certain circumstances and where and when it is abused (chap. 12.3 [7]); and
- the moral *sense for inner coercion*, i.e. the willingness and strength to jump to the aid of others, even if deliberately facing serious sacrifices (chap. 14.1).

(C) Concerning the *communication of information and knowledge*, science is the prime model, though not the only measure, for
- *fact-orientation* and *truthfulness* (chap. 13.1).

  However, since one may deceive oneself regarding facts and truths and since one may unintentionally deceive others, a healthy mistrust is also necessary here.

(D) Finally, concerning *philosophizing*, the first orientation virtue is to always consider that you proceed from a certain standpoint, and that, in order to successfully philosophize, you must remain open to other standpoints and able to determine the relations between yours and theirs. This permits self-critical instead of dogmatic philosophizing. It always involves
- *courage*, required for innovative philosophizing without relying on any final certainties, and a high degree of
- *self-control* and *modesty* (chap. 1).

All these virtues usually involve the expectation of reciprocity. When dealing with different morals, this changes. Attuning to different moralities – which is required, given the separation of all orientations, not only when living in faraway cultures, but even in your own neighborhood – is hard because it may affect your own, perhaps strong, moral convictions; your adherence to values, norms, and principles may altogether become troubled. In addition, the attunement to different moralities can no longer be a matter of reciprocity: when it comes to different morals, there are no universal values, norms, or principles that everyone is obliged to adhere to. Universal norms still exist – but only in the law, especially in the shape of human rights, which the countries of the UN Charter agreed on and which these countries are to guarantee (whether they actually do so is a different question). Ethical orientation – an ethics of moral orientations toward each other – is instead based on individuals and their individually different capacities for orientation. You cannot expect everyone to have the virtues or attitudes required here, you cannot demand them from everybody – rather, individuals ethically distinguish themselves or stand out based on them.

So, there is a further group of virtues: the specific *virtues of ethical orientation* (E). In our everyday life, these virtues begin with

- *open-mindedness* and *unbiasedness* toward others, toward their different appearances, their behavior, and their morals. Someone capable of open-mindedness is, more than others, open for moral behaviors and moral utterances that are foreign to him or herself. Whoever is unbiased is bound by his or her own morals only to such a degree that he or she can not only endure strange moral behaviors and utterances otherwise morally alienating or outrageous but may also take some pleasure in them – because they question his or her (perhaps narrowed or hardened) moral routines. Under the conditions of double contingency, this is in itself pleasant.

Beyond this, with

- *benevolence* and *friendliness*, you can be more complaisant to others: you may act in a more welcoming way toward them. Nietzsche, the greatest critic of all moral reciprocity, gives an unparalleled description of both:

> those expressions of friendly disposition in communication, those smiles of the eye, those handclasps, that comfort in which nearly all human action is, as a rule, webbed. Every teacher, every official brings this addition to what he does as a matter of duty; it is the continual exercise of humanity, as it were its light-waves in which everything grows; especially within the narrowest circle, within the family, is life made to flourish only through this benevolence. Good-naturedness, friendliness, politeness of the heart are ever-springing outflows of the unegoistic drive and have played a far greater role in building up culture than those much more celebrated expressions of it called pity, mercy and self-sacrifice. (*Human, All Too Human* I, No. 49; transl. by R. J. Hollingdale, modified)

While in the cases of open-mindedness and unbiasedness as well as benevolence and friendliness, you will, at some point, expect reciprocity – at least all these will usually soon wane without receiving reciprocity –

- *tact* or *tactfulness* is typically upheld for much longer without receiving reciprocity. Tact, literally the 'sense of touch,' is one's attention to other's indecent behavior so that their indecency remains unnoticed. You need it when helping others with their self-display (chap. 11.4); it is particularly required and particularly appreciated in cases of morally indecent judgments.

244 — Chapter 15 The Self-Reflection of Moral Orientation: Ethical Orientation

Tact then becomes

- *cautiousness* or *gentleness*, i.e. the care for those who, in their behavior or utterances, are *careless* of others. One adheres to tact even if others continue to behave in an indecent manner; and one also tries to not make them feel one's tact in order to avoid embarrassing them.

- *Politeness* makes tactfulness become 'formal.' Politeness rituals are perceived *as* rituals (by those who know them); they are signs of 'good manners.' You can also make other people feel your politeness; you can try to discipline them in this way, and you can, if this attempt fails, at least appear more cultivated than them. Politeness, as it still reverberates in the English term 'courtliness,' goes back to one's behavior at court; it was intended to convey a favorable image of oneself to the prince or princess in order to win his or her favor. Since then, it has carried the smell of hypocrisy. Ethically, it instead becomes a 'politeness of the heart,' as Goethe called it in his novel *Elective Affinities*; it is, for Goethe, allied to *love*. With it, one pays less attention to the conventional forms than to the respect one gives to others, as if they were princes or princesses.

Tactfulness and politeness, as virtues of ethical orientation, are superseded by a virtue for which there is hardly a common term. It is the virtue of being able to *silently* dispense with all favors in return, even if you may expect them; you may even dispense with the other's thanks and gratitude after having saved, with great effort, someone from an emergency situation: you rescue people from a house in flames and then leave, when the professional help arrives, without even mentioning your name. It is furthermore the virtue of not taking any countermeasures in cases when they – according to most people's opinion – would be appropriate and justified: someone responds to attacks and insults with calm objectivity and friendliness, perhaps even with complaisance, or perhaps by simply remaining silent. You may think of selflessness or of the love of neighbor; but as long as one is still driven by moral or religious engagements – to thus spread one's own morality or religion – one is not selfless. Above all, this virtue is respected if you perform it tacitly and without any ado. Here, Nietzsche spoke of

- *nobility*, or in German *Vornehmheit*. But even in German, this term has not become common in ethics. Noble is, in Nietzsche's sense, someone who is able to easily, without question, fulfill the moral demands of others, but is not in need of reciprocity – someone who is not at all in need of making moral demands to others or of fighting for the respect and recognition of others. Noble people in this sense live in the pathos of distance, without being ethically indifferent toward others.

The kind of ethical complaisance that enjoys the highest respect and that is least common is probably

* *goodness* – as far as it goes beyond kindness, cautiousness, gentleness, and helpfulness by giving others confidence to follow their own morality. This virtue we speak of – containing 'the good' itself in its name – is expressed in the rare strength of enabling others to gain trust in themselves so that they can act according to their own convictions without needing the approval of others; in short: it means to give others a hold in their own orientations – without benefitting the person who does so. It may take the shape of a piece of advice given to others about how they can cope with difficult situations by themselves. Pieces of advice, if they come from such goodness, permit those to whom they are given complete freedom as to whether they accept them or not; in such cases, pieces of advice that may otherwise appear intrusive are mostly welcome. In *The Gift of Death*, Derrida strikingly spoke of a "self-forgotten goodness." People performing this kind of goodness are self-forgotten as far as they do not expect anything from it for themselves; perhaps they do not even know of their goodness. They succeed in this without any noticeable efforts. It comes from an orientation which, on its part, found its own hold within itself.

15.4 Ethical Sovereignty: Setting Signs for Others

Moral authority is gained according to moral standards; you can also lose it again through moral misconduct. In our orientation, *sovereignty* becomes possible, and ethical sovereignty goes beyond moral authority. The term 'sovereign' comes from constitutional law: states are sovereign as long as they are not dependent on others, but ruled by laws that they gave to themselves, laws that are their own (chap. 15.4). An individual's orientation is called 'sovereign' if he or she rarely gets into an emergency but rather is able to easily master even difficult situations, i.e. if he or she can always orient him or herself with confidence. They are then pragmatically superior to others. There is something similar in ethical orientation: ethically sovereign are those individuals who can impartially, resolutely, and silently follow their own moral standards, mastering difficult situations involving others who follow different moral standards; they easily get along with others; the morality of dealing with different morals does not cause them distress but comes natural to them. It is these kinds of individuals where morality loses its coercive element; since they are rare, we are pleased that they exist.

With their ethical sovereignty, they can amplify the respect for prevailing moral standards. But they can also create respect for new standards – because it is *they* who perform these standards. They can turn an exception into a rule. As such, they can also make dominant moralities go into flux again, steering them into a good direction without obliging anyone to follow. What helps ethically sovereign individuals with this are specific abilities and virtues. In addition to open-mindedness and unbiasedness, they also perform the virtues of *jauntiness* and *levity* when fulfilling obligations to others; in addition to benevolence, friendliness, tactfulness, politeness, nobility, and goodness, they also perform the virtues of *grace* and *humor*, both of which make them attractive as persons who can incite others to ethically orient themselves to them.

John Rawls, too, in his *Theory of Justice*,[48] orients his theory beyond the "moralities of authority and association" and a "morality of principles" to the goal of a "morality of self-command," of which he speaks when the "requirements of right and justice" that usually demand "great discipline and training" are fulfilled "with complete ease and grace." This then "exercises a natural attraction upon our affections." A sovereign ethical orientation, as we call it, no longer justifies moral laws, norms, or values that are to be obligatory for others, but rather it gives (more or less inconspicuous) signs that may motivate others to ethically reorient themselves. Signs point in a direction without specifying where it leads or determining what will happen there; others must be able to recognize and follow them in their ways. Ethically sovereign individuals provide ethics with a face; we no longer only experience it as binding and coercive, but as liberating and distinguishing, as a liberation to follow one's own distinguishing ethical actions.

Ethically sovereign people may at times be so surprising and outstanding that we tell stories about them, or we write and make films about them. Ethically sovereign individuals may be delightful. Nietzsche called the sight of a "sovereign" or an "autonomously more-than-moral individual" a "feeling of human perfection as such" (*On the Genealogy of Morals* II, No. 2, our translation).

Chapter 16
World Orientation in Globalized Communication
Orientation through Standardization

16.1 Global Orientation

Our global orientation world has been increasingly 'globalized.' Today, the spherical surface of the globe is surrounded by a network of satellites that makes everyone constantly available for anyone at (almost) any place. The geographical overview of the world is thus (almost) complete. Although you can, because of the earth's curvature, still only see up until a horizon (as before), you can now, using current communication technologies, make the world completely visible from (almost) any position at all times. *Global geographical orientation is presently no longer a problem.*

This began with 'globes.' Ever since mankind understood the spherical shape of the earth and began creating models of the globe, one has been able to view it from above, and turn it (as a model) on its own axis and thus survey it from all sides (not simultaneously, but with rapid succession). One views the earth as a whole from a 'theoretical' standpoint (chap. 13.1 [3]). Today, the image of the rotating earth with its geographical and political structures has become completely familiar to us through virtual animations on daily news broadcasts. And ever since spaceships have been able to circle the earth, one's overview of it is no longer just constructed but has now become a reality (at least for astronauts). How they have seen the earth is also (more or less) how it is shown by the media on a daily basis. *The 'theory' of the earth as a globe has become an unquestioned certainty, an indubitable everyday reality.*

In addition to this 'theory' (in the Greek sense), which is based on satellite systems and space stations, there is also the *fixing of time* through the system of 'universal time' (UTC) via the 'international atomic time' (IAT): at the end of the 19th century, the globe was divided into zones of a uniform world time, and around 1970, the measurement of time was standardized according to the vibrations of cesium atoms; this allowed us to synchronize the times of the day as accurately as desired everywhere on earth. The invention of the telephone, likewise in the 19th century, permitted a (quasi) synchronous communication across any desired distance on earth; today, this has been perfected through computer- and satellite-based information and communication technologies. Whatever happens anywhere in the world can be broadcasted 'live' to all other places in the world. *The events on earth can always be represented everywhere on earth.*

https://doi.org/10.1515/9783110575149-018

In our spatially and temporally globalized world, a *world society* develops in which *everyone may deal with everyone else at any time or place on earth.* When exactly globalization began is controversial; you can re-trace its origins to various points in the past. In any case, worldwide communication became increasingly dense. The more the peoples living in separated places came in touch with one another, the more global trade expanded; worldwide military campaigns, such as those by Alexander the Great or Genghis Khan (whose name literally means 'ocean-like,' 'world ruler'), were also expeditions for discovery; mass migrations across vast regions of the world as well as colonization created mixed societies. In the case of cultural achievements, one began to view the world as a whole (to the extent that it was known): wonders were considered 'wonders of the world,' languages became 'world languages,' religions 'world religions,' literature 'world literature,' while in philosophy spirit became the 'world spirit,' views 'worldviews,' (in economics) cities 'world cities' and exhibitions 'world exhibitions,' (in politics) powers 'world powers'; worldwide human rights made citizens into 'world citizens'; and an ethos gathered from worldwide religions and moralities was to become a universally obligatory 'world ethos.' But wars, too, also grew into 'world wars.'

The hitherto strongest push of globalization has primarily arisen from the spread of science and technology, which has made everyday life easier, since the middle of the 19th century, and from the forced liberalization of markets beginning in the 1980s: i.e. the deregulation of the trade of goods and of the financial markets, including an extreme increase of economic chances and risks; the privatization of state-owned enterprises, especially postal services and telecommunication; the integration of most formerly state-planned economies into the global market economy; the growing number of transnationally operating companies ('global players'), for which only the world market is economically relevant and which establish worldwide supply chains ('global sourcing'); and, fostered by these companies, the worldwide distribution of jobs. Here, the economic orientation outweighs the political, legal, and moral orientations; *world orientation has become a world market orientation.*

On the world market, where you must act and react very quickly, the new information and communication technologies permit a globally unlimited range of business activities as well as extremely short-term interdependencies of companies on the markets. Different countries become – in the long run – competing 'business locations': natural resources, services, technological innovations, and sales markets make them increasingly dependent on each other, too. This leads to *major political reorientations:* the, so far, politically dominated world of states becomes – in the name of 'neoliberalism' – an economically dominated business world. Governments increasingly have to focus on maintaining and increasing the economic competitiveness of their respective countries. The trend of economic liberalizations, however, is also fought against with respect to other aspects (national interests, social security, fear of migrations); it can also slow down, be disrupted, redirected, or reversed.

Threats of war and terror, climate change, the destruction of biodiversity, and other dangers to the living conditions on earth – all these make *common political world orientations* necessary. As far as the responsibility for them is not taken on by single governments, non-government organizations (NGOs) draw attention to them in ever-new ways. The realm of world politics reassembles itself on a large scale. After the experiences of the political totalitarianisms of the 20th century, the notion of a world state has lost credibility; such a world state, if it existed, would indeed have a global monopoly on violence, but it could just as well abuse it with devastating consequences. Empires such as the Ottoman Empire, the Austro-Hungarian Monarchy, the British Empire, and the Soviet Union collapsed; power and defense interests have been bundled into international organizations such as the NATO (North Atlantic Treaty Organization, under US leadership) or the CIS (Commonwealth of Independent States, which emerged from the former Soviet Union, under Russian leadership); the states of Europe that were constantly caught up in wars have step by step united to form the EU (European Union), without completely absorbing the individual nations in the process. *Instead of clearly dominating political entities, one now wants to maintain leeways everywhere for one's own orientations and decisions.* As such, 'global governance' is a matter of various inter- and transnational organizations such as the UN (United Nations), including its (often paralyzed) Security Council, the World Trade Organization (WTO), the International Monetary Fund (IMF), the World Bank, and regular meetings of the leading economic powers at G8 or G20 summits. The last remaining 'world power,' the United States, is indeed for the most part a hegemonic power, but it is not the only and absolute one; it oscillates between national and international responsibilities.

For 'global players' – commercial enterprises, media, governments, NGOs, and inter- and transnational public institutions – the globalized world as a whole is the situation of their orientation; from all world affairs, they gather footholds for their decision-making. In doing so, they however follow their own matters of interest. *Global orientation, too, is pluralistic; it is bound to multiple standpoints and various leeways. The world society and its world orientation do not have a clear center, either; what becomes center or periphery depends on every single position and is newly decided on case by case.* For both the decentralized structure of the world society and the discontinuous processes of orientation, the *metaphor of a network* or a *web* has become commonplace: every 'node' is, via diverse relations, linked with every other one. Each can conceive of itself as the center, and each can also become a center for others. But a single node does not allow one to survey and control the network as a whole.

Orientation in the world society, too, does not have an overview of itself, nor does it have central (self-)control. In these networks, connections may become stronger or softer; they may be dropped or tied in new ways; and they may be torn apart or replaced. In them, (more or less) tight or loose orders develop, which hold for a longer or shorter time. *Orientation networks* are capable of self-organizations similar to those of modern decentralized electricity networks, where power, fed from multiple locations, finds the most efficient way to the costumer with the lowest number of disruptions. They organize themselves like cerebral networks in dialogue with their environments. Their hold is not based on hierarchical orders oriented toward a highest point from which they are controlled, but on heterarchies that organize themselves by the mere intertwining of contexts. The world orientation of the world society is therefore everywhere open to *fluctuance*, through which identities may completely change.

As is the case in the individual, interindividual, and societal orientation worlds, one observes all changes in the global orientation world as to what extent they promise benefits or rather bring dangers. Changes are, on the one hand, perceived with unsettlement and anxiety if one expects a stable hold but is in danger of losing acquired or inherited assets, and, on the other hand, with confidence if one wants to free oneself from hardship and gain new leeways to act. Globalization does not simply lower or abolish trade barriers. The greater the economic and political dependence of different countries, the greater the impediments for authoritarian and totalitarian regimes to stay in power: globalization *in principle promotes the worldwide assertion of human rights, the democratization of societies, and the non-discrimination of minorities* – even if we continue to experience serious and unexpected setbacks, which may likewise indicate an alternative trend.

Globalization creates, in large parts of the world, migrations from poorer to richer countries; when migrants are starving and run the risk of dying in their homeland, this, at least for a certain period of time, may morally coerce richer countries to open their borders (even if there is great political resistance). As far as the *economic* competitive pressure of globalization contributes to the endangerment of so far untouched nature, of the climatic living conditions of humanity, and of cultural goods and diversity, the *political* globalization may coerce governments to take coordinated worldwide counter measures. *Ethically*, globalization may coerce people to attune to other moralities; migration has brought about, especially in those countries that have most strongly benefitted from globalization, morally pluralistic and multicultural societies. It makes *ethical orien-*

tation, i.e. the strength to suspend one's own values for the sake of others, become a *routine* over time.

16.2 Standardizations of Global Interaction and Communication

Global exchange – through travel, telecommunication, and international cooperation – is possible only by means of a *standardization of the conditions of exchange*. We travel with standardized means of transportation across the globe; we plan travels with standardized means of communication; we identify ourselves with standardized IDs; we stay in standardized hotels; we move in standardized urban infrastructures; we eat in standardized restaurant chains, etc. *The standardized 'global culture' permits everywhere an initially problem-free orientation.* Besides standardized communication- and orientation-technologies, it also involves standardized orientation signs and a standardized orientation language (English).

(1) Standardized Orientation Signs. – To abbreviate communication in global travel, one makes use of immediately comprehensible orientation signs, i.e. pictograms or 'icons.' They work without verbal explanations and give one quick and unambiguous instructions that are independent of national languages or cultural differences. At central junctions of international mass travel, i.e. especially at airports, they first of all simplify finding the standard services and facilities (e.g. departure or arrival halls, ticket counters, terminals, gates, baggage claim, toilets etc.). Every icon stands for itself; they do not require any rules or grammar for connecting them and avoiding errors. They characteristically abbreviate the places and functions they refer to; they are designed and installed in a striking manner so that they immediately catch the eye of the person seeking orientation; wherever they accumulate, they are ordered in a surveyable manner – i.e. an *exemplary global use of signs for local orientation.* The praxis of using pictograms has been adopted not only in the instruction manuals of internationally distributed products but also – through increasingly creative modifications – in online communication, where they prompt standardized functions of communication, which are summarized in graphic user interfaces ('icon bars' and 'menus') that are likewise presented in as attractive and surveyable a manner as possible. Here, you also find, among other things, 'emojis,' i.e. abbreviated facial expressions, used as footholds for approval, disapproval, or other emotions.

(2) The Standardized Orientation Language of English. – Pictorial orientation signs, however, only allow for the simplest local, functional, and affective orien-

tations. Complex needs of orientation, in international travel and communication, still require languages; and as far as we cannot learn as many languages as we want, we need a standard language. As less and less people, even among scholars, were proficient in Latin, there were, again and again, new attempts – from the early modern period up until the 1950s – to create 'international auxiliary languages' as well as 'universal languages' in order to meet the basic needs of orientation, and they were supposed to be easy to learn (there were more than 500 such languages, including Esperanto). They were successful only to a very limited extent. Instead, after the Second World War, a natural language has prevailed as a standard language, which one can also use for more complex communication – it has superseded French, Spanish, and Portuguese, all of which became world languages over the course of colonization. This selection of one standard language, too, abbreviates communication: one no longer needs to initially inquire about the other's language; you can (largely) take for granted that you will be able to 'get by' with just this one.

In this process, the language used, now English, becomes standardized as well. 'English as a foreign language' is mostly a (more or less) reduced version of English. In many areas, e.g. tourism, a very limited vocabulary is sufficient for a mutual orientation that largely (more or less) neglects the rules of grammar. This standard language is in turn being lexically and grammatically enriched (or, as others say, 'corrupted') by the translation of other languages into English. In a similar way, in the 19th century, pidgin English was developed for the communication between Chinese and Europeans; already in the Middle Ages, Yiddish was developed from Hebrew-Aramaic, German, as well as Roman and Slavic languages, and its rich idiomatics and flexible syntax allowed its different speakers, on the one hand, to communicate with the people they lived among and, on the other, to communicate with each other; via ever-new adaptations, Yiddish is still being used to a considerable extent, e.g. in North and South America.

If a national language becomes a world language, it develops according to the world's needs of orientation and communication. At the same time, it is differentiated according to the respective orientation worlds, e.g. economic branches, academic disciplines, electronic data processing, or pop music, and these developments in turn tell you about the changes of our global needs of orientation. As an international language, English also permeates the national languages (including English as a primary language) and standardizes them in certain language fields. Since English continues to be a primary language, and since it is learned by foreigners according to the standards of primary English, it also functions – different from an artificial language – as a corrective authority with all its refined subtleties. The specific orientation world – spanning the British Commonwealth and the United States – that it emerged from remains the *standard of its standardizations.*

(3) *Standardized Orientation Technologies.* – The most important real-time locating system is GPS, the global positioning system, developed by the US Department of Defense for military purposes; later, it has increasingly been used in a standardized version for civilian purposes. The satellites surrounding the earth function as external observers of all the paths that one may walk; they thus no longer need to be identified on maps, which involves efforts and errors. For the spatial identification, they make use of time: high-precision rubidium- and cesium-clocks measure the signal propagation delay between, in each case, four satellites and the respective receivers on the ground; computers then calculate very accurately, by means of a global reference system of time differences, the location of the person orienting him or herself. *The geographical orientation is calculated with highly complex means.* High-tech locating systems thus allow for a *complete overview of the area, which can be retrieved in greater or smaller degrees of abbreviation (by 'zooming' in or out).*

But all they really allow one to do is determine locations, and they do so only if these places are already defined as targets. The standardized orientation technology simplifies only the beginning of orientation. And these secure beginnings create new leeways for new surprises: this technology now invites you more and more to go on adventures in unfamiliar areas. But they can themselves be surprising: technologies can fail, and they may reveal private information – all locations can be stored, and this data may be used by unauthorized persons. Thus, here it is true again: what is gained in orientation security in one regard is given away in another.

16.3 The Digitization of Global Communication

(1) *Smartphones.* – While high-tech real-time locating systems allow you to always know where you are (*constant locatability*), you are also (given sufficient means and legal powers) locatable by others, even if you do not want to be located; while, with mobile phones, you are discoverable or available everywhere (*constant discoverability or availability*), you also signal, if you keep them turned on, *constant readiness to communicate,* even if you do not want to communicate right now. Mobile phones (in principle) increase the readiness to communicate and act: you can always, without any long-term scheduling, arrange a meeting at short notice. And yet, you keep control of your own time: you can respond right away, but you do not have to. *By canceling the spatial distance, smartphones (as letters once did) create the leeway of temporal distance* – a new, now com-

pletely normal *space-time-autonomy.* Interactive social media combine the fastest response possibilities with the constant potential for withdrawal.

Interactive social media newly regulate the *degrees of an interaction's distance* as well. Because they are designed for high-speed communication, they are (different from letters) pressed for the brevity of messages. They constantly bring about new abbreviation idioms, which appear sober and 'cool'; at the same time, they increasingly differentiate and distinguish themselves. *Abbreviations become cultish.* As such, they create specific communication cultures, in which you use specific idioms, and where others may join or not, thus leading to a formation of groups with their own identities. On your smartphone you can specify what you want to share with some but not with others, especially your pictures, videos, or 'stories,' i.e. combinations of pictures, videos, emojis, and text; you can also choose between different communication channels offering specific functions, and you can use them in different ways. But since every message can easily be forwarded to others, and posts and pictures can easily by 'shared' in the public, you here, too, run the risk of making something private public – thus sometimes risking severe life crises.

Ever since digital communication has become less tied to (fixed) personal computers, running instead on (mobile) smartphones, it has gained its own fascinating attraction: you not only have more comprehensive possibilities for immediately orienting yourself (it is literally 'in your hand'), but you can also use these handy devices to play games, watch movies, listen to music, make video or conference calls, or as a GPS in your car, or to check in at airports with a QR ticket, search for a partner on a 'dating app,' make payments without cash or credit cards, call a taxi or a ride, buy a car or a house, or make large transactions, etc. You can, if communicating with these devices, always be social without needing (to have) other people around you; you can, at the same time, be alone and in the company of others. Your friends and followers are clearly listed; you can immediately survey how closely and frequently you are in touch with them, or whether you are not. You can increase (or decrease) the attention you receive by merely sending out (or not sending out) messages or by sharing a post; you may have to work to not be neglected on the 'attention market'; the joy of staying in touch with your 'contacts' and followers may become a compulsion or an addiction. Beyond all this, you can even use your smartphone (as you once did your personal computer) to, as it were, 'surf' the web, from (almost) any given location: on the internet, you can playfully ramble as if on a surfboard in the wind; by merely clicking on a page and going on to the next, you can move around, search and find (or perhaps not find) what you are looking for, and often find something that you were not looking for. *Your orientation in the world is concentrated within the smartphone in your hand,* and this is *orientation partly with, partly without intentions – orientation in its pure form.* This is why smartphones are so fascinating, why so many people can hardly look away from them anymore.

(2) The Internet. – The internet, to which smartphones connect, has undergone a clearly observable evolution in a short, clearly surveyable time; like never before, it has intervened in our everyday orientation and triggered a hitherto – in breadth, depth, and speed – unparalleled transformation of our orientation to other orientations. Where its evolution will lead is still completely open.

The conditions of its evolution have been, and continue to be, very multifaceted. Technologically a worldwide and decentralized network of networks that is used for the exchange of digital data, it has become *'the* net,' the epitome of a network as such, the prototype of all networks. Its physical basis is – besides satellites and transcontinental cables – the local and decentralized 'servers' of 'providers' through which internet users can access the network. 'The net' was initially developed in the United States by universities for scientific interests and purposes before it was used (prior to GPS) for military purposes. After the so-called Sputnik shock, which seemed to reveal the technological inferiority of the USA as compared to the USSR, the search began for methods by which to transmit data even in the event of a partial system failure (e.g. after a nuclear strike). A network was then most suitable as it operates independent from any central control. So-called routers were to find the best routes for data transmission in the network and, in the case of failure, detect alternative routes, to thus keep operations going. The internet is a *result of scientific and military orientation research made under the conditions of an increased uncertainty of communication.* Since 1990, it has also been made available, first, for economic, and, then, for private use.

The internet initially brought about, as with every new technological development, *new technological problems:* regarding its physical accessibility (via cables, distribution stations, transmission towers, etc. – not everyone is reached in the same way), the failing of computer hardware or software, or various smartphone 'glitches,' etc.; the potentials of technologies' use expanded very rapidly and also created new orientation problems. These problems are comparably easy to fix or 'debug,' but they at the same time require new orientation skills. As such, they create *new psychological and cultural problems:* older generations may no longer be able to keep pace with the evolution of the means of communication; they may feel 'left behind' and powerless regarding the growing technological interconnectedness of a society's communication. They must learn from the younger generations: the traditional generational privilege, i.e. that the older teach the young, is turned upside down. However, considering the speed of the evolution of communication technologies, user generations age and 'outdate' very quickly, and we cannot yet predict how this will change the structure of modern society as a whole. At least, we can assume that *digital natives*, i.e. those born after c. 1990 and having grown up with the internet, will, depending on country and place, much more easily keep pace with new developments compared to older generations: here, too, it is to be expected that *routines in changing routines* will develop (chap. 8.3).

A new source for economic, political, and socioeconomic chances and risks is *'big data,'* i.e. the collection and storage of vast amounts of data regarding every internet user that he or she discloses in some way or that can be gathered from his or her online behavior and then used to influence his or her buying or voting behavior. Big data provides economic corporations and political authorities with an extremely high and, at the same time, hardly observable power that is so far without comparison in world history. In contemporary China (in the year 2019), big data is being used for the education (or disciplining) of an entire society, through the establishment of a 'Social Credit System' that assesses any relevant behavior of individuals, according to which he or she is given or denied certain rights in society. Indeed, the idea of an 'education of humanity' is not new; you find it in many cultures, from their very beginnings. But the technological means of communication now allow economic corporations and political authorities to very concretely realize it: the economic and political possibilities of influencing an entire society are rapidly expanding – at the cost of the leeways of individuals. *Big data can reorient our interindividual, doubly contingent orientation to other orientations to a unified macrosocial orientation that is governed by specific organizations.*

Any worldwide internet communication can (in principle) be observed and stored for an unlimited time; this stored data can be used in a variety of ways. As far as it is reserved for specific uses, it must be saved in specific ways in order to make it inaccessible to others. This is in turn only possible on the internet itself, by means of *digital security measures* such as encryption. These measures ensure that internet communication and the data gathered from it continue to be safe – to some extent. Historically, places of great societal importance have been protected with mechanical means, such as fortress walls, moats, or canons, which were distributed all over the country; at the same time, they attracted greater attention, particularly if fortresses were built on mountains, where it was easier to defend them. One's security was openly protected and defended. In times of the internet, you can largely conceal control centers and security measures; but at the same time, you can easily find these control centers at *one* 'place,' i.e. the internet, which must not be locatable in only one specific country (and is therefore decentralized in its own way). While security measures implemented on the internet offer varying degrees of protection, you can never completely rule out the possibility of being hacked: over time, security gaps can be detected in any protection system and can then be used to access secured systems, exploit them, and take control of them. This creates a new kind of intelligent crime: cybercrime. Since, by now, countless vital service institutions of society (such as hospitals, public transportation systems, energy supply chains, and even nuclear power plants) are controlled through digital means, both our need for security as well as the security risks we take have increased exponentially. Our private and social communications have never been as easily and as securely protected as they are today – and, at the same time, they have never been exposed to so much insecurity. On the horizon, cyber wars are looming. *Individual and societal orientations are both more and less secure than ever before; and the need for both trust and mistrust in security systems has never been as high as today.*

The need for sufficient security to defend against ever-looming uncertainties puts us, as in everyday orientation, under the pressure of time, now a *spectacular pressure of time:* the pressure to close all safety gaps and find new, more intelligent encryption methods, while also securing reliable access to ever-more data in need of protection – until this data and the encryption methods are hacked again by even more intelligent methods. The accessibility of data grows – and becomes ever-more intricate. Security thus becomes a question of *intelligence.* The concept of intelligence is manifold; definitions are therefore controversial. In any case, it is a mode of orientation ability that involves superior and inferior competencies and that can do, in contrast to canons and bombs, without physical violence (even if it may eventually lead to it). If intelligence is enhanced by digital technologies, as is currently the case, then this brings about an ongoing competition for more intelligent orientation abilities and actions, which in turn increasingly drives the evolution of the digitization of communication forward. *The constantly looming uncertainty of the internet increases, in the long run, the intelligence of orientation.*

(3) Artificial Intelligence (AI). – The enhancement of orientation intelligence can in turn be pursued with digital methods – with appropriate algorithms that enable so-called *deep learning,* i.e. the self-referential learning of computers, their learning to learn. Self-learning robots, constructed in this way, permit making our work and everyday life easier in hitherto hardly imaginable ways; science fiction has long given us a foretaste of this. Since the deep learning of machines, constructed by human beings, is possible only in the form of complex digital network structures (comparable to those of the human brain), it again arouses the great fear that the human brain may at some point be outpaced by evolving machines, leading to their domination of humanity.

Two spectacular footholds for this are the defeats of both the world's best chess- and Go-players by computers. The so-called *internet of things*, where machines autonomously communicate with each other in order to optimize all kinds of processes, will, as we can already predict, go far beyond this and influence human life on a much deeper level. In the long run, the evolution of humanity then may turn into an independent evolution of machines. The fears are not unjustified; in them, an old fear of humankind returns on a grander scale: that a situation will be created that humankind can no longer master and at whose mercy it will then be entirely powerless. It is the *fear of the end of one's own orientation*. What is happening in this field and what will happen in the future cannot be yet predicted. It will be the task of future observation and research.

(4) Virtual Reality. – We have so far seen that the internet can also have politically liberating effects, in very different directions. The possibilities of very quickly finding new contacts are supposed to have made substantial contributions to the so-called 'Arab Spring,' when a whole range of North African peoples almost spontaneously freed themselves from their dictators. Many will also consider it liberating if those in power communicate directly with their people through spontaneous 'tweets,' thus bypassing their administrations. Both developments have broken with long-established routines, causing severe upheavals: the Arab Spring also brought about severe problems, including new authoritarian regimes and wars; where such governance, which bypasses the 'establishment' in order to connect with its supporters, ultimately leads remains to be seen.

In both cases, what was, and still is, at stake is the question of *facts*; it is nowhere easier to produce *fake news* than on the internet. This begins with the identity of each individual (chap. 11.1): online you can create, without much effort and without the restrictions of everyday interactions, your own identities – virtual or online identities are *designed identities*. However, they can just as well be created by others and for *their* interest: with the help of big data, you can, based on persons' past behavior, about which you have collected a sufficient amount of data (in 2018, the numbers reached about 30,000 attributes per person), predict, if not their future actions, then at least their usual decision behavior and thus their future orientations – and you can then also propose decisions that are tailored specifically to them. Identities are standardized on and through the internet, in a manner largely independent of the identities you design yourself. You can then choose to subscribe to the identities offered or not; it may be delightful and reassuring to see yourself continually confirmed in your usual decision behavior. Based on this, one can develop various business strategies.

It is (in principle) not easy to distinguish between *facts* and *fake news* as no one can make claims concerning definite truths; all we can do is (more or less) rely on footholds, and choose and asses them in our own orientation. This is also the case, as we have shown (chaps. 12.3, 13.1), in mass media and science. These two communication systems can offer only their own results and are thus competing with those of others; people who cannot acquire their own journalistic or scientific results can do nothing but trust some media outlets or scholars more than others.

Moreover virtual, fictitious realities can support 'real' reality with detailed animations, e. g. navigation systems that are surveyable and easy to handle or flight simulators that help prepare pilots for real flight operations. Many scientific results are displayed through imaging techniques in order to make them either more or initially plausible. *Virtualization increases the orientation qualities of information:* its accessibility, surveyability, adjustable detailedness, and currentness.

As such, fictitious and real realities permeate each other in increasingly nontransparent ways: *fictions gain their own reality.* Realities can no longer be recognized in their 'naked' form; their presentation in animated, stimulating, and plausible fictions can always be manipulated. Virtual realities can eventually take on *orientation worlds of their own*, in which you may prefer to be instead of in the real ones, as they are more fun; but they can also misorient you in real realities. Human beings have never been able to orient themselves without fictions; now they face the *challenge of continually distinguishing between whether certain fictions are reliable and helpful or holdless and misleading.*

(5) Internet Knowledge. – Information of all kinds can now be easily accessed using search engines. The downside of such easy orientability is that sources are often uncertain as well as, for a variety of reasons, only trustworthy to a limited degree. Information found online is not necessarily checked according to clearly selected standards or by professional editors of newspapers or scientific organizations. As such, this information remains, in an exemplary way, a *foothold requiring additional reviews.* The basic conditions of orientation are likewise present even in the virtual reality of the internet.

Just as older generations are being deprivileged by orientation technologies that are difficult for them to handle, so do internet searches *deprivilege experts:* most people now have easier access to expert knowledge (medical, judicial, scientific, etc.); you can, before asking experts, learn about the current state of affairs yourself so that you need personal advice only in special cases. This leads to job cuts in consulting services (in administrations, businesses, banks, travel agencies, etc.). You are now, more than ever, responsible for how informed you are; you can modify this in breadth and depth as desired or needed. In this regard, Wikipedia has become a principal source, calling itself "The Free Encyclopedia." Wikipedia is, given how difficult it is to distinguish between fact and fiction, a remarkable phenomenon: it presents the current state of our continually expanding knowledge to an unprecedented extent and in many of the world's languages, without (as most people believe) political or economic motivations; it does so (as most people believe) with great reliability, if one takes for granted that all facts are inevitably selected and presented in a certain way. Wikipedia, too, does not offer any definite knowledge; but its readers and editors continually check it for errors and gaps. And most of its knowledge is not based on its authors' own research. Nevertheless, Wikipedia creates, online and for free, a standard knowledge that keeps up with the times and that ensures all its consumers *an initially sufficient orientation at all places, at all times, and on almost every desired topic.* This knowledge is no longer acquired in the manner of classical education, which is not even remotely possible in this quantity, but now represents our *global memory*, which (almost) anyone can access anywhere in the world.

Altogether, the digitization of human orientation creates a new situation of orientation with new requirements for orientation: the potentials of orientation as well as the needs of orientation have grown in an unprecedented manner, and they pose new demands on our abilities of orientation. The capacity for orientation now also involves the ability to participate in manifold variants of online communication, and it is to a large extent replaced by this ability; e. g. the constant use of GPS systems supersedes one's former ability to geographical orient him or herself (and in fact it seems to weaken it in 'digital natives'). But participating in online communication requires not only a new orientation concerning these ways of orientation, which are likewise hardly surveyable, but also, in each case, the right decision to be made about them, and this entails: increased capacities for orientation, judging, and deciding – and all this under a greater pressure of time.

Nevertheless, people, especially young people, easily get used to it. For, our orientation also becomes simpler when communication, e. g. with administrations, traffic or travel businesses or online retailers, is guided through standardized formats, where you just have to 'click' your way through. However, the new means of communication are not only auxiliary, but are also coercive means: they are *orientation schemes* you simply have to adopt. To some extent, this has always been the case for languages and cultures; however, the prefabricated online orientation schemes hardly offer any alternatives and only in special cases provide alternative options for communication.

Orientation's uncertainty management changes and grows: on the one hand, both the interpolation of information technology and the use of machines in communication produce a new certainty of orientation in all kinds of situations. On the other hand, the functioning and interplay of machines has, for most people, never been so non-transparent and uncertain. *The old certainty paradox of orientation – the more certainty, the more uncertainty – is intensified.* All the more do we also long for completely surveyable orientations here.

16.4 Standardized Leeways for Surprises: Global Displays of Desired Orientations in Sporting Events

The standardization of our global orientation still leaves plenty of room for surprises, because of its own evolution. It even cultivates surprises – in its own standardized formats. The most attractive ones are globally broadcasted sports competitions with a worldwide audience, such as the Olympic Games, taking place every four years, or the different variants of football (such as soccer, American football, or rugby) as well as baseball or basketball, all of which are played by two teams competing against each other; they attract massive audiences, who are fascinated by them; they enjoy a cult status across continents and cultures (even if not all to the same degree everywhere), in mass media, especially during championships. The most capacious stadiums are built for them; their clubs and sports associations are run like large-scale businesses; the most important games are attended by the heads of state. Up until the 19th century, such cultic-ritualistic mega events of a similar size were solely reserved for religious or political festivals (e. g. a royal coronation).

The games are played, based on the ancient model, in 'stadiums,' i. e. in 'theaters' designed for athletic competitions (chap. 4.1; 13.1 [3]). The viewers gather in an elevated oval building, in which they can have an overview of the game while also being able to observe and react to each other. They form a festival- and cult-community; they become a community and react as a community. This community is virtually extended by radio listeners, TV viewers, and live streamers; this once again intensifies the community experience in the stadium as you distinguish yourself by being immediately present. The popularity of such team sports may (at least to some degree) be explained by the fact that they fascinate their audiences with *particularly attractive orientation achievements* – orientation achievements that are clearly distinguished from our everyday life. In team games with balls, athletic, 'theoretical,' artistic, religious, and moral orientations are intertwined. *Ball sports, as competitive games between teams on a large terrain and based on explicit rules, show in an exemplary way how orientation succeeds – according to global standards.*

- Such a competitive ball game between teams is initially a *game*, a temporally and spatially clearly limited event, in which everyone (especially the viewers) participates on a voluntary basis. The rules of the games are (at least for people familiar with the game) easy to follow, yet they still offer unlimited possible combinations, which themselves require *an extremely fast orientation*. These games are obviously played (at least in the case of fast-paced games) under a great *pressure of time*, in which every *leeway* and *opportunity* must be promptly utilized (under the strict observation of the viewers), and every player can demonstrate special abilities by doing this. *This is how you wish the conditions of orientation were in general.*

- Such a game offers excitement by means of *surprises*, but only within limited leeways. The degree of excitement is the criterion for its success. It is aimed at easily countable 'goals,' 'points,' 'runs,' or 'touchdowns,' which clearly assess the (orientation) performance of the players. How goals etc. come about is narrated and discussed after the fact – the more surprising, the more often. There are clear winners and losers in a surveyable narration that offers common *footholds* but allows for different interpretations of them – *this is how you wish the narrative orientation were.*

- Such a game is a *competitive contest:* two teams of a surveyable size try – by most effectively using their scarce resources (the number of players on the field, their running performance, their endurance, the strategic concepts of the coaches, their tactical skills in executing their strategies, their limited knowledge about the strategies and tactics of their opponent, etc.) – to snatch away the ball, which the teams possess in alternate turns, and bring it into the other team's half to either place it in their 'end zone' or kick it through the 'goal posts' (or a player advances around the bases, or shoots the ball through the opponent's 'hoop'). Competitive superiority becomes immediately visible. In football, soccer, and basketball, the 'territories' have equal size (each team has one half of the field), and the teams switch sides after half-time; the competition takes place under the same general conditions. *This is how you wish the economic orientation were.*

- Such a game is played according to *explicit rules* whose compliance is constantly observed, and whose violations are immediately sanctioned by a referee who makes a final and decisive judgment (unless they have to go to 'instant replay' to make a call) that has immediate consequences for the ongoing match. *This is how you wish the political and judicial orientations were.*

- Such a game is a *field game:* contrary to the theater, nobody knows ahead of time what course the game will take, and the players on the field can survey what is happening at each point only to a limited extent. The spectators in their elevated seats, however, have a 'transcendent,' 'theoretical' *overview* of the entire field and the action taking place on it. They are mostly (more or less) proficient at playing the game themselves; from the distance they partake in it; they are 'fully immersed' in the game; from their superior view they give (mostly without any consequence) instructions to the players ('Pass the ball!'; 'Take a shot!'); they also support (with consequences) their own team, sometimes with ritualistic chants. They experience a godlike standpoint. *This is how you wish the scientific and religious orientations were.*

- Such a game is a *team sport:* it forces you to play together and be considerate of each other. Here, *considerateness* develops into the high art of in-game maneuvering, in which each player must consistently and physically engage with their opponent's various combinations of moves; it enhances and grows more and more refined. *This is how you wish the artistic orientation were.*
- Such a team game furthermore forces each individual to make in principle unlimited *efforts for the entire team*; it requires the individual to adopt the morality of the group. *This is how you wish the moral orientation were.*
- In such a team game, the group morality is a fighting morale. But it is a fighting morale restricted by (strictly monitored) rules; it must respect *'fair play'* and will usually calm down after the game. The players can, over time, change their teams; they do not commit themselves for all time; they likewise prepare to adjust to *always new opponents*. They demonstrate how you can adopt group moralities, identify with them, and then later detach yourself from them; fans (short for 'fanatics') may learn from this too. *This is how you wish the ethical orientation were.*

16.5 Fluctuant Value Orientation in Our World Orientation: Time Values

In the course of the globalization of orientation, our values change as well. Globalization requires you to adapt to competition and to the transformations it brings about, and that means: to time and *time values*. These values demand from everyone ongoing achievements of reorientation.

- Now the fundamental value is *innovation*. Change is no longer considered to be decay but rather a chance for renewal. In global competition, companies, business locations, governments, legal systems, academic disciplines, styles of art, and, depending on the location, even religions – all these require innovation to survive. Innovations are preserved and presented, where possible, *as* innovations in museums ('houses of history'); these museums' organizations are on their part, as Hermann Lübbe puts it,[49] continually renewed.

- Innovations must be extremely inventive and also appealing (in a variety of ways) if they are to assert themselves (more or less) on a global scale: they demand *creativity.*
- They must be successful in a widely economic sense, as far as possible: *efficiency.*
- You need to go to wherever is most conducive to innovation; you must be ready to, again and again, change your place of work and residence: *mobility.*
- You must be able to adapt to always new living conditions: *flexibility.*
- You must be able to withstand the stress you face when acting upon times values: *resilience.*
- And you must, at your own peril, be willing to take risks regarding the future: *appetite for risk.*

Time values keep our value orientation itself in fluctuance.

Chapter 17
Metaphysics in Our Orientation
Disregard for the Conditions of Orientation within Orientation

17.1 The Need for a Stable Hold on Solid Ground: Transcending Orientation through Metaphysics

Blaise Pascal (1623–1662), in his *Pensées,*[50] pointedly outlines the basic situation of human orientation *avant la lettre*. He describes it as a situation of someone being "lost" in a "double infinity": on the one hand the universe, "an infinite sphere, the center of which is everywhere, the circumference nowhere," on the other hand, the infinitely little, which in turn may contain an infinity of universes. The human being must find his or her way in this double infinity, being infinitely small compared to the universe and infinitely large compared to the small universes – without being able to sufficiently relate to either: "A nothing in comparison to the Infinite, an All in comparison with the Nothing, and mean between nothing and everything," and "infinitely removed from comprehending the extremes." But at some point, in both the macro- and the microcosmic, human reason begins to grasp its first footholds – human orientation's own being limits its cognition, including its knowledge of itself: "we are something, and we are not everything. The nature of our existence hides from us the knowledge of first beginnings which are born of the Nothing; and the littleness of our being conceals from us the sight of the Infinite." Being dependent on both the infinitely great and the infinitely little, all we can do is interpret these infinities from a lost standpoint somewhere in between – in a limited horizon and according to our own footholds. As such, we are incapable of both "certain knowledge" and "absolute ignorance (*ignorer absolument*)"; therefore, we

> sail within a vast sphere, ever drifting in uncertainty, driven from end to end. When we think to attach ourselves to any point and to fasten to it, it wavers and leaves us; and if we follow it, it eludes our grasp, slips past us, and vanishes for ever. Nothing stays for us. This is our natural condition, and yet most contrary to our inclination; we burn with desire to find solid ground and an ultimate sure foundation whereon to build a tower reaching to the Infinite. But our whole groundwork cracks, and the earth opens to abysses.

The scaleless uncertainty of ever-vanishing footholds awakens man's deep desire for a firm hold on solid ground; it urges us to grasp final certainties or, if there

https://doi.org/10.1515/9783110575149-019

are none, to invent them. Pascal warns us against blindly following this desire. As an antidote, he recommends the maxim:

> Let us therefore not look for any certainty and stability (*Ne cherchons donc point d'assurance et de feremté*).

In a situation of total uncertainty you must accept and find your own means for enduring it. You must

> work for the uncertain; sail on the sea; walk over a plank (*travailler pour l'incertain; aller sur la mer; passer sur une planche*).[51]

Facing ineradicable uncertainty, you can fulfil the need or desire for certainty and a firm hold only by making efforts to find a hold in the uncertainties themselves. When confronting uncertainty, human orientation cannot do without something to hold on to, at least temporarily. We must assume that there is something permanent and firm even in changing situations – but this something need not always be the same. This is also true for concepts (chap. 9.5.).

But as soon as we get accustomed to this something that is permanent and firm, especially in the form of concepts, our orientation is tempted to forget its own conditions: then *the conditions of orientation are neglected in our orientation*, i.e.

- its situativity (chap. 3),
- its selectivity (chap. 4),
- its perspectivity (chap. 5),
- its decisions on its footholds (chap. 6),
- the leeways of its signs (chap. 7),
- the unnoticeability of its routines (chap. 8),
- the constant shifting in meaning of its terms (chap. 9),
- its doubly contingent communication (chap. 10),
- the dependency of its identities on identifications (chap. 11),
- the plurality of orientation systems (chap. 12–13),
- its self-bindings through moral convictions (chap. 14–15),
- the standardization of the means of communication, and the virtualization of its realities (chap. 16).

What was accepted as permanent and firm in *our* orientations then tends to appear as something existing, per se, *beyond* orientation. If philosophers try to put such things that seemingly exist beyond orientation into permanent, consistent, and systematic orders, then they develop *metaphysics*. Metaphysics consists in *transcending the conditions of orientation*. Through it, one looks for unconditional certainties while rejecting Pascal's understanding of orientation's fundamental uncertainty.

Understood in this way, metaphysics is not in opposition to (the philosophy of) orientation but rather a possibility of orientation itself that has its own place in the philosophy of orientation. The concept of metaphysics, too, has become subject to fluctuances; it has undergone various shifts in meaning. Originally, it was merely the title given by an editor attempting to classify Aristotle's writings on fundamental issues, which went 'beyond' his writings on the more specific issues of physics (*metà tà physikà*). Later, this librarian's title 'metaphysics' also became the term for the content of these writings, which Aristotle himself called 'First Philosophy' – the part of philosophy that deals with the preconditions of physics (as well as of logic and ethics). In the early modern era, 'metaphysics' (as 'First Philosophy') became a historical term for a specific strand of European philosophy in the 17th and 18th centuries, and, at the same time, it became, as it remains today, a systematic concept for efforts that go beyond the spatial and temporal, i.e. the physical conditions of individual human orientations, by instead relying on an alleged universal and atemporal knowledge of a reason independent of all experience. This also, but not primarily, involved first principles from which everything else could be deduced; but above all metaphysics dealt with finding final certainties where questions came to an end, where one could – in Pascal's sense – stop working for the uncertain and instead calm down by omitting further questions. Many people (philosophers included) still have this need to be calmed by final certainties.

Questions come to an end when no alternatives seem possible. Metaphysics therefore only makes sense if there is only one in effect at a time and others are excluded. Nevertheless, in the history of philosophy there have been a variety of metaphysics that were simultaneously in effect, thus functioning as alternatives or critical instances of each other. Metaphysics as a discipline of philosophy was and is a self-critical enterprise, too; for all of the different metaphysics have proceeded from certain footholds in orientation, allowing other metaphysics proceeding from different footholds to always question them. Hence, they may oppose, overlap, embrace, or (in Hegel's sense) 'sublate' (i.e. abolish, elevate, and preserve) each other.

But even the assumption of something absolutely firm in our orientation has – in the history of philosophy (but not in religion) – always been controversial. Already Plato, who was, besides Aristotle, the main initiator of metaphysics, had to grapple with philosophers following Heraclitus and with sophists such as Gorgias and Protagoras, who did not allow for any final certainties. And every new metaphysics that followed triggered its own new anti-metaphysical doubts; as such, the history of metaphysics can also be written as a history of the critique of metaphysics. After Kant's critique of all metaphysics feeding only on truths of reason, after Kant-Laplace's theory of the temporal origin and relentless change of the universe, after Darwin's theory of evolution, after Dilthey's historical description of both philosophy and science, and after Nietzsche's suspicion that any metaphysics that claims to be general and atemporal actually springs from individual and temporal life necessities – after all these critical efforts, the evidence has been reversed: one no longer has to demonstrate the temporality of the temporal from an atemporal point of view, but the assumption of something atemporal must be made plausible via temporal points of view. Today, the basic attitude of (almost) all current philosophical projects is critical of metaphysics.

As far as no orientation gets by without making temporary assumptions of atemporal holds that, if no longer questioned, are easily metaphysically reified into atemporally existing entities, there will always remain suspicions against metaphysics in philosophy. After Heidegger interpreted even Nietzsche's philosophy as a "blinded" (*in sich erblindete*) completion of metaphysics, this very interpretation likewise proved to be metaphysical. After Heidegger's student, Hans-Georg Gadamer, believed that in his philosophical hermeneutics he had freed himself from being entangled in metaphysics, his guiding principle of an 'approximation to the truth' was still a metaphysical concept of the one truth that can be approached. After Wittgenstein, in his *Tractatus Logico-Philosophicus*, pushed forward the logical analysis of language, he himself rejected, in his *Philosophical Investigations*, the guiding principle of that analysis, the concept of "an *ideal* language," as a misconception, and instead wanted to "bring words back from their metaphysical to their everyday use" (*Philosophical Investigations*, §§ 81, 116). After logical empiricism, largely following Wittgenstein's *Tractatus*, declared metaphysics to be entirely pointless, its own representatives, among them Willard Van Orman Quine and Donald Davidson, proved that it, too, was based on metaphysical dogmas. As such, it was still possible to find metaphysics even in philosophies resolutely critical of metaphysics.

This was followed by the insight that metaphysics can neither be overcome nor done away with in our everyday, scientific, and philosophical orientations. Heidegger therefore no longer called for an *Überwindung* ("overcoming") of metaphysics but for its '*Verwindung*' (something like "accepting it, coping and working with it") – metaphysics being the '*Geschick*' (destiny or fate) of Western thought. Derrida connected to him in this regard by stating that all the "destructive discourses" that metaphysics tried to overcome (Heidegger's in *Being and Time* being the most famous) remained stuck in a "circle" of replacing the 'destructed' metaphysics with a new one. According to Josef Simon's *Philosophy of Signs*, we "do not have any other concept of philosophy but the metaphysical one" – as long and as far as philosophy tries to speak about the entirety of human orientation from one standpoint beyond human orientation (and Simon included his own anti-metaphysical philosophy in this). The philosophy of orientation can live with metaphysics but only while keeping its critical distance from any firm grounds or final certainties. *Metaphysics may be necessary and helpful – in specific situations of orientation and only for a certain period of time.* One can accept metaphysics if one cannot avoid it – and then one can detach oneself from it again.

17.2 The Origin of Metaphysics in the Needs of Orientation and Their Change over Time

To be able to detach oneself *from* a situation while *within* said situation is, as shown above, a crucial achievement of orientation (chap. 9.2). As such, it can become a need of orientation (as it obviously was for millennia) to endow *thinking* or *reason*, to which this ability of distancing was and still is ascribed, with an absolute strength, i.e. to consider it capable of distancing one from *all* situations. This is not only the case for the metaphysics that began with Aristotle, the first metaphysics with systematic intentions, which shaped Western thought for millennia, but also for the modern metaphysics in the tradition of Descartes. The Aristotelian metaphysics was a *metaphysics of being*, the modern one a *metaphysics of consciousness*. The metaphysics of being proceeds from visible nature and its movements; it tries to comprehend how, in these movements, a hold in terms can be established. The metaphysics of consciousness, on the other hand, found a hold in the mere self-referentiality of thinking: the first certainty was, according to Descartes, the being of consciousness itself, and all other certainties were certainties adopted by this self-consciousness. The plausibility changed: one no longer relied on nature and, later, on God, who created and maintained it, but rather on how one could *think* nature and God according to the criteria of self-referential thinking. However, both Leibniz, connecting with Locke, and Kant, connecting with Hume, showed that the mere self-referentiality of thinking would be empty without references to nature; the self-referentiality of thinking then only makes sense combined with an other-referentiality (chap. 8.1). Hegel, in this sense, sublated the metaphysics of being *and* the metaphysics of consciousness into a concluding *metaphysics of mind (or spirit: Metaphysik des Geistes)*; 'Geist' was his term for the step-by-step exploration of the categories of other-referentiality through the categories of self-referentiality, and vice versa. The categories of this systematic guiding (self-)distinction of *Geist* constitute what Hegel called "logical science," and this logical science constitutes the "genuine metaphysics or pure speculative philosophy" (*Science of Logic*, Preface to the first edition). By developing a "system" of spirit, Hegel provided metaphysics with a new and now comprehensive plausibility, which was entirely unprecedented. It encompassed all alternatives, and as such it could no longer be refuted with traditional means; but it lost its credibility over time.

Kant and Hegel still accepted Christian Wolff's (the prevailing thinker of German Enlightenment) classification of metaphysics: he distinguishes general metaphysics (*metaphysica generalis)* or ontology from special metaphysics (*metaphysica specialis*), which he subdivides into 'general cosmology' (*cosmologia generalis*), 'natural psychology' (*psychologia naturalis*), and 'natural theology' (*theologia naturalis*). Thus, the issues of metaphysics are being as such (ontology); being as a whole, or rather, the world (cosmology); the soul as the being that thinks both being as such and existing things (psychology); and the highest being that, for Aristotle, keeps everything else in its being and that, in Christian philosophy, also brings everything into being: i.e. God, as far as He is to be thought through natural or human reason (theology). Today, the metaphysical orientation to these issues has likewise had its time; it was undermined by an orientation to science and time. Metaphysical cosmology, psychology, and theology have largely been given up on, and ontology is now dealt with only under limited conditions. However, ever-new 'realisms' and 'ontologies' that deliberately disregard the conditions of orientation continue to emerge. But they, too, are in fact philosophical approaches under the conditions of orientation. They thus describe, in many different ways, an alleged 'reality as such,' which likewise differs in each of their conceptions, as does the seemingly firm hold that they hope this reality provides.

Both classical metaphysics as well as later concepts of metaphysics and ontology indeed correspond to needs of orientation or respond to problems of orientation. *The term of being responds to the orientation problem of unsteadiness, or rather, of time as such.* Being was, for Parmenides, who was the first to conceive of it in this way, the atemporal hold in time as such. Aristotle then determined being as *ousía* or as the atemporal ground of accidentals and as the general and constant form across the ever-changing individuals of a species; an atemporal being thus became the hold of temporal beings. Descartes, in his metaphysics of consciousness, reintroduced the problem of time in a new way: for him, the being of consciousness can only consist of the temporal performance of thinking; both thinking and the 'I' that thinks exist only *as long as* they think. But since a performance like this must be, according to Descartes (still following Aristotle on this point), an accident of a substance, he again turned thinking into an atemporal substance. After Locke and Hume insisted that *that which* is thought by thinking is that which is initially available to the senses, and thus always temporary, Kant broke with the metaphysics of being too. He made, following Locke and Hume, all cognition subject to the conditions of temporality. However, he did not give up the autonomy of reason (and thus its atemporality) as being opposed to the senses: he assumed that reason can *a priori* or transcendentally determine the conditions of cognition.

Nevertheless, in practical philosophy reason reaches, with Kant, its limits. Here, reason can indeed formulate an atemporal norm of action, i.e. the categorical imperative. But in order to act in the world, reason is required "to orient itself"; it is in "need" of an orientation that it cannot provide itself as a *pure* reason, i.e. when transcending all experience. Orientation in the world and in time becomes a need of reason that exceeds its own capacities. It was, to recall, Kant, the most eminent philosopher of reason, who, though he did not introduce the philosophical concept of orientation, still needed it to complete his conception of reason and who thus made it more widely known. Given its need to orient itself in the empirical world, atemporal reason, with its atemporal view of the atemporal conditions of cognition and action, thus becomes temporal again. As far as we continue to speak of "being" as an atemporal being, we disregard that this is a need of orientation we are only sometimes subjected to.

The term of world, the first of the 'metaphysica specialis,' responded and still responds to the more specific orientation problem of each situations' unsurveyability. In every situation, everything given depends on an unsurveyable variety of other things given, which can only be explored over time. By contrast, the metaphysical term of the world refers to the totality of everything given (the world as a whole) as simultaneously present, as if one were able to have a complete overview of it. Aristotle conceived of this whole as a 'cosmos,' i.e. a beautiful order entirely surveyable so that it could also function as a model and measure for human actions. At the beginning of the modern era, the belief in the Aristotelian cosmos was destroyed; an overview of the universe was gained in a new way. Copernicus made it plausible to choose one's standpoint when observing the celestial movements; one could choose it in such a way that one would be able to calculate the celestial movements in a mathematical way as simply and clearly as possible: the plausibility relied on was no longer the aesthetic, ethical, or theological, but now the mathematical one. Since Kant-Laplace, one has found oneself situated in a continuously changing universe, whose evolution has been difficult to calculate; since Darwin, one has been situated in an evolution of everything living that can (as a whole) no longer be calculated or predicted in mathematical terms.

Instead, to gain an overview of all the world's givens, the idea of a 'universal encyclopedia' prevailed, i.e. the collection and concise display of the total knowledge of the world in books available anywhere and anytime. *The plausibil-*

ity relied on was now the surveyable orientation itself. The compilation of universal knowledge, however, also took time, in fact, decades: it thus became outdated in the process of its creation (which again and again made supplemental volumes and revised editions of the encyclopedia necessary). And over time, the systematically (i.e. according to functional groups) ordered encyclopedias were replaced by those in an alphabetical order of terms. For only this allowed for a persisting overview in light of the accelerating growth of knowledge. The alphabet is an ordering principle of the art of world abbreviation that uses signs of language. Its sequence is, once learned, easy to survey – but (as with all signs) also arbitrary. Since it has, in its entirety, become, like our language as a whole, a routine for us, we mostly overlook this.

The term of the soul was and still is a response to the problem of orientation's controllability. For Aristotle it was the 'who?' of orientation, that which perceives and thinks anything – and it was also the principle of a living body that desires and feels. As such, the soul was to also govern the body and control its passions, enabling successful exchanges between human beings – it was meant to make the double contingency of our orientations to other orientations controllable. Later, in the modern metaphysics of consciousness, one moved from the concept of the soul to the concept of free will: free will was, contrary to the soul, which was thought to also govern all unconscious physical processes, considered to be completely conscious. With it, the notoriously controversial question of the soul's immortality no longer arose, and so free will could become the sole addressee for the attribution of responsibility. For everyone to get along with each other, orientation was regarded as consciously and willfully controlled and as based on a common insight into shared norms. Kant – according to whom the will ought to be only a 'good will' and, as such, to examine the maxims of our actions on the basis of the categorical imperative with regard to their possible general legitimacy – spoke of a "causality out of freedom." Hence, everything that we face in our orientation to other orientations as well as every event in nature would have an identifiable and thus controllable cause. This is reassuring; and we therefore often disregard that we, when ascribing political, judicial, or moral responsibilities, are ourselves coerced by our own needs, and that we could ethically also dispense with performing such ascriptions (chap. 15).

The concept of God in 'rational' or metaphysical theology was and still is a response to the problem of orientation's uncertainty as such. Conceived of as the highest kind of being, equipped with omnipotence and omniscience, God is the instance of absolute permanence, overview, and control of everything; since He was also considered to be capable of completely surveying both the past and the future, He was also thought to be the instance of an absolute and eternal certainty of orientation. But since, in human orientation, there can only be uncertain footholds for His transcendent being, special kinds of proof were required which made this being's existence, just like the immortality of the soul, notoriously controversial as well – until Friedrich Schleiermacher eventually dispensed with all proofs and anchored the existence of God in the "feeling of absolute dependence" (chap. 13.3 [7]). The feeling of continuous dependence on something other is the basic feeling of orientation. This feeling comes to the fore when we dispense with metaphysics.

Chapter 18
The End of Orientation
The Death of Our Orientation in Our Orientation

In death, orientation ends. That death will occur is (for now) certain; when and how it will occur is (mostly) uncertain. It can come by surprise or as expected, in a natural way or by force, desired or undesired. You can decide to die, but not against it. You may experience the process of dying, but not death itself. We cannot imagine death, but neither can we imagine what it would be like to not imagine anything. As such, we involuntarily orient ourselves beyond death; we try to grasp it and grasp at nothing. You may, but you do not have to, think about it. It may be the most significant as well as the most insignificant thing in your life; it can be the greatest concern as well as the greatest reassurance; it can trigger anxiety and despair as well as calm us down – because all concerns, anxieties, and despair will end with it. Death is serious, but during your lifetime you can only experience the "mood," as Søren Kierkegaard puts it, when others die. You may be responsible for the life and death of others, and others can bring about your own death. You may sacrifice your life for others as well as for political, moral, or religious convictions, but you cannot expect others to do the same. Death, too, dispenses with reciprocity. You may make metaphysical statements about death, but nothing you can say about it can be confirmed. As an (always possible) ending of orientation it is a perpetual problem of orientation: one always needs to find one's way with it. As it is both certain and ungraspable, it once again reinforces the paradoxes of orientation. Death plays a role in everything we have dealt with in this book. Let us briefly review the book in this respect:

Chapters 1–5: The Primordialness and Self-Arrangement of Orientation . – Epicurus, who died a slow and painful death, famously conceived of death through his sober formula, that "as long as we exist, death is not here. And once it is here, we no longer exist." Thus, he argues, death need not concern us. This seems plausible, especially for a philosophy of orientation. Death is seen from a certain perspective – from the standpoint of life ("as long as we exist"). But Epicurus contrasts this with the standpoint of death ("once it is here"), which cannot be adopted within life. *Death is also an end of all standpoints and perspectives:* if we are dead, we can no longer say that death is here.

Within the perspective of life, Epicurus distinguished, in the ancient sense, between being and non-being. By distinguishing between being and non-being, the sage, i.e. the philosopher, differs from the foolish and deluded crowd, who

https://doi.org/10.1515/9783110575149-020

either allow themselves to be bothered by the expectation of death or expect it to be a salvation from suffering. By distinguishing between being and non-being, however, one would also be able, according to Epicurus, to gain a firm stance toward death, ridding oneself of fear and hope, allowing oneself to live a life that if not long, is at least full of pleasure. But of death you cannot say that it 'is' (or 'is not') and, in this way, make it meaningless for life. It is neither a being nor a non-being, but rather the ending of this distinction itself: a *being-an-end*. As long as we exist, death is still before us, but it continues to be delayed. As such, death is a boundary in the sense of a horizon: a *temporal horizon*. But it makes a paradox of even the horizon: at some point, the horizon no longer moves away, but is reached and then ceases; it is therefore not a mere temporal horizon, but the horizon of all temporal (and spatial) horizons: an absolute temporal horizon and thus, at the same time, no longer a horizon. It is, without one being able to draw a clear distinction, both a horizon and not a horizon.

We are always moving closer to death, but it is (for the most part) unlike any appointment that you or others have set. Our death may appear far away, but still be near, or vice versa. If it seems far away, you will think about it less, or rather, you will face it with more Epicurean serenity. If it seems closer, it causes anxiety and resistance, as far as orientation operates, beginning with the most basic orientation reflexes, in the service of sustaining one's life. In everyday life, orientation's circumspection always wants to keep death away or at least delay it; and anxiety alerts an orientation. The prospect of death can, as it were, startle you. As such, death is always a concern for orientation; death is, just as life, a primordial condition of orientation. And initially death does not appear in the form of either fear or hope, but rather as a *delay:* just as you cannot get to the beginning of orientation, as every orientation is always preceded by another, you also cannot reach its end – you continually orient yourself anew as long as you live. As long as you live, you still have time; you still have a chance to survive; pleasure and joy are still possible. Life, as far as death is certain to end it at some point, is indeed a kind of dying from the very beginning, as it has often been described. But with every day that death does not occur, *time is gained*. In light of death, time is experienced, in our everyday orientation, not as a loss, but as a gain.

Chapter 6: The Hold of Orientation. – As with the self-arrangement of orientation to horizons, standpoints, and perspectives, death also paradoxizes how we deal with footholds. As far as death is (at least until now) as certain as nothing else is, it could be the *strongest and firmest foothold* of orientation and the yardstick of all its certainties. But since it remains uncertain when and how it will occur – even in the final stages of a terminal illness, or after a firm resolution to commit suicide, or before a scheduled execution – death, like every other foothold, allows for *leeways*. However, unlike other footholds, death does not refer to other footholds; therefore, it does not form any patterns, either. It does not distinguish itself as something that you can make something of. As such, it is *not a foothold that one can hold onto.*

However, there are (more or less striking) indications *of* death: dangers, sicknesses, violence, wars, catastrophes, or terrorist attacks; you can thus still orient yourself to death – by avoiding such indications. Death is an *avoided foothold.* It is of greatest relevance if acute dangers are looming. But in everyday orientation, such dangers are mostly not imminent – and we can thus forget about death for the most part.

The everyday forgetting of death is not necessarily a kind of repression, as has been claimed again and again. We can indeed repress the looming of death; but this does not make its repression a basic characteristic of an "inauthentic (*uneigentliches*)" human being in the world (*Dasein*), as was argued by Heidegger, who perceived the "authenticity" of *Dasein* to be a "Being-towards-death" (*Sein zum Tode*). According to him, this Being-towards-death offers *Dasein* the "potentiality of Being-a-whole," as it allows us to take into account our entire existence from birth to death (*Being and Time*, §§ 46 – 51). But our orientation does not initially need to become 'whole'; rather, it is already whole and authentic in every situation of orientation, and our *Dasein* therefore does not need to first understand itself as 'Being-towards-death.'

Nor does that which is often considered a sign of the general repression of death in modern societies – namely that today more people than ever before die in retirement homes or in hospitals – mean that their deaths and death as such is being repressed. Professional care in retirement homes and hospitals (in most cases) promises that the lives of the elderly and the sick will be maintained with more professional medical attention than could be provided by traditional families (which often no longer even exist) could offer. In addition, the people dying in retirement homes or hospitals are (mostly) neither neglected nor abandoned, but taken care of with thoughtful support. Often, relatives and friends visit and provide them company. But even this is not something that every dying person wants. Montaigne already wrote that he wanted to be looked after by professionals, but not mourned by either relatives or friends: "Let us live and laugh among our friends, let us go die and look sour among strangers."[52]

And even if you spare dying persons from having to speak about their imminent death, you are not repressing it. If they themselves want to speak about it, you will surely respond and engage with it. When their death occurs, it is (mostly) not made taboo, but is publicly noted. In cemeteries, we maintain and take loving care of graves; we solemnize memorial days, etc.; even the mass murders and genocides of the 20th century are (often) not repressed, but carefully and actively preserved in the peoples' collective memories. Everyday orientation reacts, when the situation requires it, to death with focused attention rather than anxious repression.

Chapter 7 – 8: The Signs and Routines of Orientation. – The attention to death has also become part of the art of world abbreviation and the self-stabilization of orientation. We speak of 'dying' or 'death' usually in the case of living beings that have special significance and thus also a *name*. These are not only human beings, but also some animals and plants, as well as everything that can, in some way, be 'alive': biotopes, habitats, or landscapes ('the desert lives'), peoples, cities ('a city dies'), cultures, or organizations ('this would mean the death of the UN'). But whatever has a name may also be outlived by its name. Human beings receive names before they can speak; and their name is still mentioned even when they are dead. Names thus reach beyond death; to know that their name will remain on a gravestone may provide comfort and a hold to dying persons. Photos, letters, emails, and, today more and more, digital traces (e. g. on social media) remain as well; some persons are commemorated in articles or books; and for some people memorials are even erected. An orientation in signs helps us get over death in a variety of ways. But signs, too, are mortal; graves can likewise decay and be abandoned.

Rituals for commemorating the dead allow them to live on in the memory of those surviving them. Rituals are specifically marked routines. Routines around the act of dying and death stabilize how we deal with it; they create a growing familiarity with it even for whom it is not imminent. Experiencing the death of others allows those who are alive to become familiar with it, and it prepares them for their own death.

But death affects our routines as well. Even for those who deal with it professionally – doctors, morticians, criminal investigators, spiritual or psychological counselors, executioners (where they still exist), soldiers or war correspondents – death never quite fully develops into a routine, at least not when they are close to or have to face the dead. Even the most practiced executioners, those in the Nazi extermination camps, tried to avoid having to face their victims. Everyone who is dying reminds those surviving of their own upcoming death, no matter how far away it may be. If a familiar person dies, then his or her orientation worlds, which are (more or less) intertwined with yours, die as well, are irreversibly lost. Children who lose their parents at an early age or partners who, after living together for a long time, are separated by death may, no matter how they stood to each other, be severely disoriented; mourning the death of relatives or close friends involves the *horror of a final loss of orientation*. Routines that break away can be regained in one way or another; others with their own orientation worlds, which you oriented yourself to, cannot. They may leave a permanent gap in the orientations of those surviving.

Death thus becomes a *sign of absolute finality*. In life, everything may still change and perhaps get better – but not in death. You may even seek the finality of death yourself: through *suicide*. It usually happens in situations of need that seem inescapable. Whoever decides on killing him or herself no longer just looks for a way to calm the unsettlements of his or her orientation, but rather seeks a *final calming* of its needs. This paradoxizes the self-stabilization of orientation. Death is indeed the most stable state of orientation – but one where orientation is no longer possible, nor necessary.

The freedom to kill yourself, i.e. the paradoxical killing of the self by the self, brings orientation's self-referentiality to its utmost extreme. The freedom to commit suicide is a freedom that ends all freedoms, a decision that ends all decisions – a decision against all further decisions. It is therefore very difficult to discourage someone from his or her firm intention to commit suicide using reasons: he or she no longer exposes him or herself to reasons that might influence his or her decision – he or she *wants* to die. This is even more so in the case of martyrs who want to die *for* something: to testify one's faith in the greatest hardship; to burn oneself in order to draw attention to political grievances; or to kill others as well in a terrorist attack meant to cause public turmoil and anxiety and thus destabilize an established political order.

But, as bizarre as it may seem, *even suicide still follows routines:* not only in how you proceed when committing it, but also in the regularity of its occurrence. For each individual, his or her death is absolutely singular. Nevertheless, in death statistics each death is regarded like every other. If someone becomes aware that he or she fulfills with his or her suicide precisely what statistics have led us to expect, then the contradiction between singularity and countability may irritate them so much that they may refrain from committing suicide. No one wants to kill him or herself for statistical routines.

Chapter 9: Orientation through Thinking. – Kant spoke of death and dying with the utmost sobriety:

> No human being can experience his own *death* (for to constitute an experience requires life), he can only observe it in others. Whether it is painful cannot be judged from the death rattle or convulsions of the dying person; it seems much more to be a purely mechanical reaction of the vital force, and perhaps a gentle sensation of the gradual release from all pain. – The fear of death that is natural to all human beings, even the unhappiest or the wisest, is therefore not a horror of *dying* but, as Montaigne rightly says, horror at the thought of *having died* (that is, of being dead), which the candidate for death thinks he will still have after his death, since he thinks of his corpse, which is no longer himself, as still being himself in a dark grave or somewhere else. – This illusion cannot be pushed aside, for it lies in the nature of thought as a way of speaking to and of oneself. The thought *I am not* simply cannot *exist*; because if I am not then I cannot be conscious that I am not. I can indeed say: "I am not healthy," and think such *predicates* of myself negatively (as is the

case with all *verba*); but to *negate* the subject itself when speaking in the first person, so that the subject destroys itself, is a contradiction. (*Anthropology from a Pragmatic Point of View*, § 27, transl. by Robert B. Louden)

Thinking allows one to think beyond all possible situations of orientation. But we can think of ourselves *as* being dead only in a contradictory way – and you then become anxious. The "nature of thinking" itself evokes an "illusion" (or, as Kant calls it in the *Critique of Pure Reason* [A 388], an "unavoidable illusion"): what is the "natural fear of death" becomes, if thinking finds its final certainty in its self-referential performance, a fear of a "thought" – the thought of the extinction of precisely this self-certainty of thinking. To the extent that our self-referential and self-certain thinking, in Descartes' sense, distinguishes itself from everything bodily, the question of Shakespeare's Hamlet about whether to be or not be refers to the extinction of this very thinking, whereas the bodily persists and, as Hamlet soberly admits, decomposes after the extinction of consciousness into new (chemical) compounds.

By contrast, Plato, thousands of years prior, thought of thinking as saving us from death. In his dialogue *Phaedo*, which he designed to be Socrates' last conversation before his execution, he had Socrates prove the immortality of the soul solely on the basis of the 'nature of thinking.' The argument runs like this: all conceptual opposites are reversible, even the one of life and death. Hence, death can not only follow life, but life can also follow death. Because it is the soul where opposites are reversible, the soul itself has no opposite. Thus, it can only live, not die. As such, death is sublimated into the thinking soul, and thinking itself becomes immortal. For Plato, *to think is to overcome death*. Even more, through death thinking detaches itself from the shackles of bodily life, thereby becoming pure. As a result, death should be welcomed by a thinking person; *to philosophize then means learning-to-die and wanting-to-die*; and philosophy, the 'love of wisdom,' becomes a love of death. Because one cannot know, according to Plato's Socrates, what death itself is (he knows that he does not know anything), you will not seek death on your own part. But as a thinking person, you can indeed face it in a friendly manner. We are – contrary to Epicurus, who did not praise thinking as highly as Socrates did – as thinking individuals at the very place where death is.

Even if death is no longer connected to a proof of the soul's immortality, the thinking of thinking is still considered a thinking-beyond-death. While it causes fear to think of *oneself* as dead, to think of *other* living beings beyond their death reassures one's orientation: to see them 'living on' in their offspring gives you the strength to accept death. Any thinking of a form or essence that remains the same while individual beings change – the essence of a biological species as Aristotle conceived of it, taking it as the observable model for the universal in both logic and science – is a *thinking of continual death:* individual beings that relentlessly arise and die maintain an atemporal form. Aristotle, and with him the entire metaphysical tradition, conceived (just as Plato did) of the universal form in such a way that the individual is formed by it; but at the same time, he conceived of the universal form as owing its observable existence to the cycle of individual births and deaths. *Universal terms, as they have become self-evident in Western thought, live on the death of individuals.* As far as Western thinking conceives of the world in universal concepts, death is contained everywhere in it. This has made plausible individuals being sacrificed for a common or universal good, be it the matters of a family, a people, a state, a class, an organization, or an institution, or be it for the principles of a morality, religion, or ideology.

Kierkegaard compressed this thinking of thinking to a short and paradoxical formula: death is *"the briefest summary of life"*; for it offers the quickest and most comprehensive kind of overview:

> When one fears that somehow he will not be able to maintain an understanding grasp of something complex and extensive, he tries to find or to make for himself a brief summary of the whole – for the sake of a comprehensive view. Thus death is the briefest summary of life or life reduced to its briefest form. Therefore to those who in truth meditate on human life it has always been very important again and again to test with this brief summary what they have understood about life. For no thinker has power over life as does death, this mighty thinker who is able not only to think through every illusion but can think it analytically and as a whole, think it down to the bottom.[53]

By abbreviating orientation into general and ever more general terms, all the way up to an entirely abstract atemporal 'being,' and thereby gaining a total overview in orientation, thinking makes death everywhere 'at home' in orientation, without one being able to think of death itself. Thinking is therefore most strongly attracted by death: "This, then, is the ultimate paradox of thought: to want to discover something that thought itself cannot think."[54] In the face of death, Plato's Socrates was still able to calm himself through the power of thinking. The more our confidence in thinking has dwindled – as, for instance, with Nietzsche – the greater the unsettlements caused by death have grown: on the one hand, as the death of universals that seemed to exist autonomously; on the other, as the death of each individual who cannot hold on to anything but his or her own footholds and the self-referentialities of his or her own orientation.

Chapter 10 – 14: Orientation to Other Orientations. – You can indeed orient yourself to the death of others; here death is observable. One can also make general claims about death, including one's own (still upcoming) death. But just as the other's life is different from yours and just as you cannot orient yourself in his or her stead, his or her death is also different from yours. Even if we succor each other when living and dying, we are still alone in death. It is also on our own that we are exposed to the risks of death. Dangers such as floods, fires, or epidemics may be fought with joint efforts. And yet they may hit one person but not the other. And *the greatest danger for human beings is other human beings*. In nature, every life lives on other lives; every life threatens other lives. Among human beings, everyone is exposed to everyone else; everyone can afflict damage upon everyone else, use violence against him or her, and, in the extreme case, kill him or her. Even without wanting to do so, everyone can, with his or her life, harm another (e. g. deprive him or her of scarce resources, the care of third persons, or jobs, etc.); or someone may, in extreme circumstances, such as during the evacuation of a ship or during a famine, or amidst the violence of the Nazi extermination camps, only survive at the cost of another's death. The risks that human beings inevitably pose for each other require *caution* toward each other; this caution accompanies all our interactions, communications, and identifications – until *trust can calm it down*.

Trust grows through the security measures that technologies, administrations, and hygiene offer. These can contain the dangers of random, unintentional killings, e. g. those caused by collapsing buildings, street traffic, epidemics, or violent crimes, etc.; to care for an effective lowering of such hazards is one of the state's basic tasks. Technologies, administrations, or medicine can, however, also be used to purposefully make selections of life – in great numbers and justified through general norms. Over the last 200 years, according to Michel Foucault, a deliberate "biopolitics of the population" has developed. In addition to their monopoly of power over the life and death of individuals, states have seized the right to discipline those who will not submit to the community and even the right to breed both life and forms of life through systematic politics regarding migration, birth, and health as well as social and educational issues. These measures were (and still are) justified with economic necessities; today they are largely accepted without question. We currently only still dispute (more or less) rather specific issues of biopolitics, such as the legality of abortions or of genetically modified human embryos. But biopolitics has also been racially justified at times, and it led, in the Nazi period, to the most serious crimes in the history of humanity. Perhaps these crimes were not just an accident of history.

Chapter 15: Ethical Orientation. – After the Shoah, the state-run industrial killing of millions of people in the middle of Europe, Levinas questioned, as mentioned, all general justifications of ethics by recurring to the Jewish tradition and by starting afresh with the 'face-to-face' situation. In the face-to-face situation, death appears as well; it does so, according to Levinas, in two ways: as the

Other who can kill, on the one hand, and, on the other, when looking into the Other's face, which can prevent *me* from killing *him or her*. *The tension of the face-to-face* situation keeps awake, despite all the securities provided by institutions and despite all norms, the awareness that human beings may kill each other. But the unprotected face of the Other, which I look into and which looks at me, makes me hesitate for a moment and calls out to me: 'You will not kill.' This does not offer a final protection against the killing; it only *unsettles the thoughtlessness of killing.* After, during the totalitarianisms of the 20th century, all the securities that Western civilization believed it had established against the thoughtless killing of human beings by other human beings failed, it was, for Levinas, only the look into the unprotected face of the Other that would impede the murderers. The moment of hesitation before the killing may – but does not have to – halt the person resolved to kill and thus provide the time that may allow him or her to refocus on his or her responsibility to the Other – just as, in the Hebrew Bible, Abraham's killing (as commanded by God) of his own son was held up (again by one of God's messengers) (chap. 15.1). Levinas called this resistance against killing, which emerges from the Other's unprotected face, "ethical resistance." It could be extremely fragile, but still provide a hold to an ethical orientation soberly confronting the risks of killing and being killed.

Chapter 16: World Orientation. – Global media report daily on countless avoidable deaths: humans starving, dying in epidemics, expiring in traffic accidents, perishing in natural catastrophes, becoming victims of terrorist attacks, or being sacrificed in political fights. The news of such deaths is often followed by the most popular form of entertainment: action movies or crime thrillers that prepare murders in suspenseful ways. So, in the virtual world too, deaths and murders become an everyday routine, and we therefore grow (more or less) indifferent to them. *For everyone his or her own life is of the greatest significance – but on a global scale the life of a single person is almost insignificant.* This, too, is one of the abysses in Pascal's sense that makes our orientation dizzy. So, as Hans Blumenberg showed in his *Lebenszeit und Weltzeit* (Lifetime and World Time),[55] all we can do is experience as much as possible of the world in our short lifetimes and thus exhaust the possibilities the world offers us. The certainty of death suggests that we live life to the fullest.

Chapter 17: Metaphysics. – Within the horizon of death, most people seek not only to fully exhaust the possibilities of their own limited lives, but also to make provisions for those who they will be survived by, usually with the intention of facilitating their lives by leaving them a good inheritance. They can legally dispose of it through a *will.* With the help of the written word and the law, they can (in one way or another) make provisions, *beyond their own possible orientation,* for their heirs – irrevocably binding them. In his or her will, the dead person speaks once again, beyond the limits of death, to the living. He or she may oblige his or her heirs – given that they accept their heirship – to take on certain tasks and responsibilities, without him or herself being made responsible: e. g. by obliging others to continue, in some way, the deceased person's work or enterprise after his or her death. This too may ease the dying person's expectation of death.

The poet Matthias Claudius, a contemporary of Kant's, let Death speak for himself – to a young maiden, who sees him approaching as a man of bones and who rejects him in fear. The composer Franz Schubert later set Claudius' poem to music and depicted its mood through touching variations in his string quartet No. 14. Schubert himself was forced to confront death at an early age. In the last years of his life, the works he produced were increasingly meditations on death. Claudius' poem reads as follows:

> *The Maiden:*
> Pass by! Ah, pass by!
> Go, fierce skeleton!
> I am still young, go, dear one,
> And do not touch me.
>
> *Death:*
> Give me your hand, you pretty, tender creature!
> I am a friend, and do not come to punish.
> Be of good cheer! I am not fierce,
> You shall sleep softly in my arms!
> *(transl. by Robert Jordan)*

The poem opens with the maiden's horror in the face of death. Death confronts her as a man, as a "fierce skeleton," whom she may have been told of, a man of bones wandering around with a scythe and haphazardly mowing down human lives. She tries to repel him as if he were someone who wants to harm her, who wants to rape her. She experiences the horror of death as something similar to the shock of being raped by an overpowering, covetous man. But then she seems to calm down. Her defensive screams are followed by an argument appealing to the man's reason: "I am still young" – too young for death. But nobody is too young for death. The maiden's defense quiets down, weakens, and turns into a plea. Death seems to come very close to her, and now, very near, he seems to lose his horrific character. She calls him "dear" and still seems to be bargaining with him (in Schubert's adaption, the singing voice now makes leaps of fourths and fifths). But by articulating the word "dear," her feelings seem to reverse; death, whom she wanted to force away, seems to now pull her to him. Schubert makes this audible. He repeats her final, anxious "And do not touch me" and makes it heard again, in the meter of death (the consistent halves and quarters just as in the slow piano prelude in a minor key), in a way that now sounds like a released "yes, dear, touch me": she surrenders and gives herself to him. When Death, from whom she expected violence, approaches her, he becomes a lover who irresistibly attracts her; she now only rejects him out of decency, but inside she has already surrendered to him. And Death responds like a lover, too; he takes her hand and admires her tenderness and beauty; he only articulates what she already experienced when he was close to her: he is a "friend," "not fierce," and she will "sleep softly in [his] arms." She answers no more. She is completely calm, has softly fallen asleep in the arms of the loved death (the piano postlude closes in a major key). In Matthias Claudius' poem, and even more so in Schubert's song, death is erotically charged in the act of dying. With it, the question of its meaning, and thus the question of the meaning of life, quiets down.

* * *

Nietzsche, a passionate philosopher himself, as well as a poet and composer, treated philosophers in an unfriendly manner if they made a "philosopher's claim to *wisdom*." Is such a claim, he asks, not quite often "a hiding place in which the philosopher saves himself from weariness, age, growing cold, hardening – the feeling that the end is near – mimicking the cleverness of that instinct which animals have before death, they go off alone, become silent, choose solitude, crawl into caves, become *wise...*"? (*The Gay Science*, No. 359, transl. by Josefine Nauckhof, modified) Nevertheless, he had his wisest figure, Zarathustra, likewise choose solitude and crawl into caves – for a certain time. However, eventually Zarathustra, Nietzsche writes, "left his cave, glowing and strong, like a morning sun that emerges from dark mountains" (*Thus Spoke Zarathustra* IV, The Sign, transl. by Adrian Del Caro).

Endnotes

1 William James, *Pragmatism: A New Name for Some Old Ways of Thinking* (New York et. al.: Longmans, Green, and Co, 1907), p. 51.

2 Ibid., p. 53.

3 Ibid., p. 190.

4 Ibid., p. 58.

5 Ibid., p. 138.

6 Ibid., p. 185.

7 Ibid., p. 54.

8 Ibid., p. 205.

9 Ibid., pp. 53 f.

10 Friedrich Nietzsche, Notes 1884, *Kritische Studienausgabe in 15 Bänden*, ed. Giorgio Colli/ Mazzino Montinari (Munich/Berlin/New York: Deutscher Taschenbuch Verlag/Walter de Gruyter, 1980), vol. 11, pp. 223 f. (No. 26[280]). Our translation. The following notes by Nietzsche are from this edition, abbreviated as 'KSA' with volume and page number.

11 William James, *Pragmatism*, p. 186.

12 "Zur Philosophie der Orientierung: Fragen und Antworten (Nachwort)," *Philosophie der Orientierung. Festschrift für Werner Stegmaier*, ed. Andrea Bertino/Ekaterina Poljakova/ Andreas Rupschus/Benjamin Alberts (Berlin/Boston: Walter de Gruyter, 2016), p. 375–408.

13 In his survey of the "basic needs" of humans – which is foundational for more than just his functional anthropology – Bronislaw Malinowski, *A Scientific Theory of Culture and Other Essays* (New York: Van Rees Press, 1944), p. 91, lists: metabolism, reproduction, bodily comforts, safety, movement, growth, and health; all of them, especially the basic needs of comfort and safety, connect with the "derived needs" of "cultural imperatives." Orientation is missing from this list.

14 Hans Blumenberg, *Paradigms for a Metaphorology*, transl. by Robert Savage (Ithaca: Cornell University Press and Cornell University Library, 2010 [1960]).

15 Martin Heidegger, *Being and Time*, transl. by Joan Stambaugh (Albany: State University of New York Press, 1996 [1953]), p. 15.

16 Ibid., p. 74.

17 Ibid., p. 30 ff.

18 I thank Mike Hodges for the hint about John Boyd.

19 Cf. Niklas Luhmann, *Risk: A Sociological Theory*, transl. by Rhodes Barrett, with a new introduction by Nico Stehr und Gotthard Bechman (Berlin/New York: Walter de Gruyter, 1993).

20 William James, *The Principles of Psychology*, Vol. 1 (Cambridge, MA/London: Harvard University Press, 1981), pp. 397–398.

21 Cf. Wolf Singer, *Der Beobachter im Gehirn. Essays zur Hirnforschung* (Frankfurt am Main: Suhrkamp, 2002), p. 108. Here, Singer summarizes his own results and the international state of recent brain research. Wolf Singer was, from 1982 to 2008, director at the Max Planck Institute for brain research at Frankfurt/Main, Germany.

22 Thomas Nagel, *The View from Nowhere* (New York: Oxford University Press, 1986).

23 Cf. Isaac Newton, *Philosophiae naturalis principia mathematica* (London, 1687), p. 5 (Definitiones I, Scholium).

24 Singer, *Der Beobachter im Gehirn*, p. 111 (all translations are ours; emphasis added). See also (in a more popular scientific account) Gary Marcus, *The Birth of the Mind: How a Tiny Number of Genes Creates the Complexities of Human Thought* (New York: Basic Books, 2004).

25 Singer, *Der Beobachter im Gehirn*, pp. 108 f.

26 Ibid., pp. 134, 207.

27 Ibid., p. 172.

28 Ibid., p. 129.

29 Ibid., pp. 138 f.

30 Ibid., pp. 94 f., 113.

31 Ibid., p. 157.

32 Ibid., p. 140.

33 Ibid., pp. 168 f.

34 Ibid., pp. 168, 128.

35 See Josef Simon, *Philosophie der Zeichen* (Berlin/New York: Walter de Gruyter, 1989); English translation by George Heffernan, *Philosophy of the Sign* (Albany: State University of New York Press, 1995); Spanish translation by Ana Agud, *Filosofia del signo* (Madrid: Gredos, 1998).

36 Michael Walzer, *Spheres of Justice: A Defence of Pluralism and Equality* (Oxford: Robertson, 1983), differentiates in the societal orientation world between autonomous spheres of interaction and communication by means of peculiar goods and conceptions of justice.

37 Niklas Luhmann, *Die Politik der Gesellschaft*, ed. André Kieserling (Frankfurt am Main: Suhrkamp, 2000), p. 432.

38 Ludwig Wittgenstein, 'The Blue Book,' *The Blue and Brown Books: Preliminary Studies for the 'Philosophical Investigations,'* transl. by Rush Rhees (Oxford: Blackwell, 1969), pp. 6 f.

39 Erving Goffman, *Relations in Public: Microstudies of Public Order,* (New York: Basic Books, 1971), p. 154.

40 Edward T. Hall, *The Hidden Dimension,* (Garden City, N.Y.: Anchor Books, 1966), pp. 113–130.

41 Goffman, *Relations in Public*, p. 7.

42 Wilhelm von Humboldt, "Ueber die Verschiedenheit des menschlichen Sprachbaus und ihren Einfluss auf die geistige Entwicklung des Menschengeschlechts," *Akademie-Ausgabe*, Vol. VII, ed. Albert Leitzmann, reprint (Berlin: Walter de Gruyter, 1968), pp. 53–66 (our translation).

43 Georg Friedrich Wilhelm Hegel, *The Phenomenology of Spirit*, transl. by Terry Pinkard (Cambridge: Cambridge University Press, 2018), pp. 300–305.

44 Goffman, *Relations in Public*, p. 102.

45 Ibid., pp. 339 f.

46 Niklas Luhmann, *The Reality of the Mass Media,* transl. by Kathleen Cross (Stanford: Stanford University Press, 2000).

47 Albert O. Hirschman, until 1974 professor for political economics at Harvard University, demonstrates in famous empirical studies how moral involvements are subject to economic cycles, where they periodically turn into moral abstinence again; he thus initiated a socio-economic moral psychology. See: Albert O. Hirschman, *Shifting Involvements: Private Interest and Public Action* (Princeton: Princeton University Press, 1982).

48 John Rawls, *Theory of Justice* (Cambridge: Harvard University Press, 1999 [1971]), p. 419.

49 Hermann Lübbe, *Im Zug der Zeit. Verkürzter Aufenthalt in der Gegenwart* (Berlin et al.: Springer, 1992).

50 No. 199 (ed. Louis Lafuma)/No. 72 (ed. Léon Brunschvicg). Cf. Blaise Pascal, *Thoughts*, transl. by W. F. Trotter (New York: Collier & Son, 1910), pp. 25–29.

51 *Pensées*, no. 101 (ed. Lafuma) / 324 (ed. Brunschvicg); Trotter's translation, p. 113 (modified).

52 Michel de Montaigne, "Of vanity," *The Complete Essays of* Montaigne, transl. by Donald M. Frame (Stanford: Stanford University Press, 1965), p. 748.

53 Søren Kierkegaard, "The Work of Love in Remembering One Dead," *Works of Love: Some Christian Reflections in the Form of Discourses*, transl. by Howard and Edna Hong (New York: Harper and Brothers, 1962), p. 317.

54 Søren Kierkegaard, *Philosophical Fragments. Johannes Climacus*, ed. and transl. by Howard V. Hong and Edna H. Hong, *Kierkegaard's Writings VII* (Princeton: Princeton University Press, 1985), p. 37 (Ch. 3: The Absolute Paradox).

55 Hans Blumenberg, *Lebenszeit und Weltzeit* (Frankfurt am Main: Suhrkamp, 1986).

Index

A   Subjects

https://doi.org/10.1515/9783110575149-021

knowledge XII, XIV-XV, 9, 41, 58 – 59, 66, 76, 78, 83 – 84, 149, 161 – 162, 184, 186, 189, 191 – 192, 242, 259 – 260, 265, 267, 271 – 272

language, speech XVI, 12, 14, 69, 71 – 72, 75, 77, 82, 97 – 99, 105, 114, 125 – 130, 170, 183, 212, 240, 251 – 252, 259 – 260, 268, 279 – 280
law, statute 90, 156, 158, 172, 175 – 181, 219, 222, 229 – 230, 242, 245 – 246, 283
law of nature 29, 52, 76, 139, 190 – 191, 210
leeway (allowance, clearance, elbow room, latitude, range, room for maneuver, room to move, scope, tolerance, German *Spielraum*) 15, 53 – 54, 57, 65 – 68, 73 – 75, 93 – 109, 119, 129, 132 – 133, 153, 155, 178 – 181, 183 – 185, 195, 202, 208, 220 – 223, 226, 249, 253, 261 – 262, 276
limitation 27, 36, 62 – 63, 168
logic 2 – 3, 7, 9, 29, 56, 64, 76, 99, 105 – 107, 130, 139, 144, 184 – 185, 240, 269 – 270, 281

marking 70 – 71, 99, 169, 195
mass media 158, 161 – 167, 173, 175
mathematical, mathematics 2, 9, 18, 29, 48, 52, 72, 74, 99, 105 – 106, 109, 185 – 186, 190, 271
meaning of life 36 – 38
memory 69, 84 – 86, 97 – 98, 151, 166, 260, 278
metaphor 11 – 12, 20, 41, 43 – 47, 52 – 55, 97, 101, 127 – 129, 249
metaphysics *chap. 17:* 265 – 273; XV, 41, 54 – 55, 72, 77 – 82, 95 – 96, 107 – 108, 176 – 177, 275, 283 – 284
mood 45, 93, 100, 117, 123, 125, 190, 212, 275
– basic mood of orientation 29 – 33
moral, morals, morality *chap. 14 and 15:* 205 – 246; XIII, 8, 11, 15, 62, 98, 113 – 114, 124, 134, 149, 156, 159, 161, 166, 172 – 175, 180, 196, 248, 250, 263
– moral coercion see coercion

name 104

need 2 – 3, 9 – 11, 31, 36, 55 – 56, 61, 73 – 76, 82, 90 – 91, 138 – 139, 146, 148, 155 – 159, 173, 176, 179, 186 – 189, 199, 204 – 205, 207 – 208, 210 – 212, 215, 224 – 226, 244 – 245, 252, 257, 265 – 267, 269 – 273, 287
– need of/for orientation XI, XIII, 5 – 8, 14, 28, 30 – 31, 37, 80, 105 – 107, 124, 144, 150, 161, 167, 207, 222, 260, 269 – 271
net, network, internet XIV, 19, 56, 67 – 68, 172, 249 – 250, 255 – 259
norm, normative XIII, 1, 60, 115 – 116, 131 – 132, 140, 148 – 149, 156, 166, 175 – 176, 180 – 181, 203, 205 – 206, 220 – 224, 236 – 239, 241 – 242, 246, 271 – 272, 283

opportunity 5, 25, 30 – 32, 36 – 38, 167
order XI, 5, 43, 49, 56, 79, 96, 103 – 108, 116, 123, 130, 155 – 158, 172 – 173, 175 – 177, 230, 250 – 251, 266, 271 – 272
orientation (first definition and differentiation) XI-XIV, 1 – 3, 5 – 6, 15 – 16
– of animals, plants, and particles 16 – 22
– with maps and compasses 20 – 23
overview, survey, surveyability *chap 4: 35 – 42*; XI, 10, 27, 43, 45, 56 – 57, 70 – 71, 76, 89 – 90, 93, 96 – 97, 99 – 100, 105 – 106, 113, 115, 139, 156, 159 – 167, 169, 171, 174 – 175, 178 – 179, 185, 187 – 190, 200, 240, 247, 250 – 251, 253 – 255, 259 – 263, 271 – 272, 281

paradox, antinomy 2 – 3, 8 – 9
– starting paradox of orientation 28
– religious paradoxes 199
– moral paradoxes 231 – 233
– of unjustified justification 11
– of examining plausibilities 13
– of expecting the unexpected 33
– of seeing everything and nothing when overlooking a situation 39 – 40, 56, 165
– of an invisible and movable limit (horizon) 44
– of a contingent absolute (standpoint) 46
– of a regulated limit of an unregulated behavior (leeway) 53
– of a temporary atemporality (hold) 55

B   Names